A museum for the global village

A museum *for the* global village

The Canadian Museum
of Civilization

by

George F. MacDonald
and
Stephen Alsford

edited by

R.A.J. Phillips

Canadian Museum of
Civilization

Hull, 1989

© Canadian Museum of Civilization   1989

Canadian Cataloguing in Publication Data

MacDonald, George F.

A museum for the global village

Issued also in french under title: Un musée
pour le village global.
Includes an index and bibliographical references.
ISBN 0-660-10787-2

1. Canadian Museum of Civilization.
2. Museums – Canada – Technological innovations.
3. Museum techniques.
I. Alsford, Stephen, 1952-
II. Canadian Museum of Civilization.
III. Title.

AM101.H8M32 1989   069'.9971   C89-097049-2

Printed and bound in Canada

Published by
Canadian Museum of Civilization
100 Laurier Street
P.O. Box 3100, Station "B"
Hull, Québec
J8X 4H2

Cat. No. NM 98-3/55-1989E

PREFACE

The new Canadian Museum of Civilization is the creation of many, many people - architects, museum staff, consultants, and others - who have worked on the project between 1982 and 1989. A few have played pivotal roles in the evolution of the form and the function of the museum, many more have made specialized contributions, large and small. To all of these the new museum stands as tribute to their creativity, dedication, and energy.

Those people were one of the major research resources for this book, providing documents, illustrations, or verbal information. The authors would particularly like to thank the following persons for especial efforts in providing information, illustrations, or other invaluable assistance : Denis Alsford, Jean-Pierre Camus, Paul Carpentier, Michael Carroll, Frank Corcoran, Carole Cuerrier, Howard Dean, Rick Dubé, Paula Fairweather, Sandy Gibb, Tom Govier, Ian Gregory, Fred Granger, Charles Hett, Rod Huggins, Lorna Kee, Bob Kelly, Andrea Laforet, John Lomoro, Ron McRae, Rick Mandy, Sylvie Morel, Kathleen O'Neill Cole, Estelle Reed, Nancy Ruddell, Dave Theobald, Penny Trottier, Paul Trottier, Amber Walpole, Scott Windsor, Wes Wenhardt, Anne Woollam, staff of the CMC Library, and Douglas Cardinal and his staff. In addition we would like to thank Bing Wong for his layout design, Deborah Brownrigg and Heather Sinclair for their hard work on the desktop publishing system, Harry Foster and Richard Garner for some fine photography, and Christiane Saumur for illustrations research.

Much of the information in this book derives from voluminous reports and other writings produced during the course of designing and realizing the new museum. A few of these debts - landmark reports - are acknowledged in the endnotes. But the very large number of documents consulted during the research process, the varying degrees of formality or informality of the writings, and the fact that the documents are unpublished and therefore not easily accessible, have made it impractical to credit all sources.

Decisions regarding naming of spaces in the new museum were still in process during the writing of this book. Since the finalization of the main text, the Native Peoples Hall, for example, has been renamed First Peoples Hall. The reader is asked to excuse similar discrepancies that may be found.

One final note : this book discusses the Canadian Museum of Civilization within the context of the museum community, and museological developments, as a whole. Some statements may appear very sweeping. The reader is asked to bear in mind that most generalizations apply primarily to the human history museum model, and may not be as applicable to science/technology, natural history, or art museums.

George MacDonald
Stephen Alsford

Illustration credits

Harry Foster: figures 1, 21, 24, 25, 27, 39, 43a, 45, 47a, 49a, 59, 81b, 84, 94b, 103, 117a, 133, and on p.81. *Richard Garner:* figures 2, 16, 19, 20, 39a, 45a, 46, 48-48a, 50, 55-55a, 56-56a, 57, 58a, 61-61a, 65, 67-67a, 69, 73, 74-74c, 80, 90, 109, 114-114a, 115-115a, 124b, 126, 128, 129a, 131, 134, and on pp.107, 115, 222. *Malak Photographs:* figure 2. *C. Lupien:* figure 2. *Jean P. Larocque*: (graphic) figure 2. *Toronto Star:* figure 3. *National Museums of Canada:* figures 4, 5, 64-64a, 82, 93. *Canadian Museum of Civilization:* figures 6, 8, 13a, p.23, 44, 53, 63, 66-66a, 68a-68b, 72, 91, 99-99a. *National Capital Commission:* figures 9, 105-105a (Terry Atkinson). *Environment Canada:* figure 9. *National Archives of Canada:* figures 9, 17 (NMC-20966), and on pp.22-23 (C-6090, C-742, C-2984). *Tourism Canada:* figures 9, 33, 34, 62. *Bing Wong:* (graphic) figure 10. *Marc Lincourt:* (graphic) figure 11. *Douglas Cardinal Architect:* figures 12-12b, 13, 14, 18, 43. *Jack Schekkerman:* figure 15. *Howard Weingarden:* figure 16. *George MacDonald:* figures 22, 26, 31, 32, 35, 36, 37-37a, 38, 40a, 51, 60, 75a, 81c, 101, 102-102a, 113, 119, 125, 130. *Michael Bedford:* figure 23. *Photo courtesy of Children's Museum of Indianapolis:* figures 28, 97. *Stephen Alsford:* figures 29, 40, 40b, 42-42a, 70, 81a, 82a, 84a, 85, 86, 88-88b, 89, 92, 100, 103a, 104, 106, 108-108a, 110-110c, 112, 117, 118, 120, 121-121a, 122, 123, 124-124a, 125a, 126a, 127, 132. *Little World Museum of Man:* figures 30, 75. *UBC Museum of Anthropology:* figures 41 (M. Waters), 49 (William McLennan), 89a (Jacquie Gissen). *Peter Schwarzmann:* (graphics) figures 47, 50, 58, 111, 116, 129, and on pp.81, 222. *Huronia Historical Parks:* figure 52. *Peter Fortey:* figure 54. *Courtesy The Citizen* (photo Rod MacIvor): figure on p.110. *Merle Toole:* figure on p.110. *Rutenberg Design:* (graphic) figure 68. *Jean-Pierre Camus:* figure 71. *Bell Canada:* figure 76. *John Lomoro:* figures 77, 78, 79-79a. *Thomas Moore Architect:* (graphic) figure 81. *Amber Walpole:* (graphic) figure 83. *Denis Alsford:* figure 87. *Optima Photographie:* figures 94, 98, 110d, 112a, 118a. *National Museum of Science and Technology:* figure 94a. *Design + Communication:* (graphic) figure 95. *Koninklijk Instituut voor de Tropen:* figures 96-96c. *T.R. Photography:* figure 107. *Imax Systems Corporation:* figures on p.187.

CONTENTS

the museum as symbol

*Figure 1
CMC's daringly innovative
architecture makes it a major national
symbol*

Between 1983 and 1989 a sculpture of monumental proportions gradually took shape on the northern bank of the Ottawa River, on a site known as Parc Laurier. This was the Canadian Museum of Civilization (CMC).

At first only those intimately connected with the project grasped its significance. The media paid little attention. There was dutiful recording of key events such as the appointment of the architect, the unveiling of the conceptual model, the ground-breaking ceremonies. More attention was paid to transitory problems: delays in construction schedule, cost overruns, minor differences amongst those associated with the project, or the supposed sexism in the old name of the museum (the National Museum of Man). For the most part, however, the creation of the new national museum made little impression on Canadians at large in the early years. CMC's staff were content to keep a low profile. Their energies were mostly focused inwards, onto the exhausting process of designing the facilities and programmes for the new museum.

The rising building's striking design evoked the eroded landforms and streambeds of post-glacial Canada. Being on one of the most conspicuous sites in the National Capital, it began to attract the public's notice. CMC was encouraged to share the emerging dream with the museum community and the public at large. Apparently the museum was soon added to the world 'visit list' of important cultural projects for foreign delegations came to see it from such countries as the United States, Britain, Japan, South Africa, the Soviet Union, China and Australia; many were led by museum directors. Its daringly innovative design and its symbolism led to frequent comparisons with the Canadian Pavilion at Expo '86 or with the Sydney Opera House. Many felt it would be the last great museum to be built in this century.

Such descriptions barely glimpse what the new Canadian Museum of Civilization represents for Canada. Along with the many other museums in this country, it has an indispensable part to play in assuring the vitality of Canadian culture, for an understanding of the past is the foundation for the future. The Ontario Heritage Policy Review put the point well:

"In seeking to define Canada's unique cultural identity, we have become increasingly aware of the need to have a sense of who and what we are as a collective .... This sense of self in the individual or in groups is a vital sustaining force in adversity and essential for the mobilization of community resources. But it requires an

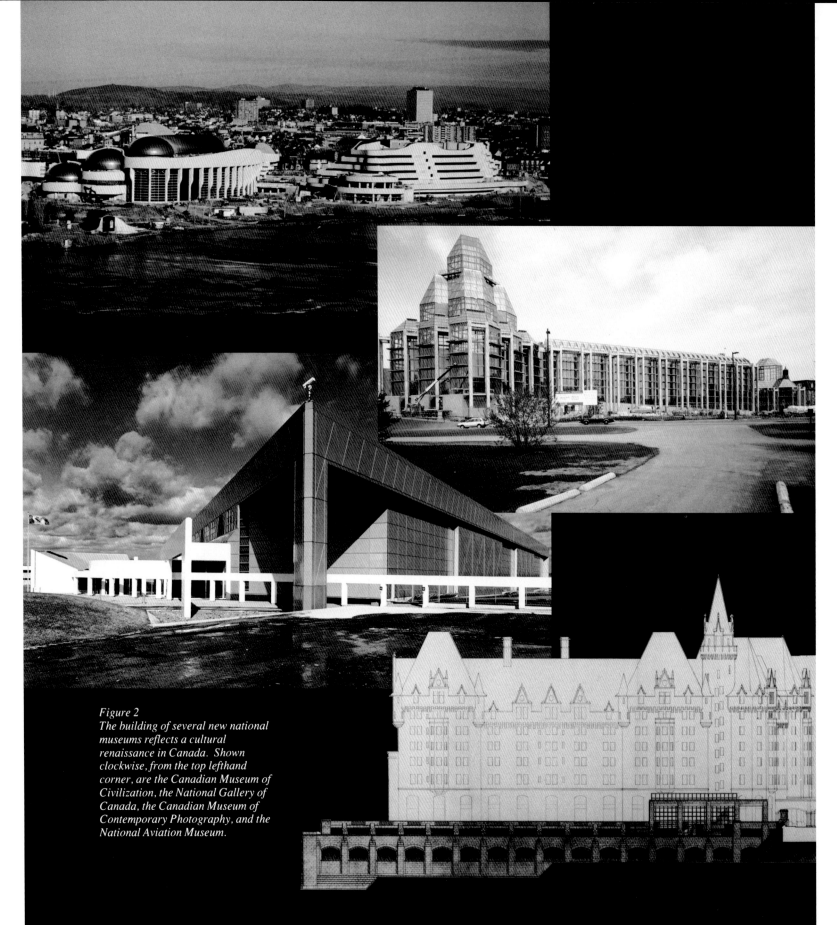

Figure 2
The building of several new national museums reflects a cultural renaissance in Canada. Shown clockwise, from the top lefthand corner, are the Canadian Museum of Civilization, the National Gallery of Canada, the Canadian Museum of Contemporary Photography, and the National Aviation Museum.

appreciation of what we have inherited, a collective memory, and a will to cultivate it."[1]

This collective memory, of the many people and cultures in the Canadian mosaic, is institutionalized in many forms. Canada being a nation of immigrants from diverse backgrounds, there is a national tendency to look to public institutions to preserve and interpret our past experiences.[2] Museums therefore have a unifying role.

What has traditionally distinguished museums from other institutions of cultural preservation is their chosen medium of physical artifacts, the material remains of the past. They are the image banks of our heritage. But even this does not express the unrealized potential within museums. The popular criticism that museums are the burial vaults for relics of the past is shallow and rarely deserved. Culture, or heritage – the two are inextricably intertwined, no matter how defined – are living, dynamic forces which reflect the past in our present, and transform that present into its future. By selecting from the remnants of the past those elements to which society attaches significance, and by interpreting or reinterpreting this past, museums are intimately relevant to the present. As Robert Sullivan puts it:

> "Museums, in and of themselves, are artifacts; social documents that reflect, present and transmit the belief and values systems of the societies that create them. Their very existence in a society begins to reveal the attitude of that people about themselves and the world around them."[3]

Museums are sometimes described as oases of the past in a rapidly changing world, a place to seek one's roots. They do not resist change, however, but show the contrasts and continuities between past and present, and thus portray change as a natural, explicable, and acceptable fact of life.

If museums generally are symbols of our society and its cultures, and as central to social development as the heritage which they help preserve and explain, what of the National Museums in particular? The National Capital is itself a symbol of national identity. This was the view of most visitors to the National Capital Region surveyed in 1985/86.[4] Next to such historic landmarks as the Parliament Buildings, cultural institutions are the major contributors to that image, and to the region's selection as a tourist destination. A national museum of human history is part of that symbolization. It helps define cultural identity and the country itself. It stimulates pride amongst Canadians in their own culture. It announces to the world that Canada is a nation with special and unique characteristics. It reflects the ways in which various peoples, bringing their own cultures, have met the challenges of the land, by shaping it and by shaping themselves to it.

CMC offers, both to Canadians and non-Canadians, an initiation into the national identity. It submits itself to the confines of scholarly objectivity and seeks to make itself of utmost relevance to present issues and concerns. In a sense, a national museum elevates culture by recognizing it and placing it in a context that can be likened to a temple or a treasure-house. As a temple of culture CMC is very much a ritual space. This fact has been a key to the types of experiences it has sought to programme into its new facilities.

CMC is also a symbol of the federal government's commitment to a role in cultural affairs. The creation of a new national museum of human history is only one element in the development of a cultural pilgrimage centre: the 'museum capital of Canada' as it has been tagged.[5] The construction of new buildings for CMC and for the National Gallery of Canada, the creation of the National Aviation Museum and the Museum of Contemporary Photography, plans for a Museum of Caricature, rehousing of the National Postal Museum and the National Archives of Canada, and the beginning search for new homes for the National Museum of Natural Sciences and the National Museum of Science and Technology: all are components of this cultural master-plan.

On a narrower level of symbolism, the museum expresses the philosophies, world-view, values, aspirations, and intentions of those who shaped its form and its function. One was the architect; Douglas Cardinal's first proposal for a design for the new museum declared:

> "Our future is optimistic and should be celebrated. This national treasure-house must welcome the people, teach them, inspire them and send them away enlightened and optimistic that we are progressing as human individuals and as a Nation."[6]

Instead of designing a structure that merely houses artifacts, Cardinal created a modern artifact. It makes statements about Canada's past and present that are highly appropriate contexts for the cultures presented within the building. His vision of what the new

Figure 3
The creation of the CMC owes
something to the visionary ideas of
both Marshall McLuhan and
Pierre Trudeau.

museum should be matched well the vision of CMC's leaders.

The Canadian Museum of Civilization, now accessible to the world, is both a product and a process. The process is the harmonization of the creative efforts of the architects of museum form and the architects of museum function. The product is a microcosmic reflection of the global village and, at the same time, its spiritual counterpart the universal church, celebrating the cultural achievements of humanity (especially Canadians) from the Ice Age shaman who painted the caverns at Lascaux to the Space Age wizards who plot spiritual pathways in fibre-optic cables. The reference here, and in this book's title, to the 'global village' is not casual. The thought of that great Canadian communication and media pioneer, Marshall McLuhan, has so influenced the direction of the museum's development that he deserves to be considered an honorary mentor of the project! It seems so appropriate that Canada's Department of Communications, which launched the

museum project, itself sprang from McLuhan's fertile mind.

It is also appropriate that, during the course of that project, the museum's name changed from the National Museum of Man to the Canadian Museum of Civilization, reflecting not only an implicit broadening of the museum's mandate but also a recognition of McLuhan's concept of a global village where all civilizations meet. Unlike the United States' Smithsonian Institution, which tends to focus on the eastern seaboard, as the cradle of the nation, and the myth of the melting-pot, CMC has necessarily taken a different position on ethnicity. Canada has never been a true melting-pot of culture. CMC celebrates the diverse ethnic origins of the Canadian people within the context of a national identity. This gives CMC a stronger link to other nations than most other national museums have, while placing it in a unique position to provide world leadership in intercultural understanding. This perspective reflects Canada's image of itself as a nation which seeks to promote world peace.

If Canada is not a melting-pot, it can be seen as a crossroads where valid cultural forms can be exchanged and built upon. Crossroads have important traditional roles as market-place and ritual centre. The first meets our needs to communicate with fellow humans, and the second recognizes our urge to communicate with our ancestors and our deepest-rooted beliefs. As Canada in microcosm, CMC uses the crossroads model to provide an arena in which different cultures meet for their better mutual understanding.

The name-change also symbolizes CMC's entry into a new arena. In the past it has lacked national presence; several regional museums – such as the Royal Ontario Museum, the Glenbow, the British Columbia Provincial Museum – built deserved reputations which overshadowed the National Museums. Now comes the opportunity for Canada's national museum of human history to take a place amongst the outstanding cultural facilities of the twentieth century. The building to house the museum has been recognized, at home and abroad, as a world-class structure. Bigger and more complex than originally planned, it is a building unlike any other the world has yet seen. The structure is 'geoform': its features are drawn directly from the landscape and the forces of nature which shaped the landscape. By contrast, it embodies many state-of-the-art technologies: from the evolution of its form within the 'womb' of a computer's memory, through its nourishment and protection by computer-controlled environmental and security systems, to its nervous system made up of fibre-optic cables.

The only valid response CMC's staff could give to a world-class building, and to the substantial investment of public funds in the project, was to 'sculpt' a prototype for an indoor human history museum of a quality that will make it a source of national pride. Much effort was devoted to gathering information on the best new developments in museums and related institutions worldwide. CMC's own experiences and practices also proved an invaluable foundation, but they were not unquestioningly perpetuated. Curatorial operations, exhibitions, interpretive and educational programmes were re-evaluated and, wherever desirable, reshaped as resources allowed.

The new CMC can perform on a more sophisticated level and at a greater capacity than was expected when the project was begun. A fundamental tenet guiding the architects of museum function was that their product should be user-driven not producer-driven; that is, responsive to all potential users of museum services, insofar as their needs could be ascertained. The main aim for the exhibitions has been to give the artifacts context. This meant re-creating the cultural settings appropriate to the displayed objects, supporting them by dynamic programmes that have cultural relevance, and enhancing the experience by interactivity that will draw visitors into a more intimate and meaningful relationship with the presentations. New techniques and technologies were employed to heighten the quality or outreach of the experience. That last point is important, for CMC cannot be satisfied with servicing only those visitors who pass through its doors every year; as a *national* museum it must reach out towards every Canadian, offering its entertaining events and learning opportunities to all.

This, then, is the story in this book: the how, why, and what of the new Canadian Museum of Civilization. It is the story of a vision en route to realization, the translation of a symbol into palpable reality. It is a story without an end, but it begins at the beginning . . . .

The New Accommodation Project

The beginnings of CMC stretch back to the founding of the Geological and Natural History Survey of Canada in 1842. Specimens gathered by its members were the basis for the collections of the future museums. In 1877 Parliament encouraged the Survey to collect ethnological and historical objects, in addition to the geological, archaeological, botanical, and zoological material already collected. An Anthropology Division was established in 1910. The same year saw the Geological Survey move into the Victoria Memorial Museum Building, whose construction had begun five years earlier unknowingly, on unstable ground; the building began to display Survey collections to the public in 1911. It was not until 1927, however, that the National Museum of Canada was formally established.

In 1956 operations were divided into human history and natural history branches. Twelve years later the National Museums Act made these into the National Museum of Man and the National Museum of Natural Sciences, under the umbrella of the National Museums of Canada; the fields of study of the National Museum of Man were organized under four scientific, or curatorial, divisions: ethnology, folk culture, history, and archaeology. This coming of age was followed by attempts to stabilize the sinking Victoria Memorial Museum Building, and by

5

Figures 4 and 5
The first home of the national museums, the Victoria Memorial Museum Building, has its own part in Canadian heritage. Parliamentary sessions were held there after the fiery destruction of the Parliament Buildings in 1916. In 1919 it hosted funeral ceremonies for Sir Wilfrid Laurier.

refurbishment of the exhibitions. The 1980's have seen the differentiation taken further: separate homes for the National Museum of Man and the National Museum of Natural Sciences; the dissolution of the umbrella corporation, leaving the component museums free to pursue their individualistic directions; and the name-change to the Canadian Museum of Civilization (symbolizing new status).

Over the decades CMC built up large and valuable collections and a staff of experts in scientific and museological fields. In the 1970's it developed a philosophy of public programming much in pace with the rest of the world; this was inspired by the National Museum Policy (1972), stressing preservation of and increased public access to heritage collections, and by the federal Multiculturalism Policy. But, as its collections grew and its public services expanded, there was no corresponding provision of the proper facilities to house them, once the Victoria Memorial Museum Building was outgrown.

Instead, collections and staff were decentralized into 17 scattered buildings, most never designed for museum functions. Many were warehouse-type structures eminently unsuitable, in terms of space, environment, fire safety and security, for housing the often fragile and irreplaceable artifacts. Too few people and too little money hindered efforts to combat the deterioration to collections which the unsatisfactory storage conditions were causing. Some buildings were so bad that the Fire Marshall condemned them. These were no proper places for safeguarding the national treasures. Furthermore, the dispersal process, separating those responsible for exhibitions, extension programmes, management, administration, collections management, and research, tended to create a feeling of isolation of each division from the others, impeding teamwork. These factors compromised the museum's ability to carry out its mandate and generally obstructed the efficiency of museum operations.

Nor was this state of affairs conducive to increasing public access. Although the collections grew, the amount of display space in the Victoria Memorial Museum Building did not. So the proportion of the collections publicly accessible was increasingly dwarfed by the proportion hidden from view in storage. Some exhibits that CMC staff wished to present were extremely large, and demanded more spacious galleries than were available. During the renovation of the Victoria Memorial Museum Building ways were sought to improve the situation.

Figures 6,7, and 8
CMC's collections and staff were formerly
housed in these and several other buildings,
scattered across Ottawa. All were designed
originally for other tenants; none was very
suitable for museum functions.

A scheme to have stratified exhibition galleries to cater to different levels of public interest – orientation and didactic exhibits would overview a subject, a more artifact-intensive exhibit for deeper study would follow, and finally the presentation of typological collections for in-depth research – was never realized.[7] In 1977, even as the renovation programme was nearing completion, museum management presented to the federal government a proposal to consolidate museum operations and services at a site on Brewery Creek, on the Quebec side of the Ottawa River, in Hull. Although the government drew back from making the huge investment necessary for a new building, the ball was now rolling.

In fact, the roots of the decision on new accommodation for CMC lie in the National Museum Policy. With its twin pillars of democratization and decentralization, it engendered optimism in the museum community that the National Museums Corporation would provide leadership and support to that community and would develop national museums of a quality comparable with those of other countries. Over the next decade this turned to pessimism, as it became apparent that the National Museums could not reach their potential within the confines of government funding, which increased at a lower rate than inflation. Nonetheless, federal politicians were finally persuaded of the long-standing deficiencies in accommodations of the museums:

• that space in the Victoria Memorial Museum Building permitted the display of only a small percentage of the total collections;

• that space was not adequate to allow for receiving major travelling exhibitions, or even to show the travelling exhibits prepared by CMC itself;

• that congested working and collections storage conditions inhibited CMC's ability to mount travelling

7

exhibitions at all, further limiting the national exposure of collections;

• that the collections required standards of safety and environmental stability impossible in their existing congested homes, and that serious damage – some irreparable – had already occurred to the nation's material heritage;

• and that all museum operations needed to be integrated, in a single facility, if they were to form a cohesive and effective unit able to provide public services.

All these factors, particularly the very real physical threat to the national treasures, made it clear that a decision could not be longer delayed. In June 1981 Cabinet approved in principle the transfer of the National Museum of Man and the National Gallery of Canada to new buildings specially constructed to meet their needs. This decision was made public in February 1982, when $185 million was allocated to build the new museums. The Canada Museums Construction Corporation was to be set up to recommend to Cabinet sites, architects, and designs for the two museums, and to manage construction. CMC pulled its specialists from their regular duties to form the New Accommodation Task Force to gather information, coordinate the production of conceptual design proposals, and represent the museum in the formulation of an architectural programme.

It is not enough to attribute the decision to build new museums to their own needs. Also significant was the effect of museum construction on the economy. It would provide employment for the construction industry, Canadian architects, designers, engineers, and various consultants. There would also be job creation in the museums themselves. And most of the materiel for constructing and furnishing the new buildings would be purchased from Canadian sources. More importantly, the new museums would stimulate the tourist industry in the National Capital Region. Buildings that were themselves works of art would be an attraction in their own right; more so if they provided facilities which allowed major exhibitions of international renown into the capital. A growing public interest in heritage over the last couple of decades has meant that places able to offer a quality cultural 'product' are often the most successful tourist destinations. Increasingly today one encounters references not merely to 'tourism' but specifically to 'cultural tourism'.[8] There are over 2000 museums, historic sites, archives, or comparable heritage institutions in Canada today. They have about 90 million visits each year, almost half to federally-administered institutions; this far exceeds attendance at professional sports events. A recent Gallup Poll ranked the importance of museums as higher than defence spending, or than performing and aesthetic arts, in public estimation.[9]

A 1979 survey by Canada's Capital Visitors and Convention Bureau discovered that 82.9% of visitors to the National Capital Region go to tourist attractions, including cultural events. A major, but underdeveloped, part of this market is people on business trips. The 1985/86 visitor survey also found that cultural edifices or activities were a leading draw for tourists, although 52% of the respondents said the capital required more content reflecting the breadth of Canadian culture; in particular, they suggested the establishment of a theme park or a major exposition, in which cultural features associated with all provinces were represented.[10]

The development of Ottawa-Hull, as a capital expressive of national identity and a source of national pride, is the responsibility of the National Capital Commission (NCC). One of its key strategies,[11] has been to bring Hull into the capital in more than just name, to enhance the image of the capital as the symbolic centre of a nation of two official cultures. Hull had been neglected while the southern bank of the Ottawa River was undergoing rapid development, and had benefited little from its nominal inclusion in the capital. Federal building in Hull was the solution proposed; a mix of cultural, administrative, commercial, and residential functions would avoid concentration of land uses. In the 1970's large buildings to serve the federal bureaucracy were erected in Hull, but there remained the need to complement them with cultural and public-oriented facilities. A further tactic in helping to tie Ottawa and Hull together was the development of a ceremonial route, circling the Core Area of the capital and passing major national institutions. Key sites along the proposed route were acquired by the NCC and reserved for institutions that are essential building blocks in establishing a strong chain of national symbols, such as the Canadian Museum of Civilization. Plans for the Capital Core Area were thus the context for the decision to build a new museum.

The Clay and the Sculptor

The first task of the New Accommodation project was the selection of the best architect and the most suitable site. The Canada Museums Construction

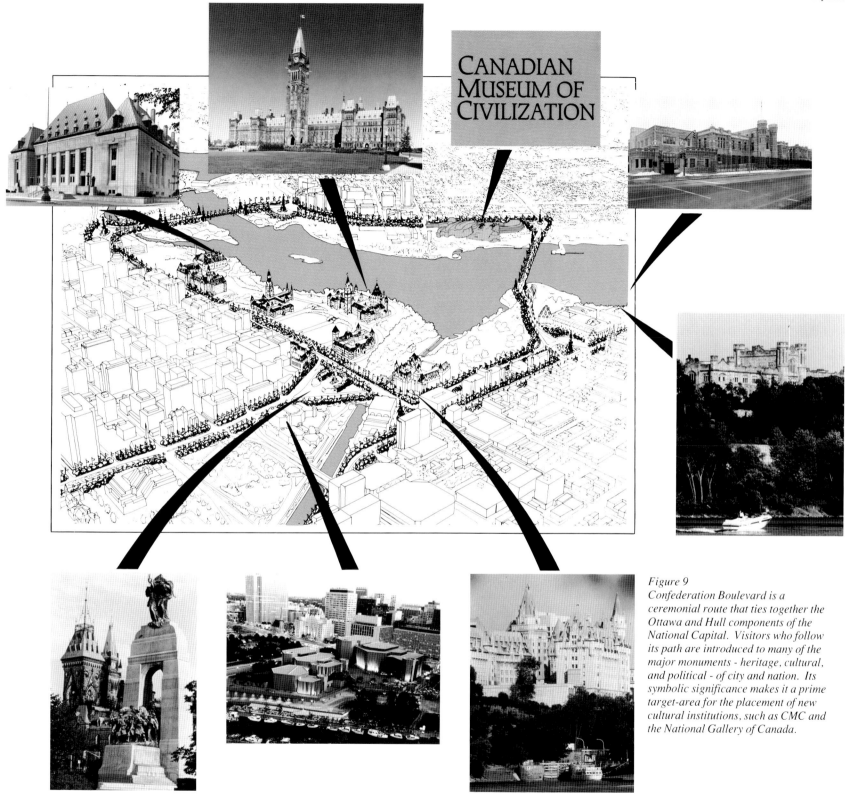

CANADIAN MUSEUM OF CIVILIZATION

Figure 9
Confederation Boulevard is a
ceremonial route that ties together the
Ottawa and Hull components of the
National Capital. Visitors who follow
its path are introduced to many of the
major monuments - heritage, cultural,
and political - of city and nation. Its
symbolic significance makes it a prime
target-area for the placement of new
cultural institutions, such as CMC and
the National Gallery of Canada.

Figure 10
The well-known view of Parliament Hill on the back of the dollar bill can be recaptured first-hand from CMC's site.

Corporation commissioned a study of possible locations.[12] It assumed that an appropriate site would be within the Capital Core Area, on publicly-owned land, linked to the intended ceremonial route, and preferably visible from both the Hull and Ottawa sides of the river. Five prominent sites were compared; any would have been satisfactory to hold a museum that was to be a symbol of national heritage, although in fact it had largely been pre-determined where CMC would be placed.

All of the sites lay along the envisaged ceremonial route, and most of them on the primary part of that route known as Confederation Boulevard. Ceremonial routes exist in many capital cities of the world, accommodating special events related to the political, cultural, and diplomatic life of a country, and linking the principal images every visitor to the capital is likely to retain of national symbols. The Boulevard being constructed by the NCC will define the heart of the capital and serve as the element unifying the capital on both sides of the river; it will be a circuit taken by tourists and dignitaries. Along its route – incorporating parts of Wellington Street and Sussex Drive on the Ottawa side, and Laurier Street on the Hull side, with bridge linkages – lie a number of landmarks. Some are rooted deeply in the history of the capital and of the nation: the Parliament Buildings, Confederation Square, the Chateau Laurier, the Rideau Locks (terminus of the historic Rideau Canal) and the adjacent Bytown Museum, and the industrial heritage complexes on Victoria and Chaudiere Islands. The Supreme Court, the National Library, National Archives, and the National Arts Centre are other major edifices on the route, while the Canadian War Museum and the Mint are just off the Boulevard. Of local relevance, but

also imposing in their way, are the Maison du Citoyen (Hull's city hall), the Rideau Centre mall and associated Congress Centre, the outdoor Byward Market, and Nepean Point offering a superb panorama up-river and summer performances in its amphitheatre. To this list have been added CMC and the National Gallery of Canada; the National Museum of Natural Sciences and National Museum of Science and Technology may join them later. It is not far-fetched to compare the Boulevard, with its attached cultural landmarks and attractions, to a 'heritage theme park' whose activities focus on the river.

Of the five sites, only one lay on the Hull side of the river: a former industrial site which the NCC had acquired from E.B. Eddy Company in 1972 and converted into a mix of parkland and parking. Parc Laurier was targeted as a prime site for a national museum even before the comparative site analysis. Both by the NCC, which desired a cultural institution in that part of the capital to attract tourists across the river and to make Hull seem more a part of the capital, and by the City of Hull, whose development plan (1980) aimed at making Parc Laurier an urban park with a transitional building form that would link the downtown buildings to the riverfront. It was a natural decision that, of the two national museums to be built, one should be on the Ottawa side and one on the Hull side. And since CMC had in the past attracted more visitors than the National Gallery, it was considered the better choice for the Hull site. When the museum site analysis showed no reason to reject Parc Laurier, its fate was sealed.

Parc Laurier had much to recommend it. By far the biggest of the five sites, it had some 9.6 hectares (24 acres), although to escape the risk of the river flooding not all the site was useable for building. It is bounded by Laurier Street, on the ceremonial route, on its western side; across the road from the south-west corner stands the Maison du Citoyen. Frontage here is 405 metres (1328 feet). On the south side is Eddy Forest Products. At the other end of Parc Laurier is the adjacent Parc Jacques Cartier, linked by a pedestrian pathway; this is recreational parkland, equipped with a marina. Soaring over the boundary between the two parks is the Alexandra Interprovincial Bridge, a plaqued heritage structure; it is like a great ceremonial arch over one river entrance to the Core Area, linking CMC with the National Gallery at its other end.

The 'jewel in the crown' is the eastern boundary, facing onto the Ottawa River. The low-lying park

slopes gently down to the river across a depth whose median is 235 metres (770 feet); the slope is about 5.5% from Laurier Street, which is at an elevation of 53.5 metres, to the river, at an elevation of 41 metres. The high-water level (47 metres, based on a worst-case, 100-years recurrence) means that almost half of depth of the property is susceptible to flooding; but this still leaves room for a sizeable building. The direction of the slope guarantees a sunny exposure, especially in the morning. More significantly it provides a sweeping panorama of the river and the

Ottawa side of the Core Area, including the famous 'dollar bill' scene of the Parliament Buildings and the limestone escarpment on which they sit, as well as picturesque views of the National Gallery, the Rideau Canal cascading through its final locks into the river, and many other landmarks between Nepean Point and Victoria Island.

Parc Laurier is also quite well served by physical access routes. Principal vehicular access is off Laurier Street, linked by bridges with either side of

Figure 11
CMC's site is bounded by a pulp products factory, downtown Hull, the Alexandra Provincial Bridge, and the Ottawa River, all of which have a story to tell in the history of the National Capital.

Figures 12, 12a and 12b
Cardinal's architecture (exemplified
here by the Grande Prairie college, the
Ponoka government services centre,
and St. Mary's Church in Red Deer)
has been characterized by his
sensuously curving forms and his use
of earth-tone materials that create a
sculpted effect reminiscent of natural
landforms.

downtown Ottawa. A pedestrian and bicycle path cuts across the park, at the river-edge, and connects to trails which not only circle around the river in the Core Area but also network outwards in several directions across Ottawa and Hull. Both these and the ceremonial route itself link up a series of green spaces developed for the public adjacent to the city's watercourses. Parc Laurier is one such space. Although the building of the museum resulted in some loss of parkland, the park was very underutilized, nor was there any significant vegetation there to be lost.

When a selection of architects was invited to submit conceptual design proposals for the new museum, the information they had to feed into the creative process was the site study, the intentions of the National Capital Commission and the City of Hull for that site, and a package put together by CMC's New Accommodation Task Force outlining the nature of the museum, its functions, and ambitions, supplemented by discussions with museum staff. Into this palette they mixed their own creative visions.

Over eighty of Canada's foremost architects were considered - their offices visited, their past works examined - in the course of selecting the right firms to build the new museums. Twelve were invited, in December 1982, to submit by 17 January concept proposals for one or other of the two museums.[13] The short-list approach was selected instead of a full-blown architectural competition because time and money for the project were very limited. Those on the list were asked to consider the context in which the museum would be placed, the role of the institution, and an *approach* to an architectural solution. The design proper would be created only after far more detailed input from the museum staffs about precise needs. Seven of the architects submitted proposals for CMC. On 10 February 1983 the government announced the selection of Parc Laurier as the site for CMC and Douglas J. Cardinal Architect Limited as design architect for the museum, in association with the Montreal architectural firm of Tétreault, Parent, Languedoc et Associés Inc.

Some eyebrows were raised in the architectural community at the selection of Cardinal, an Edmonton-based architect not yet of national stature; his works and his reputation up to that time had been built mainly in his native Alberta. Yet he had already carved a niche for himself with his distinctive and individualistic architectural style, and his Albertan works have been discussed in many books on modern architectural milestones.[14] His design for St. Mary's Roman Catholic Church (begun 1967) in Red Deer, the town where he grew up, first brought him into the spotlight; its curving forms, dramatic use of natural lighting over the altar and lectern, and his imaginative use of brick, which were to become trademarks of his style, prompted critics to note that his architecture combines the contemplative and the sensuous. In the Grande Prairie Regional College, a recreational, cultural and educational centre for that community, the Alberta Government Services Centre at Ponoka, the St. Albert Civic & Cultural Centre, and his own home at Stony Plain, he continued to design and build beautifully undulating shells. Another side of his creativity was shown in the Edmonton Space Sciences Centre, which had a futuristic appearance; the Centre included an Imax theatre.

Cardinal is a landscape-inspired architect. He considers the first step in architectural design to be to reach an understanding and feeling for the land on which a building will stand; for nature has its own sculptural forms, alive and dynamic, to which the architect can respond. In his own words :

> "Instead of viewing the museum as a sculptural problem, instead of identifying all the historical forms and making them the vocabulary for my solutions, I prefer to take a walk in nature, observe how nature has solved its problems, and let it be an inspiration to me in solving mine."

And again :

> "Our buildings must be part of nature, must flow out of the land; the landscape must weave in and out of them so that, even in the harshness of winter, we are not deprived of our closeness with nature."[15]

He responds to the land with giant earth structures which appear more to rise out of the land, rather than to be added on top of it. His curvilinear forms make deliberate use of changing moods of light and shadow, and he uses warm textures of brick, stone and tile to provide natural earth-tones for his building exteriors. This makes his style humanistic and uplifting; he places human needs at the heart of the design process, rather than designing something that is merely structurally sound and functional. He states

> "I have always maintained that the endeavours of all Canadians should be directed towards a

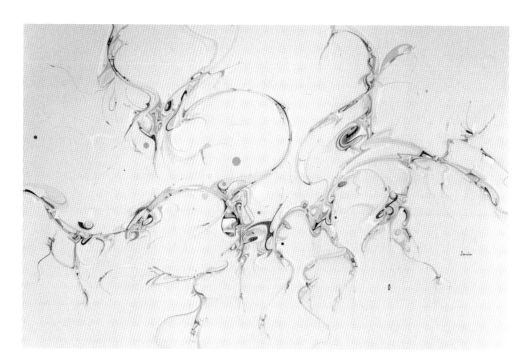

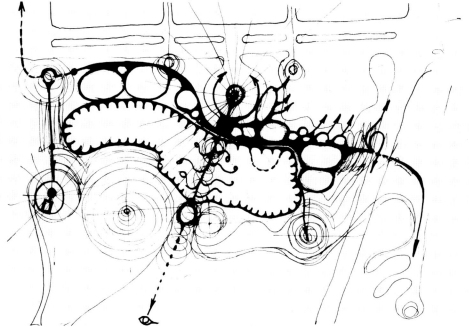

betterment of the human condition. Therefore in my role as planner and architect, and as the coordinator of technologists, I see a tremendous opportunity to petition the needs of the individual and to reinstate our humanness as the most important element in all of our efforts. I have found that by placing the needs of the human being before the systems that modern man has created, we can ensure that man is indeed served by these systems rather than becoming a slave to them."

Figures 13 and 13a
The curving forms and sweeping lines of Cardinal's early impressionistic sketches of CMC are reminiscent of the artwork of fellow-native Alex Janvier.

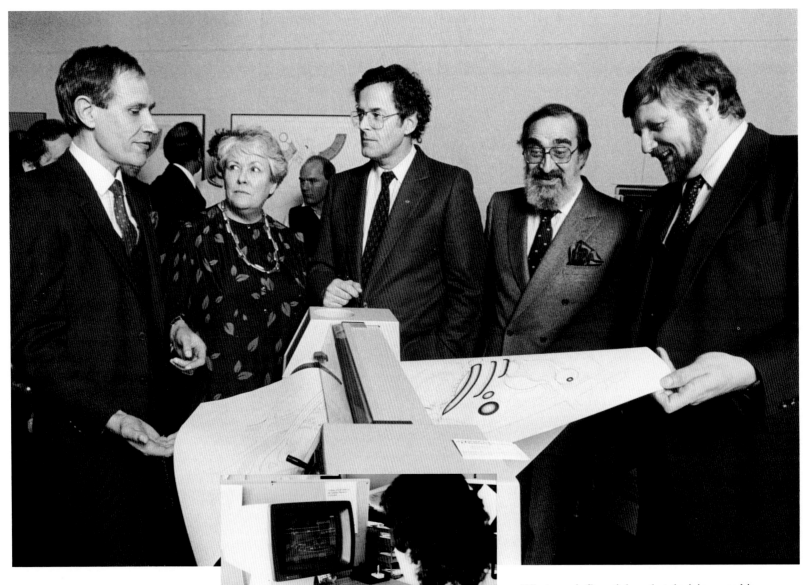

Figures 14 and 14a
Cardinal's CAD equipment facilitated
the design of the complex geometrical
forms of CMC, enabled alterations to
be made easily, and permitted quick
production of updated site plans.

These ideas hark back to his own native ancestry [16] - not least his belief that the design of a building is a spiritual act. The ebbing and flowing liquid forms of Cardinal's initial conceptual drawings of CMC are reminiscent of the paintings of the Chipewayan artist Alex Janvier : the two men appear to have the same feeling for line and form. It seems appropriate that a museum housing collections of Indian artifacts of national importance should be designed by someone with roots in Canada's native culture, although this was not a factor in the selection decision.

What *was* influential on that decision was his reputation for integrating high technology into his work. Cardinal's firm pioneered the use of computer-aided design (CAD) in Canada and was considered one of the leading firms in North America in that field, pushing CAD software to the limits of its performance and identifying new frontiers for it. The complexity of his serpentine architectural forms presents difficult geometrical problems; his church at Red Deer, for example, required 82,000 simultaneous equations to design the tent-like roof structure. To solve these and to accommodate the dynamic process of design, involving frequent changes in technical drawings and the repetitive procedures involved in producing updated sets of drawings, CAD was a natural answer. It gives accuracy, speed, and coordination, releasing staff from tedious manual drafting tasks to devote more time to design refinements. By itself, of course, it cannot guarantee a better building - that responsibility remains with the creative skill of the architect.

The project to build CMC brought Cardinal squarely into the national architectural arena. His understanding of his task was embodied in the opening paragraph of his conceptual design proposal:

"Symbols are the way we communicate. Words and sounds are symbols and writings are symbols of words and sounds. Pictures are symbols of feelings, events, and can communicate impressions beyond words in two dimensions. Sculpture goes beyond pictures to symbolize impressions. Architecture, perceived as living sculpture, symbolizes even more the goals and aspirations of our culture. My challenge is to evoke images, creating images in sculptural and architectural forms that symbolize the goals and aspirations of this National Museum."

He understood too that Canada's history and culture have been shaped by geography. The museum building had to represent this fact by appearing to be an integral part of its site, growing out of the landscape, moving and flowing with the contours of the land like a massive outcropping of stratified rock. Looking back in 1984, he declared :

"Within this great continent, wherein lies this expansive and diverse nation, I could sense the feeling of time, the rhythm of time and the way nature had shaped and formed the land - that the formations had been carved by the elements and forces of nature, by wind, rain, the movement of water, the warmth of day, the coolness of night, the seasons. I felt that the building itself should express the evolution of the natural formations."

He felt that a building in harmony with the land would be in keeping with the cultures of Canada's native peoples, and therefore thought in terms of the simple lines and forms that make up the artistic designs of those peoples, seeking to capture their grace and beauty of movement.

If the building was to symbolize the land, it also had to permit the embodiment and presentation of the many cultures that have created Canada, to capture the spirit of the country and of its people, and to serve as a cultural bridge. Not only the remembrance of the past, but the dynamism of the present, and confidence in the future needed to find expression in the new museum; CMC may have its roots in the past, but it really addresses the present, by showing that past cultures live and evolve in present-day Canada. The building interior he visualized as an internal urban park, with its inner life (exhibits, activities, visitors) flowing out into the riverside park, and along the outer terraces of the building, in one great celebration. He sought to add to these natural and human layers a technological layer, aiming at a balanced integration of human and technological needs of the building, with all systems evolving together to create a harmonious whole. Although his original mandate did not extend beyond design of the building's structure, he anticipated the unfolding conceptual designs for the interior facilities, exhibits, programmes, and indeed the mission of the museum, in his belief that artifacts should be displayed in dramatic settings reminiscent of the past. He noted:

"We all live in the bubble of our own perceptions, and we create the world through seeing, hearing, touching, tasting, smelling. If we are to fully comprehend the various cultures that are represented by the artifacts, we should bring as many of our senses as we can to the fore, so that we are transported in space and time to the era from which the artifact came; the artifact should be viewed in context of the culture. This can be accomplished not only through physical settings, but through electronic aids such as audio visual, computer graphics, holograms, lasers, and so on. Where one can witness the artifacts in use, and understand the significance of that artifact to the culture, one acquires a better appreciation and understanding of that culture."

Cardinal's vision of the museum is well summed up in his Design Statement, made public shortly after the announcement of his selection as architect :

"The Museum will be a symbolic form. It will speak of the emergence of this continent, its forms sculptured by the winds, the rivers, the glaciers. It will speak of the emergence of man from the melting glaciers; of man and woman living in harmony with the forces of nature and evolving with them. It will show the way in which man first learned to cope with the environment, then mastered it and shaped it to the needs of his own goals and aspirations. It will depict man as a creature of the earth who knows his tremendous power to change his environment, yet understands that he must live in harmony with it.
The building itself should truly aspire to be an artifact of our time, a celebration of man's

evolution and achievement. It should point optimistically to the future, promising man's continued growth to a higher form of life, exploring not just this continent or planet but outer space as well. It should endeavour to be a spiritual act, and should demand from all those contributing to its design and construction the very best of their endeavours."

The appropriateness of this vision (and the architectural forms in which it was materialized) to the site, to a national museum of human history, and to the evolving vision of the museum's own planners, convinced CMC staff that Cardinal was the right architect for the job. Of all the submissions, his seemed to achieve the best balance between the relationship of the museum to the land, and the relationship of humans to that environment.

The Process

On the day set for the submission of the architects' concept proposals, CMC staff, working with the Architectural Services staff of the National Museums corporation, completed the initial phase of deliberations of the New Accommodation Task Force (NATF) with the issue of the first edition of an architectural programme. This described : the museum's mandate, goals, history, functions, audiences, and organizational structure; the New Accommodation project; site development guidelines, access needs, use and security requirements, and landscaping concepts; general building requirements (e.g. image, functionality, circulation, conservation, security); and a brief description of each of the principal areas desired for the building, with functions, space requirements, and adjacencies specified.

Much of this document came out of the expertise of CMC staff, harnessed through the NATF. The Task Force was divided into a Public Programming Task Group and a Curatorial and Services Task Group, under which there were 12 Study Teams planning for: education and interpretation; visitor amenities; gallery requirements; thematic concepts; security and fire protection; conservation; open storage; reserve collections; office and operational spaces; building maintenance and operations; documentation centre; and new technology. To obtain ideas from a broader audience, the NATF surveyed the attitudes and wishes of the museum community regarding the new museum. Some 1400 discussion guides/ questionnaires were sent out (July 1982) to the

museum's staff, Advisory Committee, Board of Trustees, Canadian Museums Association membership, and other interested individuals.[17] By October 1983 the architectural programme had swollen into a second edition of four large volumes of over 1200 pages. They included more detailed descriptions of individual spaces in the new building, lengthier specifications relating to conservation, security, and communication systems requirements, and a visitor projection model.

The design and production of a building as complex and demanding as a major museum could hardly be a simple sequence of architectural programme, architectural design, and construction, however. It was very much an interactive process. As important to Cardinal as the written documents was the continuing dialogue between architect's and museum staffs. The latter provided initial input (the architectural programme). The former responded with a design, in the form of a model and architectural blueprints, interpreting the programme. CMC staff came back with an analysis and criticism of the interpretation. The drawings were revised and submitted to a fresh round of feedback. And so on. It was a learning process for both parties. It encouraged increasingly specific and careful conceptualization and verbalization of needs, as museum staff and architects learned each others' languages and thought patterns. Furthermore the conversational process was integral to the 'from the inside out' design philosophy of Cardinal; allowing those persons who had lived and breathed museums for years to express themselves fully and provide an informational framework for the architect's creativity. Through this process the original visions - both of the architect and of CMC staff - evolved. And it is the nature of evolution to produce an entity which is more appropriate to its environment than its forebears.

The above is still a simplistic description of the process of design. Its real complexity may be suggested by the number of parties who had a role in it. Central to the process were the architect and his staff and CMC's staff; although in a project this complex there were some disagreements along the road, as each group struggled to understand the other's viewpoint, the relationship was on the whole harmonious. Other components of the National Museums corporation - notably Architectural Services, Security Services, and the Canadian Conservation Institute - contributed to the architectural programme. The RCMP was consulted on security, and the Dominion Fire Commissioner, as

well as provincial and city experts, helped with standards relating to safety concerns. Public Works Canada gave technical information on maintenance standards and space requirements, while the NCC specified design criteria that would ensure the building complied with federal objectives for the development of the Capital Core Area. Numerous consultants helped with engineering standards, laboratory layouts, building lighting, vertical transportation, landscaping, acoustics, and many other matters, while industry was approached about preliminary requirements for products such as

high-density mobile shelving, dock levellers, etc. And, finally, the Canada Museums Construction Corporation was kept busy coordinating.

CMC staff also looked further afield for information, visiting (or consulting by phone or letter) museums and other cultural, recreational, and educational institutions, both in Canada and abroad. The new CMC is not modelled on any single institution, but it was desired to identify the most appropriate features for CMC and absorb them into the evolving design. Among those which had early influence : the

Figure 15
The architects of museum form (Douglas Cardinal, in the red hat) and museum function (George MacDonald, in the white hat) show a VIP tour group the Grand Hall in process of construction.

regional orientation of the Museum of Anthropology in Mexico City, and its role in portraying native culture to a modern society; the achievement of native involvement in the programmes of the Museum of Anthropology at the University of British Columbia; successful children's museums at Boston and Indianapolis; outstanding exhibit techniques at the British Royal Columbia Museum, and particular exhibitry in the Smithsonian's Museum of American History; the changing exhibits programme of Britain's Museum of Mankind; the use of environmental reconstructions at the last-named, in York Castle Museum, Milwaukee Public Museum, and in outdoor museums generally; interactive exhibits in science centres, notably San Francisco's Exploratorium; intriguing uses of space in museums at Santa Barbara, Nagoya and Otami (Japan), and general application of new technology in some major Japanese museums; innovative techniques and technologies at cultural centres such as France's Centre Pompidou and Parc La Villette, Expo 85 and Expo 86, and at Epcot Center. Other debts will be suggested in later chapters. From such influences CMC planners sought to synthesize a new model, unique to the Canadian experience and responsive to a wide range of audiences.

Given all the diverse sources of information, the challenge of the design process can well be imagined. The museum would be a complex, interrelated set of diverse functions; the architectural programme characterized it as "simultaneously a shopping plaza for ideas, a layman's college, a hospital for artifacts, a heritage temple, and an entertainment centre".[18] Some spaces would require maximum creative architectural expression; others, maximum restraint. Some would be detailed, sophisticated environments carefully fitted to precise functions, others would have to be highly flexible. The architect saw the design process as beginning from the inside and expanding outward.[19] First, the inner functions of the museum were studied and understood, a shape assigned to each function, and a building shell wrapped around them. The translation of a textual programme into a three-dimensional building, with vertical as well as horizontal relationships between areas, prompted changes from the original specifications, in an effort to reconcile competing needs for adjacencies.

Above all, building design had to meet the needs of the collections, the core resource of CMC. This meant environmental conditions suitable to the long-term preservation of artifacts, whether in storage or exhibition galleries. The building structure had to be capable of maintaining those conditions in a climate which has extreme temperature fluctuations. The collections need protection from theft, fire, or other dangers, and functional adjacencies conducive to effective management. Artifacts require specialized, stable environments to prevent their physical deterioration. Some are highly sensitive to light, which can cause cumulative and irreversible damage. The traditional response of museums to this problem is to reduce the duration of exposure and level of light in collections holding areas, and to create 'black-box' galleries in which filtered light is used in restricted amounts. Natural light is less easily controlled. This presented a problem for Cardinal, who had relied on the use of natural light in his previous buildings to make them vital and stimulating places. Furthermore it was desirable that the new museum have some natural light to combat 'museum fatigue' to which visitors become prone in black-box galleries, owing to a lack of visual orientation and stimulation. Advantage also had to be taken of the scenic views offered by the site.

The issue of natural light exemplifies a key problem facing the design of museums : are they to be 'artifact-friendly' or 'people-friendly'? Sometimes the provision of maximum protection for the artifacts and as much public exposure as possible of the artifacts seem mutually incompatible. In designing the museum for public use, Cardinal was instructed to ensure facilities and amenities catered to the safety, comfort, and pleasure of visitors. There was to be direct and easy access to public areas for all, and the building should encourage most visitors to enter off Laurier Street. Exhibition galleries had to accommodate large numbers of visitors, circulating at their own speeds, without congestion or over-crowding at any point. The circulation route was to permit visitors to avoid travelling through exhibitions of no interest to them or retracing their steps to re-enter central areas. Also important was that the building's architecture be a symbol of national pride and identity, and convey the image of an active and dynamic institution, so that it attract tourists from the Ottawa side of the river and draw tourists to the capital expressly to see the museum.

Once the requirements of CMC's staff had been satisfied, the next step of the design process was to apply external factors to the shell, further shaping it to the needs of the site and larger context of the Ottawa River basin. The building was to give Laurier Street greater dignity as part of the ceremonial route; on the other hand its street facade had to make the museum look inviting to passers-by, by

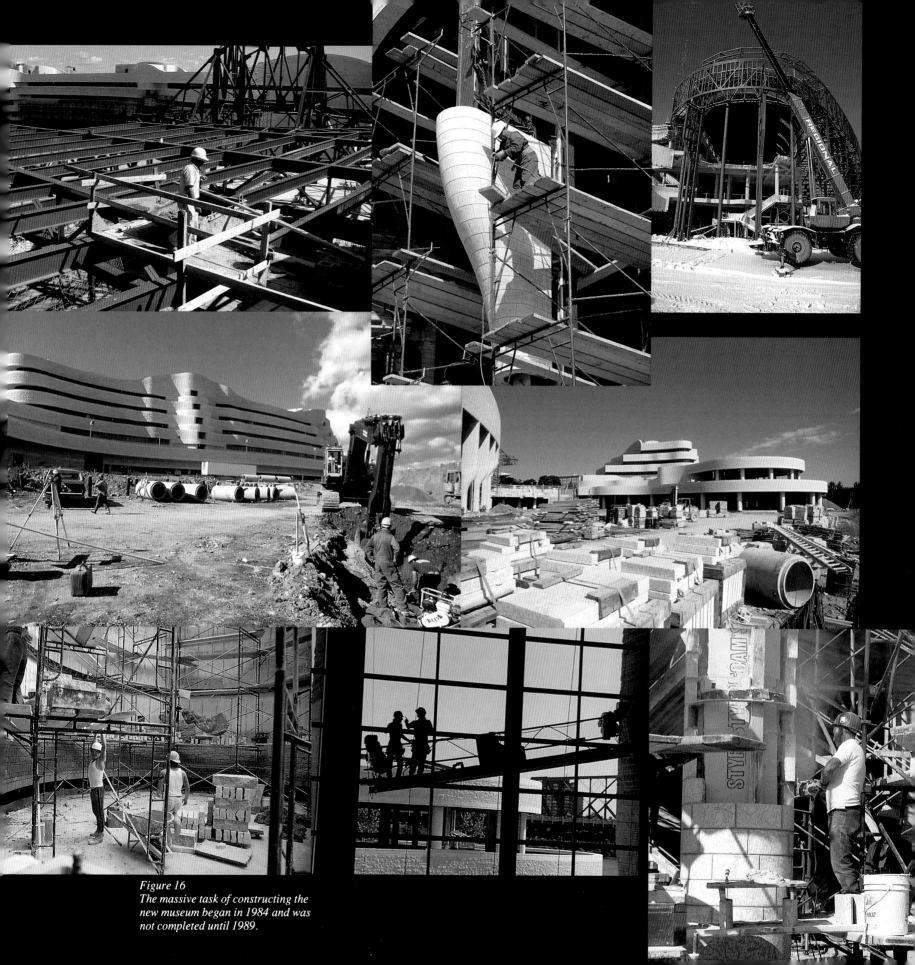

Figure 16
The massive task of constructing the new museum began in 1984 and was not completed until 1989.

providing bustle and colour. Both this and the park side of the museum were to provide a degree of transparency, to give visitors an idea of what awaited them within. The site itself had to be an attractive, hospitable, and dynamic place, with the building providing a framework bounding and protecting special areas of public activities. Above-ground parking was to be avoided, as an unattractive feature; this, together with the satisfactory integration of group arrivals and departures with the internal functions of the museum, proved one of the most persistent challenges during design. It was important to ensure the building not act as a barrier. It was not to obstruct access to Parc Laurier, making it clear that site events were public activities to be freely attended by anyone who so wished. It was not to form an apparent wall between Hull and the river, and the building height should not extend too high above street level. Nor was it to intrude on a public corridor fronting the river and the recreational trail there. Most importantly, both interior and exterior elements of the building were to protect or enhance certain views of the river and of Parliament Hill. The view-cones that the NCC delineated, and their intersection, influenced the shaping of the museum's form. Furthermore, the architectural character of the building was to make it easily identifiable as a major tourist attraction. Since the site was low, special attention was to be given to making roofs - highly visible from Parliament Hill, Nepean Point, the Alexandra Bridge, and high-rises in downtown Hull - distinctive and interesting.

As if all these requirements and constraints were not enough, it was of course expected that the design be able to be constructed within the allocated funding and schedule. This too was a major factor in the continuing re-evaluation and modification of design drawings. It was quite a task to develop economical structural solutions to complex structural forms, in the short time allotted. Cardinal's conceptual design was not approved by Cabinet until November 1983, with site excavation starting the next month and construction early in 1984. This left just under three years to meet the original deadline for construction. Because of this and the evolutionary nature of the design process, a 'fast track' method was adopted, whereby construction proceeded as design decisions were still being made and incorporated into the architectural drawings. The progress of design sometimes did not greatly outpace construction. Here, Cardinal's use of computers in the design process was a great boon; at times the computer-updated drawings were reprinted almost daily.

From the start there were doubts that the 1986 deadline could be met; the interruption of work through labour disputes did not help matters. By the end of 1984 it was apparent how seriously underfunded the two new museum projects were. The completion of their Cabinet-approved designs was threatened. Options were considered ranging from not finishing parts of the building, to finishing it on an extended schedule, to major reductions in the original standards. It was decided by the Minister of Communications to transfer control of the project and of the Canada Museums Construction Corporation to the Department of Public Works, which had more construction expertise; this was done in May 1985.[20] A project review at this stage reached the conclusions that both the Museum and the Gallery needed to be larger than originally expected, that the Museum was badly behind schedule, and both buildings were underfunded, given their size and complexity. Treasury Board therefore increased the funding for both projects to $261 million. This injection of funds allowed the construction of CMC to be completed within a year and a half of its original deadline.

The Product

From concept to opening, designing and building the new museum was a long, demanding, and sometimes frustrating process; yet also rewarding for the many persons who contributed their creative energies and hard work. The end-product is a building that will surely be acknowledged as world-class. Cardinal departed from the international style of mid-20th century architecture which expresses the collective ethos of the commodity-based society. The repetitive elements of that style, appropriate to the industrial age, are giving way in the information age to an architecture reflecting human functions and informing viewers about the nature of the activities and rituals that the building serves. Cardinal's work frees itself from the industrial age's architectural paradigm and hearkens back to an earlier, tribal paradigm, without losing sight of the great architectural achievements of this century. He relies mainly on the organic forms of Art Nouveau, but applied on a scale more monumental, and marries his creative style with that information age marker, the computer. While his earlier architecture reflected images of the Prairies, CMC symbolizes a Pan-Canadian landscape - Canada at the end of the Ice Age - and evokes native longhouses, earth lodges, and igloos.

Cardinal's first abstract vision of the museum-to-be was necessarily modified, yet the fundamental character and sense of identity remain intact. The most obvious difference is that the museum has been fanned open mid-way to provide the appearance, from Laurier Street, of two separate pavilions. The opening provides an unobstructed view of the Parliament Buildings from the street and access to the riverside. The whole building was kept low to avoid obscuring views from buildings across the street. Cardinal also drew the northern end of the museum back from the Alexandra Bridge, again to permit a clear view towards Parliament from the corner of the bridge and Laurier Street. His original design, like a reverse 'S' shape, broke into two discrete curves, one convex the other concave, which were rotated roughly 45° in a counter-clockwise direction. The northern, or curatorial, wing contains the collections holding areas, laboratories, work-shops, and staff offices. The southern wing houses the public facilities : galleries, theatres, and Children's Museum. The public wing dips towards the river more than the curatorial wing, which runs more nearly parallel to Laurier Street. Both blocks are curvaceous on the river side, to blend with the natural landscape, but present a straighter facade to the street, where entrance lobby, gift shop, and theatre foyer present bustle, colour, and activities appropriate to the urban context, and inviting to passers-by. The facade is punctuated in the centre by a great hemispherical entrance plaza, giving pedestrian access to the main entrance and vehicular access to the parking area. The two wings wrap warmly around this welcoming plaza. Under the semicircular plaza lies the parking area.

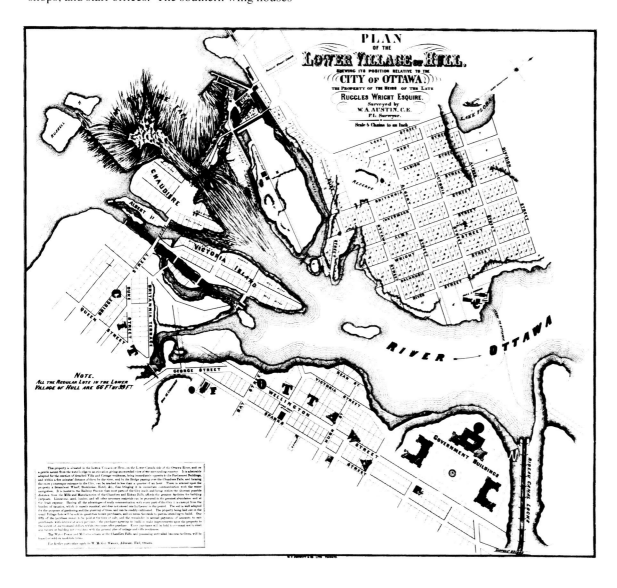

Figure 17
In 1887, when this plan was made Hull Landing was the terminus of the ferry link from Ottawa.

21

Parc Laurier

Following the selection of sites it was decided to chronicle their history before construction erased most traces of their past use. Documentary studies were commissioned in the winter of 1982/83. They paved the way for rescue archaeology projects; such projects are undertaken under time constraints with the aim of obtaining as much information as possible before a site is destroyed. The dig took place between May and November 1983.[21]

The history of the Parc Laurier site stretches far back. The region was first inhabited by humans as the glacial meltwater lakes retreated some 10,000 years ago. The site's first use was probably as a regular campsite of traders of the Archaic period, about 6,000 years ago; they travelled this part of the river, with utensils and ornaments of pure copper obtained from the open pit mines of the Lake Superior shore, en route to the territories of other tribes along the St. Lawrence, as far downstream as the Atlantic provinces.

The earliest European explorers to pass the Parc Laurier site found a large village long established there; later redevelopments, and the removal of gravel when the original Parliament Buildings were built, make it impossible now to gauge the extent of this settlement, though weapons, projectile points, and pottery have been found. When Champlain arrived (1613) it was still being used as a trade junction, for the Eastern Woodlands peoples and the copper producers from the shores of Lake Superior; locally-grown corn, shells, skins, birchbark, and copper were trade items. The local Algonquin Indians were middlemen in the fur-trade between the French and Indian hunters of the interior. Rival Iroquois middlemen contested with the Algonquins through the 17th century, and finally pushed the latter out of the area, but never moved in to settle. The site was near the impressive Chaudiere Falls. Champlain described elaborate ceremonies and tobacco offerings there. Explorers Alexander Henry and Alexander Mackenzie also described the falls and the portages necessary there. Until at least the end of the 18th century the Ottawa River was one main artery of the fur-trade route, linking the merchants of Upper and Lower Canada to the great north-west : 'les Pays d'en Haut'. Voyageurs, coureurs de bois, and missionaries would camp on the Parc Laurier site before or after a trek past the falls.

European settlement did not begin until 1800 when Philemon Wright, a Massachusetts man, purchased property from the Indians for farming, and established a colony near the Chaudiere Falls. Wrightstown was the precursor to Hull. To make his enterprise pay, Wright exploited the forest and the ready market for timber. His first timber raft reached Quebec City in 1806, inaugurating the square timber trade along the river and launching the largest lumber enterprise in eastern North America. He also established, away from the rapids, at Parc Laurier a boat-landing to serve passengers and goods travelling the upper Ottawa River; next to it he built a warehouse, an inn, stables, and sheds. The name Hull Landing was subsequently applied to

this spot, where Wright docked his two steamboats - the first on the river - which operated between the landing and Grenville. The 1983 excavations found remains of the warehouse, but all trace of the boat-landing had disappeared, and it was not possible to extend excavations to search for the inn.

Contemporary with the Hull Landing period, was the era of canal-building, represented by the northern terminus of the Rideau Canal, directly opposite Parc Laurier. The canal reduced the importance of the Ottawa River as a route into the interior, but continuing influx of settlers preserved it as a communication route. In mid-19th century a second generation of entrepreneurs established themselves in the area; they developed the lumber industry one step further, exploiting the energy from Chaudiere Falls, by building sawmills. But fluctuations in water-level made the current a less than satisfactory power-source. So, in 1868, Ruggles Wright junior and Benjamin Batson constructed a steam-powered sawmill at Hull Landing; a further partner, Currier (related to the Wright family by marriage), was later added to the enterprise. The factory was a large operation, incorporating planing-mill, pump room, carpenter's and blacksmith's shops, drying kilns, stables, administrative offices, and other components. Within a year of construction it was producing 25 million feet of planks annually; at its peak it employed some 200 workers. Excavations focused on the remains of the caretaker's residence; the mill's stone platform and various fragments of machinery were also recovered.

In 1878 arson put an end to the sawmill, and the site was abandoned. It was acquired in 1883 by Ezra Butler Eddy, a Vermont native, who settled as a young man in Hull (1851) - at first he made matches, and later baskets and clothes-pegs, by hand, selling them door-to-door. In 1866 he bought a property from the Wright family and built a sawmill. Three years after adding the Parc Laurier site to his holdings, Eddy obtained the rights to make wood fibre products, and in 1888/89 built a sulphite fibre mill there, starting paper production in 1890. This was only the third mill of its type in Canada and at the leading edge of technology for transforming wood into pulp. The operation was carried out in enormous horizontal cylinders known as digesters. The original mill used four, to produce 10 tons of pulp a day; a fifth, vertical cylinder was added in 1900. In 1925 the factory underwent a major transformation; it was by now an extremely large industrial complex, stretching beyond the Parc Laurier site, which was largely used to stockpile

timber and pulp. In 1972 the NCC acquired the site, cleared off stock and pulled down most of the by now obsolete mill. Only the vertical digester, housed in the sulphite tower, remains standing. Near this spot the principal rescue archaeology excavations took place; they uncovered large sections of the mill's foundations. At their conclusion work was done to conserve the remains and the dig was filled in to protect it from the elements.

The documentary and archaeological investigations made it clear that Parc Laurier was a site of some representative significance in the nation's history. It was one of the first sites occupied in the National Capital Region. It played a part in native trade and subsequently in the fur-trade. It reflects the role of interior rivers in opening up the country. And it documents the evolution of the lumber industry : from logging and timber export, through sawmills to world leader in pulp and paper technology. These themes suggested ways to design the museum site and interpret it to the public.

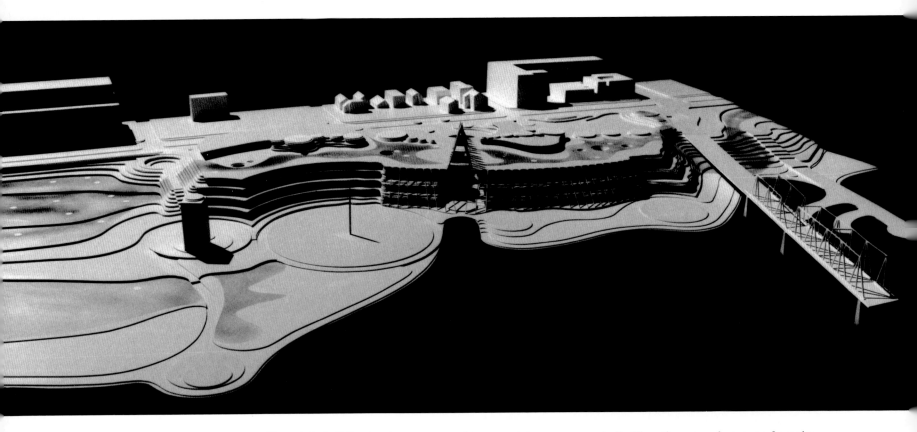

Figure 18
Cardinal's original concept, shown in his first model of the museum, was for a single, continuous building. Here the placement of public and curatorial sections was reversed from the museum's final form.

The whole building has been compared to two petals of a flower with a stamen [22]. The 'stamen' is an offshoot, between the two wings, projecting into the riverside park. It houses food services, a lounge for volunteers and Friends, an information resource centre, and the future terminus for voyages of discovery into non-public areas of the museum. Cardinal has made the roof areas varied, intriguing and, in places, accessible to the public. Three long copper vaults rise above the exhibition galleries, and domes top the Imax/Omnimax theatre and a visitor rest area. By contrast, the curatorial block is a sweeping arc that presents a terraced effect. Its cantilevered structure leaves no level exactly above the level below : upper floors overhang or recede.

Despite the physical changes, the structure's symbolism remains essentially as originally conceived. It is based on a representation of the land as it was when humans first arrived, over 15,000 years ago, and on the topographical history of the site. It is a sculptural monument to the distinctive landscape that faced the first people to come to Canada, in the epoch when the Ice Age glaciers were receding. The curatorial wing, in which are buried the collection holding vaults, is an image of the outcropping bedrock of the Canadian Shield, which itself holds the nation's mineral wealth. This bedrock was eroded and its angular forms smoothed by the glaciers which

overrode it. Then the outwash streams from the melting glaciers undercut the rock; these streams - one of which was once on the Parc Laurier site - are echoed in the watercourse flowing down between the two wings. The public wing, fronted by the huge glazed Grand Hall, is emblematic of the great wall of the melting glacier itself. The copper roof vaults will eventually turn green, and will represent the eskers and drumlins of gravel and glacial till as vegetation recolonized the land. Finally, the parkland between, and before, the two halves of the building depicts the plains over which mankind migrated millennia ago. All this seems an immensely appropriate symbolic starting-point for the story of the Canadian peoples since their coming to the New World, told inside the museum.

The building's cladding was selected to complement its architectural goals. Although variegated brick was a trademark of Cardinal, he felt that for a national monument stone was more appropriate; also it can be made to flow better with the curve of a building, lasts longer, and requires less maintenance. Brick was considered as a dressing, to save money, but injection of extra funds allowed the use of a rough-split Tyndall limestone from Manitoba. This buff-coloured fossiliferous stone is durable and easily carved; appropriately, the limestone was itself overridden by glaciers. The embedded fossils

provide an element of visual surprise in the sculpture. The copper roof cladding helps the otherwise unconventional building harmonize with the other great buildings on the south bank of the river. Roof domes and roof overhangs are lit at night by concealed fluorescent tubes. The curatorial wing, washed by soft lights from the surrounding landscape, seems glowing and mystical. The public wing is lit mainly from the inside; it is like a transparent display case, inviting glimpses into the inner world of the museum, or a sparkling gem nestled in the river valley, beckoning to people on the far bank.

The Grand Hall is the pivotal feature of the museum. Its great window was a source of problems in the design process, allowing in natural light that threatened the artifacts. Splitting the building into two wings permitted the Grand Hall to be turned so that its window faces north-east; as a result, direct sunlight enters only in the early morning. These, and other windows in the public wing, are triple-glazed, coated with a film that helps contain radiant heat, and tinted to screen out much of the solar ultraviolet. The Hall's exhibits are against the wall farthest from the window, and some particularly sensitive artifacts are shielded by specially-shaped columns that punctuate the giant window, though many objects on display here are reproductions.

The glazed front of the Grand Hall not only allows external viewers to look in but offers dramatic views of the river and Parliament Hill. It thus exploits the symbolic connections of the museum with its heritage surroundings. The museum is quite unlike traditional western architecture in which buildings are aligned in rectangular grids determined by straight-line axes. Cardinal has used two parallel straight lines and one circular axis to align CMC. One straight axis is also a line of sight down the centre of the Grand Hall, through the six-storey bay window at the river-end of the hall, and across to Parliament's Peace Tower. Along one side of this symbolic axis, and parallel to it, is aligned a diorama of the monumental sculpture of Canada's Pacific Coast Indians, to emphasize the contribution of native peoples to the heritage of the nation and the world.

It is rarely appreciated that museums are highly-charged, symbolic space/time capsules in which social value hierarchies are made manifest. Architects and artists dealing with space since the Lascaux caves or Stonehenge have understood that all space is hierarchical and symbolically loaded. This is particularly true of ritual space, which works on axial alignments. It is especially potent where a secondary axis crosses the primary one - and here the crossroads model is relevant. Ritual spaces, from the

Figure 19
This final model of the museum shows how the building was split into two separate wings, to allow for a view through from Hull to Parliament Hill.

Figure 20
The Manitoba limestone used for the museum is itself a witness to the Glacial Age whose passing the building form symbolizes; embedded fossils remind us of an even earlier stage in the evolution of life.

dragon lines of ancient Chinese geomancy, to the desert tracks of ancient America, the lay lines, megalithic alignments, and cathedrals of Europe, have embodied this rule. The axial principle has also been applied to CMC, and may inspire future alignments focusing on the museum (cultural centre) and its relationship to Parliament (political centre).

A corollary of the central axis concept in architecture, which deals primarily with interior space, is the concept of matching alignments in exterior space. Often the central exterior axis will cross the interior axis, as in cathedrals where the transept crosses the axis of the nave. Or it can parallel the interior axis. CMC's major exterior axis parallels that of the Grand Hall, and aligns the centre of the entrance plaza with the Peace Tower - a happy opportunity for photographers. Crossing the interior and exterior axes is the circular axis : the ceremonial route; the intersection of the exterior axis and this ring provides a compass point which defines the entrance plaza. Cardinal's use of circular ritual space in his architectural style means that there is no preferred point of view for the building itself; instead there are many viewing points, determined by tangents on arcs of circles. One perspective after another reveals itself as the viewer moves around and through the building, offering plenty of scope to photographers.

Even visitors not conscious of these symbolic alignments will find the museum's form intriguing, and probably gentle and soothing. The humanistic principles embodied in Cardinal's style are a very important feature of the museum's structure. The building is sensitive to human needs. Such as the way natural light has been introduced in rest areas, lobbies, and other places where artifacts are not threatened; it provides psychological relief from the controlled-light areas of exhibitions and capitalizes on the superb local views. Or the spaciousness of the exhibition galleries : high ceilings, and general increase in space (four times that available in the Victoria Memorial Museum Building); if all the floors were laid out on one level they would almost cover the whole of Parc Laurier - making CMC one of the largest sculptures in the world.

The same sensitivity is seen in the attention to public circulation. Several large assembly areas allow hundreds of visitors to group at one time. The main entrance and a tour group entrance are accessible from Laurier Street or the driveway that rims the entrance plaza, while another entrance provides access from the riverside park. The underground parking area (320 spaces) also has direct access into the museum. Escalators and elevators linking the three levels of the public wing are close to the entrances at either end of the wing, which makes it easier for visitors to identify the principal circulation route. There was particular concern for handicapped visitors; elevators, ramps, provision of lower viewing angles, and care in placement of equipment controls, are among the efforts to look after their special needs. In only a few places is universal access still difficult.

Not only the visiting public, but artifacts too have circulation requirements. It was desirable to differentiate human and artifact circulation routes, as far as possible. The separation of curatorial and public wings helps here. They are linked only on the lowest level of the museum, by a wide corridor, the Main Artifact Route. This runs the length of the curatorial block, and other corridors chiefly for artifact movement are on the higher levels of that block; smaller corridors for staff are on the far side of that block. Although there are no such dedicated routes for artifact movement in the public wing, a freight elevator there is reserved for artifacts, and connects with the end of the Main Artifact Route.

If Cardinal's design has satisfied the human needs of the building, it is no less successful in satisfying the needs of the artifacts. The separation of public and curatorial wings has facilitated the differentiation of levels of security for collections not on display. Positioning the collections holding areas in the centre of the curatorial block may be likened to placing a strong-box inside a vault, or more appropriately the West Coast Indian treasure chest which contains other worlds nested in boxes. Wrapping offices and work-areas around the collections holding rooms not only increases their security, but helps guarantee stable environmental conditions. The storage and working areas are about 50% larger than in the total previous accommodations, and provide facilities of a quality commensurate with the importance of the collections and the curatorial work.

In the public wing the choice of materials for construction and limited areas of glazing (outside the Grand Hall) provide the galleries with a high thermal inertia and relatively stable environment. The demands of communications systems, security systems, lighting requirements, environmental controls, and building maintenance equipment necessitated a heavy-duty electrical system. Power failure is guarded against by having the power supply come from not one, but two substations in Hull; if

Figure 21
CMC is linked with Canada's political centre - the Parliament Buildings - by view-lines which have a ritual symbolism.

both fail, the museum has back-up generators to support security and environmental systems.

The architecture of the building is closely integrated with the architecture of the landscape, so that the symbolic themes designed into each complement those of the other. At points it is difficult to say quite where the 'building' stops and the 'site' begins, so that the museum is a transition between the urban landscape on one side and the natural landscape on its other. The museum's plazas, terraces, parkland, and even the building roof (an exotic landscape in its own right) tie the museum into the recreational fabric of the capital's Core Area, not least for the many striking views they offer. The site is a public place of celebratory, entertaining, and recreational activities, amenable to both active and passive uses year-round. CMC's programming there will use themes suggested by the symbolism of the building and the historical significance of the site.

The museum's Entrance Plaza relates to the ceremonial route running along Laurier Street. The character sought here is dignified yet animated.

The museum has been set back ten metres from the property edge to permit ample access and circulation for pedestrians, bicycles, wheelchairs, and tour groups, and allow widening of the street as the ceremonial route is developed. Banners and flags, trees, benches, information poster kiosks, other signage, bicycle stands, and street vendors' stalls, will meet the needs of users of this area. The Entrance Plaza, patterned partly on the wonderful festive plaza in front of the Centre Pompidou, serves multiple purposes. The driveway around it allows for drop-off and pick-up of visitors, and accesses the parking garage. Its central area acts as a gathering-place and a welcoming 'people place', offering a transition from the urban ceremonial route to the museum proper and a first orientation to the museum facilities. Information about offerings in the museum, and other attractions of the capital, will be available from video terminals. The plaza offers a direct sight-line to Parliament's Peace Tower, with the view framed by the two wings of the museum. In this it is like the terrace between the two wings of the Palais de Chaillot in Paris, home of the Musée de l'Homme and the Musée de la Marine, which

Figure 22
The terrace between the two wings of the Palais de Chaillot commands a marvellous view of the Eiffel Tower, much as CMC's plaza offers a view of the Peace Tower.

commands a marvellous view of the Eiffel Tower. The features of the plaza define spaces where entertainers can perform before small audiences, and electrical and communications services are available for equipment for larger performances. Visual interest and expression is added to the plaza by swirling patterns in the walking surfaces (echoing the lines of the building) and varying textures and colour gradations in the poured concrete, by the changing levels framed by long, sinuous seating walls, by curving pools of water, and by small shrubs and other low plantings. The main lobby area of the museum and the curatorial wing, with its sheltering, cantilevered steps, define, partially enclose, and thereby reduce the scale of, the plaza.

Just beyond that plaza is the upper terrace, giving access to the museum's main entrance and to the Grand Stairway leading to a lower plaza. The terrace is where dignitaries visiting CMC will be formally greeted. It too offers a fine view of Parliament Hill. The Grand Stairway is a spectacular passageway down between the two museum wings. Its steps are broad and concavely-rounded; several of the widest form small terraces. It is paralleled on the Grand Hall side by a cascading watercourse which ends in several pools; the waterfall imagery of the stream, and of the stairway, relates to the hall's West Coast theme.

The stairway ends in the Central Plaza, defined by the sweep of the Grand Hall and arc of the extension

holding the restaurant and other facilities. At first a more intimate place than the upper plaza, it begins as a circular flat area finished in exposed aggregate with accent strips of stone at the edges. The plaza then curves outward, paving changing to lawn in a transition between the man-made architecture and the natural parkland. The primary role of the this plaza, sheltered from street traffic noises, is to provide a place for outdoor performances and demonstrations. Spectators can sit on existing benches, the Grand Stairway, and the terraces of the cafeteria and restaurant. The bowl shape of part of the plaza provides favourable natural acoustics.

Beyond the Central Plaza stretches the riverside park, along the lower-lying strip of the site. The landscaping here enhances the natural slope of the land towards the river to form a natural amphitheatre on which crowds of thousands can gather to watch events such as the Canada Day fireworks, performances on a temporary riverside stage, or events on the river itself. This area, tagged 'Theatre Canada', is bounded by the NCC's recreational pathway, adjacent to the river-edge and linking northern and southern ends of the park.

The north-eastern corner, which links Parc Jacques Cartier near its marina, will be developed in the 1990's to reflect the pre-industrial role of the site by the creation of a Waterfront Plaza. Here will be interpreted the fur trade and navigational history. A covered stage will permit animated presentations and demonstrations, such as birchbark canoe construction; there will also be a workshop area. A dock and boathouse will display watercraft from CMC's collections, including vessels acquired from Expo '86 and a three-hulled dance platform recalling the North-West Coast Indian cultural style.

At the southern end of the park, where stands the Eddy mill's digester tower, the theme will be industrial archaeology. The tower will be a backdrop for the main interpretive area : the site of the 1983 rescue archaeology excavations, which has been surrounded by an earth berm to protect it from flooding. To be developed in the 1990's, this area will operate in two modes. Normally it will be used to interpret the park's industrial history; part of the original excavation will be reopened, to demonstrate to the public the archaeological process. On special occasions it will be a staging area for live performances, demonstrations, or lectures on topics such as the industrialization of the waterways or the influence of urban development on the riverfront; the excavations will be covered with risers and platforms

Figure 23
This digester tower is the only above-ground remains of the historical Eddy pulp mill.

at these times. The protective berm, roughly 60 metres across and up to 3 metres high, will serve as seating for the audiences. The digester tower may be adapted to house audio and lighting equipment for performances at this amphitheatre. The outdoor archaeological exhibit will link the park to the interior exhibitions of the museum.

Cardinal's sculptural forms are designed to use direct sunlight to create an ever-changing pattern of shadows across the museum surfaces. At night the challenge is to make lighting effects equally dramatic, yet also a change of pace. The lighting design 23 was influenced by the need for visibility (inside and out), direction and clarity for visitors arriving at night, orientation, views to and from the site, sequencing of experiences, safety of users, and building security. The building's exterior lighting had to accommodate viewing both from close range and from above at distant locations; light sources had to be well shielded, therefore. The public wing is lit mostly from the interior, although surfaces adjacent to the Grand Hall window are also lit, to prevent interior lighting turning it into a mirror. The curatorial wing, on the other hand, is washed in light that spills from other parts of the site. This and continuous edge lighting of the overhangs on both blocks serves security needs. Pedestrian lighting emphasizes comfort and night-time visibility. To allow the eye to adapt to low levels, so that viewers can see into even deep shadows, lighting has been kept below 30 lux where possible; higher light levels create stronger contrasts and would make it more difficult to see at night. Pathways therefore are largely lit indirectly, from the lighting of the building, pools, and the landscaping, rather than by dedicated lamps. Source shielding, reduction of contrasts, and low levels of ambient light permit visitors good night vision.

A problem not yet satisfactorily solved is adequate visitor access to the site. The route directly across the river is as yet little used, but will be encouraged; there are marinas in Parc Jacques Cartier and near the

Rideau Locks. CMC's site can be seen as the apex of a 'Golden Triangle' consisting of the extreme eastern part of Ontario. The triangle is bounded on its southern side by the Lake Ontario shoreline and St. Lawrence River (Kingston to Montreal), by the Rideau Canal on the west (Kingston to Ottawa), and on the east by the Ottawa River (Ottawa to Montreal). This large tract of land is circum-navigable by craft up to 30' long - the limiting factor being the size of the canal locks - and is served by the second largest inland waterway in North America, stretching from Lake Superior to the Atlantic. The world-class potential of this triangular waterway became clear in a 1987 international conference, "The Future of Our Rivers", organized by the NCC in response to the challenge posed by the clustering of cultural attractions along National Capital waterways. The conference stimulated new programmes to provide pleasure-boat facilities between Montreal and Ottawa (by the Quebec government) and between Ottawa and Kingston (by the Ontario government); the St. Lawrence side is already well served. CMC stands as a boundary marker on the exact northern apex of the river triangle, which will be the focus for summer celebrations through performances on the waterfront.

By land there is a pleasant path for pedestrians and cyclists leading from downtown Ottawa to Parc Laurier; it too has been greatly underused. Automobile access is easy enough, via three nearby bridges and the ceremonial route, but the museum has fewer on-site parking spaces than it would wish. However, there is street parking and other parking lots in the museum's vicinity, including a 2000-spot car park in Place du Portage, an office building/ shopping mall complex close to the museum and to the Ramada Hotel built across the street from CMC. When the complex's interior walkways are linked to the museum, it will create one of the largest intercon-nected commercial, hotel, and cultural developments in North America. There are special arrangements for tour and school group buses : a dedicated unloading/loading area and off-site parking. And summer shuttle buses have been added to the public transit system to carry tourists around the ceremonial route. Yet more needs to be done to assist large crowds, drawn in tourist season, to reach the museum. The NCC has been considering a dedicated peoplemover system to serve the tourist attractions that dot the Core Area. It would tie together the nodes of the ceremonial route to offer tourists an integrated, ritual experience appropriate to their pilgrimage to the National Capital.

A peoplemover network makes more sense as an element in a general strategy of developing the banks of the Ottawa River in the downtown core into what will eventually be a continuous string of heritage, cultural, and recreational facilities. CMC is some-thing of a heritage theme park in its own right - with its main museum, its Children's Museum, its Imax-Omnimax theatre, its Médiathèque, its peoplemover mystery tour into the curatorial wing, its outdoor exhibits and performance areas. But the Core Area, taken as a whole, is also analogous to a theme park, with major and minor attractions. Well-planned parks are an important element in lengthening a visitor's stay. Walkways and special transportation connect the attractions, so that visitors can park their cars at a distance and still be in easy reach of all they want to see; the special routes also introduce visitors to minor attractions lying between the more heavily frequented sites. An approach of this type, applied to the Capital Core Area, would benefit not only CMC but all other tourist attractions.

A peoplemover system to serve Parc Laurier and other sites in the capital is an example of the willingness to consider advanced new technologies to make CMC a success. To ensure that the museum can efficiently and effectively meet the needs of the collections, of staff, and of the visiting or remote publics, it has been necessary to think innovatively and to design a complex and sophisticated building which takes advantage of high technology : to control security and environmental systems; to provide media and communications systems; to manage the information which is a central product of museum operations and make it accessible to the public; to support public programming and exhibitions. The museum must not become a morgue for the remains of a dead past, but be a place where life is celebrated and new elements of our culture and identity are generated. If CMC is one of today's most fascinating and stimulating museums, it is in no small part because the building's form hearkens back to natural roots while its functions look ahead to the most modern technologies.

Figure 25
Parc Laurier lies opposite the meeting-place of the Rideau Canal and the Ottawa River. A special ferry service offers visitors an interesting passage between the Ottawa bank of the river and CMC.

the museum as vision

The Canadian Museum of Civilization is more than magnificent architecture. That is but the visual symbol, and itself the container for the museum. What then is a museum? Everyone has a vision of the essence of a museum. Doubtless each interpretation could be supported by reasonable and well-founded arguments. Yet, within these many visions are varied and even apparently conflicting viewpoints among both visitors and museum professionals. The controversy over what a museum is, or ought to be, is now livelier than ever, at this time of significant social transformation; since at least the 1960's museums have been experiencing an identity crisis. The various viewpoints represent disparate personal values. Museums do not share a single, unalterable, dominant characteristic. No adequate definition for 'museum' is valid for the whole existence of such institutions. The goals of museums are set by people. Social change, with its concomitant shift in attitudes, prompts change in any museum that is sensitive to human interests.

When the public thinks of museums, the foremost image for many is of the artifacts displayed in the galleries. Often there are mental associations between particular artifacts and particular museums, such as the British Museum's Elgin Marbles and Rosetta Stone or the Louvre's Mona Lisa and Venus de Milo. Museums had their origins in collections of *special* and tangible objects, whether as curiosities or art treasures, gathered with deliberation. There was usually either a high intrinsic value to the objects (stemming from the materials or the workmanship), or their value lay in their symbolic representation of something in the past : they were the secular counterpart of religious icons. By inference, they were also unique or at least rare. Thus arose the image of museums as treasure-houses or temples. The treasure-house promoted the prestige of its owners. The museum as temple is an even richer metaphor. The museum is a spiritual repository of the past, a shrine for ancestor worship through the veneration of their relics, and a destination of pilgrimages.

Figure 26
The architectural forms of, and security guards at, the entrance to the British Museum of Natural History reflect the traditional image of museums as treasure-houses or temples of secular culture.

Museums acquired appropriate characteristics. Classical formats (temple facades, rotundas) were selected for the architectural monuments housing the collections. The atmosphere inside brought the visitor away from the bustle of ordinary life to an air of formality, solemnity, and ceremonial. In peace one could contemplate, meditate, muse in a direct and personal rapport with each icon. It was not a place to encourage questioning, analysis, or criticism, nor any kind of negative response that might demystify the objects. [1]

Today the image of the museum as treasure-house/temple is still very much alive in the minds of the public, particularly the non-visiting public, and often with reason. A mystical atmosphere remains important to many visitors. Yet now many museums recognize the value of seemingly trivial everyday objects (often no longer rare, but mass-produced),

Figure 27
Museums are research institutes whose principal source of information is material objects.

to tomb, to hospital (the link perhaps being the museum equivalent of cryogenics?) for artifacts.

Not surprisingly, the principal proponents of preservation as the fundamental duty of museums are the conservators and curators who have been schooled to respect and protect artifacts. They argue that a museum's unique role is custodianship of artifacts, many rare and irreplaceable, that have been selected for what they reveal of the past; if the artifacts do not survive, there is no museum. To ensure their survival for future generations, restrictions must be placed on public exposure; long-term care must take precedence over short-term use. This view holds that displayed artifacts should be kept safely in enclosed cases, for direct handling by visitors contributes to their degradation.[3] Conservators have not intentionally sought an adversarial role in the museum world, although there is inevitably some polarization between them and those who emphasize the need to use artifacts effectively to convey information. The debate is still very lively, the conservation approach having been strengthened by heightened interest in heritage preservation.

A slightly different, somewhat allied perspective, is held by research staff who consider artifacts valuable not in their own right but for the information that can be extracted from them. Museums therefore are a type of research institute, unique because of their focus on *material*, rather than documentary, evidence. Some museums categorize themselves as 'research museums' - particularly those affiliated with universities. Although researchers may disagree with conservators on the *prime* function of museums,[4] they are natural allies to the extent that, since research is a continuing process, long-term preservation of artifacts in an unaltered form is crucial. Much of the curatorial world would support the interpretation of the museum as essentially a collection of artifacts.

Reaction against this view gathered force in the 1950's and '60's. It was directed not so much against the notion of the primacy of the artifact as against the ways in which artifacts should be employed. A general increase in concerns with education was reflected in museums by an influx of trained educators. They brought attitudes that were oriented more towards the needs of the museum users than of the artifacts. They sought to make museums an integral part of the educational fabric of society. This vision was not wholly radical; museums were a product of the Enlightenment, with its ideas of educating and spreading cultural values.

that are symbolic of the present; and others collect non-material evidence of past or present. Collections continue to be the essence and core, the *sine qua non*, of museums; but do collections define museums? The past preoccupation with the collections as the be-all and end-all of museums established an image of museums as conservative, gloomy, and boring. Critics have converted the metaphor from temple to tomb, for the interment of dead things with no vital role in the present.[2] The image may be outworn, but it is hard to shake.

Museums that are dominated by their artifacts consider their prime functions to be collecting, preserving, and displaying artifacts; to this list some would add research and interpretation. Museum workers who hold this philosophy emphasize that it is the 'real thing' that makes museums distinctive, and excludes rival institutions such as science centres, theme parks, open air museums, and ecomuseums, from the ranks of true museums. The paradigm of museums as storehouses of treasures has certain practical implications. Much of their resources must be directed towards the maintenance and management of the artifacts in environments conducive to their long-term preservation. Other activities are secondary. From temple,

Like researchers, the educators emphasized that artifacts were important only as sources of information; this information, in turn, was of value only if it could be used for education. Thus research became the means and education the end.

Traditionalists do not deny that the role of museums is at least partly educational, but they tend to believe that exhibiting fulfills that responsibility. Sometimes, particularly in museums of art, *active* education is opposed as creating an undesirable intervention between museum visitor and artifact, and so threatening the direct rapport that can create an intimate and personal experience and understanding.[5] They have criticized educators :

• for introducing 'gimmicks' (such as audiovisual presentations, olfactory special effects, theatrical techniques) or exhibition designs which distract attention from the artifacts themselves, thereby making the medium more important than the message;

• for building separate, and qualitatively inferior, 'education collections' or using replicas (sometimes unannounced) to allow visitors to have hands-on experiences of artifacts;

• for, worse, exposing real artifacts to the same treatment.

One critic has declared that "Presenting any object less than unique, less than rare, or less than usually meaningful, insults the audience and degrades the museum."[6] However, the issue at the heart of the undeclared war between the education and conservation factions is "Preservation or Use?" Both sides seem as irreconcilable as combatants in religious conflicts.

Although the degree of access to the artifacts which educators might have wished has often been blocked by the curatorial interests which have charge of the collections, their interpretation of the museum as fundamentally an educational institution remains dominant.[7] Yet there is a good deal of diversity within the educational faction. Some consider the key role in the educational process to be research and publishing. Others say exhibition and/or interpretation, and still others underline more formal educational programmes. Some prefer to see museums as institutes for *learning* rather than education. Nor is there agreement on target audiences : should museums ally themselves with the school system, with universities, or should they serve the lifelong learner? And how could museums accommodate the rather individualistic learning styles and preferences of their many visitors? It is

Figure 28
Museums use their information resources to educate. Often this has meant introducing school-like classrooms and teaching methods into the museum, as this programme at the Indianapolis Children's Museum instances.

somewhat ironic that the effort to develop museums as educational institutions has been partly responsible for reducing direct access of the public to collections, because of its emphasis on selecting the most 'meaningful' artifacts to be displayed and placing the rest out of sight.[8]

The education paradigm is established well enough to have taken on traditionalist overtones of its own. A newer wave of reform has stemmed from the desire to make museums more accessible and attractive to a broader spectrum of the public. The catchwords of this wave are 'communication' and 'recreation'. A museum, it is argued, might have the loftiest educational goals, but can never hope to attain them unless it first capture the attention of the public and entice them through its doors. Museums have an image problem that the focus on education has done little to solve : they are popularly seen as elitist and, still, boring. The underlying problem, some feel, is that most museums have simply not come to terms with the modern world; perhaps their preoccupation with the past imbues them with a natural conservatism. The proposed solution is to introduce more recreation into museum programming : before the museum can gain an opportunity to teach, it first needs to entertain, to capture the imagination of potential visitors. People learn best from experiences they enjoy most. This lesson has been forthcoming from the entertainment industry and from institutions generally considered on the peripheries of the museum world (science centres, theme parks, open air museums), although it has only begun to penetrate the traditional museum core. It was also learned from surveys of museum visitors, which showed that visiting was motivated by a desire to enjoy as well as to be informed.

The integration of education and recreation necessitates some realignment of the educational paradigm. Hence the museum as communicator, which accommodates both aspects, as well as a realization that museums cannot afford to ignore modern media of communication, but must use them to promote their services and to disseminate their information resources. Museums have gradually become aware that they are competing for public leisure-time with the entertainment industry. To compete effectively they must adopt the weapons of their opponents, including public relations, media relations, and guest relations, since most museums are ever more reliant upon public support for funding - whether from public, governmental, or corporate sources. In particular the "museum as communicator" approach seeks flexible forms of presenting information, to cater to individual needs and draw visitors into the museum experience; 'education' has been reinterpreted to go beyond the didactic approach, with its emphasis merely on the acquisition of factual information, to a process of growth and development of the complete person.[9]

If the interpretation of museums as communicators is relatively new, there is yet a further innovative vision of the role of museums. Its roots lie partly in the notion, introduced in the United States in the '60's, of museums as instruments for social change (by addressing social issues), and partly in the intel-

lectual crisis of academia in the same period. This view challenges the belief that museums present an objective and accurate picture of the past. Its proponents argue that many museum artifacts are merely the random remnants of the past, while others by being collected are decontextualized - that is, taking them from their proper environment in which their use/function is evident removes their meaning, and putting them in a museum environment replaces that original meaning with some other (for example, as artworks) and imposes on them a classification system reflecting the perceptions of the classifiers rather than of the creators of the objects. Furthermore, the process of selecting objects from the collection for display further redefines the new context, according to the world-view of those doing the selection. Similarly, since the artifacts displayed by a museum are like pieces in a jigsaw puzzle, visitors are obliged to fill in the gaps with subjective interpretations offered by museum staff or with their own, at least equally subjective, interpretations.[10]

In effect, supporters of this view argue, a museum does not reveal so much about the past it seeks to represent as about the present society of which it is a part. Robert Sullivan suggests that "Museums are ritual places where societies make what they value

Figure 29
Museums can use entertainment as a vehicle for communicating knowledge, or simply to entice new audiences. The National Gallery of Canada's amphitheatre has proven a pleasant venue for a range of summertime entertainments.

visible," and thereby indicate what aspects of the past are considered consequential, while the method of presentation and interpretation define how the past is to be remembered.[11] Linear presentations in museums may reflect the view of historical development as 'progress'. Exhibitions of the settlement era in North America often tend to focus on the virtues of pioneer values (freedom, neighbourliness, self-reliance, etc.). Functional objects collected from ethnic cultures and displayed in isolation from their cultural context are portrayed merely as art forms. In Canadian human history museums there is often the tendency to create an artificial separation of native cultures (shown as part of the natural environment) and European migrants (as the 'first discoverers' of the country and founders of its history - the assumption being that native cultures have always been here and have no history!) by segregating their themes in different physical locations. Above all there is the problem of stereotyping people of other cultures.

Critics have particularly targeted art museums, for representing the materialistic values of capitalist society and, by treating all objects as high art, communicating the impression that culture is homogeneous. At their harshest, critics accuse museums of being ideological tools celebrating the values of the society that created them, or of re-creating the cultural past in their own image (or rather in the image of stereotypes formed from cultural biases). The dominance of artifacts is itself attacked as suggesting that physical objects can accurately depict a culture, when they are in fact only a poor substitute for the ideas, beliefs, feelings, and values of the individuals and societies which created those objects.[12]

How would these critics solve the problems they have identified? While there is no consensus, the general feeling seems to be that museums should acknowledge their failings, accept their true characters, and re-orient their role to accommodate reality. That new role has been variously described as :

• Social advocate. The museum abandons its traditional distaste for advocacy, assumes a symbiotic and catalytic relationship with its community, and seeks to become relevant to the present by addressing societal problems.[13]

• Forum for the exchange of ideas. Essentially the same idea as 'social advocate', but emphasizing the participation of museum users.

• Metaphor machine. Here the visitor exchanges ideas with him/herself : the museum experience becomes self-reflective and creative; artifacts are the raw materials (like theatrical props) from which each visitor creates personalized metaphors to bring about an understanding of the 'meaning of life'. The decontextualization of artifacts facilitates this process.[14]

• Theatre. The imbalance in object-oriented presentations in museums is redressed by performances which re-create cultural activities. Thus a museum can present alternatives to its own cultural perspectives and serve as a forum for the meeting of cultures. Objects are placed in their only authentic context : use.[15]

• Moral educator. By reflecting the belief and values systems of the societies that create them, museums are unavoidably making moral statements. So they should consciously seek to develop the moral character of their visitors, particularly by encouraging cross-cultural respect and empathy.[16]

There is a common thread running through all these ideas. The museum is not, as is commonly held, a mirror of the past. It is a mirror of the present with a vital role in social development through its ability to communicate (and even to generate) cultural values.

The purpose of this whole discussion is not merely to review the concepts of 'museum' now in vogue. Still less is it to espouse any of the competing viewpoints presented. The diverse perspectives suggest that museums *cannot* be slotted into a single role in society. With a wide spectrum of possible goals, some of them mutually contradictory, it seems either that every museum is expected to be all things to all people or that different museums can reasonably pursue differing roles to satisfy one or other segment or need of the public. A bewildering variety of museums does indeed exist. There have been calls for a taxonomy of museums, to categorize them by scale and type;[17] this would not be easy, for any categorization of the individualistic character of an institution is necessarily artificial and approximate.

The question asked at the beginning of this chapter - "What is a museum?" - is itself misleading. Many answers, all correct from one perspective or other, can be given. The American Association of Museums, for example, for its accreditation programme, defined 'museum' according to the *functions* of collection, conservation, and exhibition - a definition which is well-founded in general usage. By contrast, the ICOM definition stresses the *purposes* of a museum : study, education, and enjoyment.[18] To ask which of these definitions is correct, or to argue about the *primary* role of a museum is to deny the multi-faceted character and evolutionary nature of museums. Our own difficulty in tolerating ambiguity hinders us in accepting the co-existence of diverse lines of thought and assimilating them into a holistic philosophy.

All these perspectives on the role of museums are, to a point, valid. They reflect a variety of characteristics/functions/purposes/roles, some of them still in the process of discovery. These are balanced or given different priorities in different institutions; that is, one museum may select, at a given moment, to emphasize care of collections, another its role as teacher, while a third may seek to make the visitor's experience enjoyable. Yet it is also more than this. At any point it may be possible to categorize an institution by its emphasis of one of its roles over the others, but that categorization may not be valid indefinitely. Museums are institutions that cater to the needs of their society. They must be responsive to societal changes by adjusting their goals and priorities.

We are now undergoing major change that calls for a dynamic response by museums; the contemporary debate on the role of museums is an indicator of the need for a new model, incorporating revised mission, goals, strategies, organizational structure, and systems. Resistance to this notion arises partly out of the established images associated with the name 'museum', which prejudice our thinking and set up artificial boundaries that some hesitate to cross. Those institutions which have adopted different names to represent their new mix of characteristics - cultural centres, science centres, living historical sites, ecomuseums - may receive popular acclaim but, in the museum world, have often earned banishment to the peripheries, although this is beginning to change. Kenneth Hudson expects to see "out-of-date museums fade away and eventually possibly die from a surfeit of learning, dullness, obstinacy and arrogance."[19] The Canadian Museum of Civilization has elected not to be condemned to this fate.

Anticipating the future

To adapt and survive is not a simple matter of choice. It requires an ability to analyze the environment of museums, to distinguish significant trends, to assess their likely effect on the future, and to decide how museums can best respond to changing societal needs. Whether they like it or not, museums are products of their environment and their time. They cannot stand outside the inexorable process of change if they wish to remain a meaningful part of the social fabric. Early in the planning of its future programmes, CMC staff analysed the demographic trends, the social, economic, and political frameworks within which the museum would have to operate, and the competitors for the leisure-time of its potential audiences. From there they extrapolated the implications for museums. The conclusions were used in building a theoretical model which has now been realized in CMC.

The 1960's and early '70's were a period of growth for the Canadian museum community, with increases in the number of institutions, of museum professionals, the size of museums, and museum attendance. The emergence in 1968 of several separate museums out of a single National Museum exemplifies the expansion. At the risk of oversimplifying, this trend may be attributed to a buoyant economy, rising interest in national identity and heritage, and growing national self-confidence. The late '70's and '80's, however, have been a period of consolidation or retrenchment as the museum community struggles to adjust to new constraints. Most notably, since the economy could not sustain its rate of growth, the quest for funding has become increasingly competitive. There have been demographic changes. Major technological change in all areas, including the service sector, has brought new public expectations for quality and efficiency of service. Evidence on how these changes have affected public attitudes towards museums is a little ambiguous. Federal and provincial surveys indicate favourable public attitudes towards cultural activities,[20] but the public does not place cultural affairs high on its agenda for government funding. The relationship of museums to their markets - visitors, government, other cultural agencies, and the private sector - is uncertain.

It is certain, however, that the pace of change continues to accelerate and to disrupt established patterns. We are in the throes of a revolution - transforming industrial society, with its economy based upon the production of material goods, into an information society. Information is becoming wealth in its own right, a commodity to be traded.[21] In industrial society part of the appeal of museums was that they enshrined intrinsically precious objects which symbolized a society whose primary values were tied to material wealth, and which essentially validated the status of its members who possessed similar wealth-objects. In an information-based society the important feature of museums will be their ability to use objects (and non-objects) which are valuable for their *communicative* qualities, to provide experiences in which information is encoded. Museums will help people distinguish between data and opinions which masquerade as facts, statistics, and images, so they may judge for themselves the relative value of each.[22]

How much we can learn from the past, to help us cope with the trauma of rapid change, is open to question if this is an age of discontinuity. Museums can be useful in communicating some sense of continuity and enduring identity. In the industrial age smaller cultural forms were overwhelmed by capitalism. The paraphernalia of those cultures became the flotsam and jetsam of the cultural world, and museums were created to gather it up. Those objects alone, decontextualized, no longer communicate a sense of the past, or a sense of the present as inheritor of the past.

According to Dr. Robert Kelly, of the University of British Columbia, social status in the new information society will derive from people's information-providing experiences, more than from wealth objects they possess, and the quality of their experiences will reflect in the value assigned them.[23] The implication for museums is the need to rely less upon traditional exhibits using glass-fronted display cases, which both enshrine the artifacts and emphasize their value by protecting them. They must turn more to experiences of a social nature (blockbuster shows such as King Tut, although their exhibit techniques are very traditional, provide a social experience which has a status-enhancing value), or a personal nature involving a more direct experience between visitor and artifacts, whether it be by contemplative relationship or by recontextualizing artifacts in their cultural framework.

As society is transformed by technological, macro-economic, and other forces, tendencies towards greater homogenization and centralization are becoming more marked. Western civilization in particular is becoming a pluralistic society : multiracial, multilingual, multicultural. At the same time, the international traveller finds now the same airports, hotels, fast-food chains throughout much of the world. The mass media have played a major part in the homogenizing process. But because they tend to present information detached from its context they do not provide an understanding of other cultures that seems coherent, relevant to our own experience, or other than exotic. Culture usually reaches its

natural state of growth, and thrives, within a restricted locale, but media representations are inclined to strip out meanings with local relevance.[24]

Another manifestation of the social transformation underway is that in the workaday, Monday-to-Friday, nine-to-five routine of Western civilization people are increasingly reduced to categories reflecting their role in the workforce (e.g. computer programmer, primary school teacher). The counter-trend to homogenization and centralization is a growing expression of the human need to identify and define oneself according to one's cultural roots. This can be partly explained by a desire for immortality through membership in a smaller and more distinctive social unit, a particular community, or an ethnic group, or through a relationship to one's ancestors or country of ancestry; or perhaps by the wish to balance the influence that a technologized and rapidly changing world has on our lives, with a link to reference points in a more down-to-earth and durable heritage. Museums can do much to answer these basic human needs for a sense of both personal and shared identity.

A noticeable attitudinal change over the last couple of decades is a greater awareness of, and concern for, heritage and its preservation. 'Heritage' had been used synonymously with 'heritage conservation', and applied narrowly (to architecture, archives, natural or historic sites), but it has gradually taken on a broader meaning to incorporate tangible and intangible aspects of the past, both personal and collective. The proliferation of community museums, as well as of specialized museums - which are able to focus in on particular aspects of the past rather better than multidisciplinary museums - and also of museums established by corporations to validate their own spheres of operations, bears testimony to this.[25] So too does the propagation of associations, at all levels of society, concerned with the conservation or management of the physical remnants of the past, most of which remain outside the walls of museums as traditionally defined; museums are only the most highly institutionalized forms of access to heritage. In Canada more than two thousand institutions act as custodians of heritage, receiving over ninety million visits annually.[26]

Museums cannot hope to respond to the reawakening of the notion of stewardship of our cultural past, to ensure continuity of the community, by encompassing within their control all the physical evidence of the past; nor would such a monopoly be desirable. But they can enhance an awareness of cultural identities, and foster sensitivity towards our historical and natural environments, by instilling the attitudes and teaching the strategies necessary to ensure we do not lose touch with our roots. This is not a reactionary role. It is perfectly appropriate for a society which embraces change as a natural state of affairs; for heritage itself is "a dynamic process, the way we transform society without losing its recognizable configurations, conserving our inheritance not in the *face* of change, but in the *flow* of change." [27]

It has already been mentioned that museums, rightly or wrongly, are considered elitist. This is probably truer of the larger institutions than of small local museums, although the latter's stereotyping of the past is open to criticism. [28] The charge of elitism is based partly upon the notion that museums preserve high culture - wealth objects presented essentially as art forms - and thereby promote the associated aristocratic or bourgeois values. The professionalization of museums has itself contributed to the image. Critics claim that it has created a wider gap between museum staff and visitors, reflected in a special museological jargon employed by the professionals, termed 'curatorese' or 'the curator's code', which few visitors can understand. That professionalization, by providing museum staff with a common education, tends to promote standardized and highly structured interpretations of history, and conformity in methods of presenting information. That it has encouraged reduction of public access to only a very small proportion of the total collections, specially selected by staff as relevant to the messages they feel worth communicating. Professionals are said to embrace standards for excellence incompatible with popularity, and to be content to communicate with a limited audience of particular tastes, interests, and level of education; to be inclined, in fact, to design exhibits to meet the approval of their peer group more than of the general public. Thus they scorn any institutions that attempt to be more populist. [29]

This picture represents a *common* image of museums, not necessarily a *correct* one. At least, it is a mistake to tar all museums with that same brush. The existence of a counter-trend in the museum world is evidenced by the fact that it is largely from elements within the museum community that charges of elitism are most frequently heard. This counter-movement, now a very vocal part of the museum community, stresses the need to democratize museums. There are many aspects of democratization. One is to make museums, their collections, and their other information resources more accessible physically, intellectually, and emotionally. The National Museums of Canada declared their commit-

ment to this back in 1972, and it has since then been a key goal of CMC. It is easy to pay lip-service to an ideal, but harder to translate it into practice. Glenbow Museum and the Museum of Anthropology at the University of British Columbia are among the few making more directly accessible a large proportion of their collections (via 'open storage' techniques) and the collections catalogues. [30]

In public programming, democratization has been interpreted to mean : assigning larger areas to display; greater use of a variety of media to communicate the messages of exhibits, to disseminate information to wider audiences, and to promote museums and their activities; longer and more convenient hours of opening; more amenities for the comfort and convenience of visitors; decentralization of collections, whether by travelling exhibitions, or by repatriating artifacts back to the locales of their origin where they have more significant meaning. With regard to education, democratization means reducing the role of museum staff as mediator between public and heritage, or rather, downplaying the authoritative role that mediation has tended to assume. This entails increased opportunities for personalized and self-directed learning along pathways set by individual interests. Only in the last decade have information technologies made this goal of customized learning truly feasible. Finally, founded in the notion of the museum as public trust and as manager of the community's heritage, democratization means greater participation by the community in the content and direction of museums.

In the past, the museum profession has shown a deep-seated fear of possible undesirable effects of populism and democratization. At the same time there has been a conflicting desire to achieve a success that can be measured in popularity demonstrative of effective service to the community. Society places greater value today on accountability of, and public involvement with, public institutions. If museums are to remain viable service institutions they cannot keep aloof from these general trends, but must find their own ways to respond to changing social demands.

It is doubtful that anyone, whether believing museums should be populist or elitist, could argue convincingly that museums have a *raison d'être* remote from their various audiences. Yet it is only comparatively recently that museums have sought to replace assumptions on the nature and needs of their audiences by detailed examinations. Audience studies are particularly important at this time of major social upheaval. They have revealed demographic trends with important ramifications for museums. One is that the educational level of Canadians generally is increasing, owing to better access to higher education, more time available for continuing education, and greater competitiveness in a shrinking job market. That there are more people enrolled, part-time or full-time, in university today, is also partly because much of the Baby Boomer generation is still of an age to be involved in post-secondary education, while that generation's own offspring are now reaching university age; it is also due to a general growth in population. It is uncertain whether, or how long, this trend will continue.

It has long been known that the majority of adult visitors have university educations. A study of visitors to the Victoria Memorial Museum Building, when it housed CMC, showed the following features of visitor profile : that there was a higher proportion of post-secondary educated visitors than in the total population (64% as opposed to 39%); that there was a higher proportion of Baby Boomers, defined as 19-39 years, than in the total population (64% as opposed to 34%), and a lower proportion of senior citizens; that there was a higher proportion of English-speaking visitors than in the total population; and that 59% of visitors came in family groups. One might conclude, then, that as the level of education in the population rises the number of museum visitors should rise too; but matters are not quite this simple.

A more difficult problem for museums to address is the growing gap between the well-educated and poorly-educated segments of society. Museums can provide individualized and relatively unstructured learning processes at far lower charges than university fees. And while they may not be the best institutions to fight textual illiteracy, certainly they are well-equipped to teach visual literacy.

Owing partly to high unemployment and greater part-time employment, as well as to major growth in the senior citizen segment of the population, leisure time available to people is increasing. Though there is no guarantee that this leisure time will be spent on museum visits, the rising interest in heritage and greater acceptance of the idea that learning is a lifelong process will encourage attention towards the cultural sector. The majority of the population does not visit museums very frequently, but the minority that does seems to have increased its museum visiting over the past decade or so.[31]

At the same time, the tastes and expectations of the traditional (i.e. well-educated) museum audience are becoming more sophisticated and demanding. Their fuller awareness of, and interest in, cultural history can be expected to fuel a desire for increased access to more detailed information. Furthermore, in a world becoming ever more geared towards tourism, those with leisure time will be more discriminating in use of their time. They will seek qualitative experiences with greater personal participation, whether they define 'quality' by recreational values, intellectual stimulation, or cultural meaningfulness. Ironically, precisely those institutions which traditionalist museum professionals have scorned - open air museums, science centres, world's fairs, theme parks - have been largely responsible for raising expectations of the museum-going public. If museums are to attract, or increase, the presence of those with leisure time to spend, they must be able to offer experiences catering to individualized interests and values, and relevant to current issues and popular concerns. More specifically they will need to refocus their attentions away from school-age visitors and more towards such client groups as the elderly and the handicapped. The greater numbers of single persons or parents in the population may also require less emphasis on programmes for large family groups. The museum's potential audience is becoming increasingly fragmented, and it cannot safely specialize its attentions as in the past.

Another aspect of the greater sophistication of museum visitors today is their familiarity with the new technologies driving social change. VCR's, microwave ovens, video games, compact disc players, home computers, automatic bank tellers are taken for granted in everyday life. The Baby Boomer generation, with its university education, its relatively high standard of living, and greatest disposable income, has been the most influenced by the range of technologies. And again it is those institutions on the peripheries of the museum world which have played a large part in introducing such technologies to the public in the context of recreational and cultural experiences. The influence of communications technologies, especially television, on public expectations for the delivery of information should not be ignored either.

Museum visitors are much more sophisticated in the use of technologies than they were in the 1970's. Many have had some exposure to computer technology, such as retrieving self-defined items of information from large electronic databases; there is *substantially* greater exposure of university students to online searching techniques than even in the recent past. Thus they are becoming accustomed to accessing large quantities of data, often from remote locations, and rapidly extracting from them precise elements of information. The typical museum, however, has advanced relatively slowly in the technology it makes available to its audiences. Museum workers are often less adept in new technologies than many visitors. Some visitors are not merely *receptive* to the use of technology in museums, they *expect* it as an integral part of the museum experience. While museums must avoid chasing the technologically trendy, those which can successfully anticipate future trends and incorporate them into the museum experience can expect great rewards. On the other hand, museums can also counter-balance the technological bias of society by offering intuitive and mysterious experiences which are becoming increasingly foreign to everyday life.

Bob Kelly has provided a particularly interesting analysis of museums' audiences and potential audiences.[32] To discover how museums can reach the large and untapped publics which rarely if ever visit them, we must first know why people visit museums at all. Studies have shown that the obvious reason - to learn about the subjects represented in the museum - is only part of the answer. Another motive is recreational : to engage in a meaningful leisure activity. Often this is related to tourism.

Tourism is the secular counterpart, and the modern successor in the western world, of religious pilgrimage.[33] Pilgrimage has its roots in cults spread from the locale of origin to distant areas, by missionaries, traders, or other itinerants. The diffusion of the cult tends to carry with it linguistic, ceremonial, social, and technological baggage and is invariably linked with the mystification of rare objects of the cult (icons or relics). It is the veneration of such cult objects - surrogates for the once-living prophets of the cult - that leads believers to withdraw from routine daily life, leave their homes, and travel long distances to sacred sites where the relics are housed, to see (or even touch) the 'real thing'. There, or en route, the pilgrims may acquire badges, markers, or minor relics of their own to signalize their pilgrim status or the achievement of their journey. These features show parallels to tourism and to museum visiting.

Tourism is an increasingly prevalent support to the local economy; it may soon be the principal industry in Britain. It may gradually supplement or even supplant the materialistic status system with the experience-based status system appropriate for the new information age. From a sociological perspective, the needs of tourists are : to engage in meaningful leisure, to break from everyday routine, and to undergo a transformation through having visited destinations with symbolical significance. Museums are a type of institution that provide *meaningful* leisure activities, because they embrace elements of education, the arts, and cultural heritage under one roof; they are seen as arbiters of what is culturally significant, and their curators use a special academic jargon. To visit (or rather, to be known to have visited) a museum, particularly a prestigious one, is considered evidence of intellectual credentials and taste, and an activity congruent with a certain social status. Museum visitors, commonly educated in arts, humanities, or social sciences, visit museums because they offer an experience with educational content. Museum going is an important form of self-expression and an almost obligatory social behaviour for persons of their status.

Consequently, museums have had imposed upon them the role of status symbols distinct from the purposes they set for themselves. As society undergoes its present transformation, the status system too is being altered. In the industrial age it was based upon wealth. The markers symbolizing status were material possessions with high market value; conspicuous consumption and display are associated with this status. Social groups with status are motivated to support institutions that perpetuate their status. We can include museums, as temples enshrining wealth objects, among such institutions. Today educational attainment is increasingly encouraged by the conferring of social status on its holders. This is particularly true because the post-industrial society is highly dependent upon information technologies, and educational institutions focus more and more upon the competence to create or use such technologies. Status, economic reward, and power are becoming more tightly linked to educational achievements. In this new context, educational level and its associated status are not so well expressed by the display of wealth objects as by 'revealed taste' : objects or behaviours known to be associated with persons of a high level of education, and whose cultural or aesthetic significance is evident to one's peers. Such behaviours, or the acquisition of objects evidencing those behaviours, thus become necessary to demonstrate and maintain status. Tourism, and more specifically museum visiting, may be considered 'rites of passage' that produce the transformation whereby one claims social status.

Dr. Kelly, prompted by Graburn's distinction between cognitive, reverential, and associational experiences in museums, [34] has suggested three fundamental needs of museum visitors : intellectual, sacred, and social. Intellectual needs (i.e. to know or understand) are those normally catered to by curators, educators, or exhibit designers in developing museum products. How well they succeed has long been a subject for argument. Some critics have charged that information is provided at too high a level - viz. the academic level of the curators - and in too much quantity, so that visitors become fatigued (information overload) when they try to assimilate it. Others have charged, thinking of different exhibitions, that the messages are reduced to the lowest common denominator, aimed at the lowest level of visitor education, and tend towards inaccuracy through oversimplification. Evidently you can't please everybody! The visitor's sacred needs are tied to the role of museums as pilgrimage destinations : repositories of objects from the past considered to be worthy of preservation, which thus take on an iconic character. By linking us to our past they provide an opportunity for a type of ancestor worship, in a society where explicit ancestor worship is not acceptable. The sacred needs are also tied to the rites of passage that confer social status through museum visiting. The behaviours of visitors to traditional museums are much like those observed in sacred places : whispering, walking softly in respectful postures, restraining the high spirits of children. The social needs of museum visitors are for opportunities to be seen visiting by one's peers, and to be able to socialize with them there; both architectural spaces and museum events (e.g. exhibition openings, receptions) can cater to this need.

It is very important for museums to know and analyze the natures and needs of their users. Although there are very many museum audiences of diverse characteristics, Kelly has suggested one very broad, but useful, classificatory distinction : between 'traditional visitors' and 'new visitors'. We have already mentioned some of the former's charac-teristics, particularly their educational background which, being similar to that of museum curators, allows them to understand some of the curatorese used to interpret the artifacts. They are comfortable with the static exhibit, where artifacts are the focal point. They are less interested in the quality of visitor services or amenities, or special activities. They are typically frequent visitors to cultural institutions, seeing museum visiting as integral to their social status. They have been influenced by family upbringing, education, and peer relationships to define museum visiting as meaningful leisure; they are likely to condition their children to think in the same terms.

'New visitors', by contrast, are a group which is growing in society and coming into greater social prominence. They too have a high level of education, but in technical subjects appropriate to the information age. They seek to acquire social status by imitating those who already hold it, in behaviours such as museum visiting, which may not be inher-ently interesting to them and might not otherwise be defined by them as a meaningful leisure choice. Not having a family tradition of museum visiting, and not being familiar with curatorese, they tend to become bored with museums quickly. Since they visit museums mainly to acquire status, a single visit to an institution suffices and must be accompanied by the acquisition of physical evidence of their having been there : markers such as photographs, souvenirs. The new visitors group has a greater interest in non-collection services such as lounges, restaurants, film presentations. They also seem to have a greater interest in access to the technical operations in backstage areas, partly because their own technical background allows them to relate better to those aspects of museums, and partly because there is extra prestige in penetrating the inner sanctum where more 'real things' are kept.

The message that Kelly has for museums is that they have been a factor in the social stratification system in Western societies in the past but, as the industrial age is superseded by the information age, there is no guarantee that they will remain an important social institution. The new social elite may define museums out of their list of meaningful leisure activities unless museums recognize the diversity of needs of different types of visitors and cater to them all. This will involve modification of traditional approaches to exhibition, interpretation, and public programming, as well as the development of new services and use of new technologies with which 'new visitors' are comfortable.

Above all, museums must learn to communicate in terms with which the technologically-oriented sector of the public is familiar, and to anticipate and answer the different questions that those persons ask. More concretely, it may be expected that 'new visitors' will see artifacts less as sacred objects and will wish more direct contact with them; that they will wish to learn about the technical processes involved in museum work; that they will want multimedia presentations; that their tendency to question (not accepting the authority of curators) will necessitate providing access to more information; and that, having a high tolerance for uncertainty, they will expect speculative rather than authoritative inform-ation. To return to a point already stressed in this chapter : society is evolving, and museums must evolve with it if they do not wish to become the dinosaurs of the cultural sector.

It might be thought that museums' survival is guaranteed because of the unique role they play in society, as interpreters of the past via the medium of material objects. But, rightly or wrongly, the success of museums is judged, by those who fund them, in terms of the number of persons served - whether directly (through visitation) or indirectly (through outreach services) - not the quality of services or programmes. Museums, and cultural institutions in general, are consequently under increasing pressure to become public-oriented rather than peer-oriented.

In the National Museums, the pressure has come mainly from the federal government, which funds them. Policies such as democratization and decentralization of government cultural programmes, elimination of duplication, cost-recovery for public programmes, as well as multiculturalism and access to information legislation, all affect the National Museums. Also influential has been the govern-ment's growing appreciation of the importance of cultural identity in creating a sense of community, and of the importance of preserving heritage which is part of that cultural identity.

Economic conditions in the 1990's are uncertain, with modest growth apparently the best for which Canada can hope. Governments at all levels are cutting back their funding of cultural activities, while increasing money for tourism. Museums have often had to respond by reducing their own services to the public, which does not help in winning the public support so badly needed. The current political perspective is that resource allocations should be determined by market success. Museums are therefore looking more towards private sector sponsorship, or towards direct payment for services by users, but are finding that competition for these resources is intensifying.

Museums are competitors amongst themselves for public support and for funding although, as tourist attractions, cultural institutions in a given region can operate more effectively in mutual support. The combined strength of all attractions persuades tourists to select that destination over others. Cooperative relationships can be established, so that the local market is enhanced rather than diluted. The commercial sector provides more of a threat to public cultural institutions. A not inconceivable scenario of the future would be for theme parks, expositions, or similar institutions, to usurp the public programming aspects of museums, leaving the latter only to collect, store, preserve, and broker artifacts to the commercial centres. Certainly theme parks are improving their skills in heritage presentation, increasing their educational content, and are already in advance of museums in providing comfortable surroundings, entertaining experiences, imaginative uses of new technology, and in marketing and financial management skills. Museums are just beginning to cultivate such skills. In some sectors a strong feeling of scorn remains for theme park methods or anything that is at all Disneyish.

Let us take a brief look at the competition for the public's leisure time, and how museums can respond. Television is the major magnet, attracting 3.27 hours a day of the average viewer's attention, whereas in its old home CMC held its visitors for no more than one hour *per year*. It attracts 69.4% of federal funding in support of the cultural sector, compared to 1.6% that CMC received in the early '80's. TV is highly market-oriented, a major force in the economy, and able to take advantage of new technologies (e.g. telecommunications, VCR). While there can be little hope of diverting television audiences *en masse* to museums, the latter can exploit TV by providing input for its programming, and so reach a wider audience.

Cinema is a comparable leisure activity, attracting 66% of Canadians to at least one show a year; again the lesson here is to use this medium within the museum. The same could be said of music, theatre, and dance, the public already being used to travelling long distances to attend quality performances. Reading is another leisure activity through which to reach remote audiences in the same education bracket as traditional museum visitors. Sixty per cent of Canadians have a hobby, and 36% attend craft festivals or fairs; since museums hold information on traditional techniques in crafts, as well as examples, this area could be more successfully exploited for hobby-oriented audiences.

A more serious competitor to museums is sports, not least because it is another manifestation of the pilgrimage phenomenon. The super-domes that have sprung up across North America in the past decade have added impetus by providing major pilgrimage destinations. Although sports are generally better viewed on television, for fans there is no substitute for the live experience (the 'real thing') shared in the community of a host of other pilgrims to whom they are bonded by the experience. This experience establishes their status in the eyes of their peers as much as museum visiting does amongst its faithful. Furthermore, the sports world has already linked up very successfully to modern electronic media : both small-screen and large-screen presentations diffusing the message of the cult worldwide. Museums have as yet ventured little involvement in the sports world, although the latter has created its museum-like Halls of Fame. Perhaps the lesson they can most profit from here is that sports are highly marketable because of their emotional, visceral content and because the sports world, like the mass media, is event-driven. Museums, as continuous institutions, are by definition non-events.

Museums find themselves in a difficult situation as they enter the new information age. As the full diversity of needs and interests of the potential audience becomes evident, so does the necessity of responding with a much wider range of approaches, techniques, technologies, media, programmes, services, and facilities. It is no longer sufficient for museums to centre their attentions on artifacts and the static displays in which artifacts are usually presented. Expectations of museum visitors and the tourist population generally are rising, partly because of other cultural or recreational institutions with which museums are in competition. Visitors continue to seek both educational and quasi-religious experiences in museums, but they also want to be entertained, to have all their senses stimulated, and to be offered comforts and conveniences not previously found in museums, as well as to have access to the social opportunities and status symbols already discussed.

Within this spectrum of needs there are many conflicts to be resolved. Canadian museums, if they are to survive by attracting more visitors and money, must diversify their activities, programmes, and services, and adopt new missions, new strategies, new skills, and new technologies *en route*. Yet this they must do in an environment in which governments are forcing new obligations on them while reducing financial support, an environment in which they face stronger competition than ever before. And an environment in which some of their own traditionally-held attitudes and assumptions may prove obstacles, such as : that museums are

authoritative arbiters of culture; that the information they offer is scientifically objective, calling for neither questioning nor debate; that they, almost alone, are the champions and protectors of heritage; that the 'real thing', with its special mystique, is the only valid tool available to museums for representing the past. This is really too sweeping a critique of museums today, but there *are* museums that fit the stereotype to a good degree. Most modern museum directors would probably agree that museums cannot stand still in the face of societal change. It is quite another matter, however, to agree on the route of development to follow. There are many diverging visions of the museum of the future, reflecting the extent to which museums are themselves already diverging in form and philosophy.

Museums of the future : some prototypes

When is a museum not a museum? Is it really productive to define 'museum' restrictively, if that closes our eyes to the future? In formulating a model for what the new Canadian Museum of Civilization should be, its staff were not content with generalized analysis of the environment to guide them. They looked around the world for the best and the most innovative, not only in museums, but in a range of cultural, educational, and recreational institutions. A Resource Centre was set up to house and organize information materials relating to the latest thinking and developments in museological matters, archival documents relating to the New Accommodation project, and the numerous trip reports and related materials brought back by staff who travelled in Canada and abroad. It was vital to get a good idea of what was going on elsewhere, to build a composite of what the 'museum of the future' might look like. A number of museums and other institutions were identified which possessed one or more attributes that seemed to fit the new type. This section will look at some of the current trends and the general situation of museums worldwide.

With the growing prominence of Japan in economic and technological matters, its growing interest in other cultures, and renewed confidence in its own culture, it is perhaps not surprising that the most extensive and exciting museum developments are in that country. Japan's willingness to invest in the cultural sector is reflected in its hosting of three international expositions in recent years : at Osaka in 1970, Okinawa in 1975, and Tsukuba in 1985; Osaka is to host yet another in 1990. In that same period more than $Cdn5 billion was spent by the

Figure 30
A cross-cultural anthropological
approach to exhibition, and versatile
display techniques, in Japan's Little
World Museum of Man were one
source of inspiration for CMC's
planners.

Japanese to build museums. CMC staff looked particularly closely at the National Ethnological Museum (part of a cultural centre created on the site of Expo '70), the Little World Museum of Man (near Nagoya), the MOA Museum of Art (Atami), and the National Museum of Japanese History and Folklore (Sakura City).

China is surely the sleeping giant of the museum world, for it contains more archaeological treasures awaiting excavation than the rest of the world combined. It has started planning for major new museum construction all across the country, along with *in situ* historic preservation, in the hope that the tourist revenue thus attracted will help finance the transition from an agricultural to an industrial economy. The Warriors of Xian have already become a 'diplomatic corps' of a sort, promoting China's heritage abroad. An entire department of the Ministry of Culture is devoted to the promotion of international exhibitions of museum objects from China. Major new film studios under development in

Beijing are dedicated partly to disseminating Chinese history and literature abroad : a careful blend of economics and nationalism.

Australia, while it has done a modest amount of *in situ* perservation, has been mostly active in planning a suite of new National Museums. A large war museum has already opened and an even larger history museum is intended for Canberra, as part of a string of museums around a lake (reminiscent of the Canadian cluster taking shape around the Ottawa River).

It has been predicted that by the beginning of the next century Asia will be the industrial centre of the world, the Americas the natural resource centre, and Europe will be the museum of the world. Europe's economic vitality will depend on the growth of tourism into the foremost industry of the world, in place of the military/industrial complex. It seems that many European countries are beginning to accept forecasts to that effect and to invest in them.

Despite two World Wars, more *in situ* historical resources survive in Europe than anywhere else. Even countries like Germany and Poland, devastated by war, are turning their battlefields and concentration camps into historic sites and reconstructing cities like Warsaw based on historical information. Affluent West Germany is building major new museums in several cities. Financially troubled Britain is less active in building new museums, but is already well-endowed and is exploiting what it does have to best advantage in its tourist industry.[35]

The most interesting European museum developments are in France, where a great deal of eclecticism is to be found. Every idea from abroad is tested, and new ideas have developed out of the great philosophical circles of Paris, dominated by giants such as Georges Henri Rivière and Claude Lévi-Strauss. It is ironic that the Musée National des Arts et Traditions Populaires is now the epitome of malaise in the museum world. Lévis-Strauss influenced the design of its stratified presentation of collections, catering to different levels of learning opportunity. At the time of its creation it was perhaps the most philosophically sophisticated museum in existence. Now it is regarded as a curator's museum, elitist and intimidating to the general public, tomblike and almost deserted of visitors, its display cases dusty, its exhibits unchanged for years, its audiovisual equipment mostly broken down. This is indeed a model to which museums should pay heed : of the downward spiral in which a low visitation rate evidently does not justify high maintenance costs or new exhibits, and in turn the public responds by staying away. By contrast to this sad case, France has poured nearly one hundred billion francs ($Cdn20 billion) into new cultural facilities such as the Centre Pompidou, the science/cultural complex of Parc La Villette, the new opera house at Poitiers, and theme parks.

Like Europe, the New World has examples of innovation and of institutions which seem content to rest on their laurels. Latin America we can practically skip over; crippled by inflation and political strife, its countries' rich archaeological resources seem doomed to neglect and destruction, and it has never followed up on the success achieved by Mexico's Museum of Anthropology, which set new standards in display techniques a quarter century ago. Nor have Americans done much of note lately in the museum field proper, although the well-resourced Smithsonian Institution continues to expand its facilities. The world's largest museum, New York's Metropolitan Museum of Art, is succes-

Figure 31
China's rich archaeological treasures are symbolized by the famous Xian Warriors, some of which have been exhibited worldwide.

sful in terms of visitation and revenue generation, but has been much criticized for its reduction of cultural artifacts to high art. The major contributions of the Americans have been rather in theme parks. Many American museums began as university or teaching museums, but it is doubtful whether they can make successful transitions to the tourist-based economy of the future, since they are tied to universities' preoccupation with academic prerequisites and specialized terminologies and frames of reference.

Breakthroughs have been made in North America, however, in attracting larger audiences to museums. One of the first major thrusts in this direction was a response, by museum staff, to the realization that museums were considered non-events by the mass media. They began to organize special museum events. The largest were called 'blockbusters' or sometimes 'Tut shows' in deference to the Egyptian boy-king whose relics launched the genre. Such shows drew in large crowds and created billions of dollars in tourist demand for goods and services in the cities whose museums hosted them; the Ramses II and Treasures of China blockbusters, when held in Montreal and linked with shows on Picasso and Miro at another museum there, added tens of millions of dollars to the local economy. The most recent manifestations are the 'megashows', blockbusters-cum-cultural-festivals held simultaneously in multiple locations. [36] However, blockbusters have not proven to be a panacea for the museum world's headaches. They are by nature 'events', and therefore temporary. Also, they may make money for local economies but often lose money for the sponsoring institution. They usually require galleries from one to two thousand square metres, equipped with rigorous climatic controls to protect the treasures on exhibit; such facilities are extremely

costly. Furthermore, in Canada at least, blockbuster shows have not much penetrated the mass media more than regionally, and consequently have had little national cultural effect.

A more successful approach seems to have been found by the National Museum of American History. When it was created in the mid-Seventies, its parent, the Smithsonian, was already a museum conglomerate with real national presence, verging on a true pilgrimage phenomenon. The National Museum of American History took a fresh approach to exhibiting American culture; one of its innovative actions was to appoint a curator of leisure and entertainment. Under that leadership the museum turned the tables on the mass media by capturing media icons as its treasures and exploiting the media's focus on 'heroes' (or at least personalities). The lecterns from the televised Kennedy-Nixon debate; the cowboy hat that J.R. wore on "Dallas"; Fonzie's leather jacket (from the "Happy Days" series); Archie and Edith Bunker's chairs used in the show "All in the Family"; Howdy-Doody, Charlie McCarthy, and Kermit the Frog puppets. All these proved great attractions, some more so than the former star of the museum, the Hope diamond. And when the TV stage set from "M.A.S.H." was exhibited it upset all previous attendance records and required a pre-ticketing system to control overcrowding. There

may be those who scoff at such efforts, as superficial and populist, but what the Museum of American History achieved was to make itself *relevant* by providing familiar points of reference to the interests and life-experiences of a much larger segment of the public and to communicate with people who previously thought that museums were not for them. Visitors were even seen to be reading lengthy interpretive labels accompanying the popular culture exhibits - a rare achievement for museums these days! These icons are recognizable not just in the United States, but to many of the museum's foreign visitors as well.

Another approach to attracting non-traditional visitors that has proven successful, if less spectacular, is the introduction of interactive elements into the museum experience. This has long been associated with science museums and their more modern counterparts, science centres (so called because they focus on illustrating the operation of technologies or scientific principles, rather than taking an historical approach). These are particularly popular with young visitors, for the simple reason that they are fun. The interactivity is achieved by levers, buttons, hands-on contact with the artifacts : the visitor triggers a response by participating in an exhibit to experience the cause-effect association. The interpretive media used in such places are also often interactive, employing computer and laser disc technologies to allow visitors to steer their way through masses of data by calling up just that information that responds to their specific interests.

San Francisco's Exploratorium and the Ontario Science Centre are outstanding examples of institutions which, by placing more emphasis on the use (for learning purposes) than on the preservation of their exhibits, are able to adopt more permissive attitudes towards visitor behaviour and to encourage more active participation of their visitors; in reward for which the museum establishment has exiled them from its ranks, as 'non-museums'. [37] Other types of institution have followed their example, such as the San Diego Zoo. Holland's Tropenmuseum (Amsterdam) has an interactive children's museum which is very advanced. Human history museums, having largely ignored these trends, have lost their pre-eminent position as institutions of public enlightenment.

Human history museums have been less reticent in trying to increase their relevance to public interests, both historical and contemporary. One technique has been to introduce small-scale theatrical performances

Figure 32
The Smithsonian's Museum of American History broke new ground with immensely successful exhibits of icons of popular culture – props used in TV shows, such as Archie Bunker's chair.

into exhibit areas to attract visitors' attention, provide them with a more involving experience than the usual touring and label reading, and set them thinking about social issues as a prelude to their encounter with artifacts reflecting on the same subjects.[38] At the Tropenmuseum Junior roleplaying by the children is the basis for an interactive and loosely structured 'play' performed in reconstructions of foreign environments; the aim is to provide a cross-cultural living experience that will enhance intercultural understanding. Recently there has been a somewhat more extreme trend, among ethnographic museums, towards becoming socially active with the cultures they represent; the Uberzee Museum (Bremen), for example, has introduced programmes to support Third World development : establishing museums, restoring buildings, creating craft industries and markets. What these trends reflect is a growing consciousness of the need to establish better rapport between the cultures of the West and cultures that the West depicts, often in stereotypes.

Live performances are most commonly associated with historic sites and open air museums, another type of institution often relegated to the periphery of the museum world. Only gradually is it being introduced into indoor museums. Live interpretation, which includes animation, theatre, and demonstrations, often allowing for interactivity of audience and performers, has proven very popular although critics have questioned the authenticity, biases, and educational effectiveness of the technique. One impetus for live interpretation was the impracticability of changing the buildings exhibited in open air museums, making it desirable to have changing programmes which *could* attract return visitors.

Open air museums have been around in a variety of forms since Skansen was established in Sweden in 1891, although in North America most appeared during the economic boom of the '60's and '70's.[39] Their outdoor setting and the full-blown reconstructions of historical environments - an attempt to recontextualize the artifacts (as too is live interpretation itself) - provide more appeal to the recreational and nostalgic needs of tourists than do most indoor museums. Indoor museums have nonetheless experimented with environmental reconstruction : Britain's Museum of Mankind has exhibited some excellent African, Indian, and Amazonian village settings, for example, and a few museums have constructed entire urban streetscapes within their walls, with mixed success. The close association between reconstructed environments, live

Figure 33
Science centres have pioneered interactive exhibits. Here, at the Ontario Science Centre, children use a computer to discover the meaning of Chinese characters.

Figure 34
Theatrical animation is a popular method of interpretation at open air museums. At Old Fort William, for example, business meetings of the North West Company partners are re-enacted for visitors.

Figure 35
Streetscape exhibitions – such as this one at York's Castle Museum – are one way of recontextualizing artifacts. Most have failed to include the live interpretation techniques that would make them more credible and stimulating, however.

orthodoxy by highlighting peasant cultures and the class struggle. A current philosophical dilemma ın the European open air museum community is whether reconstructions should be extended back into the prehistoric past, and to what extent archaeological exhibits can substitute for standing remains. North America, with a pioneer history to celebrate, is equally well-endowed with open air museums. A survey by CMC identified 79 Canadian open air museums, exclusive of Indian villages. It found that most populated regions of Canada (especially Ontario) are well-served, and that their strength lies in live animation and totally reconstructed environments; their bias is very heavily weighted towards rural and often pioneer settlements, and they tend to portray an idealized view.[40]

A more radical trend, associated with the reform movement known as the 'new museology', is ecomuseums. Again critics charge that they are not really museums at all. There is unquestionably some similarity between open air museums and ecomuseums, but it would be an oversimplification to suggest ecomuseums are essentially open air museums comprising *in situ* (rather than reconstructed) communities. The ecomuseum arose more out of the heritage preservation movement, which has often been at loggerheads with open air museums. The ecomuseum movement began, and still finds its strongest manifestation, in France where Rivière was the founding father. It has made inroads elsewhere, particularly in francophone countries, although there seems to be no *a priori* reason why it should have a cultural bias. African and Pacific peoples are pursuing the model, although they prefer the name 'cultural centres', and it has also taken root in Quebec. It and the 'new museology' philosophy, the utterance of its ideals and goals, arose from discontent within the museum community over the failure of the museum establishment to come to terms with certain contemporary cultural and social needs.[41]

interpretation techniques, and the open air museums which pioneered them have caused the last to be dubbed, somewhat unfortunately, 'living history museums'. Nonetheless there is an undeniable potency in this approach to conveying the meaning and use of artifacts in context, for showing processes and social intangibles is difficult with artifacts alone.

Japan has over a hundred open air museums; these, and others in Thailand, the Philippines, Indonesia, Korea, and China, focus on traditional architecture. Examples in Europe number in the thousands now, with very many of them in the Eastern Block countries (as far east as Siberia) following Marxist

The ecomuseum has been described as an attempt to take the museum out to the community, rather than bring the community in to visit the museum.[42] Owing something to the heritage preservation movement and something to local museums, its emphasis is on the social mission of the museum, giving that priority over traditional aspects such as conservation, architecture, artifacts, and even a visiting public : ecomuseums, first and foremost, serve the communities which live in them, for they are regions rather than specific buildings. Their tenet is the democratization of museums in the most literal sense of having them administered and operated by non-professionals resident in the ecomuseum. This notion of involving the community in a variety of ways is something from which museums in general can profitably learn; it has implications for volunteerism and heritage preservation by making community members more directly involved. furthermore, it promotes dialogue, rather than the one-way didactic communication mode typical in the traditional museum; this can be more productive in terms both of learning and of personal commitment to ideas received. Ecomuseums point the way towards empowering the museum visitor to take an active role in the management of heritage resources of which they are part-owners, and in the process of defining their own personal and collective identities.

Yet if there is one trend which seems most over-powering in the museum world, or the quasi-museum world, it is the development of the theme park. Beginning as the travelling funfair (similar origins to some museums), laying down roots as the amusement park, influenced by the thematic orientation of major expositions, the theme park emerged in the 1950's, and finds its most respectable form in the heritage theme park. America is the cradle of the heritage theme park, but has exported the form across the world. Canada has no example as yet; although plans for Timbertown, in the Ottawa Valley, were in process of development for some fifteen years, lack of funding eventually killed the project. By contrast, the wife of the President of Indonesia has champ-ioned such a park near Jakarta that has cost close to $Cdn1 billion and caused riots amongst students who preferred that the money be spent instead on universities. It mixes traditional architecture from all over the Indonesian archipelago with military and political exhibits and high technology features such as an Imax theatre. Singapore too is launching a $400 million heritage theme park, and plans have been proposed for such a creation - Sunrise Discovery Park - in Sydney, Australia.

France too has entered the heritage theme park business with a vengeance. One park is being built at Carnac, the megalithic site in Brittany; the site's managers believe that the visitor experience can fruitfully be expanded beyond just looking at the standing stones, to include an interpretive centre and theme park, with Imax theatre at its core, displays of artifacts excavated from the site, and perhaps a reconstructed environment in which visitors could experience life in the Neolithic Age. Another park is under development near the paleolithic site of Les Eysies in the Dordogne. A not entirely dissimilar

situation is the reconstruction of the Lascaux caves, with their prehistoric paintings, adjacent to the original caves, intended to allow visitors to continue to experience the site without contributing to the deterioration of the original 'artifact'. The theme park approach seems to work quite well for archaeological sites, and in England has been adopted to interpret important medieval remains at York : the Jorvik Viking Centre features a reconstructed Viking streetscape (based on the archaeological evidence of the site) as well as displays of dig finds; the Centre was heavily influenced by Disney Corporation, particularly in its use of peoplemovers in the core experience.

In the United States itself one of the most interesting new cultural institutions to emerge is the South Street Seaport/Ellis Island complex, which tells the history of the port of New York and the immigrants who arrived there. Although not seen by its developers as a theme park, it has many of the features associated with them : elaborate multimedia presentations, peoplemover experiences (in this case, ships), extensive marketing and service industry features; it has so far cost over $US1 billion. Many of the U.S. theme parks are, culturally, disasters, but in visitation and revenue generation resounding successes. Next to America's premier open air history museum, Colonial Williamsburg, is the theme park The Old Country; in 1981 the former's attendance was barely more than half of the latter's.[43]

Museums have become increasingly uneasy about theme parks as the latter have moved in the direction of greater historical content, formal exhibits, 'living history' experiences, and collection building.[44] It is now becoming hard to determine, in a few cases, whether they are theme parks, expositions, cultural centres, or open air museums, so many are the shared features and so blurred the boundaries between those institutions.

World's fairs have stimulated museum development, particularly in exhibition techniques and special events programming. McLuhan had an indirect influence on techniques used at world's fairs. He worked with others to produce prototypes of multimedia exhibits for the Royal Ontario Museum in the late fifties. These never went far at the ROM, but took off in Expo '67; they have also been an important element in the experiences at Expo '86 and Epcot. McLuhan believed the success of Expo '67 was due to the decision not to focus on a single theme or storyline; rather it was a mosaic of discon-tinuous items from which visitors were free to extract

Figure 36
New York's South Street Seaport exemplifies a new hybrid, combining features of museums, heritage districts, and theme parks.

whatever meanings they chose. Expo '86, as a Class B world's fair, was obliged to have a theme; but it stamped its own mark on the history of international expositions, partly for its widespread use of participatory theatre - indeed, some feel the whole fair seemed more of a performance than an exhibition.[45]

World's fairs, being transitory, have offered only ephemeral competition to museums. They have never really taken on the role of museum, partly because their short lifespan gave them little concern for conservation. Furthermore, they have lately tended to produce large deficits; like blockbusters, their fiscal harvest is reaped by the host region as a whole. However, there is a general trend towards the development of more permanent counterparts. Expo '67 was succeeded by Man and His World, a scaled-down version but with most of the same elements, although this was largely dismantled during the following two decades. Expo '70 was also followed by permanent facilities on the site : the National Ethnological Museum, the International Art Museum, the Japan Folk Arts Museum, Expo Hall, and a Japanese garden were among the cultural facilities to replace the exposition. France's Parc La Villette is a complex of numerous facilities, including a cultural centre, science centre (with the Musée National des Sciences, des Techniques et des Industries), recreational park, Imax and other theatres. The South Street Seaport/Ellis Island complex might perhaps be thrown into this category, and also Ontario Place. And surely Epcot Centre, with its more mature approach than other Disney parks, its international participation, and its showcasing of new technologies, bears a strong resemblance to international expositions? *Time* magazine attributed the (relative) failure of the 1984 world's fair, in New Orleans, to the competition of the newly-opened Epcot Center. Canada's closest example is Toronto's Harbourfront, a complex which is planned to include : an aquarium of national quality, a Nautical Centre (focusing on marine activities and education), a contemporary art gallery, a children's centre/museum, a film centre, a theatre/dance educational institute, an antiques market, parklands and plazas, crafts demonstrations, participative sports activities, ethno-cultural festivals, and diverse other cultural and recreational programmes. Originally federally subsidized, it has been successful in attracting private-sector sponsorship and now relies primarily on its own financial resources. It claimed an attendance of 3.6 million visitors in 1986, which would place it ahead of all the Toronto museums, the Metropolitan Zoo, the Ontario Science

Centre, and Ontario Place and into the range of world fairs.[46]

However, the reigning champion in the realm of theme parks and other quasi-museum institutions, is unquestionably Disney Corporation. Henry Ford is credited with having integrated, for the first time, the manufacture, sales, spare parts, and service aspects of the automobile industry. His counterpart in the modern tourist pilgrimage industry was Walt Disney, who also managed to integrate that industry as no-one else did before or since. Disney Corporation earns over $US1 billion a year in direct revenue and probably generates $10 billion a year in spread-effect on the economy; its parks have been visited by a greater number of people than live in the whole United States.

Disney began, five decades ago, by weaving a mythology, using the medium of film, which served to diffuse the cult to old and young alike; this gave rise to cult objects (souvenirs) that are now themselves collectibles auctioned at Sotheby's in New York. Three decades ago Disney switched to television, which was beginning to reach a wider audience than film, to diffuse the cult; a spectrum of tastes was covered, from "The Mickey Mouse Club" for kids to "Walt Disney Presents" for family entertainment and the Disney nature series for education. Disney learned, with "Snow White", that re-releases on a seasonal schedule, tied in to major holidays, will pre-programme each new generation for the same experience. New staff at the Disney parks arrive pre-programmed, by TV and film, to the Disney ethic and vision, and require little corporate indoctrination. A major effort of the Disney Corporation during the past decade was the launching of a worldwide satellite system to link their cult centres in California, Florida, Japan, and soon Paris (and possibly China), in a live global network that will capture viewers at each location during major festive occasions. With several billion viewers as a possible goal they could sell advertising to almost any multinational corporation!

Disney's latest development is a mega-studio being built in Orlando next to Epcot Center, to produce films and videos for the insatiable broadcast networks and growing cassette markets. Prompted by public studio tours in Hollywood, visitors to the mega-studio will be able to penetrate the very cauldrons in which the Disney myths are brewed (without interfering with the production process); icons will be available in souvenir shops, the high-priest actors will be there on demand for photographs or even videotaped souvenirs, and guests will be able to have themselves electronically inserted into a videotape of a Disney film of their choice. Universal Studios is also developing a movie/TV production centre at Orlando (a few miles from Epcot) and aims to attract tourists by including an entertainment centre which will allow visitors to see movies being made and will present exhibits - including reconstructions of sets from famous movies - related to film-making.

It is the cult centres themselves that most concern museums, however. In a series of experiments Disney has perfected the theme park model. Mark I appeared in California in 1955, as Disneyland. Full of fun and fantasy, there was no notion then that it might pose a threat to cultural institutions. Mark II opened in Florida in 1971; Walt Disney World integrated the tourist industry - including airlines (Eastern Airlines became the 'official carrier'), airports, highways, accommodation, services, and marketing - with television as the diffusion medium. Mark II developed into an all-in-one vacation stop, capable of holding visitors, entirely on its own resources, not just for hours but for days; the "total vacation adventure", as it was billed, was a multi-element vacation resort : six hotels, villas, campsites, or a more exotic experience in the Polynesian Village, innumerable sports and outdoor activities, shopping and restaurant options to suit any taste, a wildfowl sanctuary, river cruises through a wilderness area, and the Magic Kingdom theme park. A decade later the facility was expanded further by building next door the Experimental Prototype Community Of Tomorrow, Disney Mark III.

Epcot has been analyzed in detail elsewhere [47] and only the broad lines need be reviewed here. It was targeted much more deliberately towards an adult population than the previous Disney parks, and comprises essentially a science centre complex (Future World) with a cultural heritage theme park (World Showcase); both, and especially the latter, are still being expanded with new pavilions. The national pavilions in World Showcase each present architectural and other monumental icons, in replica form, such as a scaled-down version of Ottawa's Chateau Laurier, representing Canada. Each Epcot pavilion is based on a formula, which Disney's previous experiments had worked out to their satisfaction. The components of the formula are :

- an environmental experience; with recreations of architecture, streetscapes, landmarks, or landforms typical of a country, in the case of the World Showcase pavilions, and environments in Future World such as space, underseas, an experimental farm of the future, and historical tableaux.

- a special film experience; using the most modern technologies, such as Imax, Circlevision, multiple screens, and so on.

- a live performance experience; musicians, street performers, narrators - both real people and animatronic robots.

- a peoplemover experience; employing automated technologies as a crucial element in circulating visitors through the presentations in Future World, or as a more nostalgic experience (employing replicas of historical vehicles) in World Showcase.

- a sensory experience; stimulation of the olfactory and gustatory senses by restaurants in World Showcase, each featuring special foods of the country associated with the pavilion, and by special effects adding realism to the reconstructed environments in the Future World pavilions.

- a marketplace experience; boutiques and shops stocked with a wide range of items suitable as mementos of the visit.

- an artifact experience; static displays of objects, much like the traditional museum.

The formula stresses an integrated, multimedia, multiexperiential approach.

The last item in the formula may strike home hardest to museum staff; it shows that Epcot is competing in the area where they are most comfortable. This competition is particularly real for museums in eastern North America, where the populace has relatively inexpensive access to Florida. Disney has recently set up a special museum branch and has approached major cultural institutions across the world - the Louvre, the British Museum, the Hermitage, the Metropolitan Museum of Art, Mexico's Museum of Anthropology, China's Forbidden City, and also CMC - to obtain on loan national treasures to display in World Showcase pavilions; most have responded encouragingly, even enthusiastically. Epcot can attract high visitation and has the financial resources to provide the most satisfactory environmental controls and security to safeguard the treasures, as well as to hire on contract all the expertise necessary for researching and designing the best exhibits, and producing superb catalogues to accompany them. Disney's venture into the blockbuster arena is a response to the understanding that they can continue to attract return visitors only if they add new pavilions and changing

Figures 37 and 37a
Epcot Center is, in essence, a
permanent world's fair. It combines
the futuristic displays of a science
centre with the cultural exhibits of a
world heritage theme park (in which
Canada is represented by a Pacific
Coast native house and a scaled-down
reconstruction of the Chateau Laurier).

exhibits regularly, and so have new 'events' to
promote each year. No individual museum, even
with a blockbuster within its walls, can compete
effectively for tourists against a centre which may
simultaneously be showing treasures - the *crème de
la crème* - from several nations, offer fun for the
kids, and sun and surf at the same time. They can
only be thankful that Disney parks are few and far
between; although Disney plans to circulate to other
members of its family the exhibitions its museum
branch puts together.

The family now includes a Tokyo Disneyland, helping the Japanese understand American mythology
(such as the frontier and individualism) on an
intimate level, and a Disney park currently being
installed not far from Paris; considering the other
developments in France, already noted, it is no
surprise Disney chose to build its European base
there. Disney's long-term plan is to mature its
image, away from that of Mickey Mouse towards
that of cultural broker.

In traditionalist quarters of the museum world
'Disney' is not a name to conjure with; it attracts
contempt, as populist, anti-intellectual, trivial, and
phony. Probably no-one in the museum world would
want to see museums mimicking Disney parks, but

it is impossible to deny that in terms of visitors attracted, visitor satisfaction, and revenue generated - prizes coveted by most museum administrators - the Disney parks are a resounding success. Museums need neither embrace nor outrightly reject the Disney formula for success. They can, however, analyze it, learn from it, and borrow what seems best or most applicable to museums.

There are several lessons for museums in Epcot and its ilk. Perhaps first and foremost is Disney's treatment of its audiences; the parks do not *admit visitors*, they *welcome guests*, and every attention is paid to ensuring comforts and services for their guests, to make them feel welcome and guarantee an enjoyable stay. Another is the technique of integrated planning, bringing together activities which in museums are too often segregated through departmentalization, all aimed at ensuring that every aspect of the visitor experience is a success. Associated with this is the multiexperiential approach, in which Disney tries to compensate for compromises it has made in the authenticity of some of its environmental reconstructions - architectural replicas are often scaled down, or merely facades (being intended more as theatre sets than accurate replicas) - by introducing interpretive elements taken from the culture interpreted. Foreign nationals are brought in on six-month work permits, to work in the pavilions of their country. Top-flight professionals are brought in to give cultural performances. Souvenir items are high-quality crafts or at least have real cultural content. The restaurants also provide culturally relevant eating experiences. Finally, Disney has long since come to terms with the need to forge strong links with the tourist, transportation, and accommodations industries, as an integral part of creating a total package to attract visitors.

Canada has no theme park on the Disney scale. Ontario's Wonderland is a pale imitation. The nearest home-grown equivalent is the West Edmonton Mall, a mega-mall that although nominally a shopping concourse has earned its fame for integrating theme park elements. Built in several phases over the 1980's it includes : a wave-action waterpark (for surfing, water-skiing etc.), hockey rink where the Edmonton Oilers may be seen practising, a reconstructed streetscape of New Orleans nightclubs and restaurants (Creole and Cajun cuisine), a European streetscape housing retail outlets for international designers of clothes, a hotel with fantasy rooms based on historical or cultural themes, a mini golf course, a two-storey aviary with ostriches, a full-scale replica of Columbus's Santa

Maria on a 2.5-acre lake which visitors may tour by submarine (the peoplemover experience) and view *en route* real sharks and robotic monsters. While all these attractions have not produced quite the boom for mall retailers that had been hoped - visitors come to look at the stores as attractions, as much as to shop - they have certainly boosted Edmonton's tourist industry, drawing mainly from the western provinces. The city's population alone could not justify the presence of the mega-mall. The close integration of tourist attractions and retail outlets is interesting; shopping in North America can occupy 25% of one's disposable time, whereas long-distance tourism accounts for less than 1%. More mega-malls

are planned, for American and possibly Canadian centres.

It is, however, Japan which really has pioneered the 'museum in the marketplace' approach, particularly the requirement for developers to build art galleries and museum spaces into shopping plazas and city centre complexes. Such plazas may prove future customers for traditional museums' travelling exhibits, perhaps on a rental basis as a revenue generator for museums. Other indicators of merchandizing possibilities for museums are exemplified by the Galleries du Louvre, a large arcade opposite the Musée du Louvre with antiquarian shops that act almost as an extension of the Louvre's own boutiques, for visitors see for sale much the same types of artifacts as displayed in the Louvre.

Figure 38
The West Edmonton Mall represents another new phenomenon, integrating entertainment elements normally found in theme parks into a shopping mall environment.

Museums need to capture this market more directly, by the use of their artifactual collections as a store of masters, and their exhibits as a backdrop for marketing replicas - a field in which the Metropolitan Museum of Art has been extremely successful.

Some or all of the developments just described, perhaps especially the new maturing of theme parks into more respectable institutions, will surely have a revolutionary effect on the museum world within the next couple of decades. Some of the trends that may result are :

- Museum collections, because of the inordinate financial burdens they place on their custodial institutions, will be managed more tightly, and exploited more fully. Museums will share their resources to a greater degree, buying less and borrowing more from sister institutions.

- Collections will be made more accessible to the public, in a variety of ways, and will be placed in more relevant, more meaningful contexts than the 'central warehouse' of the past.

- While some artifacts will continue to be primarily 'treasures' (wealth icons), most will be valued as icons in the information system, and the new electronic media will be exploited to disseminate their images and supply the contextual information to interpret them.

- Multimedia presentations will continue to develop in museums to provide a rich framework for the collections, but these will become more experiential and more interactive through the use of increased realism (e.g. holograms, sensurround film techniques) and new theatrical techniques.

- Museums will modify their established 'educational mission' by importing greater elements of entertainment into their programming. This will be done partly by placing objects in appropriate contexts and animating the contexts.

- Museums will develop an enhanced awareness of their publics' needs, improved responsiveness to those needs, and will encourage more extensive community participation in their programmes.

- In the face of reduced government funding of museums, they will exploit more successfully other help and revenue, including volunteerism, private sector sponsorship, user-fees for special events and services, cooperative efforts with the tourism industry.

- To attract media promotion, necessary to the promulgation of the image of national cultural identity, museums will develop a more event-oriented calendar.

The museum as crossroads of cultures

What then is the model for the Canadian Museum of Civilization? The elements are implicit in the discussion above; they are responses to trends, pressures, constraints, and opportunities perceived within the evolving community vision of the role(s) of museums, within the general social, economic, political, and competitive environments, and within the examples provided by a few existing museums or quasi-museums that have themselves anticipated the future. At CMC the formulation of the model centered around a document called the Vision Statement. This was produced by the Director, whose role is partly to provide a bridgehead between the museum and other worlds. Unlike an institutional mission statement, which must summarily cover all functions of the institution in responding to the questions of whom an institution is trying to serve and what services are to be provided, a vision statement focuses upon new directions that an institution must follow if it is to remain viable and responsive to a changing society. It is a *vision* of the future in the sense of an intuitive leap sensitive to the logic within the developed past and developing present. A mission statement indicates where an institution is 'coming from'; a vision statement where it is going to. Thereby it addresses, with a hopefully negative response, the doubt posed by Joseph Veach Noble : have museums lost touch with changing times and become irrelevant to society?[48]

The vision of the Canadian Museum of Civilization is based upon certain premises. One is that museums, despite their preoccupation with the past, must learn to operate in today's world and also in tomorrow's. Museums still have a role as anchor points of stability in a world that suffers from constant and confusing change. But this should not preclude their being dynamic institutions in their own way. They cannot serve society by a reactionary response to change, but must make change more comprehensible, and thereby more acceptable, by putting it in perspective. A more concrete premise is that, although it would be preferable to measure the benefits of museums in quality-of-life factors, the hard fact is that governments and the public more usually judge them by the number of visitors, or cost-per-user. A museum such as CMC will be assigned resources commensurate with the share of the user-market it can capture. Yet without adequate funding the museum cannot provide services and programmes that attract visitors in large numbers, and will fall into the deadly downward spiral of the Musée National des Arts et Traditions Populaires.

Above all then, before it can even begin to fulfill its central mission, CMC must be able to perform as a high-profile attraction, at levels far beyond those in its previous site. To achieve these levels it cannot be satisfied with a passive role, assuming visitors will come to it *en masse* unprompted (as Europeans seem to do to their museums 49). It is not the regular museum-goers whom CMC has to win over, but those who rarely or never visit museums, such as Bob Kelly's 'new visitor' segment of the population. It must entice Mohammed to the mountain, and where it cannot it must take the mountain to Mohammed.

Furthermore, in the face of government concern over continued commitment to direct financial support of its National Museums at past levels, and introduction of policies demanding cost-recovery, user-pays, and development of new sources of revenue by those museums, CMC has become even more dependent upon its users. Their number will affect resources : both the revenue generated directly from users (payments for services, sales of souvenirs etc.), and the ability to persuade other institutions - whether corporate sponsors or tourist organizations - to link their names with the museum and invest in its future. Thus, CMC must devote more attention to promoting its facilities, programmes, and services than it has in the past, in order to build the reputation of a destination of major importance to national and international travellers across Canada and in the eastern United States. And it must offer programmes and services of a type for which the public is

accustomed to paying. A third consequence is that CMC must be more sensitive to its publics' needs and wants, and respond to them within the philosophy that each visitor is a guest to be satisfied, not an intruder to be tolerated; the intellectual arrogance of too many museums has been a major factor in restricting their attraction to the better-educated elements of society : this must be swept away.

One way to diversify its audiences is for CMC to diversify its roles : to be as many things to as many people as its resources allow. Many visitors come simply to gaze upon the national treasures. They shall. Others expect a primarily educational experience. They will not be disappointed. Yet others wish for social opportunities or entertaining events, whether of a relaxed or stimulating nature. They too have been provided for.

Fundamentally, CMC has set in process two distinct modes of operation. During the day it operates in a more traditional mode, emphasizing the educational content of its artifacts (as authentic objects punctuating human history) and exhibits, directly reflecting the product of the more typical museum functions of collecting, conservation, research, and interpretation, and catering particularly to self-directed learners, hobbyists, school groups, researchers, etc. CMC feels that the daytime mode should be, for the most part, free of charge like other taxpayer-funded educational services. At night, and at certain other times in tourist peak season, programmes will make use of CMC's special

Figures 39 and 39a
CMC operates in two programming modes, characterized by educational content during the day and entertainment at night, so as to provide a wider range of experiences for visitors.

features - such as its Imax/Omnimax theatre, or its reconstructed environmental settings as theatrical sets - to provide a range of entertainments, some of them calling for audience interaction with the performers. It is important to cultivate an image of CMC as a source of enjoyable, entertaining experiences, for this is a key to maximizing the number of users of the facility. Furthermore, it is precisely such events (live performances, cinema, banquets) that the public is already accustomed to paying for; the evidence from theme parks shows common acceptance of the notion of paying for special events, even after a general admission fee has been paid. Consequently, the elements of nighttime mode operations are crucial to CMC's revenue-generating strategy.

The distinction between daytime/educational and nighttime/entertainment modes - which might be seen as manifestations of the right brain (experiential) and left brain (intellectual) dichotomy inherited from our ancestors - is not as rigid as might

seem to be implied here; it has been a useful conceptual tool to assist CMC staff in planning a range of programmes. The fact is that all forms of museum public activity combine education and leisure, in a mix which may vary according to the perspective or objectives of individual visitors. The range of needs seems almost limitless : to learn, discover, enquire, enjoy, be stimulated, entertained, mystified, inspired, or any combination. If a museum's role is to communicate, or to facilitate inter-communication, its first task is to open channels of communication by capturing the attention and interest of the audience. In the case of non-traditional museum-goers this means the provision of some kind of experience (e.g. cinematic) to which they can relate comfortably.

By offering diverse events, activities, experiences, under the two modes, it is hoped to increase the attraction of CMC for both local visitors and for tourists, so that they will visit under both modes to experience more fully the range of products available. It is important to satisfy local residents since (beside the fact that they too are part of CMC's national community!) their approval will ensure they have an image of the museum as a first-choice place to which their out-of-town guests can be taken. To make the museum a stronger pull for tourists selecting their vacation destination, it is advantageous to move CMC away from the traditional image of museums towards the more dynamic and multi-dimensional image associated with leisure facilities such as Epcot. CMC cannot be an Epcot Center, even if it wanted to (which is not the case), but it can play a key role in helping present Ottawa - and in particular the cluster of attractions being built up in the Capital Core Area - as a major tourist destination, through productive cooperation with other attractions and with tourism industry elements in the region.

Until relatively recently tourism and heritage objects were not really thought of as being interdependent; there was even some notion that they were mutually antagonistic.[50] 'Cultural tourism' (defined in chapter 1) is the concept which reflects the passing of that old view and is a response to the growth of tourism globally. Cultural tourism represents people seeking more meaningful ways of filling their increased leisure-time. Museums offer meaningful experiences; the trick is to persuade tourists of that! One way in which CMC makes itself meaningful is that, as a shrine containing the national treasures, it can be seen by Canadians as an appropriate pilgrimage destination where their experience of national culture/identity will help transform them into 'good citizens'. All Canadians should feel a certain obligation to visit their national capital, and to visit CMC as an integral part of that pilgrimage. And for travellers from abroad CMC, by the visitor experiences it offers, the publicity they generate, and its cooperation with other local institutions, can help turn Ottawa into a major tourist destination of the future, an essential part of the itinerary of all visitors to North America.

Stemming from its active role in cultural tourism, and from the need to capitalize on the volume of visitors attracted to provide CMC with necessary revenues, is the interpretation of the museum as a cultural marketplace. The marketplace is one of the oldest institutions of mankind, associated often with the crossroads on routes travelled by nomadic traders. The advent of the mega-malls suggests that, as a cultural phenomenon, the marketplace is far from dead. Despite the transition of the age of materialism to the age of information, the continued vitality of the rare commodity markets provides an important opportunity for museums. They can

exploit the 'patent' that they effectively hold on objects in their collection, by marketing replicas or authentic objects produced by bona-fide craftspeople that are comparable to items in museum collections. It is essential that the marketed items have true cultural content, by being of the highest quality; too many museums' souvenirs are cheaply produced and unconvincing. CMC's new two-storey boutique will sell articles commissioned from professional craftspeople and artists, and equivalent in quality to objects found in the museum's Massey or Bronfman collections, for example. Other, temporary marketing spaces will be tied to special exhibitions and events. Bob Kelly's analysis of museum visitors suggests that the need of the 'new visitor' component for markers of their visit - quite probably markers of a quality that display the owners' taste to their peers - will provide a growing market for what museums may be able to supply.

At the very heart of CMC's ambition is to be a crossroads of cultures, in a much wider sense than just a cultural marketplace. As a *national* museum, CMC belongs to, and serves, all Canadians and represents Canadian heritage and identity to both Canadians and non-Canadians. It has no valid choice other than to be concerned with all regions, cultures and eras in Canadian history. The multicultural nature of Canadian society seems to be the best theme for use in organizing and making sense of CMC's resources and products. This is no easy task, for in Canada the icons that may have good associations for one group are elitist status symbols to another, or symbols of oppression to a third. Many mistaken notions about the past need to be corrected, many stereotypes debunked. To give but one example, many Canadians grow up thinking that European immigrants have a real history whereas native peoples' history has all disappeared; the Haida village sites on the West Coast that have been declared national historic sites (one even a world heritage site) belie this. The traditional museum exhibition approach can also create artificial or stereotyped contexts for artifacts that may obscure the message that needs to be communicated. And most museum curators, not coming from the cultures about which they they have acquired an academic expertise, have an understanding of those cultures that might be considered second-hand. Immigration from non-Western countries can be expected to become an increasingly important component of population growth, with the resulting need to integrate foreign values and traditions into the national self-understanding.

Figures 40, 40a and 40b
CMC's chief aim is to bring together
people of different cultures so that,
through dialogue and interaction, they
may better understand each other's
cultural heritage.

It seems, then, a worthy and productive contribution to the future of this country for CMC to have as its primary aim to promote intercultural understanding in those who visit the museum or are visited by it in remote locations. This involves portraying to the museum's audiences the cosmologies of other cultures to the point where they have sufficient understanding, respect, and empathy for them to appreciate that they are (for their time and place) rational systems. By the same process stereotypes may be changed, perspectives may be influenced, and the growth of interest in ethnic roots can be catered to. Mutual understanding between cultures may not be attainable simply by displaying representative cultural items in showcases and interpreting them solely from the perspective of museum academics. Life must be breathed into the cultures by showing artifacts in their cultural contexts, including their use in rituals or everyday life, by assisting visitors to try to put themselves in the place of someone from another culture in order to develop a rapport with the feelings and beliefs of that culture, and by bringing peoples of different cultures together within the museum to communicate with each other.

There is a contemporary trend towards seeing ethnology not so much as the objective description of culture, but as the invention of culture; the same doubts as to whether the knower and what is known can ever be truly independent of each other may likewise be found in the discipline of history. It would be arrogance for a museum to present a single interpretation of a culture and claim it to be author-itative. Rather, the ideal is to present competing visions of reality and allow the visitor to understand that the imperceptible truth lies somewhere in the midst of several alternative points of view, and that 'history as truth' cannot be dissociated from the process of producing historical interpretations. It is, naturally, desirable that one of the viewpoints offered be that of the native people or ethnic group portrayed. Therefore CMC aims at engaging the participation of representatives of these cultural elements in the presentation of its programmes, as designers, demonstrators, interpreters, performers. Thus CMC becomes the point where the paths of cultures cross in time and space, and their repre-sentatives trade patterns of understanding, that all may depart enriched with a deeper feeling for their interconnectedness in the Global Village.

Frequent references have been made above to visitor 'experiences' within the new Canadian Museum of Civilization. The 'experiential' characteristics of exhibits and programmes are considered important by CMC. For example, the more intimately visitors can experience the cultures presented in the museums, the more likely the presentation is to have a real impact on them. Increasing the number of ways something is experienced also increases the likelihood of it having a significant and memorable effect upon the experiencer. The greater the amount of visitor participation in, or interactivity with, an exhibit or event, the more effective is the learning process. People go to museums not just for infor-mation or fun, but for an 'experience' which may include both these elements and more. Such experiences are generally more productive than straight information in influencing attitudes, and also more efficient since experiences synthesize many pieces of information into patterns which are grasped intuitively, as opposed to overloading people with a string of information elements presented one by one.

It has been suggested that in the Western World today we are often overloaded with more information than we can process effectively, but relatively impov-erished in experience.[51] Most of our experiences come second-hand, through film, video, television : life crises, health care and problems, religious experiences, human conflict and natural disasters, geography, sexual experiences. The breadth and extent of this personal experiential grid is unrival-

led in any population of the past and is becoming a global phenomenon. Unfortunately electronic experience is heavily edited and episodic, in half-hour segments. The British, who have in recent years been shown edited-down football games from the United States, probably think that American football is all sex (cheerleaders) and violence (scoring plays) now. Young children have all sorts of misconceptions that derive from false associations shown on TV cartoons. Their experi-ential grids are underdeveloped, rooted heavily in surrogation (through media such as TV), and lack the corrective influence of contact with the reality of situations such as those portrayed on TV. Museums have a special role in the formation of an individual's reality and experiential grids, partly because they possess the real objects that are the yardsticks against which people can measure concepts that have been communicated to them, the anchors (for experiential grids) against which we project and structure each experience; and partly because museum present-ations can add a sense of scale, real-time sequences, and context that is chronically absent from electronic media experiences.

Electronic experiences are identical wherever they are perceived in the world. Inuit elders are as fond of Big Bird, from "Sesame Street", as are the urban young of New York City for whom the programme was originally designed. Filmic mythology is becoming universal (as the name of Hollywood's biggest studio proclaims). Mickey Mouse is an internationally recognized image, and a study has found that Ronald McDonald is the next best known figure throughout the United States after Santa Claus! McDonald's restaurants are them-selves clones of each other, successful because they provide oases of familiarity to a highly mobile public. Museums are the antithesis of this trend. Like shrines, they are the ultimate site-specific feature, usually interpreting the region that created them. At best they house and protect local objects that document that region's past. Yet they strive to differentiate themselves from, rather than replicate, each other. Despite the profound differences in the museum and mass media experiences, there is nonetheless a symbiotic relationship - yet to be fully defined - between how the media and how the museum communicate with their publics. The dimension of the differences lies primarily in concepts of reality.

CMC's exhibitions provide those visitors who wish it with ample access to individual artifacts in traditional didactic settings, in arrangements somewhat analogous to the linear presentation of information in a text. But the more popular elements amongst its exhibits are sure to be those that project mosaics of images and other sensory signals from which the visitor's conscious and subconscious minds can select, prioritize, and re-order those components most relevant to his or her interests and needs. Environmental reconstructions and/or theatrical performances, and the Omnimax films which totally envelope the visitor, are the most common of these types of experience. The aim in these cases is to

Figure 41
Live interpretation programmes in the galleries will employ trickster/ transformer figures to help visitors understand the cultural past. This approach – featuring Koko and Garbanzo, anthropological clowns – has been used well at the UBC Museum of Anthropology.

dissolve the frame - a display case being a good example of a 'frame' - around the presentations, for frames provide psychological barriers which detach and distance the viewer from that which is viewed. By re-creating for the visitor the essence of significant experiences of past or present cultures, the goal of fostering intercultural understanding is more likely to be achieved.

Tomislav Sola notes that genuine communication through museums has always inspired a form of poetic experience. In such communication there can be recognized elements of magic (exhibition techniques, new media), religion (museum fetishism, the epiphanic character of the museum message), social organization and play (conventions, rules, social events); all of these are elements of syncretic, para-artistic communication which, according to McLuhan, takes us back to the total communication

of primitive societies.[52] The notion that just visiting a museum can be a rite of transformation, associated with acquiring a certain social status, has already been mentioned. A good deal of ritual content has been built into the CMC model generally, although much of it may not be apparent to the typical visitor. Visitors are initiated into the multicultural nature of Canadian identity; 'initiation', the process by which the ignorant person is converted to the knowledgable person, is both an experience and a ritual.

The theatrical presentations, of which a multitude of forms are programmed into CMC, are also initiatory experiences, for the essence of theatre is that it deals with transformations or transitions : characters undergo changes in attitude or status. The archetypal role in this process is the Trickster, an important character in myths of the West Coast native peoples, who has been assigned many forms, including Raven. CMC has positioned many Tricksters throughout its galleries and disguised them as animators, interpreters, performers; their role is to enliven and demystify, and to help visitors understand that there are many perceptual perspectives on the past, no one of them necessarily the absolute truth. Introduction of the live human agent of culture is one of the principal ways that interactivity, in the form of interpersonal dialogue, is achieved in the museum. The frequent appearance of the Raven motif throughout the museum - such as in commissioned artworks and in the Children's Museum - symbolizes the intention of CMC to be a catalyst in the process of transforming the attitudes of its visitors towards alien cultures.

Lévi-Strauss and his fellow structuralists have taught us that all actions of Mankind are in fact cultural transmissions - intended to create a sense of relatedness to fellows - using shared experiences as a bonding mechanism, refreshed with icons that are widespread, and by periodically grounding their reality via pilgrimages to cult centres. Even artifacts broadcast messages, about cultural affiliation and many other things. These 'broadcasts', in the form of myths, art, social organization, and language itself, are highly structured according to cultural grammars that are largely subconscious in the minds of participants. In order to cope with gradations - the grey zone - in cultural phenomena, humans establish oppositional sets in their minds (high/low, wet/dry, black/white, etc. - rather like the binary on/off principle used in computers); the sets bracket experiential reality in a way that allows the brain to process and store it. Even complex cultural configurations can be factored down to sets of binary oppositions, sorted, and handled thanks to the creation of 'armatures', or culture-specific templates.

One such armature is 'initiation'. It can be a group or a solitary experience, but it is predictable and relies on responses of the human brain to particular stimuli. One example from our past is 'hood-winking', whereby an initiate was hooded or blind-folded to create visual deprivation; after a while the hood was jerked away to reveal before the initiate the image of some religious icon. This sensory over-stimulation burned the image into the memory of the initiate and often produced a religious ecstasy or conversion. Museums have stumbled onto this technique in their use of darkened galleries in which those travelling through them encounter spotlit artifacts (in their display case shrines), but it has been so overused that today it is less likely to inspire attitudinal change than the notorious 'museum fatigue', which only encourages visitors to flee the experience ever more quickly.

But to return briefly to Sola's notion of museums inspiring a form of poetic experience, CMC sees itself not just as a cultural mirror of the past, but as a cultural generator of the future. Marjorie Halpin describes Canadian culture as really a multicultural conversation out of which new cultural forms can arise, presenting a model for a global conversation to follow.[53] Not all, but a select number of persons associated with the museum will undergo the types of transformation experience already described and will be inspired to create new culture. These people may be the artists-in-residence specifically engaged by the museum to communicate cultural artforms, or the Canadian film-makers for whom CMC's theatres provide a forum at which to direct their creativity, or regular visitors over whom the museum may never learn of its inspirational influence. Whether directly or indirectly, the museum can serve as a patron to the weavers of the cultural tapestry that makes, and constantly remakes, Canada. And as the hearth at which the embers of past achievements can be rekindled into the flames that drive new cultural dynamos. For, arguably, what museums are really interested in collecting are the intangibles of culture, including creativity, but they can do this only through the medium of physical objects which mirror those intangibles. The concept of the trail of history which wanders away from the viewer into the dim past is yielding to a newer concept of history as a ritual process that must be regenerated in each new member of a society. The Parc Laurier complex is designed for just such ritual experience. Its location, which faces the central icon of our country - the

Peace Tower - reinforces its role as a pilgrimage centre in the quest for both personal and national identity.

Figures 42 and 42a
CMC's public programmes will expose visitors to other cultures through a wide range of experiences, including performances of cultural rituals.

If the Canadian Museum of Civilization emphasizes visitor 'experience' in the presentations it shapes, and seeks particularly to make of itself the prototype for an *interactive* indoor human history museum, it aims beyond even this to provide the sort of multi-experiential programming which Epcot Center has pioneered and which is responsible for holding Epcot's visitors for average stays of eight hours. Museums of any size have possessed all the same basic elements that Epcot uses, but have segregated them rather rigidly. The multiexperiential model is perhaps best explained by providing a hypothetical example of special programming focusing on the foreign embassy community in Ottawa. Each programme highlights the culture of one particular country. Let us suppose that the 'country of the month' is Indonesia. The evening visitor to the museum (this programme running during nighttime mode) is greeted as a guest of the country's embassy - although in fact each will have purchased a ticket - and has his or her replica International Passport stamped with an 'entry visa'. The offering of a glass of wine or spritzer is followed by an hour in the Imax/Omnimax theatre watching films depicting Indonesia. More than a dozen countries now have films in the Imax medium which portray their cultures. At the end of the presentations the guest passes out to the lobby for a banquet of delicacies from Java, Timor, and Kalimantan, served by embassy staff, and for entertainment by a gamelan (a percussion orchestra - there are two based in Montreal). After a dessert of exotic fruits and sweetmeats, the guest is free to browse through the shops which that month feature crafts from all over Indonesia, to look at a special exhibit of artifacts from Indonesian countries, or to enquire about special package tours to Indonesia (arranged by CMC volunteers) and to enter his or her name in a draw for two tickets to Indonesia. Next the guest enters the "World Window Theatre", to enjoy performances of the Ramayana dances of Java along with rituals from Bali. The evening ends with a personal farewell from embassy staff, who have made several hundred friends that night - all potential tourists to their country. Another example of multiexperiential programming, this time involving the permanent exhibition galleries, makes use of the environmental reconstructions in history and ethnology halls to stage theatrical presentations of a multimedia and interactive nature, integrating live performances, screened films, and again dining experiences, much on the model of Murray Schafer's "Ra" or Moses Znaimer's interactive play "Tamara".

Not all of CMC's programmes involve such large-scale presentations. The museum recognizes an equal need for smaller, more personal, and more spontaneous experiences, that allow (for example) visitors to meditate upon artifacts, or converse with cultural representatives, in one-to-one relationships. Interactivity is generally better achieved at this lower level, rather than in the context of big productions. The ideal is to be able to take a variety of events, both large and small, and choreograph them into an integrated programme.

What role, one might ask, has the traditional core of the museum - its artifactual collections - in this new model? Their importance has not lessened, though it might seem so in the light of new activities of the museums that are less *directly* dependent on the display of original objects. If anything, it is greater, thanks to the fuller appreciation of the many ways they may be used to satisfy diverse user-needs : as national treasures, as icons in the information system, as reference points in our reality grids, as masters from which replicas or images may be disseminated to a larger audience, as sources of inspiration giving rise to new creative expressions, and so on; we are just beginning to understand their true value. Well-managed, well-preserved, and well-researched collections remain essential to the museum. The uniqueness of museums still rests in part upon its collections (although, as Epcot shows, not quite so much as was once the case).

Yet the fact of the matter is that the collections present certain practical difficulties for museums in a modern world of limited resources. The collectibles market has greatly raised the cost of acquiring artifacts from dealers. Gone are the days when whole museums could be created by appealing to citizens to delve into their attics and contribute their grandparents' old belongings. The cost of maintaining hospital-like environments to preserve the collections indefinitely, and registration systems to enable their efficient management and ensure at least a minimal level of research is carried out on each object, are also tremendous drains on museums' resources. Of course these are integral parts of a museum's responsibility that must be borne. The danger is that the greater part of the budget may become channelled into them, leaving little for other functions. This has happened in some museums. In others, admittedly, the reverse is true, to the detriment of the collections. As operations which have in the past remained largely invisible to the public, collections holding, conservation, cataloguing are difficult functions for which to win public support and thereby the increased level of funding they require. Museums may be able to change this by educating the public in the 'museum process', and in the value of preserving heritage; the government's decision to construct a new, better home for the Canadian Museum of Civilization itself evidences a rising awareness of these factors. CMC aims at greater efforts to see that the public understands the various functions of museums, and their importance to society.

But there remains the need to rethink collections development policies. CMC's intention is to be more discriminating in its collecting and to exploit more fully its existing resources. In simple terms, it will collect less and manage more. The need is to rationalize the size of the collections by evaluating the relevance of each artifact to CMC's mission. New technologies, based on computers and laser disc systems, are being used to improve accountability, facilitate use of the collections (by easier identification of objects relevant to any particular need), and permit greater public diffusion of knowledge of the collections. In rationalizing collection size it will be necessary to take deaccessioning more seriously than in the past; museums have come to recognize the fallacy in the optimism of the 1960's that there might be no limits to growth.

CMC has national and international obligations as a scholarly institution to support the work of visiting researchers. But, equally importantly, it has obligations to make its collections as accessible as possible to all Canadians. In this context CMC has the long-term goal of decentralizing those elements of the collections that are not identified as relevant to CMC's own reasonable exhibition and research needs, and which may be of particular interest to institutions and public in regions of the artifacts' origins. The aim is to negotiate transfer, probably loans for varying periods, of artifacts to centres (university, regional, provincial, or local) shown to have facilities for housing the artifacts according to museum standards. This is likely to prove a better solution for preservation of the artifacts than CMC producing large numbers of travelling exhibitions which take their toll on artifacts. Libraries have, for some years, recognized the growing financial obstacles to building and maintaining comprehensive collections; they have established programmes for sharing resources and thereby rationalizing new acquisitions. Museums and other heritage institutions must establish the same kinds of networks to supersede the much less structured arrangement they presently have. By

decentralizing its collections, CMC can spread across the country the financial rewards it expects to reap from increased cultural tourism.

Accessibility - to the museum, to its collections, and to the information that makes the collections and the cultures they represent intelligible - is a cornerstone of CMC's policies. It has many facets. It is ensuring that a larger proportion of the collections go on public display within the museum's galleries than was possible in the past. It is providing controlled access to even those collections held in reserve in backstage areas of the museum, wherever feasible. It is disseminating programmes, information, images, or the objects themselves across the country and abroad, to reach people who cannot come to Ottawa. It is having the space to bring in important travelling exhibitions from elsewhere in the world. It is sensitivity to the particular needs of the handicapped, of specialized interest groups, or persons whose mother tongue is neither English nor French. It is getting the public involved - participant and interactive - with the presentations by, and the operations of, the museum. It is giving ethnic or native groups better contact with the icons of their cultures, and empowering them to define their heritage and interpret it to others. It is allowing users to chart their own courses through the learning process, rather than dictating a selective version of the interpreted past. It is communicating in terms the visitor can readily understand, as well as being willing to listen to them in return. It is providing a range of experiences to cater to every need, every predilection. It is *sharing*, in one great celebration in the Global Village.

If one element of the new paradigm for indoor human history museums, that CMC believes itself to be, is to foster a sense of collective and individual identity in its visitors, another is a sense of identity for the museum itself. One of the questions that has had to be addressed is : what is a *National* Museum? Largely because it was under-resourced, CMC has lacked national presence. Much the same might be said of Canada's other National Museums. Critics charged that CMC was really only a regional museum, since its audiences were largely local. Relatively few Canadians outside that region had any real awareness of CMC's exhibitions and programmes. Except among the museum community, CMC's reputation internationally has been virtually nonexistent. The federal government's slipping confidence in the National Museums was reflected in its decision to give the National Capital Commission increasing responsibility for heritage interpretation in the capital.

During the 1980's, owing to its commitments in planning the new museum, CMC had to reduce substantially its outreach programmes, and thereby its presence across Canada. This situation it now plans to rectify. As a *national* museum it is concerned with all regions, cultures, and eras; but even with its improved facilities and resources it could not hope to cover all of these in the detail desirable. Though it must necessarily be selective in what it presents, it still seeks to be representative : an introductory overview, or a table of contents to the national heritage, attracting visitors' attention, whetting their appetites, and directing them to resources elsewhere in the country. The History Hall exhibits, for example, include cross-references to other major museum collections, to particular museums (e.g. open air museums), and especially to the National Historic Sites. CMC must interpret, in a balanced way, the various regions and cultures to each other, or rather act as facilitator in that process of interpretation by bringing together in one forum representatives of those regions/cultures. Its new name also extends its interpretive mandate beyond Canada, which is appropriate since so many of Canada's citizens have their roots in other countries. To be a national museum its influence must be felt all over Canada. It is in the process of redeveloping its outreach programming on a scale never before attempted, and of seeking the partnership of other Canadian museums so that they may share in the benefits and credit and that, by mutual cooperation, mutual goals may more easily be attained.

National institutions are national not because of their *size* but because of their *authority*. CMC recognizes its responsibility to be a leader (coordinating, not dictating) in the Canadian museum community. One aspect of this is interpreting museums to the public : their functions, their role in society, and their importance. Another is pointing out to the public that CMC is not the be-all and end-all of national heritage. The national treasures do not reside in any one place, nor should they. But it is desirable to pursue the identification and protection of the national treasures, wherever they are, through the development of formal recognition procedures comparable to those in Japan, India, Korea, and elsewhere, or on a basis comparable to that already done for other elements of heritage by the National Archives, National Library, and National Historic Sites and Monuments Board of Canada.

All Canadian museums would benefit from the founding of a heritage network through which they could air their concerns and jointly plan to solve their problems through mutual support, cooperative promotional ventures, and the sharing of such resources as collections, expertise, information, and visitor research. CMC will try to play a catalytic role in the creation of such a network, for it is well-situated to do so, and hopes to bring Parks Canada and Heritage Canada (which maintain headquarters but little or no public facilities in the National Capital Region) in to join it. Since the seat of government is in Ottawa, that city tends naturally to be a node for networks. CMC's location also allows it to serve as spokesman to the federal government on behalf of the heritage community. And it could assume responsibility for formal declaration of objects nominated as national treasures by individuals and institutions across the country. In time museums in other countries may be drawn into the network, something made more feasible today by the low cost of satellite links, to form a Global Village in microcosm within the international museum community.

CMC must also be the hub of an outreach network, with concentric rings of diffusion surrounding it, each ring well-defined according to the audiences within it and the services that can be provided them. Modern electronic technologies make this feasible. CMC considers human history museums' traditionally conservative attitude towards new technology - the notion that it is somehow incompatible with presentation of the past or that it is dehumanizing - insupportable, especially in a country characterized by great distances over which is spread a population not a few of whose members now use new technologies in creative endeavours. It plans to ship out not only artifacts or exhibits, but images and other information : via television, laser discs, video-cassettes, holograms, as well as more traditional published media of dissemination. And to provide remote access into visual and textual databanks, made available via its Médiathèque, of its own or others' creation. The museum is equipped with production facilities, for which its higher volume of special exhibitions, theatrical performances, festivals, and demonstrations will provide the content for media products. Distributed nationwide, these will increase accessibility, help to establish a national presence for the museum, build public support, and generate revenue at the same time.

At the point beyond which CMC cannot maintain physical accessibility, electronic accessibility will take over; as technologies advance and mature the latter form of access will be able to take on much the same interactive aspects as the former. They are already sufficiently advanced to indicate the feasibility of linking, by satellite, ethnic communities in different parts of the world; for example, Chinese New Year's celebrations in Ottawa, Vancouver, Beijing, and Hong Kong could be shared in an interactive programme in which participants at each site offer coordinated performances in real time. This would indeed be a Global Village in the best McLuhan tradition.

Much the same technologies, and others, will be used *inside* the museum to help recontextualize artifacts by re-creating appropriate moods and environments and to provide interpretive information in a variety of ways to suit almost every need. The costs of investing in these technologies is not small, but will certainly be outweighed by the benefits to the museum and to the Canadian community. They are allowing CMC to shift its focus towards dissemination of information - dissemination of culture itself - in a way not practicable previously, and to place the full resources of the museum more at the user's disposal for self-directed learning. Furthermore they offer the means to fuel the mass media and to provide potential visitors with previews of CMC that may persuade them to visit in person, or post-views that will encourage them to return. It is largely through television screens that the competition for people's leisure-time will be waged. Above all, it is through these technologies that we can realize the dream of the Global Village, within which we shall understand that we are all citizens of the world.

Has, then, the Canadian Museum of Civilization succumbed to the temptations of its rival, the quasi-museum, exemplified by Epcot? It thinks not. It has not lost sight of the fact that technology is only a tool, not to be made more conspicuous than the messages it is used to present. Museums retain their special role in the face of increasing competition in the cultural sector not by one characteristic but by their unique combination of several. In particular it is their collections of the 'real things', and their associated expertise in material culture, as well as their commitment to excellence in service to the public (rather than profit-making) that sets them apart from institutions such as theme parks. As the director of the Western Development Museums states : "Museums must have the open-mindedness to adopt what can be used from the competition while maintaining the principles and standards to reject that

which is not acceptable."[54] CMC has adopted theatrical techniques, but it is more than a theatre for it employs icons not props. It has introduced greater elements of recreation into its programmes, but focuses on *meaningful* leisure, through its goal of promoting intercultural understanding. Its emphasis on accessibility, and the lessons learned about hosting of visitors, make it a more populist institution; yet, as the Royal Ontario Museum's director points out, there is nothing incompatible in museums being both market-oriented and value-driven.[55] In essence, this means that there is an extra quality added to the products and services of museums which take into account longer-term cultural values than do other producers. 'Quality' is not easy to define, not being subject to empirical measurement; it is not so much an attribute as an event arising out of the relationship between observer and observed, maker and making, and occurs at the experiential level.[56] Museums cannot challenge theme parks in their own sphere of recreational fulfillment, but they can pre-empt the techniques of theme parks and outclass them with the resultant product which will have value-oriented content theme parks cannot match.

This is the vision that has shaped the destiny of the Canadian Museum of Civilization. It is no less than what it was in the past, for its traditional functions of collecting, documenting, managing, conserving, exhibiting, interpreting, are still valid. But it is greater, for it is more sensitive to the range of needs of a range of publics, and more capable of responding satisfactorily with a wider range of methods, techniques, and technologies. Moreover it has renewed purpose in its mission, now updated to meet a fundamental social want : to contribute to mutual understanding between the various cultures that make up the Canadian mosaic and ultimately the cultures that make up the Global Village as a whole. Its existence is an affirmation that we still need museums, to understand the world, our fellow humans, and ourselves, and to serve society and the process of cultural evolution. It has been, and will continue to be, criticized, especially from within the museum community; individuals and institutions who steer a course of radical change always are. Suffice it to say that the leap towards the future was necessary. And if it issues a challenge, to its own staff as well as to the rest of the museum world, well then, facing and overcoming challenges is the very essence of life.

the museum as showcase

The Canadian Museum of Civilization has been the story of an anthropology museum transforming into a history and anthropology museum. In 1910 an Anthropology Division, with archaeology and ethnology sections, was created within the Geological Survey of Canada. Its offshoot, the National Museum of Canada, was divided in 1956 into Natural History and Human History branches, with the latter comprising Archaeology and Ethnology Divisions; History and Folklore Divisions were added in the mid-1960's. Separate exhibitions in the Victoria Memorial Museum Building reflected these Divisional jurisdictions; this organizational structure was retained in early planning for the new museum. The architectural programme allocated exhibition space to the Archaeological Survey of Canada and the Canadian Ethnology Service on the lowest (river) level of the public wing, the Canadian Centre for Folk Culture Studies was given part of the main (entrance) level, and the top level was assigned to History Division. The unintentional effect, broadly speaking, was to segregate the population elements which make up the Canadian mosaic : the story of English and French colonial settlement would be related on the top level, other ethnic communities would be portrayed on the main level, and native peoples on the lowest level.

As the thinking of CMC's planners evolved, and as intercultural understanding emerged as the focus for exhibitions and public programmes, a less strict segregation of cultural elements in the gallery layout became more desirable. What was needed was a more interdisciplinary or holistic treatment, to show the integral role of all cultural elements in the formation of the Canadian identity. There was also a concern that the spatial organization might seem to symbolize a stereotypical cultural hierarchy reflecting concepts of superiority and dominance, with the cultures of Canada's two official language groups at the highest level of the hierarchy/building, native peoples at the lowest, and other cultural

minorities somewhere in-between. This connotation was never intended, although the spatial organization was designed to represent a temporal progression, from distant past to recent past.

Space limitations of the Parc Laurier site necessitated that the new museum be a multi-level structure. Splitting the building into three levels almost unavoidably encourages division of exhibitions on that basis. Efforts have been made to counteract the

Figures 43 and 43a
This cutaway – an early conceptual drawing – illustrates the different levels of the public wing, and their relationship to each other.

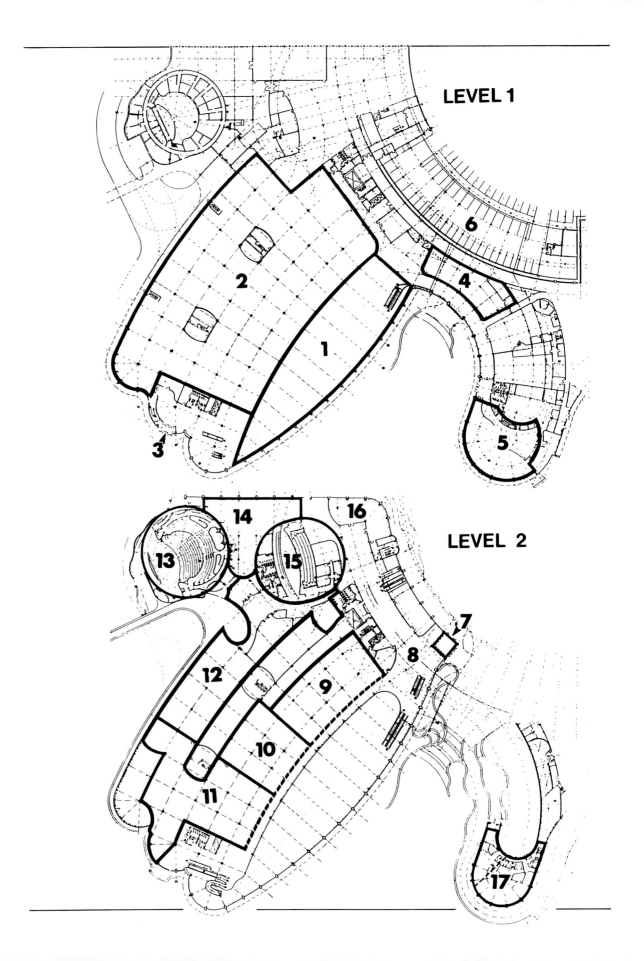

LEVEL 1

LEVEL 2

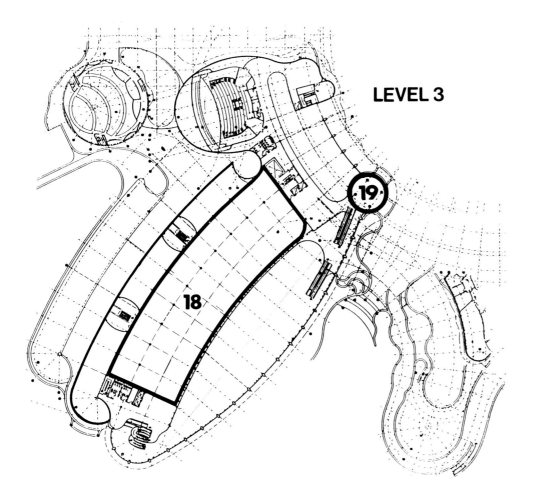

LEVEL 3

Figure 44

The three levels of the
public wing of the museum.

1	Grand Hall		11	Arts and Traditions Hall
2	Native Peoples Hall		12	Children's Museum
3	River entrance		13	Theatre
4	Médiathèque		14	Salle Barbeau
5	Cafeteria		15	Imax/Omnimax Theatre
6	Parking		16	Sales shop
7	Main Entrance		17	Restaurant and Friends Lounge
8	Main Lobby		18	History Hall
9	Special Exhibitions Hall		19	Rest area
10	Native Art Gallery			

potentially negative consequences of this. Visitors' introduction to the exhibitions, on the river level, is in the Grand Hall, where the meeting of native and non-native cultures is a key theme represented. Most of this level is dedicated to the history and prehistory of Canada's native peoples. Exhibitions here are relatively permanent; core elements may remain unaltered for two or three decades, with peripheral elements changing more often to present different artifacts from CMC's collections. The other permanent exhibition is on the top level of the public wing. Although designated the History Hall, it does not restrict itself to the story of French and English settlement but also illustrates the relationship between the European newcomers and the established natives as well as the role of other immigrant groups in the development of the country.

Sandwiched between these anthropological and historical approaches to Canadian cultural identity are exhibition halls whose contents will change more frequently; this allows for greater rotation of artifactual collections and for importing travelling exhibitions. Exhibitions based on CMC's folk culture collections occupy much of this level, sharing it with a Special Exhibitions Hall, the Native Art Gallery, and special facilities such as the Children's Museum and two theatres. Various devices are used to cross-reference exhibitions, such as light-wells at three points in the galleries, to provide visual and thematic linking between the exhibition levels. Ethnic groups are presented in the History Hall in relationship to the major issues that are important to them as Canadians. But they are also peoples with roots that go back into other continents. The Arts and Traditions Hall on the main level gives the opportunity to treat ethnic cultures, and folk or popular culture generally, more broadly than in the History Hall. The heritage of Canada, as a nation of immigrants, is closely linked to the heritage of the world. It can be argued that CMC has a mandate to portray international subjects; the changing exhibitions on the main level will permit this, to an extent. Unfortunately, the notion of an expanded mandate emerged, with the name-change from National Museum of Man to Canadian Museum of Civilization, *after* the basic design of the new museum building was completed; the means of fulfilling its broader mandate more effectively have not yet been entirely resolved.

Traditionally, museum exhibitions are viewed as showcases for the artifactual collections. This is true enough for CMC, but is not by itself adequate as an interpretation of function. Its collections are the chief physical content of the exhibitions, and are vehicles for the information, ideas, and perspectives to be presented, but it is not always easy to see into the soul of the past or the contemporary human condition through them alone. It is the traditions and world-views of past cultures that museums really seek to represent, and so preserve. Material artifacts are only one of several tools to be used in the process. CMC wishes to showcase not merely its collections but the layered ethnicity which is the cultural background of Canadians and which those collections only reflect. The metaphor of the museum as a mirror for mankind has perhaps been overused, but that does not make it any less appropriate. People come to museums to find a reference point for their identity : who they are as individuals, who as members of a social group, who as members of a national group, and so on. The principle guiding the development of new exhibitions for CMC has been to reveal those identities, allow visitors to explore them and their relationships with others, and through that process to understand the contemporary human condition. For a nation which may take pride in itself, Canada's national museum of human history is a showcase of cultural achievement : communication amidst a diversity of languages; the ingenuity and economy of environmental adaptations of immigrants; the richness of architectural, craft, and artistic styles; the enduring fascination of mythologies, religious and cosmological beliefs; the successful transplantation of homeland traditions into a new world.

Development of new exhibitions was influenced too by more down-to-earth considerations. The diverse needs of a national museum's audiences require several types of exhibit. And there was a desire to learn from experience, to avoid the problems associated with exhibitions in the Victoria Memorial Museum Building. Therefore, no single exhibition approach or philosophy dominated exhibition development. Rather CMC created a range of exhibitions and experiences to serve the range of known or predicted needs : there is, after all, no such thing as the 'general public', but instead individuals who have different reasons for visiting, and different expectations.

A traditional museum method for creating exhibitions has been artifact-driven : the best artifacts are identified and a story built around them, with labels, graphics, models, etc. added to exhibits to explain the artifacts' meaning. This allows a museum's treasures to be displayed, but risks the omission of important themes if no treasures relate to them.

CMC's past exhibits were created rather on the basis of an alternate, storyline-driven approach, didactic in nature and emphasizing cognitive learning. The story to tell was decided upon first, then the collections were searched for good artifacts to illustrate the story. The narrative of this type of exhibition hangs together quite well, but sometimes the artifacts seem merely supplementary to the textual story, and their usage contrived.

CMC now recognizes the failings in its exhibitions of this type. For one thing, educational staff were not involved in exhibition design. The labels were not very successful in persuading visitors to read them. Audiovisual elements were, with a few exceptions, unspectacular. Little provision was made for access by the handicapped. Above all, the building placed serious constraints on the exhibition designers. Some features of designs looked fine on paper but, when executed, inability to provide environmental context (due to a lack of gallery space) made them seem out-of-place or incorrectly scaled, and therefore implausible. The space confinement also influenced the design of circulation routes which often proved confusing for visitors. And inadequate space for temporary exhibitions caused repeat visitors to become bored by unchanging exhibits, a problem exacerbated by the inability to display more than a few really sizable objects - lack of variety in scale tends to create monotony. Nor did it help that most artifacts had to be presented in protective display cases, because of the poor humidity and temperature control in the building. The 'black box' gallery design, in which artifacts and their display cases are the only well-lit features, is now known to contribute to mental fatigue for visitors too long exposed to it without relief.

Both the artifact-driven and storyline-driven approaches have been employed in developing the new exhibitions, but not in excess. The dominant approach has been to liberate artifacts from the artificial frames of display cases, and recontextualize them meaningfully through environmental reconstructions in which numerous objects are seen in their relationships to one another, as well as in the context of use. The Parc Laurier building accommodates rigorous museum standards for artifact preservation (unknown when the Victorial Memorial Museum Building was erected). Any public exposure of an artifact will still contribute to its gradual degradation; the compromise between preservation and use must always be made. But environmental conditions in the public wing of the new museum reduce the need to encase artifacts in protective shields. Their removal also helps break the fetishization of objects which is, usually, inappropriate to a museum's exhibiting aims.

Eliminating the display case does not by itself solve the problem. The interior architecture of the museum

Figures 45 and 45a
The museum building itself acts as a giant display case for lifesize exhibits, known as environmental reconstructions. This is most clearly exemplified by the Grand Hall, with its huge window-wall.

73

becomes the new wrapping for the exhibit, and thus the medium whose own messages may influence, or override, messages from the artifacts. The architecture can be disguised through the 'environmental reconstruction' technique of display - manifested in indoor museums as dioramic, period room, and streetscape exhibits. This permits the messages from artifacts to be conveyed through a medium historically appropriate to the artifacts. It allows artifacts to be set in their natural and social contexts, and can offer an effective foundation on which to superimpose interpretive programmes that help visitors grasp the ways in which the components of the reconstruction interrelate and are interdependent. CMC has opted for this approach in its core exhibits : its Pacific Coast Indian village streetscape in the Grand Hall, reconstructed habitats along the central circulation route through the Native Peoples Hall, and thematic modules in the History Hall each dominated by architectural reconstructions. The space demanded by this type of exhibit was provided for in early planning. CMC is the first museum into which clearance heights of up to 55' (17 m.) along the entire lengths of galleries, and correspondingly wide spaces, have been planned to accommodate exhibits which will exploit those dimensions. Exhibits of this nature are difficult to change frequently; to compensate for their relative permanence, a much greater proportion of changing exhibits was planned for the new museum, to encourage return visitors.

Environmental reconstruction exhibits have been criticized on the grounds that the total scene may overpower, and distract attention from, individual artifacts. This depends, however, partly upon how long a visitor spends examining an exhibit. To an extent the blending of individual pieces into a larger whole serves CMC's purposes. It was important that at least the core exhibits should work as visual creations. Their function is not so much to educate as to entertain, and through entertaining to educate : McLuhan saw no fundamental difference between education and entertainment, since enjoyment is an effective vehicle for learning. CMC's educational aim for its exhibitions is less to convey a series of specific facts than to ensure that visitors leave with an enhanced understanding and respect for cultural diversity and achievement; or with an experience that has enriched their cultural perspectives and allowed them to see the world through new eyes.

Environmental reconstructions are the most prominent, but by no means the only, types of exhibits in CMC. Their contrast in scale from isolated objects in display cases, and their provision of human scale to which visitors can easily relate, will be appreciated. Yet to have only reconstructions would create its own monotony, as some museums have found. Nor would it have catered to all visitor needs : some people wish to have one-on-one encounters with artifacts, for meditation, and others are interested in comparing very similar objects (typological displays).

In broad terms, museum visitors can be categorized as 'streakers', 'strollers', or 'students'. For the first, who move quickly through exhibitions, the environmental reconstructions along main circulation routes should prove satisfying by presenting rich and dramatic images that can be taken in at a glance and yet still convey some simple messages central to exhibition themes. For 'strollers', who prefer a more leisurely pace, there are plenty of opportunities to examine the reconstructions in detail and explore exhibits in secondary areas off the main routes. And 'students' can penetrate the layers of museum information to the fullest depths, not only in the exhibits but also in visual and textual databases available in the galleries and the Médiathèque. All CMC's exhibitions are exciting : sometimes the excitement of a dynamic display in which visitors may participate, sometimes the excitement of enlightenment through contemplation.

Although people visit museums partly to see the "real thing", any museum that introduces interactivity into exhibits, as CMC has, must be flexible in employing artifacts. The use of replicas instead of originals has been criticized as cheating the public; some accept the use of replicas only if it is fully disclosed.[1] This issue stems from that inherent contradiction between the use and the preservation of artifacts. All museums draw a line of compromise somewhere between the two. CMC's position is that there is a place for reproductions within the museum. Unique, rare, or especially valuable artifacts cannot be placed in situations which will *unreasonably* hasten their deterioration; they are, after all, the heritage of our own and future generations. Original artifacts are used wherever feasible in the exhibitions, sometimes even in contexts where the public may touch them, if CMC has multiple examples. Some artifacts have been specially collected for use in ways that will eventually lead to their deterioration; these belong to the 'education collection' and are used as props for theatrical presentations, as teaching aids, or in demonstrations. In other cases - particularly the reconstructed environments with which visitors have direct contact - replicas substitute for originals.

While there is no intention to deceive visitors, it would have been counter-productive for a credible atmosphere to label replicas as such.

The Exhibition Development Process

The face of the new museum appears largely in its exhibitions, the element to which most visitors are certain to be exposed. Not everyone who sees the finished product will appreciate the energy and hard work invested in it. Exhibitions four times as extensive (once complete) as in CMC's former space have had to be planned, designed, constructed, and installed virtually from scratch. Initial funding to build the new museum, it was always understood, was insufficient to outfit it with new exhibitions as well; it was feared that the old exhibitions might have to be transplanted to the new building. Uncertainty about money made it difficult to develop exhibitions beyond the conceptual stage until a fresh injection of government funds, in June 1987, gave the go-ahead for new exhibits of a quality commensurate with the world-class building and with exhibits of national museums abroad.

CMC may still be a medium-sized museum, compared to some, but it has created exhibitions at least as exciting as any to be found elsewhere. There is over 165,000 sq.' (15,328 sq.m.) of exhibition space, with 45% scheduled to open in June 1989, and the rest joining it gradually during the early 1990's. Creating a major exhibition is very complex and time-consuming; it takes most large museums four to five years. CMC had to develop several in that time-frame, while also : participating in architectural planning; arranging for equipment, furniture, and fittings; re-developing programmes and services for clients; and ensuring the safe transfer of the collections to interim and final homes. Attention first focused on broad concepts for exhibitions and on the physical spaces for them, to guide the architect. As the first edition of the architectural programme was being completed, in January 1983, ideas for new exhibitions were being gathered for an exhibition master plan. 2

This plan could only be provisional, for various reasons. Ideally, the exhibitions would have been designed first, and the architect left to design spaces appropriate to them, but the timeline for the New Accommodation project did not allow that luxury. The architectural design would gradually become fixed whether or not it benefited from a knowledge of the intended exhibits. Therefore it was essential to supply the architect with more detailed plans for exhibitions than in the architectural programme. From that point the architectural and exhibition designs would have to evolve in unison, each sensitive to the needs and constraints of the other. Another reason that the exhibitions plan could not be regarded as 'written in stone' was the absence of a government commitment on funding. Furthermore, planning needed to allow for future developments which could not be anticipated in the early stages, such as new technologies or techniques. It also had to adjust to changes in CMC's mission, which was undergoing review as part of the New Accommodation project.

Until the injection of new funds in 1987, CMC could do little beyond planning broad concepts and themes. This is part of the reason that not all galleries were ready for the June 1989 opening. Despite this, much had been accomplished by early 1987. In September 1983 the first exhibition development team was set up, for the History Hall. Comprising CMC's senior designer, its head of the interpretation section, and one of its professional historians, this team was intended to serve as a prototype to test a particular approach to exhibition development. Other teams were phased in during the months that followed. At one point several dozen were operating simultaneously, absorbing the energies of most members of the permanent staff, some of whom sat on more than one team.

The structure and operation of the History Hall team was experimental. Experience in the Victoria Memorial Museum Building showed that exhibitions produced by either a subject-specialist or a designer were often less than satisfactory. Yet the opposite extreme of bringing into an exhibition development team many members, representing diverse expertises, would have dictated a rather formal committee approach favouring process at the expense of product, imposing bureaucratic restraints on creativity, and impeding efficient decision-making with lengthy discussions and reconciliation of too many divergent opinions. A compromise between the two approaches was required.

Essential to the team was expertise on the content (facts and artifacts) of the exhibition, on its form (physical structure, ambiance), and on its context (audience or user needs). These elements had to be developed simultaneously and held in balance. So the team was to comprise a curator/researcher, a designer, and an interpretation specialist, to represent each of the three elements. The curator was to :

Figure 46
Periodic building of scale models was helpful in allowing museum staff to visualize and evaluate the product being developed by exhibition project teams.

interpretive programming adequately met their needs; bring to the planning process a knowledge of learning theory; and propose materials to support the exhibition, such as guidebooks, posters, etc. Although each team-member brought a particular expertise, all had input to every aspect of the work, which resulted from the entire team's constant discussion and joint decision-making.

The first duty of an exhibition project team was to develop a Concept Statement : a report establishing the purposes and communication objectives of the exhibition, and possible design solutions to achieve them. These documents were to consider numerous questions. What is the subject and theme of the exhibition, and what is it to achieve in relationship to institutional goals? Is the theme best communicated by an exhibition, or would some other medium be better? What approaches to communicating the theme are feasible? Is there a real need for this exhibition and, if so, by what audience? What collection base will be drawn upon, and might there be competition for artifacts with other exhibitions being developed? Is the subject interdisciplinary? What supporting illustrative materials are available or needed? Are there special requirements, such as security, public safety or comfort, conservation?

In the exhibition development process CMC's Director acted as client for the teams, exercising quality control by approving or rejecting all aspects of the design. Once the general concept was acceptable to the client, more detailed approaches to the storyline, the exhibition's structural design, and interpretive techniques had to be written. Following stages called for increased detail, and greater attention to visitor traffic flow patterns, scripting of storyline and of audiovisual presentations, mechanical and electrical infrastructures, sound and lighting systems, assignment of specific artifacts to locations within the exhibition, and to construction and installation. The deliverables to the client were not only textual reports but also sketches, which gradually became more detailed floorplans and design drawings, and three-dimensional models showing the exhibits in their architectural context. Like architectural design, exhibit design was also, in a sense, a model-driven process. The models assisted in formative evaluation, and helped the project teams co-ordinate their work with that of the design of the spaces into which the exhibitions had to fit. The completed design details then had to be translated into construction specification and tender contracts. In the construction and installation phases the exhibition project teams served as clients to those

identify what was available from CMC's collections or from outside, or what might be replicated; ensure those artifacts were suitable for exhibiting, from a conservation standpoint; provide the research information for the artifacts; and ensure the accuracy of information conveyed through the exhibition. The designer was to : translate the storyline into a visual framework that would effectively communicate; ensure the design protected the artifacts and accommodated visitor comfort and safety; design exhibit furniture, identify component costs, produce a budget and a schedule, and coordinate exhibit installation. The interpretation expert would : set out the communication objectives for the exhibition; identify target audiences and ensure the design and

responsible for the work, to ensure that the integrity of the design was preserved in the final product.

This cursory description barely does justice to the exhibition development process, and inevitably generalizes the individualistic route that each project took. Yet it gives some idea of the involved and demanding nature of the work. During the several years of development, the first team model was modified in light of experience. The quite structured methodology had been influenced somewhat by the even more rigidly structured approach of the Royal Ontario Museum which, when the New Accommodation project was beginning, was in the final phases of revamping and expanding its own exhibitions. Membership of the CMC teams underwent changes. The leadership/coordinating function became increasingly vital, to ensure work proceeded quickly and efficiently, as the timeline for production of exhibitions tightened without funding forthcoming from the government; one member of each team was formally designated as leader. Advice was also sought from specialists outside the museum. To tap the minds of experts from within the museum world and also from outside it, consultants were engaged and seminars were organized. This was to ensure that CMC's exhibitions would be the best possible, and that they could take advantage of innovative techniques, technologies, and media with which CMC's staff had little familiarity. Moreover, the twelfth-hour funding provided by the government set in motion a fast-track programme of detailed design, fabrication and installation over a two-year period that also necessitated the museum's staff be supplemented.

Perhaps more significantly, the underlying philosophical view of exhibition development shifted somewhat. To the outside observer it might have appeared that the role of the interpretation specialist on the teams was diminished. In fact it was increasingly grasped that too much emphasis had been placed on that member as the team's main expert in communicating with the museum's audiences. Communicating with the public is what exhibitions are all about. The ability to communicate was a skill that had to be possessed, or acquired, by every member of a team; it could not be mandated to one member only. This viewpoint represents a shift towards the curator-educator concept emerging now in some museums (e.g. the Royal British Columbia Museum, the Indianapolis Children's Museum) that reconciles or integrates two roles that have traditionally been almost adversarial. It reflects a more mature attitude towards the role of museums.

The curator-communicator and designer-communicator now tended to become the core of CMC teams; the interpretation specialist was more consultative - advising on aspects such as audience characteristics/needs, special interpretive techniques, theatrical programming - and less involved in decision-making. Sometimes the interpretation role in the teams was contracted out. CMC did not possess enough internal interpretation expertise to go round, as the teams proliferated, and what did exist was needed elsewhere; the History Hall team's interpretation member, for example, had to be redeployed to live performance and special events programming.

The temporary exhibitions design teams tended to retain the three-person form more than the teams designing the permanent halls. Nonetheless, in both cases team structure became increasingly flexible and individualistic, with extra staff-members called in on consultation to deal with concerns such as conservation, security, and new technology applications. This flexibility of team structure allowed more of a free rein to creativity, the foundation of what should be a synergistic process. Since the temporary exhibitions will change the most frequently and their teams will have to be continuing, it may be *that* form which dominates the future of exhibition development at CMC.

Yet there is a need to retain the permanent hall teams too for, although these halls and their basic contents may be relatively fixed, the exhibition is not necessarily so. CMC now conceives of the total product as the 'exhibition experience' which includes not only the physical exhibits but also the interpretive programming and educational/entertainment content. From one perspective the static exhibits are a backdrop for the more dynamic programmes. The exhibition experience needs to be reviewed regularly, evaluated to assess its effectiveness in meeting the changing needs and expectations of visitors. To preserve their dynamism, exhibitions must continue developing indefinitely, with their teams dominated by the curatorial and interpretation members, concerned with adjusting content and programming, and the designer called in only if any of the physical structure needs to be altered. Certainly CMC won't be resting on its laurels once it has all its planned exhibitions in place.

Now that the reader has some idea of the thought and the work that has gone into producing the exhibitions in the new Canadian Museum of Civilization, let us proceed on a 'tour' of those exhibitions.

The Grand Hall

Upon entering the museum, through its main entrance off the Laurier Street plaza, the visitor is almost immediately confronted by a view down into

Figures 47 and 47a
The Grand Hall is shaped rather like a canoe, appropriate to its native theme. The immense size of the space is better communicated by the architectural reality than by the early concept drawing.

a breath-taking space : the Grand Hall. Its name suits it perfectly. During site tours, before the building was fitted out, that skeletal space always made the greatest impression; and when the media were shown the building during construction, it was invariably that same space that one would see on the television screen or front page of the newspaper the following day. Rising to a height of 50' (15 m.), the Hall has views into it from all three levels of the public wing. Its elliptical form is true to Cardinal's architectural style. The hall's shape is rather like a canoe; some 365' (112 m.) long and 75' (23 m.) at its greatest width, it provides 19,182 sq.' (1782 sq.m.) of floor-space : in size it has been compared to a football field, although the inward-curving walls make the river-end of the hall, when viewed from the opposite end, appear to stretch away almost to infinity.

The Grand Hall has a cathedral-like quality; certainly it offers inspirational views. Through the floor-to-ceiling window-wall visitors have a spectacular view of the Ottawa River and Parliament Buildings. The opposite wall is covered by a massive dioramic exhibit : an environmental reconstruction of a composite 'village' of houses representing six Pacific Coast Indian tribes. The hall is a space which serves multiple functions. The most significant architectural space in the museum, it is highly visible from both main and river entrances to the public wing, from other levels in that wing, from CMC's restaurants, and from the park and the far bank of the Ottawa River. What some tourists see of the Grand Hall, from a distance, may determine whether or not they choose to visit the museum. Its views to the outside will help visitors orient themselves within the building, while its natural light, contrasting with the artificial and generally lower-level lighting in the exhibition galleries, will help relieve 'museum fatigue'.

The hall is a key element in the traffic flow pattern, linking the lobbies of two entrances to the museum, and giving access to vertical circulation routes. Most first-time visitors to the museum will enter by the main entrance; from its lobby they should be naturally drawn down the nearby escalators into the Grand Hall. At the opposite end of the hall is the river entrance to the museum. Lying between that entrance and the end of the Grand Hall proper are circulation nodes to upper levels : stairs, escalator, elevators. Most visitors will begin their exploration of the museum by passing through the Grand Hall, at the end of which they have the option of touring the Native Peoples Hall or passing up to other levels.

Figures 48 and 48a
The Grand Hall can serve multiple
purposes: exhibition, circulation route,
assembly area, banquet hall, and
theatre.

The spaciousness of the Grand Hall, of which only one side is occupied by exhibits, and its conspicuous location make it an ideal assembly area, or rendezvous point for family or other groups. The Grand Hall can also serve for stand-up receptions, sit-down banquets, or as staging-area for theatrical events; for all these the village diorama provides a dramatic backdrop.

The last of the Grand Hall's functions is as the introductory exhibition of the museum. The reconstructed Pacific Coast village is a feature striking enough not to be dwarfed by the sheer size of the hall, or its vast expanse of window. CMC chose to focus on that particular culture, as an introductory exhibition, for several reasons. It was decided that the core of the museum's mission, to enhance intercultural understanding, could be well represented in this exhibition, one of whose key themes is the meeting of New World and Old World cultures.

The Pacific Coast village exhibition also allowed the presentation of objects which have particularly dramatic visual qualities and which are monumental, both in scale and in cultural significance. Claude Lévi-Strauss declared, in *Time* magazine, that the arts

of Canada's West Coast native peoples rank with those of ancient Egypt and China as world-class in their uniqueness and refinement. This was one sign of the increasing world recognition of the Pacific Coast Indian culture. The Haida village of Ninstints, on the Queen Charlotte Islands, was recently declared a World Heritage Site by UNESCO. And the Haida master-carver, Charles Edensaw, was one of the few Canadian artists recognized by the National Historic Sites and Monuments Board of Canada as a national historic figure, for his artistic achievements in traditional Haida style. CMC possesses the best collection in the world of monumental sculptures from the Golden Age of West Coast Indian art, and will add to it examples of the equally fine dramatic arts of those native cultures, by engaging their representatives to give traditional performances in front of the streetscape. In the Victoria Memorial Museum Building CMC's Northwest Coast Indian gallery, labelled "Children of the Raven", was the feature for which the museum was best-known and won the only three-star award by *Michelin Travel Guide* to any attraction in the National Capital Region. The closure of that hall, as a result of environmental threats to the national treasures there, set the ball rolling to persuade the federal government that a new home was needed for CMC's collections. Thus it was through the help of

Figures 49, 49a,
CMC has commissioned new works from native artists such as Tony Hunt, Bill Reid, and Bob Davidson for display in the Grand Hall and elsewhere in the museum.

Raven that the new museum came about; so it seems appropriate that his people should be accorded a special place in the museum. The shape of the Grand Hall and the character of its contents have led to the adoption of the image of Raven's Canoe for that space.

The Grand Hall exhibition will help give Canadians and visitors from abroad an understanding of the contribution of Canada's native peoples to the heritage of the country. That this contribution is not merely historical, but also contemporary, is reflected in the artworks which CMC has commissioned from present-day native artists such as Calvin Hunt, Bill Reid, and Robert Davidson. Reid's huge bronze casting "Mythic Messengers" is to stand outside the building. Hunt's great carved feast-bowl will be a centrepiece of potlatch-type banquets held in the Grand Hall. At one end of the hall Davidson's gold-on-bronze sculpture "Raven Bringing Light to the World" gazes down onto the Pacific Coast village. His sculpture is appropriate to the theme of the exhibition : Raven - whose role in myths was at once trickster, creator, wise man, and fool - stole the box of daylight (a metaphor for the Grand Hall) and released it to the world, thus establishing the conditions essential for human life.

The cultural clash from the first period of contact between native and non-native cultures is still in many ways unresolved. Hopefully the exhibition may help pave the way towards a resolution, by allowing visitors - both those with their roots in the Old World and native peoples themselves - to explore and apprehend the complexity and richness of Pacific Coast Indian culture and also the effect on that culture of the encounter with Europeans, to examine stereotypes from our past, and to reach an appreciation of the value of native cultures to the national culture. True to the museum's philosophy, the Pacific Coast village exhibition provides opportunities both for entertainment and for learning, by layering information in successive degrees of detail and by employing dynamic interpretive techniques while remaining faithful to the spirit and fact of Indian culture and history.

The organizing element of the Grand Hall exhibition is the village. Although its houses are arranged in a row configuration found, historically, in villages throughout the Northwest Coast, CMC's village is a composite in which each house represents a different coastal people; it would therefore never have existed in that precise form. Each housefront replicates a particular chief's house which stood in a particular

Exhibition evolution

The Grand Hall has undergone many changes over the years of development. Cardinal's original concept was of an interior park-like space, with ramps, cascading waterfalls and crystalline roofs, symbolizing the melting glaciers; much of this survives in the Grand Hall window-wall and the landscaping just outside it. Nor did the architectural programme envisage the hall as holding a fully-fledged exhibition, although some of CMC's monumental artifacts - such as the Pacific Coast house-posts - might be displayed there. Rather it saw the hall as a place of orientation and a major circulation route, with potential to host receptions and performances. A later notion proposed facades of Pacific Coast houses along one wall, as portals into the Native Peoples Hall. This idea, and the integration of the hall and introductory exhibit areas, were the core of the Grand Hall's streetscape exhibition.

It was once intended to include in the hall a second reconstruction, to emphasize the theme of the meeting of cultures, in the form of a ship such as Captain Vancouver's Discovery or the Spanish galleon Santiago (one of the first European ships to explore the Pacific Coast) or Sutil. Various obstacles presented themselves to this plan : the Discovery would have had to have been reduced in scale to fit into the hall; another group was already planning a reconstruction of Santiago; and, whichever ship was selected, its absorption of space would have interfered with the hall's other functions. It is hoped now to present a full-scale reconstruction of the Sutil outside the museum, in Parc Laurier, in the early 1990's. The theme of the clash between cultural paradigms is now depicted in the hall through other objects - such as the flagpoles, and the skiff from a visiting schooner.

Another once-planned, major feature of the streetscape was a full boardwalk. This was intended to add authenticity and to double as a stage for performances. It was also a device to raise the houses above floor-level, to increase their visibility from outside the hall. However, a raised boardwalk would have created a barrier to visitors seeking direct access to the exhibits from the centre of the hall, and vice versa. Furthermore, to satisfactorily accommodate large-scale performances, as well as circulation of large numbers of visitors at peak periods, the boardwalk would have to be so wide as to intrude seriously into the reception area. It was decided instead to present the houses as facing

immediately onto the shoreline, which presents less of an obstacle (ramps at either end allowing for wheelchair access), while retaining the elevation of the houses and providing adequate space for performances. This option also makes an architectural statement more strongly integrated with the rest of the Grand Hall, where the boardwalk might have been competitive.

village at some time during the past two centuries. The village's temporal setting is the 1850's to '90's, as it is from this period that CMC's collections mostly date. It was also in this period that key ethnological accounts were written and that the dilemma posed by the meeting of two worlds became acute. The reconstructions are based upon photographic evidence and incorporate original artifacts : some house support poles and frontal poles are from CMC's collections, many never having been displayed before. They are supplemented by commissioned reproductions of structural or decorative elements to complete the facades. As visitors pass down the Grand Hall, with the village to their right, they will travel northwards along the Canadian Pacific Coast through the different cultural regions. In this direction the houses represent Coast Salish, West Coast, Kwakiutl, Bella Coola, Haida, and Tsimshian cultures. Each region had its own architectural style; differences between the houses are visible, and accentuated by the colourful housefront decorations. But common to all was the construction of houses from a framework of adzed cedar logs and walls of cedar boards.

The houses vary in width between 30 and 40 feet. They also vary in depth (20 to 44 feet) since only those of the West Coast, Kwakiutl, and Tsimshian have been fully reconstructed, for various reasons. CMC's collections are not complete enough to allow all houses to be fully furnished with representative artifacts. Even had that been possible, it would still have been desirable to avoid overtaxing the visitor with excessive content, and to avoid the spatial intrusion of six full-length houses into the Native Peoples Hall behind the streetscape. Nonetheless visitors will be able to experience the different character of each culture in the houses.

Although the underlying theme of the exhibition is the disjunction in beliefs, values, and expectations between the culture developed over thousands of years by the Pacific Coast peoples and that transplanted on the coast by Europeans, each house will present different sub-themes. The Salish house deals, for example, with navigation and fishing skills and with the supernatural (such as the guardian spirit of the household). In the West Coast dwelling aspects of family life, social rank, and ownership of resources are touched upon. The Kwakiutl reconstruction is represented as being no longer a family dwelling but a place where supernatural beings convene for the winter ceremonial; the Potlatch, and its banning by non-native authorities, are examined. The Bella Coola house allows visitors to rest and

assimilate what they have seen in the previous houses; a film presentation explores Bella Coola territory and the integration of natural environment with supernatural beliefs. The Haida building has been restored as a carver's workshop, to illustrate the carving of house-posts and totem poles, to relate the meanings of their images, and to consider the role of art in New World and Old World cultures. The Tsimshian is the largest house; only here has there been space to include the central fire pit typical of Northwest Coast dwellings. Many aspects of Tsimshian society are portrayed; the clash of cultures is depicted through the physical destruction of tribal houses outside Port Simpson in the 1830's. As much as possible themes are presented through the experience of individual natives, through their knowledge, their words, their perspectives; and often presented in a dynamic fashion, such as by the use of living representatives of the cultures to provide first-person interpretation, or by demonstrations of crafts and skills, story-telling, and performances of rituals.

The village is set within a larger environmental reconstruction which adds ambiance to the exhibits and expands the interpretive potential beyond the house interiors to the general physical environment of the Pacific Coast cultures. A village was usually located between the dense rain-forest of British Columbia and the sea, its houses in a row facing the beach; some had boardwalks passing by, and connecting, the houses, others faced immediately onto the shore. These elements have been represented in the reconstruction. The shoreline has been symbolized within the Grand Hall floor itself. The main part of that floor is finished in a dark matte granite (the sea) in which honed lines, rippling in echo to the curves of the building, represent the waves. Closer to the village the floor alters to suggest a shoreline : at each end of the hall are three terraced steps, giving access to the houses, and rock outcrops lie between them. Here the floor is a lighter, textured granite. This beach provides space for theatrical or ritual presentations, while a small section of boardwalk - resembling a dock sitting in the sea - in front of the Kwakiutl house offers a better elevation for performances viewed from the Grand Hall floor. Performances will take place not only along the shoreline, but also inside some of the houses.

The rain-forest has been simulated through theatrical techniques. Three layers of scrim (a lightweight, mesh-weave fabric used in theatres to portray scenery), comprising several dozen independent sections, hanging all the way down from the ceiling and stretching along the length of the hall, encase the houses in a gigantic illustration which does justice to both the scale and the beauty of the coniferous forest. The front layer, a photomural scrim of translucent cotton, covers the Grand Hall wall, interrupted only where penetrated by the housefronts. The second layer is hung intermittently, at varying intervals and varying distances from the front scrim. The back-drop mural also appears to cover the wall. Between them, the layers convey a feeling of depth to the forest; the darker material of the back layer contributes to this impression.

The scenery has been enlivened in several ways. Special projectors, on the Grand Hall ceiling near the great window, can create effects on the forest scrim such as rain or mist, and so give a sense of environ-mental change. In the gaps between the intermediate scrim sections, and above the houses, several large, specially created figures which relate to Northwest Coast mythology (e.g. the Thunderbird) are positioned. At programmed intervals these will 'magically' appear to people in the Hall and be accompanied by sound and light effects; some of these props will appear to be moving through the forest. This element illustrates dramatically the relationship between natural and supernatural in Pacific Coast native cultures. When the lighting of the forest scrims is dimmed, they become transparent and the back, opaque scrim can be used for rear projection. Several large-screen projectors will show multiple presentations on that scrim, at second-storey level in the hall. The projectors are along a corridor, on the main entrance level of the public wing, which separates the Grand Hall from the main level's exhibition galleries. These animation techniques aid in the creation of a mystical atmosphere essential to the evening theatrical spectacles.

Other elements of the exhibition help enhance its authenticity and support the communication of its themes. Totem poles associated with some houses offer focal points within the exhibition. Poles in front of the Haida and Tsimshian houses had previously been displayed in the foyer of the Victoria Memorial Museum Building. Another pole is a new creation commissioned by CMC from the Bella Bella. While in front of the Kwakiutl house stands the famous Wakas pole, unofficial emblem of British Columbia; CMC acquired it on long-term loan from the Vancouver Museum. The 40' pole, carved in 1893, is a unique example of openwork carving in West Coast totem art and is a centrepiece of the exhibition. There are ten poles altogether, and the

number may be increased later. By contrast, the Coast Salish house is fronted by flagpoles, bearing the Union Jack and flags of other trading nations which frequented the coast, to show the infiltration of non-native elements. The realism of the beach is enhanced by : nets, fish traps, fish-drying racks, canoes, and a skiff loaded with trade goods. There are also berry-drying racks between the houses, and activities such as woodworking along the shoreline just outside the houses.

The uses planned for the Grand Hall, and the demands of its exhibition, necessitated outfitting the hall with audio and lighting systems beyond the requirements of most museums' galleries. The lighting system has to be able to illuminate not only the exhibits but also the theatrical performances in front of them (or, when they are unrelated to the exhibits, *only* the performances). It must equally accommodate the functions of the scrims and their 'inhabitants'. As much coverage from as many angles as possible was required. During the day natural light provides much of what is needed for the programming. But, to protect artifacts from the harmful ultra-violet of daylight, Cardinal reoriented the hall (from his first conceptual plan) to face northeastwards, and other steps were taken to prevent direct sunlight from falling on the artifacts. So, despite the hall's huge window, both diagonal and overhead artificial lighting are still necessary.

Similarly, the sound system has to serve the exhibits, the rear-screen video presentations, and the theatrical performances. Sound-imaging techniques are used to project, between and in front of the houses, effects to augment the environmental depictions, such as waves and forest animal noises, and to entice visitors into the houses. The huge size of the Grand Hall and the fact that its surfaces are all hard - granite floor, drywall ceiling, and curved glass expanse - make for an extremely live environment. Reverberation time was discovered to be more than what had originally been estimated, which would have caused problems for large-scale performances. Therefore efforts have been made to upgrade the acoustical treatments in the hall, to make the problem more manageable. Reverb-eration might have been entirely controlled, if at some expense, but it would have seemed odd for such a large interior space to lack echo. The aim is to find, by experimentation, a workable balance.

The Native Peoples Hall

Many visitors will proceed from the Pacific Coast streetscape to the Native Peoples Hall, once that hall is ready in 1991. Developing the exhibitions here has been a major undertaking, for it is the largest hall in the museum, taking up 60,000 sq.' (5574 sq.m.); this would have accommodated all the exhibitions CMC had in the Victoria Memorial Museum Building. And the planning here did not begin as early as that for the History Hall, the next biggest gallery. At this time of writing the detailed plans for the Native Peoples Hall are still evolving; but a general idea can be given of what visitors will encounter.

Visitors will be encouraged to enter the Native Peoples Hall at the end of the Grand Hall, through an entrance immediately next to the Tsimshian house. There are other access points, at the southeast and northwest ends of the hall, but the latter is strictly a secondary exit point, while the former (lying directly opposite the river entrance to the museum) is intended only as the Native Peoples Hall's main exit. This arrangement provides a logical transition from the Grand Hall, through the part of the Native Peoples Hall dedicated to Northwest Coast culture. This section of the hall was in fact transferred, for planning purposes, to the jurisdiction of the Grand Hall project team and is almost an extension of that hall's exhibition. The boardwalk once intended for the Grand Hall will now serve as the main circulation route through the Northwest Coast component of the Native Peoples Hall. On display here will be CMC's 55' Haida war canoe, shown at Expo '86; one of the largest Pacific Coast dugout canoes in existence, constructed from a single, huge cedar log, this exhibit will link the Grand Hall and the transition area, drawing visitors from one into the other. Also in this section will be "The Dig" a popular feature in the Victoria Memorial Museum Building; this is the only exhibit to have been transferred from the old to the new building. "The Dig" is a reconstruction of an archaeological excavation of the shell midden of a Tsimshian village site in the Prince Rupert Harbour area; overhanging boughs of cedar trees, a scenic diorama in the background, and sounds of ravens, frogs, and the sea re-create the environment of Digby Island where the excavation took place.

Emerging from the transition area at a spot near the hall's exit, visitors will then encounter a multimedia introductory/orientation presentation showing how native peoples arrived in North America and spread across Canada, and overviewing the central themes of the hall. To avoid impeding circulation, the presentation will exist in two versions : a brief form during peak visitation, and a longer form for off-peak periods.

The exhibitions for such a large hall have had to be designed to accommodate a variety of experiences. A central circulation spine will act as a fast and distinguishable through route, and as an orientation device, leading visitors around the hall past a number of sub-halls (theme areas) each focusing on a particular region of Canada and its associated native cultures. For visitors with little time to spend, the central route will take them past key exhibits introducing the main themes for each region. Those with more time, or a deeper interest in particular topics, may detour into the sub-halls where main themes will be explored in greater detail and secondary themes will be presented. Each region will be represented by a major exhibit in the form of an environmental reconstruction; these habitats, punctuating the central route, will be important elements in the interpretive programming, supporting live animation and dramatic presentations. Three will be positioned under the light-wells that pass through to other levels of the public wing; these exhibits have been designed for good overhead views.

The sub-halls will offer more traditional display-case exhibits and audiovisual presentations, but again with animated elements to enliven some exhibits. Each regional theme area will incorporate three compon-ents, whose exhibits vary from region to region depending on the richness of CMC's collections from the region, current developments there, and other factors. One component of a sub-hall will use CMC's archaeological collection to outline the environmental and cultural change and exchange in the prehistory of each region. A second element will feature Golden Age artifacts produced by each culture. CMC's collections are rich in late nineteenth and early twentieth century objects; the term "Golden Age" is used for that period even though native cultures were largely past their golden age of development by then, and suffering the effects of epidemic diseases and cultural disorientation. The third element will deal with present and future prospects for the survival of native peoples' traditions, which are a valuable national heritage and a Canadian contribution to the heritage of mankind; for example, the remarkable adaptations of the Inuit tell much about our species' ability to cope with extreme and shifting environments like the High Arctic.

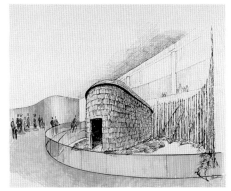

Figure 50
The Native Peoples Hall will have a central route, along which reconstructed habitats illustrate the key themes explaining each regional culture;
these and other themes will be explored in more depth in sub-halls off the main route.

Goals for the Native Peoples Hall of course relate to CMC's concern for intercultural understanding. One is to demolish stereotypes of native peoples. For example, the 'noble savage' notion; the idea that Indians are either 'bad' (primitive, lazy) or 'good' (uniformly peaceloving, living in perfect harmony with nature) will be replaced by a more balanced and realistic presentation that emphasizes diversity in past and present. Also to be discredited are the common misconceptions that : all natives are the same, reflected in the blanket term 'Indian' used for the many different peoples; that their cultures had been static until changed by the advent of Europeans; or that their belief systems are merely unsophisticated responses to their physical environment. It is important to show time-depth within the sub-halls, to demonstrate that native peoples do have a history and rich oral culture, and to illustrate the changes in their cultures over time. Native peoples today are the result of the merging of their past, their traditions, and contemporary society of Western civilization. The exhibition is really about the modern Indian. It will therefore constantly reflect current issues of concern to native peoples.

An equally important goal is to present native cultures in a way with which native peoples themselves feel comfortable. CMC will obtain their cooperation in presenting their perspectives in person; the hall offers them a forum for communicating with visitors of their own or other cultural backgrounds, partly through live interpretation programmes. Furthermore, it is vital to present to visitors the core features of the world-view, or cosmology, of each native group, since this feature provided group-members' orientation within their specific culture. Parts of their world-view are reflected in each piece of their material culture - tools, weapons, clothing, personal adornments, etc.; but all these messages are brought together in their houses. The very form and orientation of their dwellings reveals much about their world-view and which elements of it they consider paramount. Environmental factors mediate cosmological concepts, as seen in the Inuit snowhouse which shares many such concepts (although virtually no construction materials) with the Plains teepee. All the reconstructions of native houses and their decoration will be done in close association with natives, who will also animate the habitats with their presence.

The first regional area that the visitor will encounter in the Native Peoples Hall represents the Arctic peoples. Its focus is the flexibility of the Inuit in adapting to the harsh Arctic environment. The habitat exhibit will incorporate a snowhouse, with its residents and their dog-sled, set against a huge Arctic panorama in which special lighting effects simulate the Aurora Borealis. This exhibit will be positioned under a light-well, to provide scope for the special sky effects.

The next sub-hall will be divided into western and eastern Subarctic sections. The former will centre on the Athapaskans and particularly linkages between their environment, their complex supernatural belief system (animal ceremonialism, shamanism) and their middlemen role in trade from prehistoric to modern times. The core exhibit may show a reconstructed Hudson's Bay Company trading post. The eastern Subarctic theme is the persistence of the region's culture in the face of change. The habitat will be a summer scene, with canoe and tent as prominent elements.

The Atlantic Coast cultures sub-hall is also in two sections. The smaller part will investigate the extermination of the Beothuk Indians from Newfoundland, while the larger will look at native

Figure 51
Visitors will encounter in the Native Peoples Hall traditional types of display, such as this on the Inuit (from Manitoba's Museum of Man and Nature)...

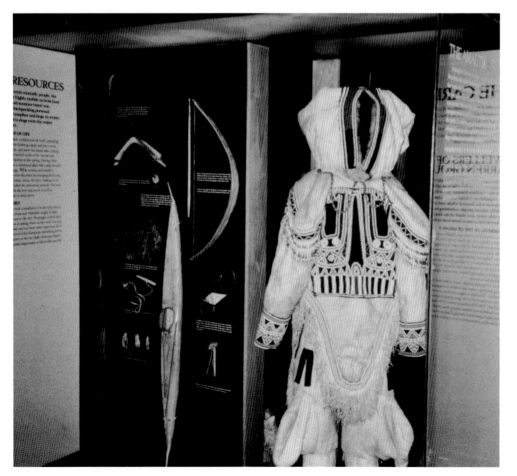

peoples of the Maritimes, emphasizing the development of a rich and complex culture focused on the sea, and what it means to be an Indian in the Maritimes today. The habitat is a summer dwelling on an estuary shoreline, set between forest and sea.

The next theme area deals with the northern Iroquoians, its habitat a full-scale, furnished reconstruction of a longhouse and part of the settlement's stockade. This too will be positioned under a light-well. The exhibition's focus is the agricultural revolution and the effects this change from a hunter-gatherer society had on the culture. The seventeenth-century longhouse also is a symbol of cultural continuity, for longhouses are still the meeting-places of present-day Iroquoian communities.

The Northern Plains theme area will highlight the central role that the bison played in the life, society, and world-view of the Plains Indians, and the effect of its near extinction (in the late nineteenth century) on that lifestyle. The associated habitat will be placed under the third light-well and will show either a teepee encampment, or a buffalo jump.

The final theme area is to examine the all-pervasive belief system of the Plateau peoples : how they perceived their world and their highly-defined place within it.

After leaving the Native Peoples Hall, our tour may proceed from the river-entrance lobby to the next (main entrance) level of the building. Here is much less use of large-scale environmental reconstructions. They may be the showpieces of the exhibition structure, but it is equally important to provide more flexibility and changeability than was available in the Victoria Memorial Museum Building, so that CMC can show through rotation a greater proportion of its collections, and so that it can host important travelling exhibitions. In contrast to the huge task of preparing the Native Peoples Hall, it was possible to ready almost all of the exhibitions on the main entrance level for the museum's opening. All halls lead off a main circulation corridor running parallel to the Grand Hall, but there is no prescribed inter-gallery circulation route on this level. Considering whence we have just come, it seems appropriate to visit first the Native Art Gallery.

The Native Art Gallery

In the early 1980's there was public debate whether contemporary native artworks properly belonged in the Canadian Museum of Civilization or in the National Gallery of Canada. The mandate to collect native art was assigned to CMC by the National Museums of Canada Board of Trustees many years ago, but native people themselves - particularly their artists - felt the very best pieces of their work, chosen only on aesthetic principles, should appear in the National Gallery. CMC agreed; its own focus is upon contemporary native art portraying the continuity of native art traditions and their interplay with other artistic traditions, including modern western art.

CMC has gathered one of the finest collections of contemporary Indian and Inuit art in the world; since the 1970's its curators systematically and actively collected works of every major native artist in Canada : prints, paintings, drawings, sculptures, and fine crafts. There are almost 10,000 items in the collection; the Inuit Print Collection is the most complete archive of any museum. Native artists combine the heritage of traditional styles with modernist trends and personal innovations in developing individualistic new works of art. From CMC's collections native artists, and Canadians

Figure 52
... and full-size environmental reconstructions animated by native interpreters, like this longhouse from Sainte-Marie among the Hurons.

Figure 53
The Native Art Gallery allows visitors
to contemplate works by mostly
contemporary native artists; it shows
that native culture remains vibrant and
creative, blending tradition with
innovation.

three examples from the repertoire of each. The pieces, some very large, are in a variety of forms : paintings, sculptures, papier-maché, ceramics, assemblage, jewellery, installations, and mixed-media works. Some are bold, colourful, powerful, others are quiet. They show a variety of influences in often unusual artforms. Most date from the 1950's to the '80's, although some masterworks of earlier date are included. Together they offer an overview of contemporary native art, by artists with the training and education to understand and compete with what is happening in the international art world today. This exhibition should accomplish much in obtaining international recognition for the participating artists, and for Canadian art generally, as well as help dispel myths, here and abroad, about the contemporary state of native culture.

"In the Shadow of the Sun" stays at CMC for four months, then is followed in November 1989 by a borrowed exhibition. Some of the artists whose works are displayed will be visiting the museum. This is an example of the type of supportive programming planned for the Native Art Gallery. Typical features of exhibitions here will include : audiovisual presentations, to supply more intimate and in-depth experiences of native art; lecture tours by native art history students (arranged between CMC and academic institutions with programmes related to native art); seminars by native artists, curators, and academics; artist-in-residence programmes, for live demonstrations; and 'performance art', both in the gallery itself and elsewhere in the museum. CMC's sales shop will support the exhibitions by selling works by leading contemporary native artists.

The Arts and Traditions Hall

A hall adjacent to the Native Art Gallery presents, through several exhibitions, artifacts from the collections of the Canadian Centre for Folk Culture Studies; it consumes 16,038 sq.' (1490 sq.m.) of space. The exhibitions together look at Canada's ethnic groups (except native peoples) and the general concept of multiculturalism, from the perspective of creativity more than of history - the latter is dealt with in the History Hall. The patterns for cultural identity, and the processes which built them, are revealed; that is : the heritage brought by immigrants from their country of origin, the dynamic process of adaptation to the new environment, and above all the continuing expressions of culture in which creativity

generally, can reach a better understanding of their artistic and cultural heritage and can chart the progression of particular artists.

It will be noted that CMC displays the art in a *Gallery*, rather than a *Hall*. This distinction emphasizes that the exhibits are treated first as art and only secondarily as artifacts. That is, the principal communication goal is to show, through exemplary works, the aesthetic qualities of native art and its contribution to world art. It is also important to demonstrate the continuum of artistic expression between historical and modern native cultures, and how their art reflects their view of the world; contemporary native art is an excellent window into the current cosmological beliefs of native peoples. The gallery's 8396 sq.' (780 sq.m.) of space is divided into two sections. The smaller is a permanent exhibition in terms of the spatial design, although the objects displayed from the collection will rotate. This area introduces the more traditional and historical native art forms. The larger section is for changing exhibitions, mainly of more recent artworks; greater flexibility has been designed into this area.

The Native Art Gallery opens with CMC's travelling exhibition "In the Shadow of the Sun". This first opened in Bremen, in 1988, and travelled in Germany before coming to Ottawa. The show, divided into Indian and Inuit sections, comprises some 250 artworks, from private collections or on loan from other museums and corporations across Canada. It features the work of 80 artists : at least

uses traditions as a springboard and the new environment as a driving force.

The contrast between the exhibit design approaches here and in the Grand Hall or History Hall is striking. The latter are highly structured, with environmental reconstructions which will remain in place for decades. The Arts and Traditions Hall is designed for maximum versatility, to accommodate with ease exhibitions which will change far more often, and to allow for the wide range of interpretive programming desirable to communicate forms of cultural expression. In respects the aim was to transplant the flexibility and functionality of theatrical space into museum space. The entire hall has been outfitted with a modular infrastructure, a three-dimensional grid built up from 1 cubic metre cells. Each cell is assembled from 12 struts and 8 dry-joint type connectors, which create the framework of a cube. The cubes can be assembled and reassembled in any grouping and quantity to form vertical or horizontal planes, columns, or beams, in simple and complex structures; innumerable spatial configurations can be composed. The hall has space for roughly 7000 such cubes to be constructed, although it is necessary to remove some to provide passage for visitors. The space for the hall was accepted from the architect in a cosmetically neutral state; that is, most surfaces were left as raw concrete, although the two ceiling vaults over the hall (one of which gives almost as much height as in the Grand Hall) are of drywall-type finish. Therefore the deployment of artifacts and means of contextualizing them are not limited by stylistically rendered environments, and redeployment and retrofitting are relatively easy tasks when exhibitions change.

Any plane of a cube can be fitted with transparent, translucent, or opaque surfaces, rigid or flexible; or it can be left open. The cubes may be used singly or in any combination as display cases, ducts for mechanical and electrical services, audiovisual equipment containers, support frames for environmental reconstructions, floors, walls, ceilings, ramps, railings, and so on. Selected areas in the structure can be left open to allow for visual cross-referencing from one thematic area to a related one, or to expand the visitor's visual perception from micro to macro context. The structure's flexibility also facilitates fluctuations in the relative sizes of each of the three exhibition areas, or can permit live animation simply by creating space as required. The design is, in short, a standardized form delivering unlimited variable content and context without overpowering those elements.

One of the sub-halls of the Arts and Traditions Hall is the Fine Crafts Gallery, which celebrates contemporary craftsmanship as both an enduring aspect of our cultural heritage and as a constantly evolving art form. As the name suggests, there is some emphasis on the aesthetic qualities of the objects displayed.

Figure 54
Versatility is the keynote of the Arts and Traditions Hall. The cubic modules of its infrastructure can be assembled in various combinations to create display cases, walkways, performance spaces, and so on; ease of construction and dismantling allows the exhibits to be reconfigured at will.

Although the Canadian Centre for Folk Culture Studies has always dealt with aspects of cultural life on a broader scale than is suggested by the term 'folk', it had no great commitment to collecting *contemporary* works of craft until the donation of the Massey Foundation's contemporary craft collection in 1981. This was expanded by the Jean A. Chalmers Canadian Craft Collection (donated by the Canadian Crafts Council), and the Bronfman Collection of works by winners of the annual Saidye Bronfman Award for Excellence in the Crafts. [3] CMC's collection now represents a worthy cross-section of Canadian craftworks, both functional and decorative, produced in the last two decades. Not only the Fine Crafts Gallery but other parts of the museum will showcase handcrafted fittings and furnishings, obtained through commissions made possible by sponsors; the crystalline glass ceiling of the entry vestibule of the museum, for example, is a product of this programme in which the museum is not only a preserver but also a patron of Canadian culture.

Figures 55 and 55a
The Fine Crafts Gallery, depicted here in models, showcases the work of Canada's outstanding craftspeople.

A Fine Crafts Gallery became realizable out of the acquisition of the Bronfman Collection, made possible by the generosity of the Bronfman Foundation. The opening exhibition there features the work of the first ten recipients of the Saidye Bronfman Award : three potters, three textile artists, two metalworkers, a bird carver, and a bookbinder. The themes around which this exhibition are organized are : the working of the creative process in craft, and the contributions of ten individuals who have produced works critically acclaimed for their excellence and innovation in relation to traditional methods. Accompanying the exhibition are : a book about the careers of the award recipients, with photographs of their works; a video, for broadcast; educational packages on the production of handbound books and on the intricacies of bird carving; an audiotour giving descriptions of the exhibits by the artists and others, and information on their techniques, tools, and materials; and various audiovisual presentations.

Exhibitions in the Fine Crafts Gallery will be hosted for varying periods, averaging one to two years. The Bronfman exhibition remains until autumn 1990, and will then tour to other museums in North America. Future exhibitions may show the products of particular regions, the work of individual craftspersons, or developments in a specific medium, such as ceramics, jewellery, glass, or textiles. Most will tour Canada, to increase public access to the national heritage. Supportive programmes such as those listed above, or a craftsperson-in-residence programme, will be typical features of the gallery. The goals of the gallery are to introduce audiences to the work of outstanding craftspeople, and enable them to appreciate the geographical, cultural, and technical diversity of Canadian crafts; attention will be paid also to conveying underlying traditions (both Canadian and international) and influences that shape the crafts. CMC hopes, through its exhibitions, to encourage practitioners, develop the general public's critical eye, and stimulate a wider appreciation of fine crafts as an expression of personal and cultural identity.

A second sub-hall is the Folk Arts Hall. The temporary and travelling exhibitions hosted here focus on forms of expression of the plastic and performing arts; one example will relate the musical instruments and costumes in CMC's collections to living traditions found throughout the country. In this way CMC will celebrate the ethnic traditions that are part of Canadian cultural identity, the creative genius of individual Canadians, and the richness of their forms of expression. Artists and performers will regularly be brought to perform in this hall or in one of the museum's theatres.

The opening exhibition illustrates dance in Canada, exploring both the forces of tradition and of innovation. It reveals influences - geographical, social, cultural - that have shaped the evolution of dance forms and demonstrates how the function of dance has changed; for example, symbolic themes stemming from performances of fertility or healing rites have lost their original function and undergone a cultural adaptation. Displays, supported by sound effects, re-create the vitality of this complex art form and explore its expressive techniques : rhythm, choreographic figures, movements, make-up, masks, costumes, and so on. Within the range of dance forms different cultural and popular traditions can be conveyed and the values and emotions expressed through the art can be perceived. A book of essays on dance and illustrative material accompanies the exhibition. Video presentations also support the exhibits, and video games stimulate an understanding of dance forms. This exhibition will remain at CMC until 1991, when it will circulate across Canada.

The final sub-hall, the Cultural Traditions Hall, showcases the historical, social, and cultural development of Canadian ethnic groups. Each exhibition will pay homage to a specific group, highlighting its resources and distinctive characteristics, and demonstrating its influence on Canadian society. The aim is to explore general themes of the Arts and Traditions Hall in a more concrete and comprehensible fashion by focusing on a single, identifiable group.

The opening exhibition is dedicated to Chinese-Canadians, one of Canada's largest and most visible ethnic groups. That group is well represented in CMC's collections and has been well researched. Furthermore, it presents a microcosm of themes

important to the Arts and Traditions Hall as a whole : the Old Country, transition (through immigration), and adaptation of a culture in contemporary Canada. As the Chinese have been in Canada for almost a century and a half, it is possible to demonstrate the process of transition over an extended period of time. The exhibition looks at the Chinese community from both an inner perspective (the Ying) and an outer perspective (the Yang); that is, its inherent cultural

Figures 56 and 56a
The first exhibition in the Cultural Traditions Hall focuses on the Chinese-Canadian community.

traditions and those cultural elements which are perceived by Canadian society. It traces the development of that community from the arrival of its first representatives to the appearance of Chinatowns in a number of cities; it highlights traditions such as its festivals, folk medicine, art and dance forms, Chinese foods, martial arts, and it shows the cultural changes the group has undergone in adapting to Canadian society without losing its vitality. The exhibition is supported by : a book on the cultural life of the Chinese-Canadian community; live performances of drama and dance, and re-enactments of ceremonies (such as a Chinese wedding); demonstrations of skills such as cooking, acupuncture, Gong Fu, calligraphy, kite-making; puppet and magic shows; video interviews with members of the community; videos showing Chinese cultural elements in the Canadian context; and an audiotour. This exhibition will move on in 1991, to travel around Canada for two years, and will be replaced by an exhibition on the Ukrainian community, to mark its 100th anniversary in Canada; following that, the German community may be showcased.

The Special Exhibitions Hall

This hall is a particularly welcome addition, for its large size (10,764 sq.', or 1000 sq.m.) permits CMC to host blockbusters; or it can be partitioned to accommodate several small exhibitions at one time. Changing exhibition space allows CMC to offer a national showcase to Canadian museums for their exhibitions, and to capitalize on a growing world-wide trend towards greater sharing of collections among museums. It is not possible for CMC to build its own world-class collections of artifacts from other countries, but it can borrow the best the world has to offer. This will allow it to : deal with subjects not covered by its own exhibitions; portray foreign cultures; bring the major historical treasures of the world to local audiences; or support themes in its main exhibitions by showing related collections from other institutions. It also gives incentive to CMC to create temporary exhibitions from its own reserve collections, in the knowledge that these can be shown in the National Capital before being sent to other centres in Canada and abroad. This type of flexibility is vital in a museum; it ensures there is always something new to bring back visitors time and time again.

The Special Exhibitions hall is intentionally the closest hall to the museum's main entrance, enabling visitors to go direct to the new exhibitions area if

Figure 57
The hall where special exhibitions are hosted was designed to allow as much flexibility as possible; it can be used to mount a single blockbuster or partitioned to accommodate several small exhibitions at once.

they wish. Of course temporary exhibition space has not been restricted to this hall. Exhibitions in the Arts and Traditions Hall and the Native Art Gallery are also mostly changing. Much temporary exhibitions space has been built into the History Hall, and a section of the Children's Museum is also dedicated to this purpose. The total space for changing exhibitions in the museum is four times the size of the Special Exhibitions Hall! As these were easier and less costly types of exhibitions to produce in the short time after funds for exhibiting were granted in 1987, it was possible to have almost all these areas ready for CMC's opening.

In contrast to the other changing exhibitions areas, the Special Exhibitions Hall will host shows that are generally shorter : from six weeks to three months will be typical. Not only exhibitions, but also special openings can be hosted here thanks to the flexibility given by movable walls (floor-to-ceiling modular partitions), acoustic baffles, etc. The hall is a large, open, rectangular gallery with a ceiling height of 16' (4.9 m.). At opening it provides extra space for the exhibition "Dance in Canada", which is also featured in the Folk Arts Hall. "King Herod's Dream", an exhibition produced by the Smithsonian Institution, appears in late '89 featuring archaeological treasures dating from 22 B.C. to 1300 A.D. found at Caesarea. "The Maple Leaf Forever" will mark the 25th anniversary of the selection of the emblem for Canada's flag, and is to run during the winter of 1989/90. "Images of the Inside Passage", a show of photographs and artifacts relating to Alaska, is scheduled for part of 1990. So too is "In Search of the Canadian Image", which will reflect the Canadian cultural mosaic through archival film, video, still photographs, and artifacts. A drumming festival planned for 1991 may be supported by a special exhibition of drums. That year also sees the arrival of a major exhibition, co-produced by the Smithsonian Institution and the USSR Academy of Sciences, called "Crossroads of Continents". This opened in Washington in 1988 and is to travel both in North America and the Soviet Union. It looks at the hunting/fishing peoples of the North Pacific and Bering Sea areas, at the surprisingly complex form of their culture, and at their contact with the Western World; some artifacts have not previously been seen outside the USSR.

Much present activity is directed at preparing for the premiere of "A Coat of Many Colours", an exhibition highlighting the Jewish Canadian community. This will open in April 1990, to coincide with Passover, and will begin travelling in September of that year,

first in Canada and subsequently to the Museum of the Diaspora in Tel Aviv. Funded largely by the Friends of Beth Hatefutsoth, the exhibition incorporates artifacts from many sources, such as : CMC itself; provincial museums of Alberta, Saskatchewan, Manitoba, Ontario, New Brunswick, and Nova Scotia; the Glenbow Institute; the Beth Tzedec Museum, Toronto; the St. John's Jewish Historical Society Museum; the McCord Museum; the Jewish Historical Society of Western Canada; the Canadian Jewish Congress Archives; and many private collections. The theme of the exhibition is the influence of the Jewish community on the development of Canadian society over the last two centuries and the way in which Canada, in return, has shaped the identity of that community. The focus is more on secular life than on religious traditions, in order to emphasize those aspects of Jewish culture that relate to what it means to be Canadian. "A Coat of Many Colours" exemplifies the multiexperiential programming CMC seeks to create. The central feature may be the exhibits of fine and decorative arts, as well as items from everyday life, but there will be many supporting components. Performances of works by Jewish composers and playwrights will be featured in local theatres. It is also hoped to arrange a local festival of films by Jewish writers and filmmakers, or with Jewish Canadian themes, and to have some Jewish rituals performed within the museum. Jewish cuisine will be featured in CMC's restaurant, and appropriate items sold in its boutique. "A Coat of Many Colours" is an appropriate title for this kind of multiexperiential exhibition.

This concludes our tour of the central level of the public wing. We now go to the top level and the last of the major exhibition galleries.

The History Hall

This is another huge space, incorporating 43,558 sq' (4046 sq.m.) divided between the structural floor and the mezzanine levels that exist in certain parts of the hall. Most of this area lies under the great copper vault (350' long by 60' wide) which stretches the length of the topmost roof of the public wing, and provides a five-storey ceiling height, up to 55' (17 m.) at its highest point. About a third of the hall, however, lies beyond the vaulted area and has a ceiling height of 21' (6.4 m.). The History Hall is bounded on one side by the upper area of the Grand Hall and on the other by the light-wells. At either end there are circulation nodes to other levels; at the Laurier Street end there is also a domed public rest

Figures 58 and 58a
The History Hall's curving expanse is large enough to house full-size structures as big as a church or a grain elevator. In fact it holds numerous partial or full reconstructions, in several theme areas which trace the route of Canada's development and reflect all regions of the country. Changing exhibits are mounted in mezzanine areas atop the first storeys of several buildings.

area with excellent views across Parc Laurier and the Ottawa River. Like the Grand Hall, the History Hall is a long and relatively narrow space, 97' (29 m.) wide; this suggested the type of exhibition for it.

When the architectural programme and the exhibition master plan were produced (1983) it was already being proposed that environmental reconstructions such as period rooms, workshops, offices, courtrooms, and even barns or factories, might be suitable for the history exhibition. This was a logical extension of a display technique already used in the galleries of the Victoria Memorial Museum Building, where there were quite popular period room exhibits such as a Victorian drawing-room and a Depression kitchen, and a coal-mine reconstruction which suffered from space constraints.

During 1983 members of the New Accommodation Task Force made first-hand investigation of exhibitions and other facilities of numerous museums and related institutions in North America, Europe, and Japan, to discover and learn from their examples. Among the strong impressions made by some of the places visited were : the extensive use of reconstructed environments in the newly-opened

Epcot Center, particularly the architectural replicas in the World Showcase section; the New York Metropolitan Museum of Art's interior display of a multi-storey urban building facade, the Dendura temple, and a Ming garden with porticos and pavilions; the Jorvik Viking Centre, with its re-creation of an early medieval streetscape, and (in the same city) an extensive reconstruction of nineteenth and twentieth century streetscapes inside the York Castle Museum; the British Museum's ethnological environmental reconstructions; a series of similar, but historical, reconstructions (including a streetscape) at the British Columbia Provincial Museum. By the time that the History Hall project team was set up (September 1983), the idea had taken root that CMC's long History Hall, stretching away into the distance around the curve of the building's architecture, might be eminently suitable for a streetscape exhibit.[4]

Further streetscape examples were now identified and investigated : at the Henry Ford Museum (in Michigan), the first American museum to try that type of exhibition, contemporary with York's; the Milwaukee Public Museum, whose example prompted the British Columbia Provincial Museum's foray into the field; Abbey House Museum (near Leeds, England), its streetscapes created by a former employee of York Castle Museum; the Manitoba Museum of Man and Nature; and the Western Development Museum branch at Saskatoon. These examples exerted an influence - teaching both what might be achieved and what should be avoided - on the first conceptual plans drawn up by the History Hall team in January 1984. The early concept was repeatedly refined as the team gathered more information from staff and from outside museum experts, designers, and historians, who critiqued the ideas through organized seminars and review panels.[5]

The evolving concept was exciting, but there were problems. Streetscape exhibits have proven popular with visitors, but have been criticized by historians and museologists on a number of counts. Authenticity and realism is difficult to obtain when modern construction materials are used; when buildings must be placed indoors; when they must be scaled-down through lack of space; when lack of animation programmes makes the buildings seem lifeless; and when conformity to museum standards demanding low lighting of artifacts makes it seem as though it is constantly evening in the street. Similarly, a desire to be authentic makes it difficult to provide facilities for the handicapped; or to use modern technologies for interpretation, for fear they

Figure 59
The Victorian drawing-room exhibit in the Victoria Memorial Museum Building.

will intrude into the historical ambiance. Critics have also suggested - not always with justification - that streetscapes cater to nostalgia rather than to the teaching of historical 'truths', that (like open air museums) they tend to romanticize the past by ignoring its unattractive aspects, that the complex make-up of environmental reconstructions distracts attention from the individual artifacts, and that their unchanging nature makes them boring to return visitors.

CMC also faced its own particular problems with the concept. The accurate reconstruction of a numerous historical buildings would be prohibitively expensive. Yet to transplant original buildings might have had an adverse effect on heritage preservation - CMC prefers to support *in situ* preservation of heritage structures - and would have been an obstacle to visitor interactivity with the exhibits. The floor-loading capacity provided by the architect for History Hall would not support a streetful of buildings constructed from authentic materials. Even more seriously, as a national museum CMC has the obligation to represent a wide range of periods,

Figure 60
CMC studied numerous examples of streetscape exhibitions - such as that at Epcot Center - in the early stages of planning its History Hall.

regions, and historical themes in its exhibitions. An urban streetscape would make it hard to deal with non-urban themes; yet most Canadians lived in rural areas before this century. And to collapse the breadth of Canada (5630 km.) into 106 m., would present a difficult process of selection of representative elements from the past.

Despite all this, the History Hall team remained convinced that, by learning from the experience of other institutions and by developing a more vibrant and flexible approach than any tried before, the problems might be overcome. There seemed much to be gained. Streetscape exhibits are popular partly because they offer a change of scale from the individual, relatively small artifacts in traditional displays; and partly because people feel comfortable in that type of environment. They are used to navigating through urban streets, in contrast to the restrained, temple-like atmosphere of the traditional museum. Environmental reconstructions allow a very large number of artifacts to be displayed in relatively small areas, which gives visitors access to a greater proportion of a museum's collections; it also enables visitors to focus on elements of their choice and even to reconfigure and reinterpret the presented information elements in other ways, seeing new patterns and connections. Display cases place a barrier between visitor and artifact. Environmental reconstructions allow visitors to penetrate the exhibit, thus increasing the potential for that participation and interactivity which enhances both the enjoyment and the learning process. Furthermore, within the context of CMC's expanded definition of the 'exhibition experience', the use of reconstructed environments offered great potential to enliven the physical setting, by overlaying performances, presentations, and animation programmes; in many instances the physical setting could be treated as a theatrical set. These added elements would be the key to communicating concepts and themes that could not be presented through material objects alone, and would also ensure that the streetscape not become boring to visitors during the decades of its existence.

The streetscape concept was developed into a more balanced and more carefully thought-out form, and solutions found to many of the problems. The final design was a mix : entire buildings, building facades, fully furnished environments, exhibits employing traditional display cases, and multimedia presentations. The basis for the hall remains the reconstructed environment; this is the principal canvas on which the past is painted, but no longer restrictively so. Mitigation of the total reconstruction approach makes it possible to employ a wider variety of interpretive tools, such as interactive video. And each historical setting in the hall can more reasonably be used as a stage set for theatrical performances or as a television studio for educational and entertaining productions to be broadcast across Canada - thus sharing the museum with a wider audience.

Three types of 'environments' have been incorporated into the hall : realistic, stylized, and symbolic; these are the building blocks over which the other design and interpretive elements are layered. The realistic environments re-create all aspects of a particular historical setting, as far as is feasible. The stylized environments visually suggest settings, such as a forest or a townscape, but deliberately leave room for the visitor's imagination. Symbolic environments contain only icons (e.g. building shells) without a surrounding setting.

The architectural structures are mostly typical examples, rather than replicas of specific buildings, yet accurate in their details and their represent-ativeness of Canadian architecture. They are full-scale reconstructions, regardless of which of the three settings they inhabit. Authentic construction materials have been used on the first-storey levels, but lightweight synthetic materials above. The layout has been influenced by the need to overcome floor-loading problems by conforming to the ten-metre grid of supporting columns in the hall. However, parts of the floor have been reinforced with steel plates, to support the heaviest structures. Displayed in context within the environments are objects such as tools and equipment in a workshop, or barrels and a cart in the town square. Visitors do not have full access into all areas of the exhibits, but may move through and around many of them; where direct access is not possible, barriers integrate visually within the environment. In a similar way there are no separate rest areas for visitors : these instead take the form of period furniture in the streets, benches in the train station, seats in the garden, and so on.

To ensure the environments do not appear static, various techniques and programmes provide them with a sense of habitation, activity, and change. For example, authentically furnished building interiors, positioned under some of the mezzanine slabs, are settings for demonstrations, live animation, and theatre. Light, sound, and special effects have been carefully orchestrated and paced throughout the hall to create liveliness, particular moods, and general

Figures 61 and 61a
These scale models, made during the
exhibition development process, show
some of the exhibits to be encountered
in the History Hall.

atmosphere. For example, the sounds of tumbling water and wildlife in a forest, morning light in the market square where townspeople may be heard conversing and church-bells pealing; special effects create drifting fog among the trees near the Norse boat, fire and smoke under the cauldrons in the tryworks. There are different, and sometimes adjustable, light levels from area to area; settings that particularly benefit from natural light have been put near the light-wells. Multimedia presentations - employing film, multi-image slide shows, special effects, large artifacts, and partial period settings, in various combinations - help develop themes in certain areas, or set the scene and heighten a sense of drama. Exhibits other than the reconstruction type exist at various locations on the main floor, often adjacent to and supporting environments, and on the mezzanine slabs. They include artifacts, scale models, graphics, texts, audiovisual presentations, and interactive video programs, and may be changed occasionally to present different sub-themes; those on the mezzanines are particularly intended as temporary exhibits.

Where the main level exhibition is a mix of experiential and thematic exhibits, the mezzanines provide for a more reflective relationship between visitor and artifact. They also give raised views of main floor exhibits, from various angles, and allow visual cross-references between the exhibits on the two levels. In some of the mezzanine areas, and also in the Native Peoples Hall, photo mural 'tents' have been created. Using new digital paint gun technology, historical photographs have been greatly enlarged and printed on room-sized plastic scrims that can be 'wrapped around' visitors. This is another of the techniques intended to give visitors a more realistic sense of the past.

A thousand years of history is covered in the History Hall. Its organizing theme is "New Beginnings", the story of how generations of Canadians have faced new and challenging situations as they moved from one frontier to another : the waves of immigration, the spread of people from many cultural backgrounds across a wilderness, the growth of settlements, the adaptations to the environment, and the far-reaching changes in technology and in the character of

society. Visitors can travel through the hall in either direction and still understand the exhibition's narrative. However, the chronological sequence begins at the river end, with the era of early exploration; here the visitor encounters a Norse longship (observed, from the forest, by Amerindians), can explore the life of mariners aboard a sixteenth-century European ship, and look at a Basque whaling station where oil was extracted from blubber. In the next section early settlement is presented in two main exhibits : one interpreting the Acadian settlement, the other representing New France through both a rural setting and a town square (with tavern from the Fortress of Louisbourg, artisans' houses, and convent hospital surrounding it). The wilderness life in the nineteenth century is depicted by a fur-traders' encampment on a lake-shore in "les pays d'en haut", while frontier development is also shown through a sawmill, logging, a frontier dwelling, and a British blockhouse. The development of urban centres and an affluent Victorian middle class is interpreted in an exhibit on ship construction, commercial storefronts, a merchant's house, customs house, and railroad

station. From that eastern station the visitor is transported westwards to a Prairie railroad station, beyond which a grain elevator towers, its interior used to interpret farm life and the mechanization of farming at the turn of the century. The sixth section of the exhibition portrays elements of life in an industrial city (1890-1940) including a garment factory, commercial establishments, a private home, a labour temple, a Ukrainian Orthodox Church, and the world of childhood and adolescence. Modern Canada, of the last half-century, is the focus of the final section. Here is a dockside scene depicting the Home Front during the Second World War; opposite it, a Newfoundland house - an exhibit commemorates the province's entry into Confederation in 1949. Further along are scenes or structures from the other side of the country : British Columbia (including a cannery/net-loft) and Dawson City. And, finally, a view of Canada's far north, its last frontier. About half of the hall has been completed for CMC's opening.

It is no coincidence that many exhibits in the History Hall represent what may also be found at the national historic sites maintained across Canada : for example, the Norse village at L'Anse aux Meadows (Newfoundland), the whaling station from the Gulf of the St. Lawrence, the Louisbourg tavern, historic structures from Quebec City and Dawson City. The duplication is intentional. For decades Parks Canada, which is responsible for the National Historic Sites Service, has conducted painstaking research on all such sites; this information on the history, structural details, and animation scenarios of the sites CMC has been able to exploit for its exhibits. Parks Canada has also assisted greatly in the direct research for the History Hall by making its experts available to CMC; the cooperation was much appreciated. Arrangements have been made to link CMC's environmental reconstructions more explicitly to the corresponding national historic sites by borrowing, each season, a few of those sites' costumed animators to offer interpretation and dramatic vignettes in the History Hall exhibits. These guest-interpreters can tell visitors not only about the CMC exhibits but also about the historic sites they represent. In this way the History exhibition acts as a table of contents to historic sites across the country. CMC's overview of Canadian history may be experienced in a single visit, but will hopefully encourage visitors to make future trips to explore the original sites in other regions of Canada.

Along a simple, linear circulation route (with sidetrips to the mezzanines, if desired) visitors can retrace the path of Canadian history, in either direction, at their own pace. They will encounter diverse historical settings, each creating an illusion of habitation, and heightening the experience through dramatic live performances and multimedia presentations, as well as opportunities to interact with the exhibits and participate in some of the activities taking place. Streakers, strollers, and students will find in the hall subjects of interest, different levels of interpretation, and opportunities for changes in pace and in degrees of intimacy with the artifacts, that will appeal to all their desires : to learn, to enjoy, to ponder, to commune with the past.

The History Hall offers visitors a true exploration of Canada's history and of the life of those who

inhabited its past and who people its present. It also gives them a chance to feel, for a time, the fundamental truth that they too are a part of history's tapestry, intimately tied to the past. The exhibition is not a series of isolated segments, but an integrated presentation with common themes running through it : notably that colonial legacies have shaped the character of national life, and that the human sense of spirit and adventure moved immigrants to spread from frontier to frontier until the whole land was settled. Everyday people from the past tell their own stories through the exhibition. And the exhibition says that 'Canada' is people of many different backgrounds : the interaction of their cultures has both changed those cultures and produced at their meeting-point - their crossroads - our national community and national identity.

Figure 62
CMC's history exhibits act as a table of contents to heritage sites across Canada, such as Louisbourg; costumed animators from some of those sites will occasionally make guest appearances in the History Hall.

the museum as treasure-house

The Canadian Museum of Civilization considers exhibitions to comprise not only the artifacts displayed and their display furniture, but also the interpretive programming, the educational and entertainment content, and the technologies that support display and interpretation. This definition is not intended to downplay the importance of artifacts, but the modern museum has broader horizons than its predecessors. It looks beyond the physical remnants of the past to the less tangible aspects of cultural heritage which museums also ought to preserve and make accessible. The role of the physical artifact in museums has not been diminished, but supplemented.

The national heritage is our collective memory. Much of the information that makes up that memory is embodied in the material remains surviving from the past. Artifactual collections are, historically, the reason for the existence of museums and are still their chief, most valuable, and most irreplaceable asset. Museums are not unique as collectors, preservers, and communicators of the material past : much exists *in situ*; a great amount is held by private collectors; libraries collect realia; archives' documents are artifacts in their own right; even recreational institutions like Epcot are showing interest in the 'real thing'. Nonetheless, it is their collections of original artifacts that have hitherto been the trademark of museums.

Museums cannot collect everything. They have always collected what they considered *special* objects, selected according to criteria that were more or less consciously understood. Early museums acquired curiosities, antiquities, or treasures. As their perceptions matured, curators expanded collecting to everyday and often mass-produced objects, which may be neither aesthetically attractive nor unusual nor intrinsically valuable. Yet this interest in representativeness remains balanced by a bias towards unique, rare, or atypical objects.

In all cases the artifacts destined for a museum are thoughtfully and deliberately chosen for what they reveal about the past. By their selection, they become a foundation for our understanding of history. This alone suffices to make them 'treasures'. We perceive them as valuable not so much in a monetary sense but for what they contribute to human knowledge. Their value is seen in the expenditure museums lavish on them : to find and to buy them; to conserve those which are deteriorating; to restore some to as near an original condition as possible; to store them consistent with the needs for preservation and access; and to study and document them. These are the inalienable but costly responsibilities behind the public exhibitions and programmes.

Though the museum is no longer just a treasure-house, displaying precious objects without

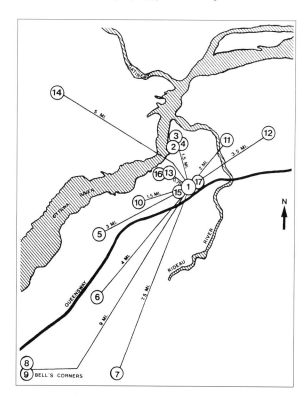

Figure 63
This diagram shows the geographical dispersal over the National Capital Region of CMC's former accommodations.

101

interpreting their significance to historical or cultural themes, that metaphor seems still applicable to collections management functions. Every artifact, regardless of intrinsic value, is treated by CMC as a treasure in terms of the money and effort devoted to preserving, storing, documenting, and keeping it safe. CMC's curatorial block is its treasure-house. Inside it lie the treasure-chests in which are cached the artifacts, 'guarded' on all sides by the offices of CMC staff. Part of the rationale for a new building was to house the national treasures appropriately. But treasures are not meant to be hoarded, hidden away from sight. Ensuring public access to the collections, and to the information that makes them meaningful, was a major concern for CMC's planners. The exhibitions answer this, partially; yet, even in the larger space of CMC's new galleries, only a small proportion of the collections can be displayed. Other, and more innovative, ways had to be found to offer access to the remainder - the reserve collections.

The first concern was to look after the collections properly. The geographical dispersal of the collections, in the 1970's, impeded their effective management. Some research staff were not in the same building as the collections it was their job to

Figures 64 and 64a
Some of the problems with former collections holding areas are illustrated here. Crowded storage conditions sometimes made it difficult to retrieve an artifact without moving others or dismantling shelves. In one building CMC inherited from the previous tenant an overabundance of electrical services - a potential fire hazard immediately adjacent to the collections.

study. In some cases artifacts had to be transported from one geographic location to another for conservation treatment. Conservation staff often had to work in areas not designed as laboratories, to operate with equipment not up-to-date, or to store potentially hazardous chemicals in areas too close to the collections for comfort. Security was also complicated by the many buildings that were essentially insecure warehouses. Their alarm systems were unreliable; at one place police finally refused to respond to repeated false alarms.

A thorough survey of accommodations was carried out by the Canadian Conservation Institute in 1981.[1] It reported : leaking roofs and windows; blocked drains during spring flooding, with consequent seepage; dust, made worse by uncoated floors and poor air filtration equipment; unreliable controls for temperature and humidity, with occasional resulting structural damage. The buildings had many windows and doors, which could not be secured satisfactorily and which contributed to environmental instability and insect infestations. Some buildings were shared with other tenants; lack of fire walls increased the museum collections' vulnerability to fires starting in areas beyond CMC control. Growth in the

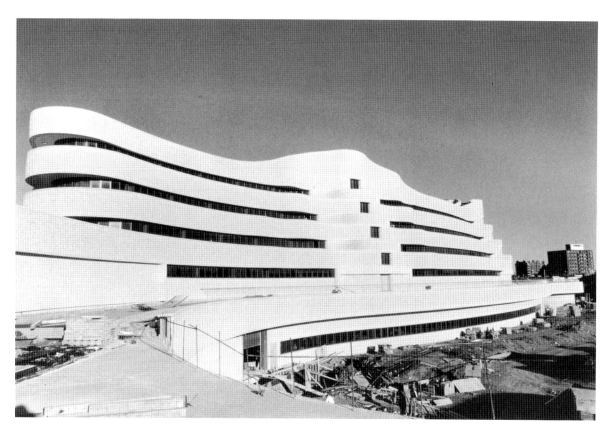

Figure 65
The curatorial block of the museum was designed to be the best possible home for the nation's treasures. In addition to the environmentally controlled rooms holding the artifacts, the block houses facilities for collections management, research, and conservation, as well as staff offices and workshops.

collections, with inevitable overcrowding in the holding areas, impeded access to artifacts, and necessitated overflow storage into non-secure areas. The character of these buildings thus created many of the conditions in which artifacts will deteriorate; many objects had already sustained damage, and much time and money was being spent on restoration efforts. CMC lacked the money and staff to overcome all these problems.

The federal government's decision to build a new museum stemmed partly from the recognition of the damage being done to the national treasures in their former repositories. It gave the opportunity to leave past disasters behind and to custom-design facilities for safe-keeping of the collections. Preservation of the collections is perhaps the single most critical factor governing the design of a museum building. The organic and inorganic materials of artifacts' construction are subject to deterioration from fluctuating atmospheric conditions, environmental pollutants, inadequate storage conditions, and the need to make them accessible to view or to touch. Preventive conservation and the ability to manage the collections efficiently and without damage are important in planning a museum.

Storage and display are the two museum functions most demanding of space. The public wing is dominated by the exhibition halls, the curatorial block by the collections holding areas. The New Accommodation project provided the chance to create collections holding facilities to meet museum standards : ample space for storage, precise and reliable environmental controls, and a storage system customized to meet the peculiar character and needs of museum artifacts. Both access and preservation are well served by the new collections management system.

Collections holding

Planning for the housing of museum collections is not simple. Part of the goal is to minimize environmental conditions which contribute to the degeneration of artifacts. The best solution might be to shut away the artifacts in an airtight, lightless room surrounded by sturdy walls impenetrable by fire, vermin, dust, and people. This would be foolish: artifacts are worthless if the information they hold cannot be revealed because the protection accorded them is uncompromising. So collections holding areas must allow for human access and the retrieval of artifacts. The character of museum artifacts complicates matters. Unlike commercial warehousing operations, which deal with objects of comparatively standard sizes and composition,

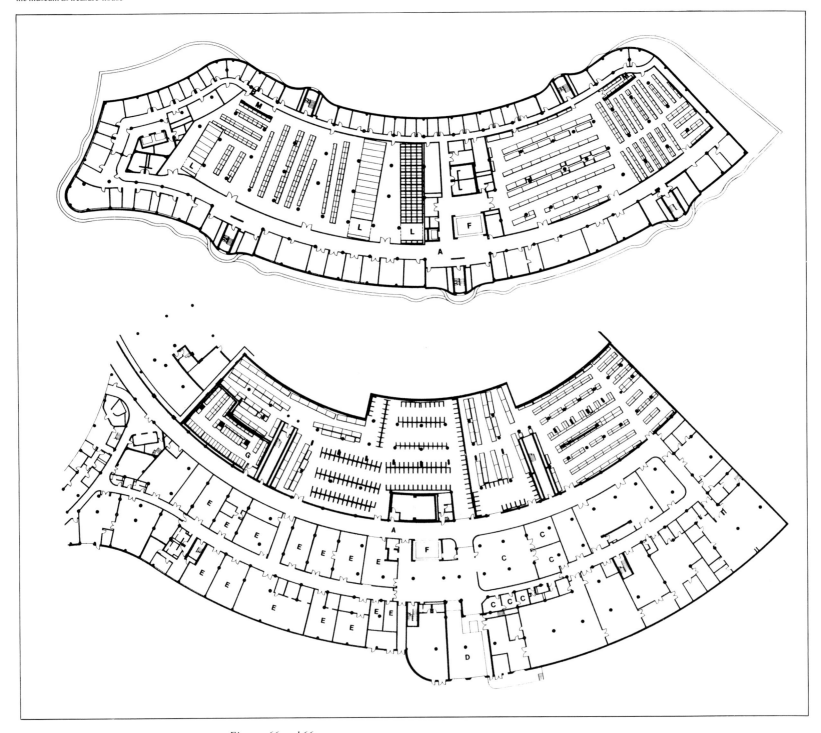

Figures 66 and 66a
Seen here are plans of two of the six levels of the curatorial block - levels one and five - with the layout of collections storage furniture shown. Level five exemplifies the cocoon concept.
KEY

A Artifact corridor
B Staff corridor
C Collections Services
D Loading/receiving docks
E Conservation

F Freight elevator
G Cold Store
L High density mobile storage
M Refrigeration units
N Artifact research and cataloguing

museums deal with what tend to be one-of-a-kind items, varying in size, weight, and material composition. CMC holds almost three million artifacts. These range in size from tiny fish-hooks to a huge Haida war canoe, although most are archaeological finds (microliths, potsherds, etc.) which fit into a compact space. The tremendous variety among the artifacts makes it complex to work out how much space is needed to store them and which artifacts should be stored where. Different types of organic or inorganic materials require different environmental conditions to ensure their preservation. This is one reason why CMC's collections are not held in a single gigantic storage room, but in a series of rooms : different rooms can be provided with different environmental conditions, and the collections divided so that each artifact can be suitably stored.

To design a collections holding system it is important to know how many artifacts are held, and to estimate the foreseeable growth of the collection; it is even more useful to discover what volume of space the collection will consume. There needs to be not only adequate dedicated space for the artifact at rest - so that none leans against or lies on top of another - but also ample space for easy retrieval without risk to artifacts or staff. Proper design of furniture can provide for space-efficient storage while ensuring dedicated space for, and safe retrieval of, every artifact. Knowing the weight of the collections allows calculation of floor-loading and shelf-loading. Attention must be paid to materials in the construction and finishing of collections holding areas or storage furniture, as some may give off fumes that cause adverse chemical reactions in sensitive artifacts. Sources of dust (e.g. the fabric of the building, footwear of visitors to storerooms) must be controlled and air filtration equipment installed. A thorough maintenance programme is required to check for the presence of vermin and to reduce the dirt that encourages their presence. The building must be designed to facilitate the maintenance of a stable relative humidity - essential to inhibiting degradation of artifacts. Unnecessary exposure to light must also be minimized. And fire safety measures are no less critical.

These considerations are common to all museums. One that was specific to CMC, however, was the curvature of the building. This influences the interior areas in two ways. First, they too curve : large collections holding areas have a pronounced curve. Second, building support columns were structurally required to be placed in a rayed pattern, with the result that the lines of columns are not parallel. Thus Cardinal's design, though aesthetically pleasing, created functional problems, such as laying out storage furniture in rooms which are not square and in which columns seem irregularly spaced. Yet it was this challenge that led to a new design for storage furniture, customized to museum needs and representing an important advance over other furniture on the market. [2] An additional complication arose in 1988 when the National Postal Museum artifactual collections were transferred from Canada Post Corporation to CMC. This placed unforeseen demands on space for storage and exhibition.

Offices and workshops in CMC's curatorial block are distributed on six levels. Most are around the outer rim of the building, surrounding the collections holding areas, an arrangement very deliberate. The outer rooms provide a protective envelope around the collections that help ensure year-long maintenance of a stable relative humidity. This cocoon, or room-within-a-room, design provides a vapour barrier that inhibits migration of humidity from the storerooms; it is the only cost-effective solution to that problem in the Canadian environment. The collections holding areas have structural floors on the first, third, and fifth levels of the block, and each extends upwards the height of two levels of offices. At the intermediate levels mezzanine floors (of an open grating type) can be installed to expand the storage space. When most of the collections are transferred to Parc Laurier, in the early 1990's, some areas of mezzanine will already be in place. Others will be added as collection growth demands.

Compartmentalization of the collections, for security, fire safety, and environmental needs, led to the creation of seventeen separate storage rooms. They range from 172 sq.' (16 sq.m.) to 15,500 sq.' (1440 sq.m.). Whereas, in CMC's previous accommodations, it was more convenient to segregate the collections according to the jurisdictions of the curatorial Divisions, it is now possible to group them primarily by size and material composition. This allows for more efficient use of space and more rational allocation of artifacts to specialized environmental conditions in the different rooms. The bulkiest items in the collection, most difficult to transport, will be kept on the lowest level of the curatorial block, served by the largest corridor - the Main Artifact Route. It runs the length of the block and provides access to the public wing and the loading docks. Objects such as large furniture, canoes, totem poles, will be stored on this level (Level One/Two); the loading docks are equipped to enable safe handling of such items. The Level One collections holding areas are buffered on one side by the corridor, conservation and other work-areas, on another by the underground parking area, and by being below-grade on the remaining sides. A special Cold Store on that level will preserve furs and other rapidly decomposable artifacts, while a second cold room is for archival photographic negatives.

The higher levels (Three/Four, Five/Six) show the cocoon principle in the inner storage rooms enveloped by offices and workrooms. On each level are two pods of storerooms, separated by a central corridor which accesses the freight elevator; work-areas for cataloguing, collections research, and artifact layout are also in the central section. The main collections holding rooms on these levels, as on Level One, will be maintained at a 50% relative humidity and a temperature of 21°C (with minor temporal or spatial fluctuations permissible). By contrast, the Cold Store will be kept at -4°C, and a room for metals, china, and glass on Level Five at 30% relative humidity. Other special rooms include an archival storage area on Level Four, and two vaults - one for artifacts made from precious metals, the other for particularly valuable or delicate organic materials - on Level Three. One pod on Level Three is being used to mount an exhibition based on the National Postal Museum collections. In part of Level Five the cabinets holding the archaeological collections will be placed on high-density mobile storage units, to use the space efficiently; nearby will be special freezer units for organic arch-aeological materials from the Far North and for historical artifacts made of plastics, which degrade unless kept at low temperatures.

The equipment maintaining temperature and relative humidity is monitored by sensors which report all fluctuations to a computer which in turn activates dampers and valves controlling a complex system of air distribution. The computer will alert staff to unacceptable fluctuations which cannot be com-pensated for immediately. Similarly, dust in the air is reduced to two microns by finely-tuned filtration equipment which is state-of-the-art. The adverse effects of light on artifacts have been controlled partly by lamps with a minimal ultraviolet content, and partly by reducing the exposure of artifacts. For inspection or retrieval, a relatively normal lighting level will be available in localized areas of the storerooms. For security or walk-through, the light will be kept at a much lower level and directed only at the aisles. When no-one is in a storage room, it will be left in darkness. Insects have been a major

problem for CMC in the past. In the new building all incoming artifacts will undergo a period of isolation and regular inspections; where necessary, an artifact will be given appropriate treatment such as refrigeration, to eliminate insects, before it is allowed into the collections holding areas. A variety of traps placed in the storerooms will detect the presence of insects. And rigorous janitorial and inspection programmes will find and remove insects and the dirt in which they thrive.

Fire can have devastating and widespread consequences. A fire safety programme must cover prevention, detection, containment, and suppression. Prevention is the most important. Unnecessary flammables, such as conservation or packing supplies that museums often negligently keep in their artifact storerooms, will not be allowed into CMC's collections holding areas. Those areas will be restricted to artifact holding and retrieval/inspection functions; all other activities (potential causes of fire) have their own separate, dedicated areas. The new storage furniture is constructed from non-flammable materials. Where possible, electrical equipment has been eliminated from the storerooms : environmental control equipment is outside those areas (with processed air fed in through trunks), as are fuse-boxes and breaker panels; electrical lighting is mounted on the ceiling at a safe distance from (combustible) artifacts; and electrical outlets, switches, and lights inside the storerooms will be deactivated by master-switches, outside the rooms, when those rooms are not in use. These precautions have significantly reduced the likelihood of a fire ever starting.

If one does, there are cross-zoned early warning sensors to detect smoke and heat. If both types of sensors agree there is a problem, they will auto-matically activate the water-sprinkler system in the zone of the alarm. It is hoped this stage need never be reached, for the water itself will not do the artifacts any good. Halon gas will be used for fire suppression in the Cold Store (since water would freeze), but this is not practical and too problematic an alternative for the main storage rooms. The collections are compartmentalized to restrict the spread of a fire. Two-hour fire-rated walls, ceilings, and doors, and also zoned air-handling systems, will help contain a fire and retard its movement.

The key to the storage system is the new, custom-designed shelving. It responds to the need to utilize space cost-effectively and to accommodate the curvature of the storerooms and irregular spacing of

Caring for the treasures

In the mid-'80's most staff and a large part of CMC's collections were consolidated at the Asticou Centre, in a 'dress rehearsal' for the move to Parc Laurier. The former school's gymnasia were converted into two-storey collections holding rooms by building inner walls, installing environmental controls, and erecting the F-post shelving. The main aisle of the room shown in the photographs is 8' wide, the cross-aisles 4'. Support beams, at 4' intervals, for the mezzanine floor grating are attached to the upper parts of the shelving units; the grating is easily installed simply by laying it across the beams. An open grating makes it easier to fight fires with the water sprinkler system, and to distribute environmentally processed air. Asticou provided the venue for testing the new shelving; testing led to improvements and the design of additional, innovative features.

This was not the first time that CMC had employed the cocoon principle, however. It happened that the storeroom of ethnological collections was located in the centre of the building that housed Ethnology Division in the '70's. This made it feasible to control temperature and relative humidity more effectively by upgrading the environmental control equipment. The encouraging results of this experiment prompted CMC's request to Cardinal to embody the cocoon principle in his museum design.

Once artifacts are stored above eye-level, special precautions must be taken in their retrieval. It is difficult, and potentially dangerous to artifacts and staff, to retrieve high-stored objects by hand. CMC has had a special forklift made to retrieve large artifacts from heights of up to 15'. This manual side-reach stacker makes it possible to use vertical space in a storeroom more efficiently, and to place large, light objects on high shelves. For safety, large, heavy objects will be kept on lower shelves. Forklifts available commercially required aisle widths of 6'6" or more; this would have meant dedicating unnecessary space in the collections holding areas to aisleways. By having the stacker, capable of manoeuvring down 4'-wide aisles, custom-built at a cost of $27,000, it was possible to save hundreds of thousands of dollars in storage space.

Figures 67 and 67a
CMC's custom-designed storage
furniture stands two storeys high, with
grating installed to provide a
mezzanine floor. Although basically
an open-faced shelving, the furniture is
highly adaptable - drawers can be
fitted in, for example.

the support columns. The flexibility of its structure will permit easy future changes without the need for major building alterations or high expenditures. Because it was designed specifically to accommodate the particular needs of museum collections, it represents a real advance and an important contribution to the museum world. Known as the F-post system, from the shape of the cross-section of its upright supports, it was developed jointly by CMC staff and the materials handling industry, and is currently available from commercial suppliers. Prototype units were tested in CMC's interim home during construction of the new building.

The F-post system is a free-standing, modular, open-faced shelving, capable of rising to up to three storeys, although CMC employs it only to two storeys. The mezzanine floor grating can be supported from the shelving units, which makes for a very simple structure and easy expansion. The grating can be laid with little effort and a second storey of shelving installed by attaching extra support posts to the tops of the lower-storey posts. Flexibility is one of the most important characteristics of the system. Support posts and shelves in a wide range of sizes allow optimal use of room-height and the design of furniture layouts which can manoeuvre around obstacles, such as building support columns. The variation in shelf sizes also allows for individual storage areas (based on back-to-back units) ranging from 4 sq.' to 48 sq.', which can accommodate most

items in CMC's collections. The shelves are smooth and present no features that might damage artifacts during retrieval. They can be adjusted at one-inch intervals, to permit highly efficient use of space without requiring the stacking of artifacts one atop another; each of CMC's Chilkat blankets, for example, can now have its own dedicated shelf without wasting storage space. The system also permits easy adjustment of shelves without necessitating their tipping or the movement of neighbouring shelves. The lowest shelves are six inches from the ground, to protect the artifacts from flash floods and to facilitate cleaning beneath. Shelves come not only in different sizes but also in different weight-loading capacities (400-1200 lbs.).

Other special fittings can be accommodated within the F-post system. Drawers of varying sizes can be inserted to turn part of the shelving unit into cabinets, which can be mixed with shelving in any combination. Lightweight sliding shelves have been designed to hold flat, fragile artifacts, which should not be unduly handled and can be moved from place to place on the slide-out shelves. Special rollers hold textiles which are best stored rolled up. And telescopic cantilever arms can be fixed to the uprights instead of shelves, to allow for storage of kayaks and canoes.

The F-post system enables museums to make optimal use of their storage space, particularly vertical space.

Its strength and stability offer safe storage for precious museum collections. The high flexibility permits configuration of units according to need, thanks to the system's 'mix-and-match' character. Its easy adjustability and expandability mean that it will not become obsolete, and need to be replaced by other furniture, as the collection grows. A spin-off is its ability to be adapted to use as display furniture : transparent or opaque panels can be attached to the upright posts and shelves to create display cabinets of diverse sizes. In fact, it was one inspiration for the design of the modular display framework used in the Arts and Traditions Hall, exemplifying the cross-fertilization of ideas that occurred during planning of the new museum.

Consolidation has made it practicable, for the first time, to establish a Collections Services Division which centralizes collections management functions previously decentralized among the different curatorial Divisions. This rationalizes functions and human resources; Collections Services will provide common services to the curatorial Divisions. Its principal responsibilities are in : collections handling - receiving and unloading incoming artifacts, and packing and shipping of outgoing objects; preliminary registration of artifacts; control and tracking of the movement of artifacts inbound to, or outbound from, the reserve collections areas; artifact identification photography (for security and insurance purposes); and inspection and janitorial operations, for vermin control, in the collections holding areas. Cataloguing operations remain decentralized within the curatorial Divisions.

Conservation

As with the Collections Services Division, consolidation at Parc Laurier has enabled CMC to bring together all its conservation facilities. This makes it easier to service the collections, and permits staff to concentrate more on their specializations. The diverse characters of museum artifacts provide a challenge to conservators; even within one category of artifacts there can be considerable variety : e.g. forms of clothing include elaborate Ukrainian folk costumes, Peruvian mummy wrappings, fur mittens, and intestine raincoats of the Inuit. Conservation and restoration calls for a range of skills. Any given artifact may require several types of work performed on it to make it structurally sound and to restore it to its desired condition. Totem poles, for instance, pose knotty problems : their size and weight makes them difficult to handle; their wood often suffers from dry-rot and must be consolidated; structural reinforcement may be necessary if a pole is to be displayed standing up; and the paintwork usually needs restoring.

The Conservation Division has two principal roles. One is the continuing care of the collections : pursuing the metaphor of the museum as hospital, the conservators are its doctors. 'Continuing care' means ensuring that environmental conditions are optimal for the artifacts and stable, and that artifacts are protected from unnecessary harm. This entails periodic checking and reporting on the physical condition of artifacts, and on the performance of environmental monitoring sensors.

The second role is to prepare artifacts for storage, exhibition, or loan to other museums. Incoming artifacts must be checked for insects or mould and, if need be, treated. Immediate conservation work may sometimes be necessary to protect a new acquisition from further deterioration. For loans, conservators must advise on packing materials and procedures which will best protect artifacts from the stresses and dangers of transit. They must also ensure that host museums provide suitable conditions for displaying CMC's artifacts. For exhibition, conservators must assess the suitability of each artifact to be displayed; some are too fragile, while others require special support for display. They must conserve and restore artifacts before display when necessary, and advise on non-harmful methods of display.

The New Accommodation project has provided the opportunity to design proper conservation laboratories and to purchase the most up-to-date equipment necessary. It has also provided the *need* for these better facilities, since the increased use of more artifacts in exhibitions will make the role of the conservators even more important. Conservation Division occupies a suite of labs, work-areas, and offices on Level One of the curatorial block. It incorporates areas for initial examination and photography (for condition reporting) of artifacts, for detailed examination and analysis as a prelude to deciding on treatment, and labs specializing in the conservation of different types of materials. Special equipment in the laboratories includes vacuum freeze-drying equipment (for water-impregnated objects), microblasting and ultrasonic cleaners, humidity chambers, electrolysis tanks, a laundro-meter (for dyeing textiles), book restoration equipment, and gold finishing tools.

Museum 'medical centre'

Conservation staff have been kept very busy over the last couple of years preparing the artifacts selected for the new exhibitions. The Wakas pole, for instance, underwent considerable treatment to make it fit to display as the Grand Hall's centrepiece. It had stood for decades in Vancouver's Stanley Park, a famous landmark; but the elements and the abuse of visitors, who would climb on it to have their photograph taken, left it in a state of decay. CMC came to the rescue by acquiring it on loan, in return for the carving of a replica for the park (raised in a traditional ceremony in May 1987). After the original was brought to the museum it was placed in a hermetically-sealed environment to stabilize it and to get rid of moss that had grown in crevices. The original, faded paint was removed, very carefully so that the cedar not be damaged. Missing parts of the pole - such as the totem's huge lower beak, which opens to provide entrance to the Kwakiutl house - were rebuilt with new wood or synthetic materials. And, finally, the pole was repainted. Repainting rights belong to artists from the native family which owned the pole, so this task was undertaken by the grand-nephew of the chief who ordered the pole's creation.

CMC's conservators employ many methods and techniques to diagnose the problems artifacts have and to treat them. One of the advanced techniques they use is 'shrinkage temperature measurement'. Developed for CMC by the Canadian Conservation

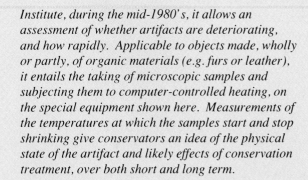

Institute, during the mid-1980's, it allows an assessment of whether artifacts are deteriorating, and how rapidly. Applicable to objects made, wholly or partly, of organic materials (e.g. furs or leather), it entails the taking of microscopic samples and subjecting them to computer-controlled heating, on the special equipment shown here. Measurements of the temperatures at which the samples start and stop shrinking give conservators an idea of the physical state of the artifact and likely effects of conservation treatment, over both short and long term.

The use of such techniques may sometimes incidentally produce information of interest to researchers. For example, during the treatment of birchbark baskets found at the Nadlok site (near Bathurst Inlet, in the Northwest Territories), it was discovered that the diameter of the trees from which the bark came was greater than the diameter of trees in the area of the site. Archaeologists concluded from this that the baskets likely evidenced trade between the Inuit peoples of the Bathurst area and the Yellowknife Indians several hundred miles to the south. Thus the conservation analysis threw light on an aspect of the trading relations of native peoples in this region about which little was previously known.

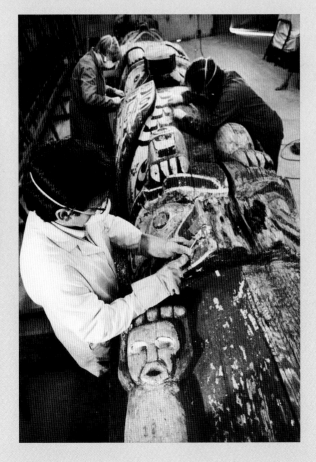

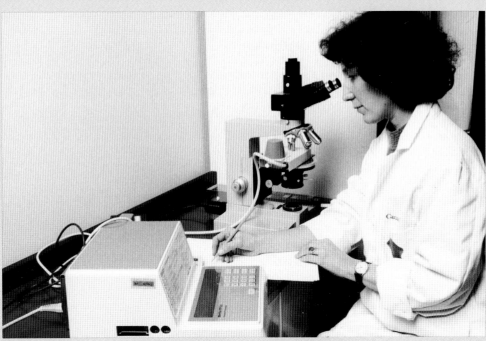

CMC's conservation staff are taking advantage of new technologies to perform their work more effectively and to share its results with others. Laptop microcomputers aid condition reporting, for example, and it is hoped to use CMC's optical disc system to keep a visual record of the changes in artifacts' conditions. Laser-recorded images made at different times, and stored together on optical discs in digital form, could be superimposed to enable cracks, expansions, colour shifts or other changes to be identified, and allow the life-expectancy of an artifact to be predicted. The ICARUS database, developed for the Canadian Conservation Institute by the Canadian Heritage Information Network (CHIN), is being used by CMC as a management tool to maintain a continuing record of the conservation treatment of each artifact. An associated database provides information on suppliers of the chemicals that conservators need for their work.

Conservation Division will share its expertise in various ways. With the public through videos showing, for example, the restoration of the Wakas pole, or the work done on the Poulin Trailer maquette, a carved ballroom scene whose figures are mechanically animated. And with the professional community through a periodical, by training interns at the museum, by an exchange programme with other museums, through public workshops, and by establishing a resource network in which conservators, students, and interested members of the public may participate. As a national museum, CMC wishes to provide for an exchange of information and ideas in many areas, including conservation.

Security

The newly-named Protection Services covers not only the security of the building and the collections, but also staff and public safety, fire protection, and emergency planning. Its work touches most other operations of CMC. Both security and conservation representatives participated as advisors in many exhibition project teams as well as in the earlier study groups of the NATF. Their planning has ensured CMC has a state-of-the-art security system.

Public penetration into the new museum was clearly defined in zones. For instance, most of the public wing is accessible to visitors; access to the curatorial block is more carefully controlled. The security system works according to the 'onion-skin' concept : concentric layers of security, each ring with barriers to penetration, so that any malefactors must pass

through several barriers before they can reach the most closely protected element : the 'treasure chest' collections holding areas. The outermost skin is the park and other grounds surrounding the museum, supervised at intervals; landscaping has been designed to offer no places for concealment. The next layer is the building's shell itself, providing steel-reinforced, concrete walls, sturdy doors and good locks supported with intrusion detection systems. Next comes the area protection layer, encompassing specific rooms or other areas within the building. Again, good walls, stretching from floor to ceiling, and stout doors are important. This layer is also protected by modern security technologies. A fully integrated and computer-controlled closed-circuit television system covers sensitive internal areas and exhibition galleries. Other intrusion detection systems in use are passive infrared, microwave and ultra-sonic motion detectors, as well as units using a combination of technologies. Access to collections holding rooms, and to certain other restricted areas, is controlled with a proximity card reader system. Each staff-member's ID card can be presented to wall-installed readers; authorized cards deactivate the door locks. The computerized system lists which persons/cards have authorized access through which doors, and records what cards have been displayed to a reader and when. This system offers a high degree of access control while easing authorized movements. The areas it covers are also protected by secondary high security locking systems used during 'silent hours'. Innermost security is supplied by point protection devices which relate particularly to elements within rooms, such as display cases and artifacts within them, safes, the precious metals vault. The principle behind CMC's security system is that the greater the number of barriers through which an intruder must penetrate, the greater the likelihood of detection and capture. Museums must expose their assets to numerous threats. It is impossible to eliminate all risks; the aim is to reduce them to a manageable level.

Protection Services also monitors the environmental control, fire protection, and water detection systems. Their uniformed staff, comprising public security (most obvious to visitors) and building security (operating largely behind the scenes), provide the eyes and ears of the museum's protective systems and the first response to security problems. A control centre is constantly staffed by trained two-member teams; they operate the microcomputers that monitor sensors and detectors. In the event of an alarm they alert protection staff, collections management staff, the fire or police departments. Protection Services has ensured that the local police and fire departments visit the museum to acquaint themselves with its facilities, the locations of emergency equipment, and the museum's special needs. An emergency organization includes representatives from all divisions of CMC. Each level of the building has a designated emergency warden : security staff in the public wing, non-security staff in the curatorial block. All Protection Services staff are equipped with the latest walkie-talkies, light and compact. The wardens would direct an evacuation, with the control centre coordinating. Particular attention has been paid to evacuating the mobility disadvantaged : evac-chairs allow difficult or dangerous evacuations (e.g. of wheelchair-confined persons).

Protection Services trains staff in the use of emergency equipment, evacuation procedures, handling the mobility impaired, and first-aid. All Protection Services' supervisors and officers are trained in first-aid, and most in cardio-pulmonary resuscitation and oxygen therapy, as well as in basic fire-fighting.

The change of name to Protection Services contributes a softer image. A human security presence is required in a museum; although electronic systems carry out surveillance, they cannot intervene. However, it has been found at CMC and many other museums that the obvious presence of unsmiling security guards, in military-type uniforms and equipped with bulky radios, can be an impediment to enjoyment of the museum visit and even intimidating. The problem has been compounded by inadequate training in human relations skills. In its public areas CMC's emphasis is now on the 'guest relations' aspect of public protection, aimed at making the museum visit as pleasurable as possible. The name-change was accompanied by less obtrusive, portable communications equipment, navy blue blazer, white shirt, and grey flannels replacing the old uniform. Public security staff are trained in human relations and communication skills, and to answer common questions such as major themes of the exhibitions or other museum and National Capital attractions. Thus the emphasis in their roles has changed from an artifact orientation (guards) to a public orientation (hosts). They bring credit to the museum and help its guests gain a favourable impression of all aspects of CMC.

Providing access to the collections

The director of a major Canadian museum has declared that "Physical access to museums and their collections is a prerequisite to intellectual access."[3] There is fairly broad acceptance in the museum world that the public has a theoretical right of access to all the collections. However, the practice in the vast majority of museums has been to allow visitors to see artifacts only through exhibition; few visitors are really aware of the far greater proportion stored in areas to which there is no public access. Problems of space, security, conservation, and limited staff have in the past made it hard to offer such access to CMC's reserve collections. This situation has become increasingly intolerable; CMC's commitment to accessibility reflects a general trend in the museum community to seek improved access. Now it has found at least a partial solution.

A very few museums in Canada have experimented with open storage as a way to 'democratize' collections. The University of British Columbia Museum of Anthropology brought parts of its reserve collections into exhibition areas called 'visible storage galleries'. To save space, no labels or other interpretive materials were presented with the artifacts; visitors had to check printouts from the computerized catalogue to get information. Furthermore, the more light-sensitive objects in the collection were still excluded from display.[4] Glenbow Institute has experimented similarly. There some didactic exhibits were supplemented with 'accessible study collections' compactly stored in furniture providing visual access to all the contents; interpretive information was available through computer terminals linked to the museum's collections catalogue.[5]

Criticisms have been levelled at open storage, notably that it exposes collections to increased environmental and security hazards, and that too many artifacts are shown without adequate interpretation. CMC considered open storage and typological exhibits to enhance access, along with possibilities such as window-in-the-wall visual access to collections holding rooms, or enclosed, transparent tunnels to lead visitors through those rooms. However, it has opted for a somewhat different course.

A commitment to accessibility implies an equal commitment to good collections management. Accessibility is impeded if the museum's artifact inventory is not carefully controlled (so that the precise location of each item cannot be determined at any given time), if the collections holding areas are crowded and cluttered, and if there is uncontrolled access into those areas. That last point is not the contradiction it may seem. Effective access depends upon the ability to find and retrieve artifacts when they are needed. Experience has shown that it is easy for even the most conscientious staff-member or external researcher, if given free and unsupervised access into the storerooms, to remove artifacts from their storage units for examination and to return them to the wrong place. A 'misfiled' artifact can be tremendously difficult to locate. There is also some risk of vandalism or theft. CMC does not have enough collections management staff to accompany and supervise everyone wishing access to the reserve collections. Instead, the intention is to limit access to those areas (with a notable exception, described later) to conservators, Collections Services and Protection Services personnel, and designated members of the curatorial Divisions who will be responsible for retrieval. Others wishing direct access to artifacts - researchers, cataloguers, photographers, etc. - will normally have them brought out to dedicated examination areas. Controlled access into the collections holding areas is the best guarantee of the efficiency of the retrieval system, upon which accessibility relies. It also reduces fire risks - by restricting functions performed in the storerooms to storage, retrieval, and inspection - and helps preserve the collections by reducing the amount of unnecessary handling and the amount of dust tracked in or disturbed.

A method for locating and tracking artifacts will rely on a computerized system, replacing the manual recording which sometimes proved deficient. When the collections were decentralized each curatorial Division had its own system for organizing, classifying, and identifying its artifacts; these continue to be used for cataloguing. But, for purposes of storage and retrieval in the new building, bar-coding technology has been adopted for inventory control. Bar codes have found a growing number of applications in recent decades, but have yet to make serious inroads into the museum world. Optical scanning converts machine-readable symbols - alternating dark and light bars whose widths are read by light-wands - into a digital form for computer manipulation. Each artifact, when first received by CMC, will be assigned a unique, sequential number and the bar code label which corresponds to that number. Numbers/labels will also be assigned to storage shelves, exhibition halls, conservation and

cataloguing areas, as well as to staff-members for security control. Whenever staff change the location of an artifact, the numbers assigned to it, the old and new locations, and the staff-member, can be quickly and accurately entered into a portable bar-code reader, which is a miniature computer. The information can subsequently be uploaded into the microcomputer-based inventory control database, from which the current location of any artifact can be identified.

No matter how well-planned the physical organization of artifacts in a storage area and how efficient the retrieval system, it remains impracticable to satisfy all information needs through direct access to the original artifacts. Staff involved in exhibition development, for example, may need information on a very large number of artifacts, from which to select the best for display. Researchers may wish to study all objects from a particular culture or sub-culture, others a specific type of artifact (such as footwear from different cultures or geographical regions), still others a variety of objects all related to a particular topic of study, and so on. Such study of the collections is not feasible when the artifacts are in storage, for they can be physically grouped in only one way. But not all needs for study of the collections require direct, tactile access; many can be satisfied by visual access and/or by access to textual descriptions. Therefore CMC has created a surrogate collection in the form of a pictorial database.

Textual information on CMC's collections has been available in the past from the registration systems and archives of the curatorial Divisions. But these are in areas not directly accessible to the public; their limited capacity accommodates authorized researchers only. Nor, until now, was there any library-type facility accessible from public areas of the museum that could provide in-depth information about CMC's collections. CMC's Médiathèque now enables anyone to access such information; its location, between public and non-public wings, symbolizes the ability of visitors to penetrate the treasure-house of information behind-the-scenes in CMC : something conceptually akin to a window-in-the-wall approach. CMC's collections catalogue is accessible to other museums via the CHIN database, PARIS (Pictorial and Artifact Retrieval and Information System); but this, providing purely textual information on what is a *visual* resource, is often inadequate to meet needs. There is an archive of artifact photographs but it, like PARIS, does not provide comprehensive coverage of CMC's collections.

During exhibition development for the new museum, the shortcomings of these sources of information became more apparent. PARIS is a collections management tool, not designed to support fast, open-ended access by researchers or the public; nor is it particularly user-friendly. One way to identify artifacts appropriate for exhibiting was to retrieve from PARIS a list of candidates, and select on the basis of their descriptions. It proved time-consuming and tedious to work through the lengthy printouts of PARIS records; and textual descriptions alone can be unsatisfactory for identifying suitable artifacts. One alternative was to obtain copy prints from the central photographic archives, but this was slow and expensive. A third option was to browse through the collections holding areas to make a selection; but the physical organization of artifacts does not lend itself to this approach, nor is it good for the health of artifacts to be examined thus.

Needed was a system to integrate both visual and textual information on the entire collections and make them available conveniently, efficiently, and cost-effectively to those needing the information. Such a system would have to be : readily and directly accessible to all; faster than existing methods of information retrieval; able to accommodate an anticipated increased demand for information (from on-site visitors, and from remote personal computers); able to provide information on any item held by any Division, in any format (artifact or mentafact). This was a tall order! To fill it CMC investigated laser discs, a new technology that has taken many forms including audio compact discs, CD-ROM, and videodiscs. The technology is establishing itself quickly in a variety of applications. Libraries have adopted it quite extensively, significant use has been made of it by recreational/cultural centres such as Epcot and Parc La Villette, and several museums in the United States have developed applications for it; in Canada, however, CMC is almost alone [6] in using laser discs as a museum tool.

Laser discs offer a number of advantages over other media for information storage and retrieval. Their already high storage capacity, relative to small physical size, is growing fast; this saves space and money. They have excellent durability, being less susceptible to damage or deterioration from handling, use, or accidents than paper, photographic, microform, or magnetic media. Their manageable

size, lightweight but sturdy materials, and cheap per unit cost when mass-produced, make them suitable for distributing information. Diverse forms of information - audio, video, graphics, text - can be stored on one medium. And computer-control provides for great speed, precision, and flexibility in information retrieval - including random access to any element of information; combining a computer and a laser disc player permits the creation of an interactive system.

CMC envisages numerous applications for a laser disc based inventory of its collections. A system which combines visual images of the artifacts and textual information about them offers a workable solution to the dilemma of access versus preservation. In collections management a comprehensive and easily searchable visual/textual catalogue of the collections is invaluable. The availability of high-quality surrogates will greatly reduce the need for that direct examination of artifacts that is detrimental to their preservation. Many researchers' needs can similarly be satisfied by access to the surrogates; much of their time can be spent just in identifying objects relevant to their interests : a laser disc catalogue will speed up this part of the work, allowing more time for the study of the information retrieved. The application in conservation has already been described. The data recorded on the inventory discs can be edited, and customized discs produced to service interactive terminals in exhibition galleries; from these visitors can obtain more information about artifacts on display and pictures of artifacts still in collections holding areas. The sale of discs, or loans to other institutions, will contribute to CMC's goal of national accessibility to collections.

In 1985 a pilot project was begun, with the assistance of CHIN and the National Film Board, to find the best system for creating a laser disc based collections inventory, and to test the linking of a microcomputer-based textual database - edited versions of the PARIS records - to the laser disc images. [7] The study identified an analogue system produced by Panasonic as the best for CMC's needs; this would permit in-house recording of images of the artifacts, via TV camera, directly to disc, and provided a very satisfactory picture quality. The recording of selected artifacts from the folk culture collections, as part of the pilot study, immediately switched to an operational phase. By late 1987 five master-discs, holding images of the entire collection of the Canadian Centre for Folk Culture Studies, had been videorecorded. Meanwhile a second team had

Optical disc system

CMC's interactive laser disc system offers the user two routes of access to collections information : through either the visual or the textual databases. Users could search for a disc visual corresponding to a photograph of an artifact, and then call up the tombstone record on the second screen, as is shown here. Or search through the textual descriptions and then call up the visual. It is easier and faster to scan a series of images than a series of textual records. Up to 15 discrete visuals per second can be discriminated by the eye and brain of the average viewer; it would take several seconds for that same viewer to scan a tombstone record. This supports the old adage that a picture is worth a thousand words! Actually it reflects the fact that our brains are better programmed to perceive and interpret an image than a textual passage (which must be converted to an 'aural' message within the brain). This is why museums can be effective vehicles for education, since their predominant medium is of a visual nature.

The system selected by CMC's pilot project comprised a standard microcomputer, holding the textual database, and the Panasonic TQ-2024 Optical Disc Player with monitor. The monitor was the weak link in the system - although the quality of the recorded image is very good, this will only become apparent as High Definition Television monitors are substituted in the system. A standard computer keyboard is shown here as the controlling device, but in different applications CMC may employ keypads bearing only the function keys, or touch-screens - which employ that very natural human technique, pointing.

CMC is not committed to any single branch of laser disc technology. Factors influencing the selection of an analogue system included the ease of recording images of the artifacts in an in-house 'studio', set up adjacent to the collections storerooms, and the system's ability (at that time) to store visual information more efficiently than digital media. Already CMC has moved to a new generation of Panasonic recorder/players. Different future purposes will encourage the transfer of the collections data from the optical disc masters to other media, such as videodisc or compact disc, according to what is most appropriate for the application. CDI (Compact Disc Interactive) offers particular promise, as its capability to store data of diverse types - video, audio, graphics, text - efficiently in digital form is developed.

begun to record the ethnological collections, and in 1988 recording of the historical and archaeological collections commenced. It is expected that by the end of 1989 CMC's entire artifactual collections will be captured on disc. All these analogue discs serve as the masters from which edited versions, designed for specific projects (e.g. exhibit support, thematic discs for publication) are being produced; this transfer can be made to other disc formats, both analogue and digital, as individual needs dictate.

Each artifact is recorded with at least five different images : one overview and four shots showing different angles or details. The images are linked with a textual database of tombstone records, in an interactive computer programme that CMC had written for the system. The menu-driven programme has been designed for use by persons with minimal experience of automated retrieval, yet sophisticated enough to permit retrieval of individual records or images from the database. It enables users to select any disc or any subject of interest, to gradually narrow down the search, and to develop a 'hit list' of records/images. When calling up any of these hits, both the image and the related textual record are shown simultaneously, on adjacent screens. Alternatively, users can browse through either the pictorial or textual databases and, when an item of interest is found, call up the related item from the other database. The computerized retrieval system allows users to delve deeply and freely into the reserve collections in ways that the collections storage system itself cannot accommodate. The latter would require researchers to move from storage room to room, or staff to bring quantities of objects out to an examination area. The interactive laser disc system allows faster, easier access to all collections from a single point, whether within the museum or outside.

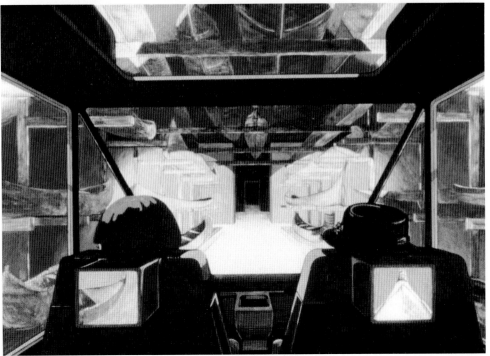

CMC's use of laser disc technology is not restricted to recording only its artifactual collections. The curatorial Divisions also hold some 14,000 hours of audio recordings, such as interviews, ethnic music, oral history, much of it stored on media too fragile to be played frequently (e.g. wax cylinders) or with a limited lifespan (magnetic tape). In the past working copies had to be made periodically on tape, and maintained by frequent rewinding. This was expensive and labour-intensive. Now those recordings are being copied onto optical digital disc. Each disc holds 512 minutes of audio and costs half as much as equivalent magnetic tape. There will also be a significant saving on storage space. More importantly, maintenance and copying of the audio recordings can be substantially reduced; their transfer to digital form even allows the sound quality to be enhanced, by processing out extraneous noise. CMC's photographic archives too are intended for transfer to laser disc, to make them more accessible.

Digitization can enhance the photographs by sharpening the images or adding colour.

CMC is interested in cooperative projects with other organizations to take advantage of laser disc technology to make Canadian culture more accessible. For instance, it is engaged in a major effort to preserve hundreds of thousands of Inuit artworks, dating from the last thirty years, which are stored in flimsy sheds in ten Inuit communities in the central and western Arctic. One shed was lost to fire in 1985. To ensure we do not lose the remainder of this heritage treasure, CMC and the Department of Indian and Northern Affairs are cooperating to provide the personnel, training, and equipment to record the artworks on an optical disc system; copies of the discs will be made available to all Canadians through the Médiathèque. Similarly, CMC has arranged to make the technology available to Bata Ltd.'s Shoe Museum, to record its collection of some 6,000 shoes from cultures and eras dating back to 2500 B.C.; CMC's reward is a copy of the disc, whose contents can be shared with the public.

For all its many benefits, laser disc technology gives access only to *surrogates* and not to the original artifacts. Therefore CMC has also sought some form of access to the 'real thing' that does not unnecessarily jeopardize security and preservation of the collection. The interest of visitors in penetrating the treasury of museums - the collections holding areas - is one manifestation of a growing public awareness of, and interest in, the purposes, roles, functions, and processes of museums, and a desire to observe, understand, and even participate in the behind-the-scenes activities. For many years museums have realized the value, both for education and promotion, of allowing visitors some access to non-public areas.[8] CMC has offered pedestrian tours of the collections holding rooms to VIPs, volunteers, and special interest groups, and found them popular. But supervision needed expensive staff time. Even this supervision did not stop people from touching artifacts or picking them up from the shelves. To avoid this difficulty, two alternatives presented themselves : encase the storage shelving, or encase the visitors.

Encasing the storage would inhibit collections management. Encasing the visitors was the unlikely answer to increasing the number of artifacts directly on view to CMC's visitors. The solution was inspired by Epcot, Jorvik Viking Centre, and Hershey's Chocolate World, institutions which

Figures 68, 68a and 68b
Plans are in progress to enable visitors to make exploratory forays behind-the-scenes into the reserve collections areas. These tours will be in automated vehicles known as 'peoplemovers'.

117

employ automated (i.e. driverless) peoplemover vehicles to carry visitors through most of their exhibitions; these applications have proven successful and popular. Theme parks and world fairs have been employing this technology since the 1950's. The technique has never been applied behind-the-scenes in museums, but a feasibility study showed no reason to prevent it. [9] Plans are now gradually proceeding for public tours of parts of the collections holding areas on Level One of the curatorial block. Starting from a room that links the public and curatorial wings, visitors will be carried on a voyage of exploration, along the Main Artifact Route and past the conservation laboratories. CMC's treasure-vault will be specially unlocked for these modern-day voyageurs, and they will see a cross-section of artifacts periodically selected from the reserve collections. The peoplemovers will then pass to a second room, holding some of CMC's largest artifacts, such as totem poles and watercraft, before returning to the terminus. The tour will take about twenty minutes, incorporating several stops en route, and with interpretation by on-board audio. The opportunity to have a peek at the backstage section of the museum, to see a larger proportion of CMC's collections, and to travel in comfort while doing so, should make the automated guided tour popular.

Each car will be capable of holding four seated passengers, or two passengers and a wheelchair; vehicle size is limited by the narrow storeroom aisles down which they must travel and by their need to navigate around the ends of shelving rows. The need for precise track-following and manoeuvring prompted the use of an automated guidance system; it has a reputation for high tracking precision - that is, negligible deviation from the track laid down - and an excellent safety record. The peoplemovers travel at walking speed and have obstacle-sensing devices. Thus there is much less risk of collision than with a manually-driven vehicle. The route will be defined by a floor-mounted guidewire, whose electromagnetic radiation is detected by the vehicles' electronic sensors; special 'markers' built into this track can signal the vehicles to make pre-determined stops. This type of track leaves no permanent scars

on floors, and creates no hazards for pedestrians. It makes re-routing easy without digging up the floor and creating dust. Its flexibility could permit extension of the odyssey to other levels by using the freight elevator to carry peoplemovers.

Since their power-source is electricity the vehicles will not introduce pollutants into the collections holding areas. Their lighting system - fluorescent lamps for the immediate vicinity, and intermittent floodlamps for more distant objects - will ensure that artifacts are not unnecessarily exposed to light. The little heat generated by vehicles and occupants will be easily dissipated by the environmental control equipment. The vehicles also meet security needs. By enclosing visitors the cars prevent touching of artifacts, yet their transparent sides and roofs still permit optimal visual access. For human safety the barrier to egress will be psychological rather than absolute, but onboard detectors will warn of security breaches, and museum personnel will be on-hand in the event of a problem. The guidewire acts as a communication channel between vehicles and a central console for monitoring the progress of the cars around the route and alerting staff to problems. The operation of the peoplemovers will be arranged so that it interferes as little as possible with collections management; the tours will be restricted to afternoon and early evening (except on weekends) to allow necessary work, such as moving of artifacts, in the early hours of the working day.

Neither peoplemovers nor laser discs offer an ideal solution to the need for public access to CMC's collections. There is no ideal system. All solutions for reconciling preservation concerns with increased public access will offer a compromise of some sort. Laser disc systems permit free and unfettered access to the whole collection, but only to surrogates of the original artifacts. Peoplemovers enable direct access to a portion of the reserve collections, but at the risk of introducing an otherwise undesirable human presence into the holding areas. These are not final solutions, but they demonstrate CMC's commitment to a continuing search for ways to enhance the public's access to the treasures it holds in trust for all Canadians.

the museum as memory

The museum is a treasure-house not only of artifacts, but also of information. The popular perception of museums is closely tied to images of the artifacts they collect, preserve, and display. Yet the real value of an artifact to a museum is in what that artifact tells of its period, the individual or group that made it, the culture in which it played a role, and the system of beliefs and values which it reflects. Were it possible to extract from an artifact all the information it could convey, the artifact itself would perhaps no longer be needed. A CMC collections manager, when asked which artifacts he would try to save first in a storeroom fire, wisely declared that he would not give priority to the artifacts, but to the collections catalogue which summarizes the knowledge of all the artifacts. In fact, it is impossible to be certain when all possible information has been extracted or deduced. Furthermore, an artifact may retain value as a dramatic device for communicating the information inherent in it, or for allowing the viewer to experience personally the discovery of that information.

The fact remains that museums collect artifacts today for the reason that the latter hold some 'meaning' that helps us understand our past. For whatever reasons, one of society's values is the desire to build and maintain a knowledge of its heritage; museums institutionalize the need to ensure access to this knowledge.[1] Therefore museums - and perhaps particularly national museums, which must reflect all regions, cultures, and periods - are an indispensable component of the collective memory of national heritage. This collective memory, in all its forms, material or otherwise, is our primary legacy from the past.

The mandate of the Canadian Museum of Civilization is to make known the cultural legacy of all Canadians, and thereby promote the advancement of intercultural understanding. It must therefore conduct research in all areas related to the collections, preserve the knowledge thus generated, and disseminate the information gathered. Much is involved in these functions. The artifacts and their historical contexts must be studied, analyzed, and documented. The documentation must be organized, stored, and maintained in forms that facilitate the retrieval and consultation of information. And this knowledge must be communicated and disseminated to CMC's various publics, in Canada and abroad, by a variety of means including exhibitions and associated public programmes, facilities for researchers to explore the informational resources, and publication of information for loan, gift, or sale.

These functions are long-established. What is new is the unprecedented potential to reach greater and previously untapped audiences, and the shifting interests of audiences in the Information Age. Their needs and expectations are becoming more demanding. To satisfy them, museums must make greater efforts to ensure physical and intellectual accessibility of the full range of their informational resources, including the collections themselves. To know and to understand have long been fundamental needs of museum visitors - CMC used to receive something like 43,000 enquiries annually. The intensity of the motivation to satisfy this need for information varies from visitor to visitor. The classification of museum visitors as streakers, strollers, and students implies that they are willing to absorb different amounts of information from their museum experience. Streakers are highly selective in the information they seek, interested only in the most general messages from the exhibitions. Strollers are more inclined to read labels, to stop and watch audiovisual or live animation presentations, talk with interpreters and penetrate into secondary exhibit areas to select more detailed information (on elements of the exhibitions that most interest them). They are less likely to seek information beyond the galleries. Students have a more avid desire for background information on exhibits and collections; they require facilities enabling them to explore the museum's informational resources in depth.

Figure 69
Diverse vehicles for communicating information are required in a museum to respond to different levels of information need. Some visitors are satisfied with the general messages they can receive simply by viewing exhibits. Others wish more detailed information, while a few come to learn about a topic in depth.

Visitor information needs are, typically, not completely satisfied in museums. The conventional approach to exhibition development tends to cater to the level of the stroller : there is an attempt to provide moderately detailed information within the exhibition, but not to enable further investigation. It is not enough to establish a museum library open to the public; there must be clear interlinking of such a facility's resources with the exhibits, through cross-referencing. The standard approach to exhibition development fails to take into account the variation in ability and inclination of visitors to assimilate information. The streaker may find it hard to pick out key information from all that is presented, and leave without a coherent understanding or with a false one, while the student may find the thirst for knowledge unquenched. Sociologists estimate that an individual in Western society receives 65,000 more pieces of stimuli daily than did people in the last century! Museums have an important role simply in synthesizing elements of information into patterns that can be more readily perceived and understood by visitors. 2 But they must communicate on various levels, to ensure that visitors are not fatigued by information overload and that sufficient information is available to satisfy all needs.

In planning to accommodate its users' "need to know", CMC has had to take into account the different levels of client need. Its public facilities and programmes are designed to make its informational resources (its memory) available in

layers, so that every user may choose how deeply to penetrate to obtain the degree of detail desired. Information must also be readily at hand when and where needed. While some visitors, notably students, may be prepared to seek out library or archives remote from the galleries, most will not go to this trouble. It is necessary therefore to provide, near the exhibits, portals into more detailed information resources, which will encourage further exploration. This is perhaps particularly important for Kelly's New Visitors, one of whose characteristics is a reluctance to accept on faith the interpretive narratives which support exhibits; they prefer to investigate information sources themselves, and make up their own minds.

A further planning factor is the increase in demand for information that CMC expects in its new home. For the new museum will attract more visitors, partly because it *is* new, partly because it is better, and partly because it is being promoted more vigorously. Its larger and more numerous exhibitions and other public facilities, and its more exciting and adventurous public programmes, will inspire in its audiences many more questions. So too will its more active travelling exhibition programme and its enhanced levels of educational programming. More leisure-time, combined with growing public and media interest in heritage, will doubtless contribute to increased exploration of museums' information resources. The new technologies of the Information Age themselves encourage greater demand for information : personal computers make it easier to access machine-readable databanks from home, school, or office; cheap transmission via satellite makes it more feasible to disseminate data in electronic form.

This permeation of new technology into all levels of society also influenced CMC planning : 45% of Canadian homes are now equipped with VCR's, 16% with microcomputers; compact disc, large-screen TV, laser light shows, and Imax theatres are no longer exotic technologies. Increasingly adept at using computer-based devices, people are becoming accustomed to fast-paced activities, electronic access to large volumes of information, and instant response to demands for information. All this adds up to a growing sophistication in querying and understanding the environment, and higher expectations of institutions to which queries are directed and from which understanding is sought - including the expectation that the latest technologies will be used in satisfying information needs.

Inevitably, CMC seriously considered ways to harness the new information technologies to meet its own and client needs. Some argue that technology has no place in museums of human history or culture; 3 yet it is impracticable for museums to fulfull their obligations to their users economically and efficiently without new technology. Faced with a growing volume of information queries, a diversity of user needs, and higher expectations for efficiency of response, museums that cannot increase their staff ten-fold can only turn to automated technologies for help. The trick is to avoid becoming preoccupied with the medium, or container, of information at the expense of the message, or content. The use of technology must enhance, not clash with, the aesthetics and atmosphere of the exhibits; at CMC new technology supports displays, but is not itself on display. It would be a fruitless, and endless, effort to pursue the latest technological trends purely to amuse a public that is increasingly technologically-oriented. On the contrary, mystery and intuition are becoming more exotic elements which museums may exploit to better effect. New technology must serve genuine needs, facilitate rather than discourage access to information, and should be one among many tools for learning about cultural heritage. CMC was aware of all these facts in planning for new technology in the museum. There was little precedent in its previous accommodations for its use of innovative technologies in the new building. The drastic change is attributable to the coincidence of the New Accommodation project with rapid advances in information technologies, to a willingness to adopt whatever approaches would allow CMC to fulfill its mandate and its audiences' expectations, and to receptivity amongst its staff to employment of new technology wherever there were benefits.

Few, even of CMC's own staff, can appreciate just how vast is the museum's memory - that is, the information it has generated. This information had been dispersed among many repositories, each with its own individualistic organization of collections, with little or no coordination or cross-referencing. The former physical decentralization of CMC's Divisions made it impractical to establish a central repository, nor would this have been generally necessary when staff relied primarily on the sources of their own Division. Each curatorial Division maintained its own collection of artifact registration data (accession and catalogue records, and supplementary files) and most had their own documentation centres holding archival and research manuscript materials. The public programming Divisions similarly had their own collections of

information materials necessary for their operations. A 1982 survey of divisional repositories produced the following estimates : 237 popular/educational publications; 1,415 graphic/cartographic items (drawings, maps, posters, etc.); 16,500 photographic slides and prints; 5,070 microform items; 552 cine-films; 431 video tapes; 15,255 audio tapes; 2,773 audio discs.

Not included in the survey were the resource centre of the public programming Divisions, with some 2,500 publications, nor the photographic collection - 40,000 slides, prints, and negatives - of the Public Relations Division. In the years that followed, the New Accommodation project gave rise to other resource centres. One was dedicated to holding museological materials of use to planners of the new museum, and archival documents relating to the project : approximately 7300 items, in a variety of media formats. Another of comparable size was set up to serve the new Information Systems Division. Beyond this, there were tens of thousands of items in the museum's library, an equally large photographic archives serving all the national museums, and the registry holding records produced by museum staff in daily operations. Furthermore, staff researchers and curators - whose own knowledge is part of the museum's memory too - had their own, often extensive, office collections of information materials.

Figure 70
CMC's information resources are vast, but were in the past dispersed and often not widely accessible. Shown here is part of a collection developed to serve staff designing the new museum, and to preserve key reports produced in the planning process.

This gives a general idea of the rich resources of information within CMC. They have been greatly underexploited in the past, both by staff and by the public. As in most museums, some collections were accessioned but not inventoried; only those who regularly used them had any idea of their contents. Where collections *were* catalogued, the listings were generally manual and not interlinked. This fact and the geographical dispersal of the collections could make it hard to find information without time-consuming searches. Matters were even worse for the public. If questions engendered by the exhibitions could not be answered by the interpretive materials adjacent to the exhibits, the visitor was at a loss. Curatorial or interpretive staff were rarely in the galleries to elucidate. None of CMC's inform-ation collections were in the same building as the exhibitions, nor was there reference in the exhibits to those sources of information, since most were really intended for use only by staff or by bona-fide researchers. Only a determined member of the public was likely to pursue a query to the museum library which, until now, was inconveniently situated on the city outskirts. As in the case of management of the artifactual collections, the opportunity to bring together all elements of the museum into a new building made it possible to rectify the failings of the past.

Most museums - not just CMC - have difficulty in coping with problems in managing their information resources and satisfying the information needs of clients. Those needs are highly individualistic, varying according to clients' education, socio-economic background, personal interests and experience. Few museums have been able to make more than a small percentage of their collections-related documentation accessible to the public. CMC's commitment to the principle of accessibility applies not only to its artifacts but also to its other information resources : to the artifact catalogue records; to the unpublished research by the mus-eum's staff; to the records stored in photographic, audio, or video form; to its subject-specialized library collections; and even to the expertise in the minds of CMC's staff. With these resources accessible, CMC's users can answer their own queries through self-directed routes of discovery.

Implicit in federal Access to Information legislation is the notion the members of the public have a *right* to access information generated through their tax dollars. CMC's own policy is fully in the spirit of that legislation. Yet it also stems from an appreciation that information is the museum's most vital

resource, upon which depends the effectiveness of its own operations and the fulfillment of its obligations to its audiences. Efficient management of that resource is therefore crucial to CMC objectives. Between them, the centralization of museum functions in a single place and the availability of new technologies have provided the foundation for such management. Divisional resources are pooled, principally through the Médiathèque, furnished with tools necessary for cost-effective storage and rapid retrieval, as well as the means to diffuse the information throughout the museum and beyond.

Museum research

The life-cycle of information is, in simple terms :

1) New information is created through research; this information may incorporate data never before recorded or it may be a new synthesis of existing knowledge.

2) The information is then organized by establishing its relationships with other elements of information, and is stored in a retrievable form (this is equally true of the facts in a book, the data in a database, or the information materials in a library).

3) The information is disseminated - that is, made available for use by as wide an audience as possible - and so becomes a source for the generation of new information (process 1).

Research is well-established as a basic function of a museum, and is an integral base for all its other activities. CMC's origins lie in a research institution: the Geological Survey of Canada. Researchers associated with CMC since that time - Dawson, Sapir, Jenness, Barbeau, and others - have, through their enduring contributions to Canadian studies, done much to give the museum an international reputation. Small museums cannot generally afford to conduct research unless it is directly related to the documentation of their artifactual collections. Major museums such as CMC are centres of learning which undertake research on a number of fronts. Some is directly related to the artifacts : it is needed to define the criteria for acquisition, to authenticate artifacts collected, to discover further information about them, and to interpret each artifact's historical and cultural context. Other research investigates the contextual background in which artifacts had their origin; for example, general studies of an ethnic group, an historical event, or a cultural process, all contribute to the recontextualization of artifacts that is so important to conveying their meaning.

Finally, there is research for internal purposes, such as : to assess needs of museum audiences and establish audience profiles; to evaluate the effectiveness of an exhibit or a programme in achieving its objectives; to investigate and develop products or techniques necessary to museum operations; to examine options, and their consequences, before important decisions are made. Although much of the research by the curatorial Divisions is eventually made public through scholarly journals or CMC's own publications, few visitors can be aware of the tremendous amount of research necessary to support functions such as conservation, collections management, exhibit design, fundraising, or the development of public programmes. Little of this is ever published or made available to the public through the museum's library.

The New Accommodation project, with its major overhaul of existing programmes and the design of new facilities and programmmes, has generated an exceptional amount of research; a small fraction of its reports are identified in this book's endnotes. The early years of the new museum will see evaluations of facilities, services, programmes, and exhibits, to ensure they are meeting the needs of CMC and its users, and to identify new needs. For this, CMC will rely on feedback from its visitors. Through an electronic Visitor Feedback and Demographics System, visitors will be invited to use a keyboard to type in free-form comments and suggestions; to participate in surveys or opinion polls, using touch-screen technology to vote or select answers from lists of alternatives; and to leave information about themselves for demographic studies to help CMC find the needs of its users. Participation will be anonymous, but participants will have the option of leaving their names and addresses if they wish to be informed of the results of a survey. In this way the public will be more involved in charting the future course of what is their museum.

A somewhat longer-term goal, for the late 1990's, will be access to the research conducted by all Divisions through a single, integrated, computerized system. Staff engaged in such research maintain in their offices filing cabinets and bookshelves full of related materials; some have created machine-readable databases. Public access to this information is either via the researcher personally or eventual publications. An Omnibus Research System would

provide an index (including thesaurus and data dictionary) to the documentation of museum research projects - be it internal memoranda, external letters, working notes, reports, papers, publications, or electronic files. It might include the full texts of the more important documents, downloadable to personal computers. This would give both public and staff a better idea of research being undertaken, facilitate sharing of results, and reduce duplication of

Figure 71
Research is an essential component of museum work, whether performed in libraries and archives, in laboratories where artifacts are examined, or out in the field. For example, to obtain background material to support its exhibit on the Chinese-Canadian community, a team was sent to video-record scenes in Chinatowns.

Figure 72
CMC plans to learn more about its visitors and their needs, through electronic surveys. Visitors will be able to leave information about themselves by answering questions posed by computers placed in the public wing.

effort. It is also hoped to link this system, via an intelligent network or gateway, to others developed in the museum : for instance, the artifact images and audio recordings databases on laser disc, the conservation records system, the exhibits information system, and others.

Informatics in the new museum

These new computerized systems will be part of CMC's informatics structure. Informatics refers to electronic means of collecting, storing, retrieving, producing, manipulating, displaying, and disseminating information; it takes under its wing technologies affecting the handling of information, such as electronic data processing, telecommunications, and office automation systems. A coherent informatics structure will be critical to the realization of CMC's goals for the exploitation of its information resources. But since CMC is a relative newcomer to informatics, a building-blocks approach will enable staff to gain experience gradually. CMC embarked on informatics in 1984 - although it had already experimented with Telidon - ranging from the development of microcomputer-based applications to requirements analysis and systems planning. In 1986 a Strategic Information Systems Plan was approved, an Information Systems Division created, and consultants were engaged to develop a conceptual plan for an informatics structure.[4] One of the first steps was to phase microcomputers into the

Figure 73
CMC has been experimenting for several years with laser discs, as an effective tool for information storage and retrieval. Many of the new technology applications developed for the new museum employ this medium.

everyday work of the museum - word processing, electronic file transfer, electronic messaging, electronic mail, and other applications - and to train staff in computer use.

In the modern philosophy of Information Resources Management [5] all information controlled by an organization is perceived as assets that must be managed uniformly with strategic planning. Not only the production and handling of the information itself but also the media and the technology are part of the management process. All systems must be able to interface and exchange data with each other. One of the strategic dimensions of information is its accessibility. CMC intends to use informatics to provide unprecedented public access to the layers of information which its corporate memory comprises. A further strategic dimension of information relates to its value. Since CMC has to derive some of its funding from self-generated revenue, it must recover the costs of improved accessibility of information by developing that information into saleable products. The informatics goals are : to create a multimedia facility able to integrate information in diverse formats; to enable public access from the museum or elsewhere to CMC's information resources through user-friendly and interactive systems; to establish systems that will support its programming and enhance the efficiency and effectiveness of its operations generally; and to provide the means to tie CMC into national and international information networks.

The numerous applications of informatics cannot all be implemented at once. This would strain fiscal resources and staff, who need to adjust their work habits and mind-sets to an automated environment. Nor are all the components of the technologies fully mature. All new technologies progress from invention to mass marketing through several stages. During its maturing a technology moves from being experimental to being stable. A stable technology works reliably and predictably. It embodies protocols, standards, and codes that have been established by national or international agreement. It demonstrably supports, better than most other technologies, applications with real benefits. It can be mass-produced in quantities and at costs that suit market demand. And it has established itself in a market, so that manufacturers do not abandon it through lack of demand. Stable technologies may move towards obsolescence as newer technologies, performing the same applications better, enter the market. Thus, some laser disc technologies are now stable, such as videodisc and CD-ROM, while L.P.s are losing their stability through the challenge from compact discs; microcomputers are stable and so too are videotex (though it may, in time, be superseded by laser disc) and large-screen film technology. Yet for any technology to become stable there must be daring institutions willing to lead in developing applications. CMC is prepared for this role when the situation warrants it. Since much of CMC's memory comprises elements that are essentially visual, such as artifacts and exhibits, the adoption of image-based technology is a priority. CMC has already committed itself to innovative laser disc applications; it will experiment with holography in future exhibits.

In its adoption of new technologies CMC has to bear in mind the ability of its users to assimilate them into the museum experience. As some internal systems will be linked to public systems, there is a fundamental need to standardize system structures, information encoding, communications methods and so on, across all systems, whether they are intended primarily for staff or for public use. This necessity for integrating systems and sharing data makes the design of the informatics infrastructure more complex, but worthwhile if the result is in better access to information.

Studies have shown that most museums infrequently satisfy the information needs of visitors, who want more detailed information on exhibits or artifacts, directory-type information related to museum facilities or services, and local tourist information. They have also shown that visitors, of any age or background, are receptive to information services based on new technology, so long as they are easy to use, available where needed, do not involve line-ups, and do not intrude upon the ambiance of the museum. Such services are appearing in shopping malls, public transportation centres, and libraries. Most people are not interested in the technology itself, but in the information it provides. It is therefore important to superimpose over different technologies standard approaches to information retrieval. CMC is especially interested in touch-screens as a simple, no-skill-required method of using information technologies.

Thus, in creating an informatics structure as a foundation for many museum operations, CMC must balance the tremendous opportunities of new technologies, the risks inherent in immature technologies, the museum's capacity to adjust to new ways of operating, and the receptiveness of its users to the technologies. The end-result, which it hopes to attain by the year 2000, is a fully integrated data,

text, voice, and video network that can be accessed from any point on the globe. However, starting from a limited technological base, CMC's informatics structure will have to evolve in a gradual, controlled manner, each application building on its predecessors. This has encouraged adoption of a distributed processing architecture based on micro-computer and super-microcomputer technology, with the staff and public workstations able to function as stand-alone units, but all interconnected to communicate with each other through a high-speed Local Area Network (LAN). Some of the super-micros will act as file servers - the units for storing databases and controlling access to them from other workstations, via the LAN - or as gateways through which network workstations can access external systems (e.g. CHIN). One of the most advanced features of this network is that it will be based on fibre-optic cable, which is already being installed throughout the new museum.

Earlier thinking had been that two minicomputers would be the foundation of a centralized architecture. However, a decentralized system offers advantages. The building-block approach makes the mini-computers unnecessary in the early phases of informatics development; but once major applications requiring their power and storage capacity have been developed, they can easily be added to the network. In a decentralized system it is easy to develop stand-alone applications without affecting the network as a whole; this will suit the different needs of CMC's Divisions. Similarly, if any computer breaks down, the repercussions on the network are minor, compared to losing a central computer. Furthermore, the processing power and peripherals of decentralized workstations can be configured to meet the needs of each; portions of the larger databases stored in the minicomputers will be able to be downloaded by any authorized user from a personal workstation.

In preparation for opening the new museum, CMC's goals have been to : install the hardware and software necessary to support the exhibitions and the Imax/Omnimax theatre; install the fibre-optic foundations for the network; continue development of the laser disc inventory of artifact images and the spin-off products serving programmes; accustom staff to an automated office environment; encourage individual computer applications in the Divisions; and experiment with localized networking using the new generation of IBM computers. Medium-term strategy, covering the early 1990's, looks towards more significant linkages of the systems then

Figures 74, 74a, 74b, and 74c
CMC unveiled its first Public Access Terminal to the public at "The Spirit Sings" exhibition in 1988.
The kiosk allows visitors, through touch-screen technology, to call up video previews of exhibitions in
the new museum or to obtain tickets for the Imax/Omnimax theatre. The ticketing process is simple :
users touch appropriate areas of the screen to enter information (such as when they wish to see a film,
and how many seats they require), and pass their credit card through a reader to pay for the tickets,
which are issued from a slot below the screen.

existing. Local applications will be developed into museum-wide systems to facilitate data-sharing amongst staff. More priority will be given to systems that serve the Médiathèque and to the outreach of the video network and its potential for live interlinking with other, similarly equipped institutions around the world. Existing elements of the system will have to be upgraded, such as the LAN (to allow for an increase in traffic and to accommodate fuller use of the video network), or monitors used for video. High Definition Television (HDTV) will form the basis of CMC's public display video system, and perhaps even of live productions; as image quality is a matter of importance to CMC, it is committed to implementing high-resolution video as soon as is feasible. HDTV and fibre-optic cable will together ensure better video, with less interference and noise.

By the mid-1990's it is hoped to have all systems in place or under development. Strategy will then focus on completely integrating these systems, further upgrading the LAN, video network, and workstation technology to permit optimum use of an integrated network, HDTV components, and inexpensive commercial large-bandwidth communications systems. The museum expects to offer direct remote access to high-quality video services. Network architecture will remain basically decentralized, but with greater reliance on the minicomputers, and the nature of the LAN will be changing to a large-bandwidth, high speed, fibre-optic, multimedia network. This system will support full colour holographic projection, if that technology is ready by 2000.

At the core of the fully integrated research, collections, and public programming network will be a multimedia databank providing information on CMC's artifactual collections. This databank will be founded partly upon the laser disc recordings of artifact images, audio materials, and photographic collections already being created. These will be supplemented by : the textual records of basic artifact information from PARIS; a database of more detailed contextual information on selected collections or artifacts, built up over time from staff research; and the Omnibus Research System. Thus, a user interested in a certain ritual performance would input the appropriate descriptors into the system and be presented with audio or video recordings of the ceremony, images of CMC artifacts relating to the ritual, descriptions of those artifacts, and references to supplementary sources (most available through the Médiathèque). In this, as in

many of the other information-providing systems envisaged by CMC, selective and interactive capabilities will be important features. A purely sequential display of information outside the viewer's control - as in the case, say, of the textual news channel on cable TV - can prove frustrating to a viewer interested only in certain items. It is therefore important to build in the means for users to choose just what information they really want, to control the progress of presentations of large quantities of information, and to direct their own courses through the many layers of information available. The laser disc technology to which CMC has committed is a medium eminently suitable for interactive applications.

Brief mention may be made of other systems that are, or will be, part of CMC's informatics structure. For collections management operations, besides the systems noted above, there will be the conservation records system (now using ICARUS, although this may not prove of long-term use to CMC); also the artifact location and tracking system, to follow the movement of artifacts removed from collections holding areas, and account for the whereabouts of artifacts loaned to CMC by other institutions. In the long term, all the systems supporting research and collections management, which hold all the physical and contextual information known about the artifacts, will be brought together in a single network.

Systems supporting public programming operations are the most numerous. One subsystem manages ticket reservations and sales for CMC's theatres, while a second provides a similar function and scheduling assistance for special events. Electronic kiosks issue personalized tickets when presented with major credit cards - they are rather like automatic bank tellers; it is hoped to provide this service from other systems' kiosks elsewhere (e.g. in hotels). Further subsystems support the scheduling of group tours and booking of rooms, facilities, and equipment by staff or visitors. Creation of these systems was assigned priority in the informatics plan, since they are vital to the smooth operation of CMC's public facilities. A lower priority was accorded subsystems to support education and exhibition projects. These will offer : computerized project management; a 'diary' providing a text/graphics trail of the history of a particular exhibit (and references to relevant documents stored elsewhere); a record of exhibit proposals; and assistance in administration of travelling exhibits. Other databases will keep lists of contacts - such as

Figures 75 and 75a
Information kiosks using new computer and video technologies are becoming increasingly common interpretive media in exhibition galleries, as instanced here at the Little World Museum of Man and the Indianapolis Children's Museum.

graphic images of the items where appropriate. This system will be made available on-site and by outreach to Canadians and to other museums worldwide. The multimedia database of artifact information will be made accessible in the same way to all who have the necessary hardware; libraries and schools may be prominent among early users, but access from Canadian homes will also be feasible. A Museum Directory system will assist visitors in several ways : electronic signs and labels; information to tour groups (meeting times, staging areas, etc.); time and location of museum events, with ticket costs, if applicable; and interactive terminals which visitors may query on matters such as hours of availability of services, location of attractions, and upcoming events. There will also be a service offering information on local tourist attractions, along the lines of public access videotex services such as Teleguide, CapitalVision, and InfoVision.

In the exhibition galleries, scattered kiosks will enable visitors to retrieve supplementary information on nearby exhibits. Some information elaborates on the historical or cultural context of the artifacts displayed; visitors will also be able to call up images, and related descriptions, of similar artifacts not on display, as well as to request a list of references to other related exhibits and relevant information sources in the Médiathèque. Some kiosks will be integrated into the exhibits and housed in customized enclosures designed to blend with their surroundings; others will be near enough to be convenient without clashing aesthetically with the exhibits. In addition to these kiosks the informatics structure incorporates a system controlling 'electronic labels' used in the galleries to provide information on the exhibits or to create special effects (e.g. simulation of smoke rising from a fire) giving the illusion of movement or habitation. Laser and new video projection technologies are now employed for this, but holography will be a future option. The electronic labels for some exhibits can be turned off, so as not to be obtrusive when those exhibits are backdrops for special entertainment.

volunteers, sponsors, media organizations - and produce mailing lists automatically; most of these have already been created.

Still other systems are intended for direct consultation by CMC's users. An Electronic Catalogue falls within medium-term objectives. It will list all items available from the museum by loan, for sale, or free, and will include descriptions, price, suggested audiences and uses, order information, and

With some systems the public will have little contact, for they serve the administrative needs of the museum. Many existed before informatics planning. Systems for managing finances, personnel, and materials were inherited from the National Museums of Canada central administration. They are being augmented by systems : to maintain statistics on revenues from donations, sales, theatre admissions, etc.; to manage contracts; to provide a computerized index to registry documents; to store museum policies, procedures, and management directives; and to deal with building management matters (e.g. space allocation, security, the internal communications network). Finally, there are office automation systems, with features such as correspondence control, electronic mail, and electronic calendar.

The Médiathèque

Creation of the Médiathèque was inspired by both philosophical and practical considerations. In part it arose from the wish to make more accessible not only the artifactual collections but *all* CMC's information resources; the principle of accessibility was expressed in the National Museum Policy of 1972, reinforced by the federal Access to Information Act of 1982, and is a key to democratizing museums. Yet it also offers a practical way to satisfy, more fully and effectively, the information needs of CMC's enlarged audiences, including off-site enquirers. Since the size of museum staff has not expanded to the same extent as its physical facilities or its clientele, the much larger volume of enquiries anticipated could not be responded to without informatics technologies, or without centralizing information resources into one repository to which the public has direct access and through which enquirers can find for themselves the answers they need.

Even before the New Accommodation project, when the possibility of a new museum at the Brewery Creek site was being mulled over, a scheme was proposed for stratified exhibitions in which each gallery included a component holding parts of the reserve collections for in-depth study, assisted by reference works and a computerized collections catalogue. Conceptual planning at the beginning of the New Accommodation project, however, envisaged a single centre - a Museum Documentation Centre - to combine with the existing library and an electronic data centre to form an integrated facility housing copies of all CMC's information resources, excepting the artifacts. 'Documentation' meant information in any format : catalogues, artifact accession records, unpublished manuscripts, published books and journals, photographic items, audio and video materials, machine-readable data.

This early vision remains essentially intact in the character of the Médiathèque. It is an amalgam of information collections previously independent of each other. The library is there, with its collection of published books and journals. The Divisional archives are brought together, in the form of copies of their original manuscripts and audiovisual materials, the latter transferred to laser disc. CMC's huge photographic collections are equally available for consultation, or purchase of copies. And the Médiathèque is the home for copies of the laser disc visual inventory of the artifactual collections. Although these separate collections will retain a certain independence in the early years of the Médiathèque's existence, the process of converting them to electronic form will cause distinctions to blur. The end-product will be a wholly integrated, multimedia information resource from which a client, from a single workstation, can access a range of materials on a specified subject. A single laser disc can now hold information in a variety of forms, making it an all-purpose medium; the ability to update recorded information is being perfected, and will strengthen the central role of laser discs in information systems.

The Documentation Centre was subsequently renamed the Information Resource Centre, and later the Museum Resource Centre. To reflect the adventurous spirit of the new museum and the futuristic character of the centre, as well as to find a title workable in both official languages, in 1987 a shortened form of the French title - Médiathèque du Musee - was proposed also as its English title. The term does not appear in English dictionaries, although it conforms to the appending of the French suffix -theque to media formats, as in cinematheque or discotheque (originally, a record library), both of which may be found in English dictionaries. French-speaking peoples have also long used bibliotheque, phonotheque, and phototheque. At the beginning of the 1980's, 'médiathèque' found its way into official dictionaries in France, and a little later into official usage in the province of Quebec. Since then, many Quebec resource centre type institutions - particularly school libraries - have adopted the name médiathèque.

A further influence in CMC's choice was the example of the Cité des Sciences et Techniques et de l'Industrie. When it opened, at Parc La Villette in Paris, a key component was its multimedia library called La Médiathèque. It has an advanced informatics structure, using an integrated library system (supplied by GEAC, a Canadian firm in origin) to control its internal operations and provide an Online Public Access Catalogue for clients. All photographic, audio, and video materials are stored on laser discs. These are to be made available to as many as 180 users simultaneously by means of a unique carousel disc-delivery system capable of handling, some 10,000 discs - a phenomenal amount of data! - although so far only 1,000 discs have been produced, and difficulties have been experienced in getting the full system up and running. [6] Anyone in France can access this information through the telephone lines, via Minitel, a videotex-type technology operated by the French national telephone company. France is well ahead of Canada

Figure 76
Presently undergoing field trials, Bell's ALEX - named in honour of Alexander Graham Bell - will provide interactive directory and transaction services (such as banking, shopping, education, news, and travel) in Canadian homes. Museum information, coded as digitized images, could also be distributed nationwide by this type of system.

in wiring the general population into textual and visual databanks, although Bell Canada is currently testing in Montreal a similar system, inspired by Minitel; this is one route through which CMC's information resources might be made nationally available.

CMC may lack the resources to create a Médiathèque on the *scale* of the one at Parc La Villette, but it can certainly match the *quality* of service and of content. Its Médiathèque represents a collaborative approach to the development and use of CMC's intellectual assets. It is a way of thinking about the inter-relationship of key museum activities, such as exhibitions, education, research, archival preserv-ation, and national outreach. It is the crossroads of diverse elements in the museum : the storehouse of the knowledge accumulated by staff during CMC's past existence, and thus a vital tool for future staff research; a facet of public programming, providing

supplementary interpretation of the exhibits, of the reserve collections, and of CMC's functions; the point where staff and public meet and freely intermingle, in a common voyage of intellectual exploration. It is a marketplace for receiving and exchanging museum-related information, a laboratory for developing and testing new technologies for storing and disseminating CMC's memory of the national cultural heritage, and a beacon for transmitting this information to distant audiences.

More specifically, its major roles are to : build and maintain, as a resource of national importance, outstanding collections of print and non-print materials in the subject-areas with which the museum is primarily concerned; to support the exhibits by fuelling the interactive information kiosks in the galleries; to make accessible further resources from which clients, with questions that cannot be answered in the galleries, can discover the responses they require; to support the studies of academic researchers and educational outreach to schools and homes, by creating customized and targeted informational packages, finding aids, and general reference databases; to be at the forefront of innovation in the development of the museum's informatics. The Médiathèque is also an important element in catering to the *variety* of information needs of CMC's clients. Many visitors will be satisfied with the level of information provided in the exhibition halls, and willing to accept the interpretations presented there. Others will seek additional information from the kiosks near exhibits. But there will remain enquiring minds which desire more direct and unmediated access to the full range of CMC's informational resources; for them in particular the Médiathèque has been created.

A very wide clientele for the Médiathèque is anticipated. It will include CMC's own staff, the staffs of other museums, other government agencies and cultural institutions, media representatives, the private sector, scholars and students, those with leisure-time (e.g. retired people), and children working on school projects (although this group's needs will largely be met by the Children's Museum resource centre). There are no restrictions on who may use it. Special attention is being paid to catering to audiences that, for whatever reason, are not able to visit the museum in person.

The Médiathèque will fulfill the diverse needs of these clients through various resources and services. For viewers of the exhibitions it will provide supplementary information, and access to images of artifacts not on display. It will enable them to create thematic menus to guide tours defined by their personal interests. And it will modulate the ambient mood in the galleries through the electronic special effects. For knowledge seekers attending the museum it will give access to major study resources, such as the library collections, Divisional archives, detailed information on the artifactual and menta-factual collections, databases holding the work of CMC's researchers, and (ultimately) databases of external creation. Finding aids and customized bibliographies will alert them to information sources both inside and outside the museum. It will also make available facilities for comfortable and convenient in-depth study of these resources. Furthermore, it will create interactive computer-assisted learning modules that bring together data on selected subjects of common interest (e.g. 19th century industrial technology); the modules will present textual and visual information on relevant items in the collections, and give the ability to branch into related sub-topics of interest, or to play a game testing the user's knowledge of the subject. To knowledge seekers beyond Parc Laurier access will be offered to the same information, if deliverable through telecommunications channels; special packages for institutions and individuals, as well as written and oral enquiry services, will also be provided. To the staff of CMC, other museums or institutions, it will furnish much information useful in their regular duties or special projects, for it is the corporate memory of a national museum, holding museological knowledge built up by the institution over time. Finally, through a separate but adjacent facility, users will be given opportunities for direct study of artifacts from CMC's collections, under staff supervision; this hands-on centre will also hold identification clinics, where the public can bring objects they have collected and discuss them with CMC's resident experts.

The Médiathèque will be developed over the course of the 1990's. At first it will be mainly a repository of separate collections, which will gradually be integrated into a single multimedia facility in which most materials will ultimately be in electronic form, stored in computer memory and on laser discs. The conversion will save storage space while giving the flexibility in manipulation and diffusion that electronic data offers. It will not be a public lending institution; it is not practical, for example, to lend a laser disc which holds large amounts of information that numerous users may need to consult daily. How-

Figure 77
The Mèdiathèque will combine CMC's library collection with information resources accessed by new technologies.

Figure 78
Study carrels in the Mèdiathèque will be equipped with electronic workstations.

ever, it will be equipped to provide hard-copy, for clients to take away, for a small fee.

Not quite all of the information of the museum will be available in the Médiathèque. Restrictions on some documentation ensure informant confidentiality or protect data on artifact valuations; thus there must be editing of some documents publicly accessible. Registration and archival documents will be available in the Médiathèque only as copies which may or may not be edited. Furthermore, one of the museum's major resources is the knowledge in the minds of its curatorial and research staff. The Médiathèque should be able to handle up to 90% of the enquiries directed to it, and so will reduce the need for visitors to enter high-security areas of the curatorial block. Nonetheless, clients with queries that cannot be answered by the Médiathèque will be referred to Divisional staff and record offices, where they can discuss their requirements with CMC's experts and seek clearance to consult restricted documents.

The role of the Médiathèque as the crossroads of CMC's staff and its public is reflected in its location in that part of the building lying between the two main wings of the museum. Public access to it is from the corridor connecting the Grand Hall and the cafeteria; staff entry is at the opposite side of the Médiathèque, from a corridor off the Main Artifact Route on Level One of the curatorial block, while a stairwell provides access to other levels.

Users will find in the main public area of the Médiathèque many of the features they would expect in a library : an orientation desk where staff will direct enquirers to the resources relevant to their needs; public reference catalogue; shelved reference works; displays of new publications and recent periodical issues; casual seating for relaxed reading; tables for more intensive study activities. The focal point of this half of the lower level, however, will be a less typical library feature : Information Resource Stations. The principal workstations of the Médiathèque, they are multi-mode electronic study carrels which give access to the computer and laser disc databases. Up to 30 such stations may be installed in small clusters. Until the integrated, multi-user databank is set up, the stations will house stand-alone units of equipment such as micro-computers, microform readers, tape decks, and laser disc players. In one corner of the main public area are three rooms that will serve as booths for the On-Call Interpreter service; until this service starts, the rooms will be staff offices.

Figures 79 and 79a
Future plans include a question-answering service combining the efficiency of computer technology and the personal touch of live inter-pretation. Inspired by Epcot's WorldKey Information Service (shown here), CMC will have an audio and video link between visitors in the galleries and museum interpreters in booths in the Mèdiathèque.

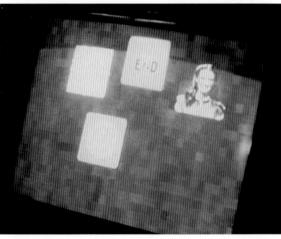

Separate facilities accommodate the viewing of audiovisual materials by small groups, as opposed to the individual access provided by the Information Resource Stations. There are two film screening rooms, one with a projection booth, the other for video. Adjacent is the order services desk, where visitors can request access to library, electronic, or audiovisual materials. The desk, with built-in switching and control over the laser disc players, will send signals to selected Information Resource Stations or the screening rooms. Visitors may place orders here for copies of museum documents. A duplication laboratory on the upper floor of the Médiathèque can copy microforms, floppy disks, photographic materials, videocassettes, and laser discs; adjacent are photocopiers. Most of the upper level, however, is taken up by the library proper : stacks, a rare books room, and a reading area equipped with study carrels and armchairs.

The non-public half of the lower level of the Médiathèque is the Network Control Centre, where entry is controlled by the electronic card access system. This is the computer-equipped hub of the museum's informatics system, controlling not only the Médiathèque systems but also those sending electronic information to the exhibitions, other public areas, and points outside the museum. In an adjacent room are the banks of laser disc players; up to 300 may be used eventually for visual images, while jukeboxes will play the audio laser discs. Because of the extensive use of electronic equipment on the lower level, most of that area has been equipped with a computer-room type raised floor, to enable technicians to carry out repairs, move units, or add new equipment with minimal difficulty. The space beneath the floor houses electrical power and communications signal distribution systems. The Médiathèque is operated by a small permanent staff, assisted by a corps of volunteers, who will help visitors use the facility and its equipment, answer queries, and assist students with their research.

Dissemination of information

The Médiathèque is the principal manifestation of CMC's memory and a place where visitors are encouraged to explore the labyrinthine network of information and discover more about the museum and its collections. Yet it is also a centre for active dissemination of that information. The Electronic Network Control Centre will send signals to the information kiosks in the public wing, to provide orientation or interpretive information to visitors there. The On-Call Interpreter service will provide a two-way video/audio link between public information stations in the exhibition halls and three of the museum's interpreters in booths in the Médiathèque. This service, not to be ready until the mid-1990's, will help answer a need identified by visitor surveys for the presence in galleries of staff able to answer questions about the exhibits. Special interpreters will be available to talk with visitors at core exhibits, and some questions will be answered through the kiosks. The interactive On-Call Interpreter service will provide a further option, catering to information needs not handled by the other sources. By touching the screen of the station's monitor, a visitor will be able to summon (like Aladdin's genie) the live image of an interpreter and pose a question. In some cases immediate answers may be given. In others the visitor will be asked to call back later from any call-up station; meanwhile the interpreter will seek the answer from the Médiathèque or CMC experts. Epcot Center has used this technology to good effect in its WorldKey Information Service.[7]

The system that will transmit data to the information stations within the museum will, in due course, be used to disseminate it to distant locations. A two-way satellite communication connection, via earth stations installed on the roof of the curatorial block, will link the Médiathèque to schools, community libraries, offices, and homes so that CMC's information resources are truly accessible, 24 hours a day, to every Canadian within reach of receiving equipment. CMC is seeking to become a 'museum-without-walls'. A *national* museum must be able to serve all members of the national community. Owing to distance, illness, or physical handicap, it is not practicable for everyone to visit the museum often. Therefore the museum must be able to visit them, through outreach programmes. Information may be given to remote audiences by response to phone or written enquiries. The Médiathèque will bear much of this responsibility. It will also be a point of distribution for free

Figure 80
CMC's publications - including this book - are now produced using desktop publishing units.

publications of CMC, and the point of access to the Electronic Catalogue of materials available from CMC.

Publishing documents about the museum, its exhibitions, its collections, and its research, is a traditional but fairly effective way of disseminating information. CMC's publication programme had to be severely cut back while most of the museum's resources were diverted into the creation of the new building. Now that programme is undergoing a renaissance. The face of publishing worldwide is slowly changing in the Information Age. CMC has taken the first step along the path of electronic publishing, by its acquisition of a desktop publishing system; this allows camera-ready copy to be produced more quickly, permits printing in shorter runs (which makes for greater cost-efficiency), and attractive formats can be created with the laser printer. For example, the Mercury Series of scholarly publications has been redesigned with more colourful and eye-catching covers, a better text lay-out and print style, glossy paper and numerous half-tone illustrations. Subjects scheduled in forthcoming issues include contemporary Canadian native art, Icelandic folklore in Canada, and historic furniture from Ontario and Quebec. Similar improvements are being made to CMC's other publications, including two new series : one on museological topics and the other on artifactual collections. These series will help CMC fulfill its responsibilities to make collections information more accessible and to share information on its techniques and technologies with the museum community.

The creation of the new museum has been the stimulus for many one-time publications. A general guidebook is under production, as well as separate guides to the Grand Hall and History Hall. Also planned are specially-written, large-print guides for children as part of a particular emphasis on this audience. Catalogues or books with supporting information and high pictorial content have been, or will be, produced to accompany temporary exhibitions such as the Bronfman exhibition, A Coat of Many Colours, In the Shadow of the Sun, the Dance and Chinese-Canadian exhibitions, and others. A booklet on the Bergeron Circus, one of CMC's recent acquisitions, will describe the creation of this unique Canadian example of miniature circus model building. The series of illustrated histories of Canadian cities, in which CMC has already issued numerous volumes, will continue with publications on Quebec and Regina. This is just a sample of the future plans of CMC's Publishing Division.

Publishing is expensive - particularly when some products are free (as with some Mercury monographs) or sold at low price. Despite the advent of electronic publishing, costs continue to rise. A cost is attached to CMC's commitment to produce documents in both official languages, and some materials in non-official languages for minorities with a special interest in the subject. Nonetheless, publication is a crucial element of CMC's outreach mission. The expense - particularly in marketing and distribution - can be reduced by co-publishing. Since 1972 agreements of this nature with publishers such as McGraw-Hill, Ryerson, Boreal, Van Nostrand Reinhold, and Macmillan, have ensured that the results of museum research be available to scholars and the general public. CMC will continue to pursue cooperative ventures.

CMC will also publish in non-print formats. The current markets for audio and video cassettes, and a market with future promise for laser discs, are suitable for exploitation by museums, whose message is high in visual and audio content. They will add another dimension to varied publications, ranging from free pamphlets through gorgeous coffee-table type books, to highly specialized monographs embodying scholarly studies. CMC needs this wide range to communicate with the diverse audiences interested in museums. One past lack has been items describing what CMC is and does, or that provide mementos of the museum visit. Particular attention has been paid to filling that gap.

Such markers of the museum visit will be available from CMC's Boutique. As Sir Roy Strong has pointed out,[8] museum shops have an important part to play in communicating with the visiting public :

they communicate the museum's collections by means of interpretive works, postcards, reproductions and suchlike, and communicate the creativity that produces many museum objects by selling contemporary works of art or craft of similar quality. In other words, they sell precisely those objects that the museum might like to collect for itself - and in some cases does, as CMC's fine crafts collection or its contemporary native art and specially-commissioned artworks witness. These are as much part of the museum's memory as objects of some historical age.

Epcot Center again presents a leading example of the type of cultural marketplace that CMC seeks to create within its walls. It has more of the 'real thing' in its World Showcase pavilion boutiques than it does in its exhibits. Its partnerships with particular countries in creating the national pavilions have enabled it to secure authentic and high-quality crafts from them to sell. Museums have long been involved in producing and selling replicas of original artifacts, but the quality is not always what might be desired. Besides, why should museums insist on showing only the real thing in their exhibits, yet offer only replicas in their marketplaces? Even when authentic crafts are offered for sale they are frequently trivial and of poor quality. The current trend towards increased investment in the decorative arts and rare commodities gives an opportunity for museums to promote present-day cultural creativity while generating revenue to support their own cultural programmes. CMC's sales shop sells auth-entic fine crafts of the same high quality as those in the museum's Massey and Bronfman collections. Ties with the Canadian Crafts Council allow it to reach some 25,000 Canadian craftspeople, many making objects based on the same styles, materials, and methods that produced CMC's artifacts. Simil-arly, the creations of contemporary native artists are featured in the boutique. The Boutique's merchan-dize will include products from demonstrations and artists-in-residence programmes conducted in the museum.

The Boutique is on the main entrance level of the public wing across the main lobby from the Imax/Omnimax theatre. The location makes it convenient for visitors to make purchases just before leaving, or to pick up exhibition catalogues upon entering the museum. The L-shaped store's exterior windows, which are full-height clear-glazed panels, front onto both Laurier Street and the Entrance Plaza. Its broad window to the exterior gives it potential as a showcase where arts and crafts will be displayed to

A. RETAIL STORE – LEVEL 3
B. RETAIL STORE – LEVEL 5
C. MEZZANINE
D. EXTERIOR ROOF

*Figures 81, 81a, 81b, and 81c
CMC's sales shop offers visitors a
chance to acquire a special reminder
of their visit, gifts for family and
friends, or information products that
will let them learn more about the
themes introduced in the exhibitions.
There is something for most tastes and
interests, ranging from inexpensive
souvenirs to handicrafted items of the
same quality as objects in the
museum's collection.*

advertise special exhibitions and draw in passers-by - either to tour, or simply to shop. The Boutique's blend of sales-display and museum-display seems appropriate for a museum store. The main level stocks souvenirs, general gifts, books and other information products. Higher quality, and more expensive, arts and crafts items are on the upper level boutique, which covers only one end of the store; the two levels are connected by an internal staircase and an elevator. The upper level also has its own entrance from a balcony walkway overlooking the main lobby. Between the two levels is a small mezzanine where patrons can rest or watch demonstrations.

A section just for children at one end of the lower shop will create a special interest for them, and isolate their potential disruption of other browsers in the shop. The display furniture here has been scaled down for children, and holds items such as colouring books, model kits, puzzles, dollhouses, costume patterns, puppets, posters, publications for children, child-oriented native and ethnic arts and crafts, educational toys, whimsy and nostalgia. This is a colourful, fun place where children will feel welcome and at ease. In fact the whole shop is bright, spacious, and relaxed for browsing and shopping. Or for learning more about the museum and its exhibitions - for most products sold in the boutiques reinforce exhibition themes with information on the history, cultures, and lifestyles of Canadians past and present.

The intimate connection between the items for sale and objects on display is most evident when the two are physically close for direct visual comparison. The desire to buy exhibition-related items tends to be strongest when the exhibits are being viewed : a single-location store does not always serve visitors' convenience. Therefore, not only will museum artifacts be displayed in the Boutique, but extensions of the shop will be deployed throughout the museum. Specialty shops will be set up in enclosed spaces within the permanent galleries, and temporary boutiques created adjacent to special exhibitions or special events. They will sell items like catalogues, books, and videotapes providing information on the nearby exhibits. A specialized video shop will sell or rent subject-related tapes and, eventually, laser discs. Another device to turn the whole public wing into one great cultural marketplace is themed mobile stalls. The wide hallways adjacent to the Boutique on both levels make it possible to extend merchandizing into this area and beyond, with the carts wheeled into the galleries. The stalls will be designed to match the themes of the exhibits they serve, to add a nostalgic feel to the merchandizing. They will be used during peak visitation periods and, when not needed, stored safely out of the way.

Meeting public expectations is not only fundamental to attaining the goals inherent in CMC's vision; it is also varied, complex, and in many cases new, with little precedent or experience to guide. To encapsulate the diverse sources of information that constitute the memory of the museum, and to impart what it remembers of the past to others, CMC has had to import technologies previously foreign to it. While busy designing a new museum, CMC's staff, bolstered by a few experts in the new technologies, also had to learn to apply those technologies to traditional museum operations. Although some applications are almost unique, and the timing of these applications may make CMC, at least temporarily, a world leader in what might be called 'museo-technology', the general benefits of these technologies are not so very different for CMC than for other institutions using them. By providing staff with information when needed and close at hand, instead of obliging them to spend time searching for it, increases productivity. By providing flexible and powerful ways of storing, organizing, and retrieving data, the technologies meet a greater *range* of needs, through different levels of information into which users may penetrate in directions and to depths that they themselves define. And by being able to provide fast and cost-efficient dissemination, CMC's dream of becoming a museum-without-walls seems within reach.

Accessibility is the theme which underlies this chapter, and much of previous chapters. Access to information, access to collections, access to cultural heritage : it all adds up to access to *understanding*. Before we can understand, we must first remember. The human brain is biodegradable, but humanity has invented a series of tools that give its memories a life beyond individual deaths : writing, printing, and now computer-based media.9 As the capability of these tools has improved, particularly for disseminating knowledge, so they increase the amount of synergy among humans and increase the human potential. The Canadian Museum of Civilization, as an institution dedicated to the service of society, is not committed to new technology *per se*, but to any means that meet the needs of its users for a better understanding of the past, the present, themselves, and their neighbours.

the museum as communicator

Most museums appeal to a relatively narrow spectrum of the public : the "traditional visitor" defined by Bob Kelly : middle-class, university education in humanities or social sciences. The messages museums present and how they present them are designed to satisfy the needs and tastes of that type of visitor; this helps explain why others have difficulty imagining that museums are at all relevant to their interests or their world. There is an unfounded, but deeply-rooted, fear in the museum community's mainstream that developing a popular appeal inevitably means lowering standards of excellence; this has encouraged a conservatism which resists new methods or new technologies tainted with populist traits, and which ignores changes in our society. It has been left largely to institutions outside the mainstream - such as ecomuseums and science centres - to pursue directions responsive to social change, and for theme parks and their ilk to draw in the large numbers of visitors that museums would really like to attract.

To continue as elitist institutions when there is widespread need for the benefits museums can offer to society - particularly in this time of rapid social change - is unethical. Museums have a vital role in guiding social change by helping people acquire a respect for heritage, an appreciation of the value of preserving it, and an understanding of the diverse cultural elements that are integral parts of our heritage. The success of that mission depends on cultivating a public willing to listen to museum messages, and this they cannot achieve while perceived as elitist.

The key to the process of cultivation is learning to communicate better with all the audiences museums would like to reach. This involves persuading people who rarely or never visit museums that they have good reason to come, providing attractions that appeal to diverse tastes and interests, finding a variety of ways to convey the museum's messages, and taking the museum to those who cannot come.

"The museum as communicator" is a title applicable to several other chapters of this book, so fundamental is it to museum functions : exhibition, research, publishing, education, entertainment, marketing, and public programmes of all sorts. None of this work can bear fruit unless the museum is able to communicate effectively with its audiences. Much of what we have said about the dissemination of information was particularly relevant to the museum as communicator. This chapter focuses on CMC's approach in communicating its core experiences - the exhibitions and related programmes - to both those who visit and those who do not.

To develop larger audiences, museums must use channels of communication with which they have little experience. As the then director of the Victoria and Albert Museum noted : "We cannot afford to stand aside from the means of communication of our own age."[1] He was thinking of the mass media and their ability to give museums a high public profile. Other cultural institutions have already found that television, that most pervasive mass medium, is a powerful device for influencing their actual or potential publics. Museums need to develop more effective uses of, and master the skills related to, all kinds of communication techniques and technologies: television, radio, video, satellite transmission, publications, lectures, computer database sharing, theatre, storytelling, and of course artifacts themselves; all are tools to provide access to heritage and to intercultural experiences. Yet this by itself is not enough. Museums must redefine the image they communicate, to ensure they capture the attention and engage the interest of audiences; this is a prerequisite to communicating their more serious messages. It is even necessary, CMC believes, to redefine 'communication' in a way that empowers the audience to play a more active - indeed, interactive - part in the process, for participation promotes discovery and facilitates the incorporation of new knowledge or experience.

Figures 82 and 82a
The traditional image of museums is one where captured tropies of dead cultures are displayed in sanitized environments dominated by glass-front cases. The principal interpretive medium of this environment was labels of text: impersonal, scholarly, and rarely read in their entirety. Although display cases remain well in evidence, indoor museums are increasingly creating exhibits that set artifacts in realistic environments. These photographs show exhibits in the Victoria Memorial Museum Building in 1934 and 1988.

turn to theme parks, which already emphasize the experience-enriching qualities of their attractions. Museums cannot survive in their traditional role of simply preserving exotic items, displaying them in a showcase, and converting them into status-validating wealth objects by surrounding them with glass and electronic surveillance systems. They must instead demonstrate what the sources of those objects were like as living, functioning cultures. This can best be communicated by recontextualizing the artifacts, by re-enactments of culture-specific rituals and other activities, by offering interpretation from a variety of viewpoints and especially the viewpoint of representatives of those cultures, and all in ways that allow visitors to interact with what is being expressed. In other words, to reincarnate and reanimate the essence of the past meaningfully for today's visitor.

There are two ways of communicating knowledge and experience : through the senses and through the intellect. CMC uses the latter method through databanks, research facilities, and vehicles for dissemination. Its exhibitions also cater to intellection, but more to sensation and emotion. It is by engaging the visitor's feelings that the museum experience is most deeply imprinted in memory. CMC's foremost goal is to develop a new kind of human history museum which encourages intercultural understanding by giving its visitors an interactive experience of past cultures (and thereby an orientation towards the future) that is profoundly moving, both emotionally and intellectually. A range of methods, techniques, and technologies has to be used to communicate that experience to visitors of differing needs, expectations, and abilities. And CMC's communications planning has also had to respond to its mandate as a national museum by developing means to reach out across the nation - and in time across the globe - using electronic media to provide universal access to the experiences the museum can furnish.

This is why CMC seeks to give many of its exhibits an experiential character, to help visitors become active participants within highly realistic exhibits, rather than passive viewers from without. This is also why it offers multiple opportunities for visitors to query live interpreters or computer terminals about what they experience, and to pursue information along self-directed paths, rather than be obliged to accept unquestioningly limited information on labels. Audiences are becoming increasingly accustomed to this approach to interpretation of exhibits, or of any recreational/educational activity, and are coming to expect it. If they cannot find it at museums, they will

Orienting the visitor

As soon as visitors arrive at the museum, channels of communication must be opened. It has been correctly pointed out that "One of the most pernicious problems in communicating with the museum visitor is orienting him to the museum environment."[2] This is true of all museums, but especially of large ones, such as national museums. Effective orientation ensures visitors get the most out of their museum experience; it is the process of acculturation of the visitor to the museum context -

that is, to its physical environment and to its content (which embodies messages to be communicated).

Spatial orientation concerns itself with familiarizing visitors with the physical, or topographical, layout of the museum and its exhibitions. Conceptual (or interpretive) orientation provides visitors with an introduction to exhibition themes to prepare them mentally for what they will experience. Museum visitors - especially first-time visitors - often do not know, or do not seem to know, what there is to be seen or done in the museum, where its attractions are, where they should begin their tour, how to find a certain area, or what are the central themes presented. Orientation measures can give visitors a sense of place and purpose, to help them adapt to a new context and make decisions about what they want to see or do, and in what sequence. This is part of making visitors feel welcome and ensuring their visit is enjoyable and rewarding.

Direction-finding is a basic instinct; to accomplish it humans create "cognitive maps" : mental represent- ations of their external environment which they use to find their way around.3 Museum wayfinding tends to be more leisurely than movement in other buildings, incorporating an element of discovery. Often visitors prefer to wander rather than be told where to go; others come to see specific things and need accurate directions. To ensure spatial orientation, it is necessary to influence the creation of visitors' mental maps through museum floor-plans or guidebooks, directional signage, guided tours, and landmarks which can be incorporated into cognitive maps. People rely on architectural statements, other visual cues, and personal interactions to find their way about. Not a few museums are housed in buildings constructed when little attention was paid to the needs of visitors. The Victoria Memorial Museum Building is an example; to the lay person the neo-Gothic structure is just what a museum is *expected* to look like. Yet that building is in fact quite unsuitable, not only for housing artifacts, but also for catering to the physiological and psycho- logical needs of visitors. The confined space of the galleries made it difficult to design exhibitions that could present fairly complex themes yet employ a clear and coherent circulation pattern for visitors. The difficulty with knowing which way to proceed through the maze was compounded by inadequate directional signage and a shortage of printed guides. For some visitors, this gave rise to disorientation, contributing to the notorious malady "museum fatigue", and helps explain why visitors often did not stay very long at the museum.

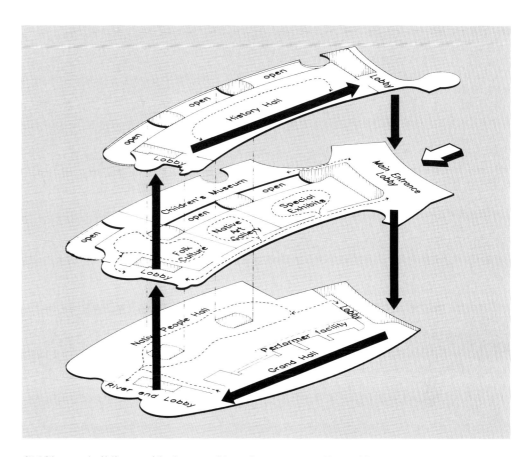

CMC's new building avoids those problems by supporting cognitive mapping. Its external appearance - the longitudinal shape - reflects the main interior routes through the galleries. And its design incorporates landmarks by which visitors can orient themselves. Windows extending from the main entrance lobby and the large rest area above it, along the Grand Hall, to the river lobby, by offering views of surrounding urban features, will enable visitors to get their bearings. The Grand Hall is a landmark in its own right; visible from every level of the public wing, it will serve as a lodestar in visitors' cognitive maps, helping them make sense of the organizational layout of the galleries within the museum.

The Grand Hall is also an important element in the circulation route. The main entrance lobby is a major decision-point for visitors, who may reach almost all of CMC's attractions directly from it. However, the most obvious element confronting visitors, upon entering, is the Grand Hall; it should therefore draw most first-time visitors into it, as the introductory experience of the museum. Its exhibition is designed for linear circulation - although random exploration of the houses will not detract from the messages presented - and will lead visitors to where they may either enter the Native

Figure 83
An ability to understand easily the layout of the galleries, and their spatial relationship to each other, is integral to visitors feeling psychologically comfortable as they find their way about a museum. CMC's simple circulation route, and periodic views to the outside, help keep visitors from becoming disoriented.

139

Peoples Hall (as a logical continuation from the native village), or proceed to other levels. The sole escalator at this end of the hall goes upwards, to encourage traffic flow to the upper levels. The second level exhibitions can be experienced in any order. The History Hall is intended to be entered at the river end of the wing, although, like the Grand Hall, it can also be explored in reverse direction. The History Hall and the Native Peoples Hall incorporate landmarks that will orient visitors within those galleries : the environmental reconstructions. There is no need for views to the outside from these galleries; what could be more familiar, to most visitors, than navigating through a streetscape?

Maps of the galleries will show the organization and layout of exhibitions, and indicate the most direct route to specific attractions. These are available from the information desk just beyond the main entrance of the museum, and from a brochure rack at the river entrance. The interests of, and time available to, visitors of course vary on an individual basis. Special routes through the building have been identified for large guided groups, VIPs, and the mobility-impaired, for example. There is a growing demand for very precisely timed tours; Japanese tour groups, for example, tend to be on rigid schedules - their length of stay at any destination may be timed down to the minute! Business visitors to the city also have limited time, usually in the evening, to see local attractions, and yuppie couples who may find free time together only on weekends similarly expect to get the most out of that time. These "streakers" are not inclined to wander aimlessly, to follow story-lines, or read labels. They want carefully designed tours showing the highlights within the time-frame available. Subsidiary information they will seek through information products that they take home to digest at their leisure. It is a major challenge to meet this type of need.

Ample signage is in place for identification and directional cueing. Signage is a very important element in wayfinding but, if overdone, can clutter and distract. CMC's has been carefully designed and placed so as to be clearly visible without detracting from the overall visual experience of the building. Passive signage is augmented by electronic marquees that present changeable messages, such as the times of theatre shows, and by touch-screen terminals to provide interactive assistance. Human assistance can also steer visitors to where they want to go, and help organize their visit.

The goal is to design customized tours for visitors that are responsive to individual needs and time available. Under development is an automated system which will create a map of the museum showing a recommended tour tailored to the visitor's requirements. The layout of the galleries ensures that visitors need not backtrack or travel through exhibitions of no immediate interest to them. Particular care has been paid to designing traffic flow patterns that minimize crowding in any exhibit area; attention to pacing also involved provision of frequent rest areas to offer relief from what can be an intellectually and emotionally demanding experience.

The need for conceptual orientation is perhaps greater than normal in a national museum, which must deal with a range of topics and offer a variety of experiences and attractions. Visitors must be introduced to the themes that will be presented, and be made aware of the full range of opportunities available. Disorientation results from constantly encountering the unexpected : as an unlikely example, if one entered an exhibition billed as a streetscape and encountered a series of prehistoric habitats of nomadic peoples, the confusion would create a mental state unreceptive to messages that the exhibition sought to communicate. Thus it is necessary to pre-programme visitors, to induce the appropriate expectations *before* they encounter an exhibition, thus increasing the likelihood of them leaving with a clear understanding of what was experienced. This is not to say that elements of surprise incorporated within exhibits cannot be employed to good effect, so long as they are not overdone.

Maps and signs will help provide visitors with an indication of CMC's features and its highlights. The visitor information desks distribute brochures giving menus of the exhibitions, facilities, and services of CMC, a calendar of special events, hours of opening, instructions for booking tours or buying theatre tickets, etc.. Some of this information is also available on video terminals inside and outside the museum; this electronic Museum Directory system will be further developed to provide interactive visitor assistance, answering questions posed by visitors, providing selective information to meet individual needs, and designing customized itineraries. For persons away from the museum, a 24-hour telephone enquiry service furnishes recorded information, with a bypass number for further information during opening hours. Audio-tours also facilitate conceptual orientation, and will be discussed later. The Grand Hall contributes to orientation by introducing visitors to the central theme of the museum : the meeting of different cultures.

Exhibit interpretation

Traditionally, in museums the dominant medium for conveying information is the displayed artifacts. Some museums (particularly art museums) consider this sufficient and may offer no further interpretation in their immediate vicinity. Most human history museums, however, consider that the non-verbal language of artifacts is intelligible only to a small group of academics and well-informed lay persons. The museum, whose specialty is translating the language of artifacts, must mediate between artifacts and the public by interpreting the former in a way that reveals their meanings and their relationships to their cultures of origin. The conventional method has been labels. An increasingly popular alternative is to recontextualize artifacts within partially or entirely reconstructed environmental settings; there each artifact's meaning is clarified through its visible connection to related objects : the whole is greater than the sum of its parts. The former approach caters to intellection, the latter more to sensation.

Too often interpretation is confused with education. There has been a tendency to use it for teaching (in the worst sense of that term) : that is, of conveying information in a didactic manner that implies the given interpretation is definitive. Labels are particularly prone to this error, for they impose information without allowing visitors to participate in the process of discovery by bringing their own initiative, judgement, knowledge, and values into play. Reconstructed environments may also reflect to an extent one or more experts' perception of a setting from the past; but they give visitors more scope for self-initiated discovery and an opportunity to see for themselves patterns of reality within presentations.

This is not to say that education has no place in a museum. 4 Far from it. But education and interpretation approach the learning process from different angles : whereas the former is an active process initiating or transmitting prescribed ways of thought into its recipients, the latter is a facilitator that merely builds a bridge between artifact and observer that may be crossed to allow for a more intimate and more meaningful interaction. It is human nature to seek pattern in interpretation as a

Figures 84 and 84a
Getting museum visitors to interact more intimately with the agents of interpretation can be a powerful tool for communicating experience. Here, for example, children help a magician carry out a trick, and at a performance of Northwest Coast dancing audience members are invited on stage to dress in native costumes and try the steps for themselves.

way to understand the past; but understanding alters as human perspectives and social values change. History is not merely what happened in the past, it is

141

Figure 85
A battle reenactment, sponsored by the Canadian War Museum, in Ottawa in 1988, included the opportunity for spectators to visit the encampments and learn about military history through conversations with the uniformed actors - hobbyists very knowledgable in the subject.

style exhibits. But its greatest efforts have been directed to interactivity wherever this has seemed an appropriate method of communicating. With any successful exhibit, the medium affects the visitor, but with an interactive exhibit the effect can be magnified or intensified through feedback. An interactive exhibit requires intellectual or sensory participation from the visitor to maximize the information obtainable from the exhibit. An example in museums is resource centres (sometimes called Discovery Rooms) where visitors may handle artifacts, to expand the sensory information gained. In the words of two exhibit designers :

> Exhibitions exist to teach, but they must do so without the advantages of the captive learning situations of the schoolroom.... A boring exhibition, and there are lots of them, has no alternative but to be a failure. The most important function an interactive exhibit can have is to establish a physical connection between the visitor and the media. This connection serves to break down the barrier of disinterest and impatience that may exist between the visitor and the intended message. [5]

The push-button-pull-lever and more complex forms of interactive exhibits found in science centres are another well-established type.[6] Interactive computer games are becoming commoner in museums. Interestingly, most of these devices seem aimed at children. Interaction most commonly provided for adults tends not to involve physical activity so much as intellectual activity, in the form of opportunities to query electronic databases or live interpreters stationed at exhibits.

CMC offers the same full opportunities for interactivity to all its visitors, of whatever ages. It hopes to break through the barrier of inhibition that controls most adults when they enter museums and to encourage participation. Museums are seen as intellectual institutions; but CMC strives to be more, by engaging the senses and emotions as fully as the intellect. Only thus can it give its visitors a complete experience of their heritage and of other cultures. Its principal strategy is to 'dissolve the frame' which traditionally separates the visitor from the cultural experience, whether that experience is conveyed by artifacts, by film or video, or by live presentations. By constructing well-researched and detailed dioramic environmental settings that engulf the visitor (instead of display cases that distance visitors from artifacts); by introducing the live human agent of culture - be it the scholarly researcher, the tribal

who tells you what happened. Museums are coming to realize that interpretation should be tentative in tone, suggesting possible views of the past rather than claiming to be definitive, offering alternative versions from which the museum's audience may choose what seems best to each of them, or (better) creating opportunities for close interaction between visitors and elements of the cultural past so that the former are enabled to reach their own understanding. For a meaningful experience, participation and interaction are more conducive than passive receipt of information, so CMC has often incorporated these elements in its exhibits and interpretive programming.

The change from observer to participant creates profound changes in the human brain. People do not generally develop a deep interest in, a commitment to, or a feeling of responsibility for, matters in which they have no participative role or over which they have no influence. If a museum wishes to be a bridge (or crossroads) between different cultures, to foster intercultural understanding, and to stimulate appreciation of the need to preserve our cultural heritage, it must involve its audiences more intimately in the museum experience. This is a lesson that indoor museums have been slower to learn than ecomuseums, open air museums, historic sites, and theme parks. Some museum visitors prefer a relatively passive role : to look, to be informed, to leave. To cater to that need, CMC has traditional-

elder, the storyteller, or the trickster/performer; by creating opportunities for tactile or other sensory contacts with artifacts; and by offering film presentations (Imax/Omnimax) which are the nearest thing to being there : these will make CMC's visitors part of the exhibits and the activity surrounding them, establish a more interactive relationship between visitors and artifacts, and thereby heighten the museum experience.

This is CMC's approach to communicating with its visitors. Yet 'communicate' is itself an inadequate term in an interactive context. Duncan Cameron came closer to the right concept in wishing that museums "will become explorable, unedited, responsive resources, open to question and prepared for discourse." [7] Interactivity implies a dialogue between participants, whether a visitor-artifact or visitor-interpreter relationship. Gene Youngblood distinguishes between communication and conversation. [8] While communication is a participative process to the extent that information is shared, the term generally implies a one-way flow of information. Furthermore, it presupposes a common context of definition, a domain of consensus, that determines the meaning of what is communicated. As a tool for intercultural understanding, communication has limited value, for different cultures may not share the common idioms on which communication is premised. To establish the common basis that makes effective communication possible requires *conversation*. The Latin roots of this word, meaning to turn around together, implies a two-way exchange of questions, ideas, and perceptions that establishes a consensus of meaning, a shared understanding of reality. CMC seeks to make itself the meeting-ground of representatives from different cultures, a neutral place offering the means to encourage and facilitate conversational exchange, and subsequently communication. Mass media communicate, they do not converse, and so cannot solve society's contemporary problems; museums, on the other hand, can make a real contribution by creating an environment that promotes intercultural dialogue. Out of this process museums may even generate new culture for, as Marjorie Halpin points out, Canadian culture is really a multicultural conversation out of which new cultural forms are constantly arising - presenting a model for the global conversation that the growth of tourism and of telecommunications are making possible. [9]

Goals for CMC's interpretive programmes arise out of this wish to encourage intercultural dialogue. One is to present multiple perspectives on exhibition

themes, to indicate that each perspective is but one of many possible interpretations, and to provide visitors with the means to examine and explore the different interpretations and understand how the truth lies somewhere between all these viewpoints. One of the perspectives presented will be the scholarly community's; here, one culture will be represented from the viewpoint of another. It is as important, however, to allow a culture to be interpreted by its own representatives; CMC has actively sought to identify and engage persons from native and ethnic backgrounds to serve as interpreters of exhibits relating to their cultures. Visitors can interact, converse, and communicate with these living elements of culture, within the physical setting of an exhibit which re-creates a cultural/environmental context appropriate to the past.

The History Hall provides examples of interpretive goals formulated for exhibitions. [10] The intention has been to create evocative environments which project strong visual images of time, region, and theme, as well as a sense of adventure, discovery, and expectation. The exhibits offer both learning and entertaining experiences. They aim at evoking emotional responses and at encouraging physical and intellectual participation by visitors, to increase their appreciation of the Canadian heritage and to give

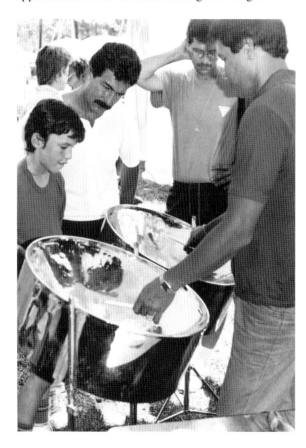

Figure 86
Whenever possible, CMC will employ living representatives of a culture to offer one interpretive perspective on the exhibited material objects of that culture.

them a sense of being intimately connected with the past. The hall has been designed to give an impression of activity and change, yet to offer different levels of experience and of information to meet the needs of different types of visitors. All elements have been orchestrated to provide a cohesive exhibition experience arousing interest, ensuring enjoyment, and thus maximizing understanding.

Conventional labels and panels of text and graphics have not been abandoned by CMC, but they will not be overused as in the past. These remain effective tools for interpreting individual artifacts displayed in traditional ways, and some visitors still feel most comfortable with this approach. For those left unsatisfied by labels, there is the electronic information from the kiosks. For most visitors, reading labels becomes tedious and is abandoned, or scanning of texts becomes cursory and little is absorbed. People prefer to absorb information through their senses. The value of CMC's reconstructed environments stems partly from their ability to engage all the senses : auditory, visual, tactile, and olfactory. They are, in themselves, an interpretive device, for they place artifacts in contexts which make the uses, functions, and roles of those artifacts more readily apparent. In some exhibits in the History and Native Peoples Halls visitors are completely surrounded by architectural structures and/or photomural scrims, to help them

suspend belief as they are whisked back through time and space.

Yet environmental reconstructions can become boring if they are static - a problem some museums have encountered with their streetscape exhibitions. To give them a dynamism that constantly renews visitor interest, CMC uses various techniques to animate the settings, increase the realism, and suggest a human presence; for example, changes in light levels, sounds and odors natural to the environments, and special effects such as animatronics and rear-projections onto dioramic scrims. This relates to conceptual orientation : people have expectations of what they will find in real environments, and if those elements are absent from the simulated versions, a negative response may make visitors unreceptive to exhibit messages.

Even more important are the live interpretation programmes. Environmental reconstructions offer excellent and plausible backdrops for theatrical presentations. The Smithsonian has found that : "Live interpretation is an enormously successful method for getting visitors involved in the museum experience. Visitors are unanimous in their requests for more of this programming in the museum."[11] This fact has long been known by open air museums, historic sites, and theme parks, where live animation is a mainstay of the interpretive programming. It is a relatively new technique for indoor museums. It offers visitors a change of pace, encouraging them to pause from their normal touring to watch, or even participate in, a presentation. Live interpreters enhance the intimacy of the experience, for people find it easier to relate to other people than to inanimate objects; and good drama can be gripping, particularly when its theme is controversial or an issue dear to the hearts of the audience. Some matters are very difficult to convey through static displays and labels. Showing is often better than telling; demonstration of an object's use, or re-enactment of a cultural ritual, reveals more than seeing the relevant objects sitting in a display case. Theatrical presentations are a powerful vehicle for conveying - and personalizing - ideas, feelings, and values that might otherwise elude a visitor exposed only to artifacts; they are an excellent way of interpreting native legends or cultural belief systems, and for presenting a culture as a vital entity. Furthermore, they furnish the means for interaction and dialogue between performers and audience; in some of CMC's presentations, the distinction between actors and audience may become quite blurred.

Figure 87
A human presence within environmental reconstruction exhibits helps animate the setting and adds to the realism. Demonstrations such as this woodturner gives (in Sherbrooke Village) restore artifacts to a more comprehensible context, by showing how they were made, or were used to make other things.

Several types of live interpretation and animation have been programmed into CMC's exhibits. Stationed interpreters, often in period costumes, will be on hand at many exhibits to answer questions, engage in discussion, give guided tours of their areas, or demonstrate crafts and skills. Some interpreters will assume the characters of specific historical personages and speak and behave accordingly; this is referred to as 'first-person interpretation'. At another level of interpretation will be 10 to 20 minute vignettes, cameos, or historical re-enactments, involving one to three costumed actors; themes such as Captain Cook's meeting with Maquinna or the banning of the potlatch are appropriate to these mini-dramas. Each show will repeat several times a day during peak visitation periods, some present-ations scheduled (for school or other group visits), others as 'guerilla theatre' - unannounced and

seemingly spontaneous occurrences at no fixed location. Larger-scale, more formal theatrical pieces and concerts, in fixed settings such as CMC's galleries, theatre, and outdoor plazas, are also scheduled.

Effort has been made to engage the services of natives as actors, artisans, singers, musicians, dancers, and storytellers during the summer, to ensure that the exhibits in the Grand Hall (and later those in the Native Peoples Hall) are enriched by a full range of interpretive activities such as totem pole carving, demonstrations of food preparation and fishing apparatus, enactments of myths, and performances of cultural rituals. Other natives will participate in the artist-in-residence programme of the Native Art Gallery. These programmes should help foster native crafts, plastic arts, and performing arts. Similar programmes, employing representatives of ethnic cultures, are part of the Arts and Traditions Hall. The use of artists allows for another type of perspective, quite individualistic, in interpreting cultural identity.

CMC has planned many opportunities for visitors not only to witness but to take part in activities and performances; for example : "Play a drum, paddle a fifteen-metre Haida canoe, dance a jig, participate

Figures 88, 88a, and 88b
Some of CMC's interpreters will re-create roles, of actual or typical figures from history, and present performances that communicate heritage information in entertaining formats. A particular effort has been made to involve natives in CMC's performing arts programmes.

period costume - to put themselves into the shoes of people of the past - and play a role in an unfolding drama; their participation may influence its outcome. This type of involvement can provide an emotionally-charged experience which is thought-provoking, challenges one's culturally-biased assumptions, stimulates discussion, and deepens interest in an issue, thereby establishing a setting for better intercultural understanding.

A dynamic approach to interpretation also helps ensure an information-rich environment. Those museum visitors accustomed to new information technologies tend to assess every environment they enter for its information potential, and abandon any found wanting. Museums using traditional interpretive media are judged as information-poor environments. World's fairs, science centres, and theme parks are relatively rich in information, thanks largely to their programmability - that is, the ability to change their information content often. Labels rarely change, but films, soundtracks, live animation and demonstrations can change regularly. Most of CMC's exhibition areas have been designed as programmable spaces. Part of the History Hall's information content is embodied in the building reconstructions, which will change little. Extensive use of live interpretation, to vary messages through different performances, compensates. At the other extreme the Arts and Traditions Hall is almost entirely a multimedia environment. Here the artifacts are only one element of communication; projected images and sound are just as important and are highly reprogrammable.

The environmental reconstructions are stage-sets for programmable interpretation. Museum dioramas have long striven for realism - often quite successfully - through attention to detail, devotion to accuracy, and the skill of their creators. But the suspension of disbelief demanded from their observers is difficult to maintain for long. Their static nature soon makes it apparent that they are not the 'real thing', especially when they are of a reduced scale. CMC has made its reconstructions life-size, and large enough to fill the angle of vision of the onlooker. Not only live interpreters, but also new video projection technologies give the reconstructions the same dynamic character that the real thing would have. Video projection has advantages over traditional film projection technology which is more common in museums. The hardware is more durable. And there is the possibility of interactivity when the source of images is laser discs. One application would be a selection of environmental

Figures 89 and 89a
There will be opportunities at CMC for visitors to dress up in costumes of other cultures and other periods, as an aid to experiencing aspects of the lifestyles of other peoples.

in a fur-trade ceremony, attend an 18th-century wedding, join an immigrant family as they step off the train into a new world and life in 19th-century western Canada." [12] Some exhibits allow for handling and use of artifact replicas. At times visitors will be invited to don a reproduction of a

backgrounds projected in each section of the History Hall. Visitors then could choose to see, for example, the New France section in a siege context, with explosions and flames surrounding the market square. Or the Prairie environment might be viewed either in a winter snowfall or in spring with flocks of geese passing overhead.

Combined, the screens of its two theatres and Médiathèque, the projection scrim and rear projection screens in the Grand Hall, the vault ceilings in the History Hall, a projection wall in the Children's Museum, and similar facilities in other exhibition areas, will give CMC almost 100,000 sq.' (9290 sq.m.) of projection space. In the History Hall the ceilings have been finished in double layers of drywall to make them suitable for projection; even the water-sprinkler nozzles have been inset and equipped with white covers. This helps make the Hall programmable. Video projectors, linked to laser disc image-banks, allow projection of different backgrounds to support theatrical performances there or re-create environmental effects of visitors' choice. This special use of moving images at CMC will continue the successful documentary film tradition of the NFB and CBC, on which Canadians have been raised.

A further medium for interpretation, particularly useful for customized tours, is the technology referred to as audio-tours or acoustiguides. Museums have found them a quite popular service; audio-interpreted exhibits arouse higher than normal visitor interest.[13] A survey of visitors to the Victoria Memorial Museum Building in 1986 identified a wish for audio-tours. They are not an alternative to visual interpretive techniques but rather to textual labels. The latter's problem is the difficulty of looking at both label and exhibit simultaneously; switching back and forth can become tedious. Audio interpretation, by appealing to a sense other than that used to view exhibits, is less distracting. It also makes the museum less reliant on human tour-guides, usually in shorter supply than audio-tour devices. Furthermore, these devices make it possible to produce a range of tours that meet personal needs, whereas guided tours must focus on what interests the group as a whole. Theoretically museums could customize tours for every individual, taking into account the language and the interests of the user, time available for the tour, the visitor's attention span, and the desired level of complexity of the message. In practice it is difficult to create the

number of different tours needed to accommodate all possible variations.

Cassette tape players are commonly used by museums for audio-tours, for various reasons. They are relatively inexpensive and their rental generates revenue for the institution. Most people are familiar with their operation. Members of a group can rent individual machines yet all be exposed to the same information for later discussion. Different tapes can be created to give a variety of tours. And the machines are adaptable to the needs of the hard-of-hearing. However, taped narration is a strictly linear and sequential form of communication obliging those taking an audio-tour to follow a precise, inflexible route. An alternative are audio devices installed in the exhibit areas themselves. Infra-red induction loop or low-power FM systems transmit messages to local area receivers, which may be stationed by the exhibit or carried about by visitors. They allows users to go from exhibit to exhibit in any order desired. The FM system can also use several channels to provide different messages (e.g. levels of complexity, languages). But the cost of these technologies is relatively high, the looping of the messages obliges the visitor to wait while they cycle back to the start before listening to the messages in their entirety, and sometimes messages broadcast from neighbouring stations interfere with one another.

Figure 90
Cassette tape players are available to provide audio guided tours through CMC's exhibitions.

CMC is presently using tape players for audio-tours; a rental counter is opposite the main entrance. However, the potential of a new option - referred to as a Personal, or Portable, Curator - is also being explored. One design is based on compact disc technology, another on magnetic computer memory. The latter is a device about the size of a walkman and can be clipped onto a pocket or belt. When in range of an exhibit prepared with supplementary inform-ation, it automatically loads the exhibit's data (via digital broadcast) and informs the user, by a beep and the illumination of the unit's LED, that the information is ready to be played back at leisure. This system permits users to select their own tour routes, or follow a route prescribed by a customized printed itinerary which CMC would provide, and it allows for easy updating of the information at local exhibits. It solves the drawbacks of the tape player and broadcast loop systems, but is still in the conceptual stage.

Outreach

So far, most of this chapter relates to CMC's efforts to communicate with its *visitors*. Yet its potential audience is far greater than those who come through its doors. If its messages, and the opportunities for people from different cultures to converse and reach mutual understanding, are to have any impact on society then CMC needs to reach beyond the minority that traditionally considers museum-going a worthwhile leisure activity. It must attract larger audiences to visit. It must provide content of sufficient interest and variety to encourage visitors to return repeatedly. To those who are unable to come, it must reach out and share any programmes capable of being exported beyond its walls. This is a huge challenge, but no national museum can rightfully turn away from it. CMC's travelling exhibits and the electronic databases of its Médiathèque represent outreach efforts. An even more powerful tool for mass communication exists, although few museums have ventured beyond sporadic minor excursions into its exploitation : television.

In the Information Age museums must define their place within the evolving electronic network; new models are needed to deal with the classic problems of outreach, both national and international. The solution lies in the electronic highways being laid to convey the information products of the new age. The mass media, and particularly television, offer tremendous opportunities for museums to raise public awareness about themselves and the heritage they protect, to attract audiences in greater numbers, and to make museum resources and experiences available in homes and schools.

We are beginning to appreciate the pervasive effect of television on Western society. Thanks to the combination of satellite, cable, and traditional broadcasting technologies, 99% of Canadian homes receive television signals, and 78% receive more than 20 channels; the fact that almost half of Canadian households own VCRs further suggests the prominent role of television in our lives. It is the most successful competitor for our leisure-time, attracting each viewer for an average of three hours a day (twice as long for children). Over two-thirds of the funds allocated by the federal government to the cultural sector are for television. Cities such as Toronto, Vancouver, Montreal, Seattle, Dallas, Indianapolis, New Orleans have spent millions of dollars to create super-domes. Why? Not merely as shrines or pilgrimage destinations for the North American sports cult. It is because television makes it possible to diffuse the message of the cult, to nurture and develop an audience of millions, and to capture that audience's interest long enough for sponsors to sell them goods and services. Fans go to the big dome not only to witness the event or to win the peer-recognition and status that their pilgrimage earns them, but also to be part of a new commun-ication experience shared by thousands. Disney Corporation happily admits that much of its success is owed to television preconditioning people the world over to feel that Disney creations are an intimate and indispensable part of their life, and that a visit to a Disney theme park is nothing short of a cultural pilgrimage. Television is now such an integral part of our heritage that, as the Smithsonian has found, relics associated with television shows or personalities have a tremendous attraction for museum-goers.

Television is thus producing icons of the type that museums employ to anchor the experiential grids we use to comprehend day-to-day experiences. Also, it is itself a major input to those grids, offering experiences not normally available in everyday life. It is an interpretive - a mediating - phenomenon, allowing us to relate various experiences into our mental framework.

Yet television has serious drawbacks as a mediator. It is rarely possible to test the reality of video experiences : we must accept what is offered on faith, or not at all. While it offers sensory experi-ences, it does not necessarily teach judgement, is no guide to ethics or values; indeed, it tends to decontextualize information and so make it incoherent to its recipients and therefore irrelevant. By transmitting the same context-free information to everyone, it has a homogenizing effect upon culture; there can be no response to the centralized, one-way communication of the broadcast networks which are television's reigning paradigm. The International Synergy Institute points out that this homogenization, by stifling diversity, is counter-evolutionary and results in greater vulnerability; yet a planetary television network could be used to facilitate the harmonious development of a global society, by providing a forum for intercultural communication. [14] To realize this are needed : two-way, interactive, video-based telecommunications; and a form of image-based communication, which will not obliterate cultural diversity by superimposing a limited set of linguistic perspectives. Television is a medium that needs qualitative content; museums have that content, and need instruments of expression. The obvious solution seems an alliance; for CMC, this could contribute to its goal of becoming a museum-without-walls.

Corporate broadcasters do not have the only approach to the use of telecommunications technology. The telephone is as fundamental to our daily lives as television, and there has long been a desire to augment it with visual two-way communications. In the mid-'70's Canada and the United States built a Communications Technology Satellite to test the feasibility of one-way and two-way video communications. This experiment paved the way for present-day communications satellites which make possible videoconferencing, although only large corporations can afford the expense of analogue video transmission. As digital compression techniques improve and integrate with the emerging broadband digital networks, costs will become more affordable. [15]

Teleconferencing technology has been put to a number of creative and humanistic uses, with control over content often in the hands of the users. As long ago as 1965 the Early Bird satellite was the vehicle for a two-way teleconference between high schools in France and the United States; students were to discuss language teaching on either side of the Atlantic, but became caught up in a more free-ranging discussion on cultural topics close to their hearts. In 1976 New York University set up a two-way interactive cable-TV system for senior citizens of a Pennsylvania urban community. It connected three neighbourhood centres, City Hall,

the local Social Security administration, courthouse and high schools; programming was also transmitted to cable-equipped homes, so seniors could participate by telephone. There were government, social service, and educational programmes, as well as composite-image sing-alongs, quiz shows, poetry readings, and programmes of oral history and folklore. The 1980's have seen more projects creating 'space bridges' between different countries, for real-time interactive video communication; the best-known is the 1985 Live Aid benefit in which rock groups in London and Philadelphia held simultaneous concerts, beamed live to six continents. [16]

Prominent in this field are Kit Galloway and Sherrie Rabinowitz, operating under the corporate name of Mobile Image. They have engaged in innovative projects exploring and developing the visual possibilities and interactive communication potential of two-way satellite transmission, to allow free and creative expression for participants. As artists using telecommunications technology as their medium, their canvas is 'virtual space' : locations having no physical or geographic reality, but existing only within the electronic environment - conversational networks - in which live interaction takes place, viewable only on video screens where separate images may be merged. [17] Their first effort was the Satellite Arts Project (1977), which brought together in virtual space two sets of dancers - one in Maryland, the other in California - to perform scored improvisations in unison on-screen; each pair could see the composite image on screens surrounding them, and develop their performance in response to what they saw. In the Hole in Space project (1980) a live, two-way, interactive satellite connection between the Lincoln Center in New York and Los Angeles' Broadway store allowed passers-by to see full-sized images of each other and to communicate if they wished. This unannounced programme ran for three evenings and offered viewers no information on the nature of the project. At first it aroused only curiosity and naive playfulness; but, as people realized that they had stumbled on a live link across the nation, interest grew and more sophisticated communications took place. Strangers played charades, casual flirtations occurred, divided families held reunions, friends passed messages. On the last evening crowds gathered for a chance to participate in the cross-country communion. For the arts festival accompanying the 1984 Olympic Games, the Electronic Cafe project connected restaurants in culturally distinct communities of Los Angeles : Korean, Hispanic, Black, Venice Beach, and the international community (via the Museum of Contemporary Art, which commissioned the project); computer-video equipment linked each location to the others through telephone lines. Restaurant patrons could develop cross-town conversations through images, drawings, and the written word; they could communicate, or create together, ideas, jokes, poetry, or line drawings, and save their creations by recording them on computer and optical disc databases. More recently, Mobile Image's Light Transition experiment brought together live video of horizon views off the east and west coasts in a split-screen image that was inserted every half-hour into the afternoon programming of a satellite superstation.

These projects illustrate the potential for using telecommunications technologies in non-standard ways : not to perpetuate stereotypes or cultural values of the establishment, as corporate TV networks are often accused of doing, but to empower users to communicate on their own terms, to give them a tool to describe themselves to others. For museums this offers one means to bring into contact different cultures from across the globe and help them understand each other. CMC's experience with the television industry has not been extensive, although in 1980 its experimental programme, Telemuse, tested the potential of Telidon (Canada's videotex technology) to provide information, promote the museum, and create educational outreach packages. Packages of texts and colour graphics were distributed via databases such as TV Ontario's OECA, CBC's IRIS, the Department of Communication's Genesys, Parliament's OASIS, and Infomart. Telidon had drawbacks, however : it was not a truly interactive system (viewers could only control the flow of information, and respond to questions through a keyboard); low-resolution screens called for large lettering, which obliged textual elements to be kept brief; only computer graphics, not photographs or moving images, could be used; and the system was slow. For the types of uses that interest museums, interactive laser disc systems and the telecommunications technology used by Mobile Image have far greater promise.

The full potential for use of television, to enhance the museum experience and as an outreach tool to help achieve CMC's national mandate, was not apparent at the beginning of the New Accommodation project; it became so as construction progressed. Fortunately not too late to prevent installation of the necessary infrastructure to allow the museum to become a "universal" facility for television production and transmission. CMC augmented its existing video production unit with new expertise and equipment. Its fibre-optic, universal network plays a vital role in the television system, allowing the whole museum to be the television facility, with projection equipment and monitors at many locations : lobbies and lounges, cafeteria and restaurant, reception areas, core exhibits, and the theatre. The system needs no central point to which signals must be channelled. Each of over 1000 Universal Cable Outlets can independently receive or transmit and, via the network, can be connected to any or all of the other outlets on either a temporary or a permanent basis. Thus audio, full colour video, and TV signals can be fed directly to and from numerous locations throughout the museum, or to the outside world via the common carrier, broadcasting services, or satellite. A TV studio in the curatorial block provides post-production facilities for mixing and repackaging (if desired) the signals from video capture points, before sending them elsewhere in the building or outside.

This decentralized design removes the restriction of having to create productions within a single studio. The whole museum is the studio, and any event occurring almost anywhere can be easily captured and transmitted. The main exhibition halls have tailored TV facilities to permit more professional productions, and CMC's theatre has a fully contained, self-supporting production centre. The curatorial block and the external site are also part of the network, while a further facility permits the Médiathèque's visual and audio databases to be integrated into the diffusion system. The theatre and Grand Hall, and to a slightly lesser extent the environmental reconstruction exhibits in the History Hall and Native Peoples Hall, will be the major sites for television transmission and recording; camera positioning, shooting angles, lighting requirements, and cabling had to be taken into account in designing the exhibitions. The numerous performances scheduled for these locations will be a principal source of CMC's television productions. Their video-recording will allow them to be shown to visitors not present at the events, to be transmitted live to distant locations, or to be packaged for national or global sale and distribution.

The system will give a good deal of flexibility : images and sound can be captured anywhere in the building and redistributed for display elsewhere. For example, visitors in the museum's eateries can be given indirect access to special events then going on elsewhere in the museum; or, programmes in

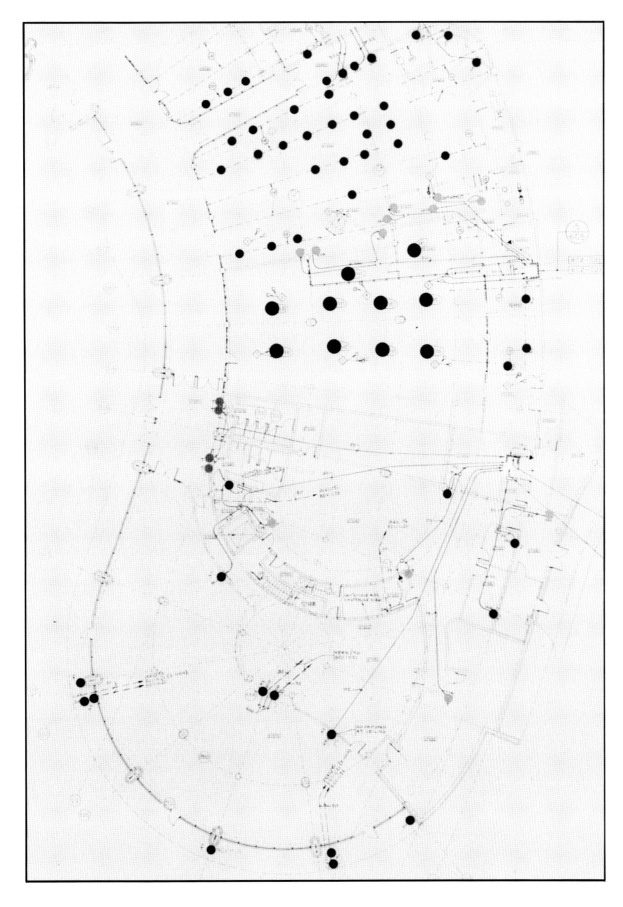

Figure 91
The whole of CMC is wired up in a communication network that will allow transmission of TV (or other data) signals from any node to another. This plan of the offshoot wing containing the cafeteria and the Network Control Centre shows the numerous locations of such nodes (Universal Cable Outlets) in that part of the building.

different exhibitions can be sampled and shown in the lobbies, to make newly-arrived visitors aware of events underway which they may wish to hurry on to watch in person. It will also be possible to capture several events occurring simultaneously, in the museum or outside, repackage them, and redistribute them. There are many ways in which CMC can put a system of this nature to good use. At first, as it accustoms itself to using this technology new to it, CMC will concentrate on mini-productions for internal use. But it will increasingly seek partners across Canada and around the world to create cooperative productions and live transmissions linking different communities and different cultures. Other national or provincial museums, open air museums, heritage sites, or cultural performance centres, would be natural participants in a growing electronic network for cultural diffusion. There is not yet a single museum anywhere that has full television capability within its facilities. CMC will be a prototype that may encourage others to follow its example. A handful of museums in Canada have auditoriums which, at relatively little cost, could be equipped for satellite downlinks. Worldwide, perhaps 10% of all museums could afford the few thousand dollars necessary to acquire downlink facilities. There is a smaller, but growing, number of centres around the world with uplink capabilities.

An intermuseum satellite network could conceivably be only a decade down the road; CMC intends to help bring such a network into existence.

Some of CMC's productions will be live, to give them a freshness, immediacy, and spontaneity that over-edited commercial television programmes lack. Live presentations are essential to interactivity, accomplished along the same sort of lines as the projects of Mobile Image; it is desirable to build the audience into the productions, to allow audiences in different locations to see each other and their reactions to events being shown. To reach larger audiences it will be necessary to package pro-grammes for delayed transmission. This may range from electronic news gathering (ENG), for furnishing broadcast networks with video news releases on museum events, to major products incorporating recordings of spectacles performed at the museum combined with archival material from CMC's laser disc databases, or other elements. In the former case the freshness of the information is important, as ENG material on museums is likely to have a lifespan of only a few days.

CMC is not entering the broadcasting business, however. The large commercial broadcast networks are not greatly interested in culture (excepting

Figure 92
The numerous performing arts events put on by CMC will provide some of the content for television transmissions.

popular culture), since it doesn't sell to large audiences. Certainly CMC will be able to produce some programmes attractive enough to interest the major networks, preferably through cooperative (cost- and profit-sharing) ventures, or by hosting a network production - that is, providing the event and the space. But it is more interested in special-audience markets, served by narrowcast or direct institution-to-institution transmission; educational TV, PBS, university and local community channels, the culture network of Pay TV - these are the closest existing models. Another option is to sell videotape or laser disc copies of programmes to participants (for whom the recordings validate their experience) and to the public at large. Outdoor festivals, cultural ceremonies, concerts, receptions, VIP visits, dramatic performances set against the backdrop of the re-created historical environments, lectures, con-ferences, seminars, craft workshops or demon-strations, documentaries on museum operations, all provide ample content for diffusion; some take the form of the 'events' which drive the mass media. CMC will never have the money to buy sufficient media time, but by offering quality information, strong visuals, topical commentaries within the museum's expertise, and a range of cultural and heritage events, it can make itself attractive to the media.

Television is a tool of use to CMC in achieving many of its goals and its central mission of fostering intercultural understanding; this is equally true for other museums. Mobile Image has demonstrated the potential for live, interactive telecommunications to erect bridges between cultures and allow their representatives to interpret themselves to each other in free and creative fashions. Language differences are no longer such a barrier when communication is through a visual medium. The educational potential of television has long been known and successful application of interactive communications techno-logy has already taken place in distance education. Universities offer an important target for joint ventures, since many already possess television or telecommunications facilities, special collections of information capable of electronic diffusion, and a rich resource of expertise to disseminate. Models for satellite link-ups are being planned for institutions such as the proposed University of the Common-wealth, and the Smithsonian Institution's intended University of the Air. The latter will use television, interactive laser discs, and printed materials to take educational programmes into people's homes and create an educational system convenient to the student, not the institution; the project takes

advantage of the dominance of television in the lives of North America's youth. Closer to home, the Commission Scolaire Outaouais-Hull has broken new ground (for schools) in using computers and telecommunications to allow its students to conduct electronic correspondence with African pen-pals. This intercultural communication system lacks the means to support its textual transmissions with visual imagery; CMC could, through a cooperative project with the schoolboard, fill that gap.

The opportunity exists - if we will only grasp it - to take the museum into the classrooms and into the homes of the nation, linking students and the general public with information on a scale never before conceived, and sharing with them whatever of the museum experience can be captured in audiovisual form. For CMC this opportunity provides a key to achieving national presence, by extending its physical accessibility with electronic accessibility to regional, national, and international audiences. This outreach, not feasible until now, can communicate with more people than travelling exhibits ever could. In this way CMC can truly be a resource for every-one to exploit : the personal electronic museum can exist in every household. At the same time national outreach is important to CMC as a means of building public support and attracting visitors to the museum itself in greater numbers. To do so it must advertise its attractions more effectively, to let people know the rich information resources, the stimulating exhibits, and the entertaining events they can encounter there. This will pre-programme them for a visit, much as Disney does for its theme parks, whetting their appetites for a taste of the real thing.

In the early 1970's a survey of the Canadian museum-going public found that most respondents believed that more advertising and information about museums would increase the probability of them visiting more regularly. Televised promotion of the Tutankhamun blockbuster at the British Museum stimulated increased visitation.[18] The competition for the leisure-time of tourists is already becoming noticeably more intense, and the trend may be expected to continue. This competition will likely be waged primarily through the most popular mass medium, television. Since museums cannot afford to buy a significant television presence through commercials, they must respond to the needs of television programmers for what the latter consider broadcast-worthy content. The cost of acquiring the necessary production equipment and media skills, and in creating the types of events that interest television networks, is not inconsiderable; but it will

153

be offset by its promotional value to the museum, and in revenues from sales of subscriptions to museum programmes. The costs could be further lessened through cooperative ventures by museums to promote each other and jointly seek media coverage.

Television is only part of CMC's efforts to communicate with its visitors and non-visitors. Commitment to one medium does not imply neglect of others; diversification is important to reach the widest audience possible : different jobs call for different tools. It is important to take advantage of all technologies, all techniques that might bring members of the public into a greater, and more rewarding involvement with the museum. We learn best through *participation*, whether intellectual, physical, or emotional, and through direct experience. We learn best from each other through interaction : through communication and conversation, be it verbal or visual. The museum is a facilitator here, providing a forum, channels of communication, and settings which provoke questions and stimulate discussion; it is a mediator between human and artifactual representatives of different cultures. By playing this role, the museum can help its users shape their sense of reality and their sense of possibility. If we are to see a planetary society in which many cultures can survive and co-exist harmoniously and in mutual understanding, it must come through interaction and communication. McLuhan's dream of a Global Village, in the best sense of his meaning, may arise from the intercultural communication that museums can nurture, if only they are willing to see themselves as nothing more than bridge-builders.

the museum as mentor

Many argue that museums' fundamental mission is to educate. This is probably the predominant paradigm for museums now, although it has been broadly interpreted so that education may range from the display of artifacts to the creation of highly structured educational programmes. From this perspective, other museum functions such as collections development, research, and exhibition are not ends in themselves, but means to serve the educational mission; publications, tours, special events, interpretive techniques are all seen as educational tools.[1] It is true that museums have long engaged in efforts to educate the public, well before it became common to view education as their driving spirit. Since the 1960's there has been a proliferation of museums founded with education explicitly as their primary goal; science centres and children's museums in particular have this character, reflected in their emphasis on experiential, interactive, hands-on exhibits, and a consequent devaluation of artifact preservation which might otherwise be an obstacle to those exhibit techniques.

While it is easy to view museums as a significant element in the educational fabric of society, there has in recent years been a growing concern that the education paradigm has led museums somewhat astray. Visitor surveys have made it abundantly clear that people have a variety of motivations for visiting museums. Education is one, but the need for recreation is just as strong, and there are other needs for social opportunities and for affirming a link with

Figure 93
The National Museums of Canada have, for decades, provided educational programmes for school groups such as this one, gathered in front of the Victoria Memorial Museum Building. Less attention was paid in the past, however, to programmes for adults.

the (sacred) past. Concern has arisen within the museum community that over-enthusiasm for the educational function, and an associated professionalization of museum education, have compartmentalized that function when it should be an integral part of all aspects of museum operations, and have transplanted educational methods from schools to museums to create a *teaching* environment there. As a result, educational programmes have tended to be directed predominantly at children, since they seemed in greatest need of educational instruction. Correspondingly, adults were neglected.

With new perceptions of education has come increasing discussion about "de-schooling" museums - and in fact de-schooling education generally. Like museums, education has acquired a poor image, with connotations of prerequisites, dictatorial instruction, mandatory attendance, assignments, exams, and so on. Schools have become relatively impoverished in experiential content, compared to newer types of educational institutions offering a more interactive and stimulating environment. There is a growing need and demand for re-education, as social and technological change make old skills and old knowledge redundant more rapidly, and as im-proving educational levels of one segment of the population stimulate the desire for more learning opportunities. At the same time there is a growth in verbal illiteracy amongst the underprivileged - or at least an enhanced awareness of this problem - while *visual* literacy is also growing in this age of TV and videos, yet wants guidance. Part of the problem is that the underprivileged lack access to knowledge, in its institutionalized form of higher education. The widening gap between the 'haves' and 'have-nots', which undermines the democratic roots of society, is partly a consequence of the equation of knowledge and wealth in the new Information Age.

Education, broadly interpreted, is the development of knowledge, understanding, skills, and character, to programme values into its recipients and thereby influence their behaviour. In essence its role is to transmit culture. However, its popular image associates it with formal schooling and the negative image that too often has. While schools have captive audiences, museums do not and should not cultivate a school image by emphasizing education. In the context of current societal changes it is increasingly appreciated that we must develop a new educational environment which is not based upon the scholastic paradigm but which recognizes that other institutions - such as museums - have an equally critical part in

creating opportunities for learning, especially lifelong learning.

Like the distinction between communication and conversation (in chapter 6), it is useful to distinguish between education and learning. Learning is a continuing and permanent process, an activity inherent in living which helps us to survive and progress - to come to terms with, and to exploit, our knowledge environment. It is an interactive process in which one encounters something different from what one knows and reaches an understanding of the experience.[2] Learning is essentially a self-directed, personal process, not limited to activities or experiences occurring within the framework of scholastic programmes. The school-based paradigm of education compartmentalizes, and implicitly limits, the learning process by assuming that leisure-time is non-learning time. The de-schooling philosophy seeks recognition that learning is not something over which the formal educational system has monopolistic control. In the process of lifelong learning other socio-cultural institutions have an equally vital role to play. The knowledge and expertise they have to offer is as valuable as that acquired in school.

Museums are essential components of this new educ-ational paradigm. The Commission on Museums for a New Century, considering the future of North American museums, committed itself to the concept of learning, rather than education, as fundamental to museums' mission :

> Learning in museums is a spontaneous, indiv-idualized process; it cannot be imposed on the visitor. When museum education emphasizes teaching and verbal communication it does a disservice to the museum as a learning environment .... Museums provide a learning environment and incentives fundamentally different from those provided by schools. These differences produce different effects. Museums stimulate the imagination, sharpen powers of observation and enrich thinking. They encourage an appreciation of other cultures, other times, other world views .... They more directly involve the visitor.[3]

Museums are informal learning centres, where people can spend their leisure-time in activities related to their personal interests and goals, where they can find entertainment and education in the same package. As with communication, the museum is a facilitator in the learning process. It creates the opportunities for people to expand their knowledge and broaden their horizons. It provides the tools, and imparts the skills to use them, for exploiting the opportunities. It stimulates and encourages the desire to learn. The task of museums is not to impose values or ideas on its visitors but to empower them to formulate their own opinions and shape their cultural sensibilities through self-conducted exploration and discovery. What may need to be *taught* are not the products of knowledge, but the skills to interpret data (e.g. artifacts) and to synthesize information into understanding. The purpose of this teaching is only to make museum-users self-sufficient in applying the museum's resources to meet their own needs for knowledge.

In facilitating learning, certain principles are important : accessibility, participation, interactivity, democratization, free choice, and responsiveness to individual needs; CMC is committed to delivering all of these to its users. For example, its strong interest in employing interactive video in the museum is not motivated by fascination with a trendy new technology, but by the public access it gives to vast quantities of information. Through it users can chart their own voyages of exploration, according to self-developed agendas based on personal interests and aptitudes, and make discoveries which leave a lasting impression because of the active role the user has played in the process. How far to plunge into the information resources of CMC is left to the individual visitor.

CMC makes a distinction in its programming for different periods based - like the streaker/stroller/student classification - on the belief that museums must respond to different needs of visitors. Educational programmes dominate its daytime mode of operation, and entertainment its nighttime mode. This distinction is partly artificial, representing not a true segregation of educational and entertaining elements, but different mixes of those two complementary qualities. Daytime mode - which applies during weekdays from opening to 5.00 p.m. - is directed primarily at visitors overtly seeking learning experiences. Formal programmes for school groups, hobbyists and others will be run mostly by day, and self-directed learners may tour the exhibits, converse with interpreters, witness or participate in animated presentations high in information content, delve into the databases created by the museum, and so on. Daytime programmes will be mostly free, so that their educational opportunities are accessible regardless of ability to pay : this is a keystone of democratic society. The federal government - faced

with enormous demands and competing priorities for resources - can no longer provide the level of financial support national museums need to carry out all their functions to the highest levels of quality, and has encouraged the national museums to seek funding through admission charges. CMC has resisted this approach to revenue generation. Part of the rationale for the daytime/ nighttime modes is that the latter, by incorporating more conventional (as well as some quite unconventional) entertainment events for which audiences may be charged, will help pay for the free experience available during the daytime.

Educational programming

The museum's shift of emphasis from educational institution to learning resource - from teacher to mentor - does not imply the abandonment of formal, structured educational programmes. They remain an important tool for facilitating museum-users' access to, and for guiding the exploration of, informational resources. Furthermore they are a necessary vehicle for collaboration between the museum and schools. Programmes for schoolchildren have been museums' most frequent educational offering; consequently school groups have made up a large part of the visitor population.[4]

CMC's former home, the Victoria Memorial Museum Building, did not adequately provide for the needs of school or other organized groups. A teachers' evaluation of the exhibitions there concluded that : more environmental reconstructions and greater opportunities for hands-on activities were desirable; exhibit themes should unfold according to a recognizable, logical progression; more space was needed for group circulation; and core exhibits ought to be clearly visible to at least fifteen students at a time. These needs have been met in the new museum and adequate facilities have been provided for school groups, including reception areas, five classrooms, and a group lunchroom. While designing programmes for school-groups, CMC consulted with eleven school-boards and provincial Ministries of Education in Ontario and Quebec, to obtain information on curricula and on innovative teaching methods applicable to the museum's programmes.

Museums' educational programmes tend to be directed mostly at elementary school audiences. Since the habits these children learn often set their future tastes and attitudes, it is to museums'

*Figures 94, 94a and 94b
Demonstrations are a common feature
of educational programmes. But it is
also important to give children
opportunities to participate; through
participation they may discover things
for themselves and develop an interest
in pursuing knowledge further.*

advantage to win a place in their hearts. CMC has
taken pains to plan for this audience, which includes
a variety of groups. It expects regular visits from
regional school groups, from junior kindergarten to
Grade 8, within a 100 km. radius of the National
Capital : regular classes, gifted/enrichment classes,
and language immersion classes. Programmes have
been designed for special education classes (e.g.
emotionally disturbed, slow learner, or handicapped
students), classes mixing handicapped and non-
handicapped children, and classes mixing students
of different ages. Various children's organizations
also send groups to visit museums; CMC can offer
programmes to enable Guides and Scouts, for
instance, to earn Nature or Culture Lore badges.
Cultural exchange groups, day-care centres, summer
camps, are other audience segments at which CMC is
targeting programmes. Finally, children who visit
with their families, mostly on weekends, require
programmes that they can share with adults.

Programmes for these groups have numerous goals.
For example, to enhance children's understanding of
their own cultural heritage and the cultures of other
peoples. And to provide opportunities for children to
participate in active discovery, and the means to
develop skills in interpreting material culture, thus
equipping them for independent study and observ-
ation on return visits. The programmes have to
complement the curriculum in social studies,
language arts, music, drama, and the visual arts, yet
be flexible enough to respond to the precise needs of
every school or other group.

Most programmes will operate from October to
April, in a variety of forms. Guided programmes
will be developed in consultation with individual
teachers and will employ teaching methods involving
enquiry-based learning, such as hands-on use of
artifacts, 'discovery visits' to the exhibitions,
roleplaying, group discussions, problem-solving,
dramatization and model construction. Live

animation activities in the exhibition halls will be
incorporated in programmes where appropriate.
Half-day visit workshop programmes will explore
topics such as native art, ethnic crafts and skills,
creative writing, dramatic production, or may be
geared to specific research projects; later they will
be extended to one- or two-day guided workshops.
Unguided school groups can engage in self-directed
programmes that their teachers organize from a
package that includes floor-plan, treasure trails,
suggested themes and tours, and worksheets. They
also have access to the audio-tours. Special
programmes will allow for more extensive use of
museum resources; for example, several visits to the
museum to complete a particular unit of study, or to
research, write, and perform a roleplaying scenario in
one of the reconstructed environmental exhibits. To
teachers alone, on their professional development
days, CMC will offer workshops and seminars
showing how to use the museum as a learning
resource.

At the beginning of the tourist season (May - June),
CMC's resources will be diverted froms schools to

tourists. In place of guided programmes for school groups, there will be pre-booked (or drop-in) presentations in CMC's theatres, audio-tours, the self-directed programmes mentioned above, and the greater volume of in-gallery animation activities planned for the summer. Emphasis will be on content suitable for older children.

These programmes will be conducted by volunteers trained by local teachers or specialists in animation and communication. Their users will have access to the specially-developed educational collection of artifacts, which allows for hands-on activities here, in the Children's Museum, and in the animation or demonstration activities in the galleries. The database of visual/textual records of CMC's artifacts will be accessible. So too will be materials such as teachers' guides, gallery guides, activity sheets, and audiovisual aids, to help teachers plan their visits and make most effective use of museum resources. A collection of props, costumes, models, and other teaching aids is being built up for roleplaying and other theatrical activities. CMC hopes to discourage the roller-coaster tour, from which students learn very little, and encourage school groups instead to spend a little time, interact with the exhibits, and discover what the museum has to offer.

Timetabling constraints make it more difficult for secondary school groups to make extensive use of CMC's educational programmes. To justify the expense and time out of the classroom, secondary school groups require programmes that are highly pertinent to their studies - general overview tours are not appropriate. Guided programmes will be more carefully geared to curriculum-related themes; roleplaying and improvisational drama will be used to help students better understand the cultural contexts of the museum's artifacts. A possible linkage between CMC and high schools would be through a drama programme involving the museum's collection of masks and ethnic puppetry or the theatrical productions it will host. CMC could offer courses through local universities and colleges, or provide mentors (resource persons) for independent study projects, at the enriched level. Another link to high schools will be through cooperative work/study placements. For students who cannot visit, outreach programmes will give access to CMC's educational resources.

Children's educational programmes have long been a feature of CMC services; now these services are extended to adults and to the casual visitor. The decision to aim programmes at adults was influenced by a number of factors. Adults in the 40-64 age group are becoming a larger and better-educated segment of the population, with greater expectations from their leisure-time activities. Their growing demand for more learning opportunities and the contemporary pressure for on-going re-training also call for positive action by institutions which foster the learning process. Adult, or continuing, education is attracting increasing attention from academics, educational organizations, and the public. Several museums, mostly American, have demonstrated that popular adult programmes can be operated that enhance the museum's image as a dynamic place offering a variety of interesting activities. These programmes permit closer links between adults and museums' artifactual collections and research findings.

Like children, adults also need to be taught the skills to make effective use of museum resources and to interpret material culture. The emerging information-based society is a learning society in which lifelong education is the norm. Museums can play an important role in this society, for they have no stringent admission standards or prerequisites, demand no attendance for fixed terms or at times which suit the institution. Rather they informally provide the learning resources and the tools to exploit them, for all to use according to their own curricula and timetables. For those who wish it, participation in programmes could be recorded to qualify for a 'diploma' in heritage studies from CMC.

Thus CMC is developing a wide range of programmes for diverse target groups; for example, single events for tourists, series events (with pre-registration) for the local population, special guided tours for VIPs, dignitaries, or special interest groups. For tour groups that pre-book CMC will create customized packages : tours organized according to particular themes, behind-the-scenes visits, scheduled Imax/Omnimax presentations, and food services. Workshops, seminars, lectures, field excursions, audio-tours, customized self-guided tours, the live animation events in the galleries, the special visual and performing arts events, credit courses through universities : all are elements of CMC programming plans. The emphasis is on self-motivation and self-direction, with programmes to enhance visitors' ability to adapt CMC's resources to their own interests and needs, and again on participatory and interactive activities wherever possible. CMC seeks cooperative ventures with tourist agencies, educational institutions, and special

159

interest organizations, to develop and implement these programmes.

The Children's Museum

CMC's Children's Museum is separate from its other educational programmes - almost an independent satellite within the main museum. This is Canada's largest museum facility dedicated to children. The New Accommodation project gave the opportunity to re-examine the nature and level of services that CMC had long offered to children, and a facility designed specifically for children was proposed.

Why a Children's Museum? It is important to generate a liking for museums - an image of them as

sources of pleasure - in children from an early age; by so doing, museums ensure themselves of a future audience with some understanding of museum resources and how to use them. A second reason was that children make up such a large portion of CMC's total visitation that it seemed appropriate to create facilities especially for them - something not possible in its former, cramped quarters. In the early 1980's CMC booked over 15,000 students a year into its programmes, and 36,000 other schoolchildren visited annually in groups without pre-booking. Many more visited in family or informal groups. Most museums (CMC included) find that children make up between 40% to 60% of their visitors. The exhibits children encountered in the Victoria Memorial Museum Building were designed largely for adults. The

Figure 95
The Children's Museum is a very special part of CMC, a hive of fascinating, stimulating, and fun activities and experiences. It is being developed in phases, with half open in 1989 and the rest to follow shortly.

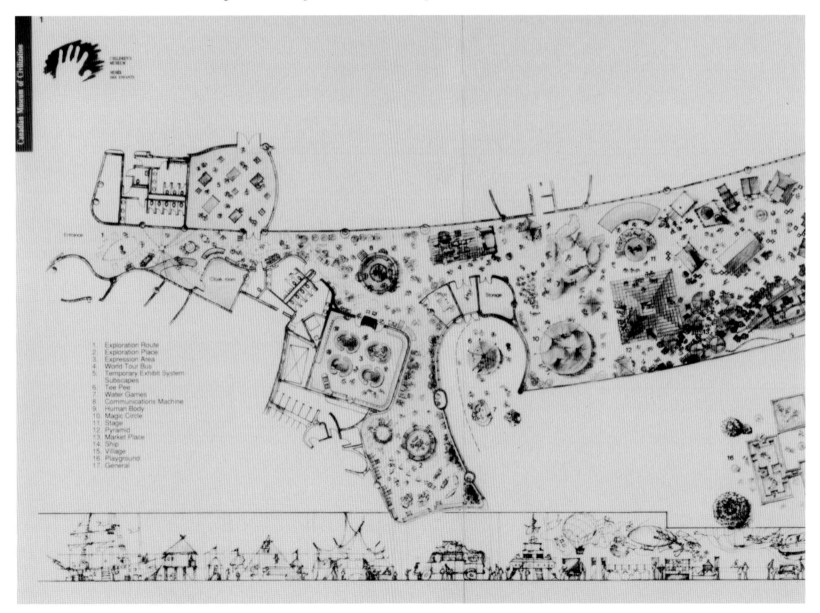

1. Exploration Route
2. Exploration Place
3. Expression Area
4. World Tour Bus
5. Temporary Exhibit System
   Subscapes
6. Tee Pee
7. Water Games
8. Communications Machine
9. Human Body
10. Magic Circle
11. Stage
12. Pyramid
13. Market Place
14. Ship
15. Village
16. Playground
17. General

complex concepts, vocabulary, physical character-istics, and types of barriers between visitor and exhibits, all made it difficult for pre-adolescents to understand fully the exhibition messages. Children can and do learn from adult-oriented exhibitions, but do so in a way different from adults. Since they do not think in complex or abstract terms, the abstract concepts symbolized by artifacts are often lost on children. Concepts mean little to children unless they have an experience to attach to them; they learn best not by simply being exposed to information but rather by sensory interaction with their environment. Physical and intellectual access by children to CMC's exhibits, artifacts, and research-based knowledge can be improved by providing exhibitions designed specifically to meet their needs.

The success of other institutions in meeting young audiences' requirements indicated that children's museums provide a very accessible, useable learning environment. There are over a hundred independent children's museums, or museums with special facilities for children, around the world. Most are in the United States; Canada has only a few. CMC's staff, looking for innovative exhibition techniques, visited children's museums at Boston, Indianapolis, Washington, Hamilton, London, Winnipeg, and Quebec, discovery rooms at the Royal Ontario

Museum, the Smithsonian, and Boston's Science Museum, and a number of other institutions dedi-cated to children. Others were investigated through their literature or contacts with their staff. Experts in children's fields were consulted during the design process. And input was sought from the intended audience : flyers asking children what they would like to see in CMC's Children's Museum were distributed by staff at Halloween, and through schools in Ottawa and Montreal.

Some children's museums are world-renowned, notably those in Boston and Indianapolis; these, together with such museums in Brooklyn and London, San Francisco's Exploratorium, and the Royal Ontario Museum's discovery room, served as the early inspirations for CMC's Children's Museum. Later a particularly exciting example was encountered in the Netherlands, and became another of the models used in CMC's design. This was the Children's Museum TM Junior, a satellite of Amsterdam's Tropenmuseum, an ethnological museum. In the late '60's the Tropenmuseum abandoned the didactic approach to exhibit interpretation in favour of allowing visitors to discover things for themselves; at the same time the display technique shifted from conventional showcases to environmental reconstructions, and the

Figures 96, 96a, 96b, and 96c
One source of inspiration for CMC's Children's Museum was the Tropenmuseum Junior. There children engage in cultural roleplaying, as a means of experiencing and under-standing the lifestyles of other peoples. Programmes are designed to bring into play all their senses, to reinforce the learning process.

emphasis from the artifacts themselves to the life-styles they reflected - cultures represented frequently from the viewpoints of their own members. When the museum set up its Children's Museum a few years later, all those philosophies were embodied in it. Its exhibitions highlight Third World cultures, notably those which have established emigrant communities in the Netherlands. They try to correct misconceptions and prejudices about these peoples, and to nurture a better intercultural understanding. The museum is filled with environmental recon-structions which incorporate interactive exhibits and hands-on opportunities. Through roleplaying, simulation games, and creation of vignettes, children are encouraged to put themselves in the places of people of other cultures, perform the daily tasks characteristic of those lifestyles, and thus reach an understanding of their values and perspectives. Sensory stimulation is an important part of the programmes; for example, food and cooking experiences bring olfactory and gustatory senses into play. So too is the temporary employment of living representatives of the culture, to research, animate and interpret the exhibits.

This is an approach that should be emulated. North American children are shown all sorts of horrors - abysmal poverty, starvation, race riots, warfare - daily on television, in the comfort of their homes; how can their inexperienced minds make sense of these events? A survey conducted by the Boston Children's Museum found that most children assumed they themselves would be caught up in one of the disasters they were used to witnessing on TV and die prematurely. That museum planned a special exhibit to prepare children for the likely bloodbath in South Africa. The Indianapolis Children's Museum also tries to promote better understanding between peoples of the world; for example, it has negotiated for an exchange of staff with the Soviet Union and China. A special exhibition by that museum, called "Kids Connect", is being brought to CMC's Children's Museum. Based on the Indianapolis Children's Museum Caplan collection of folk, fantasy, and play objects, and items from its Passport to the World gallery, the exhibition combats traditional stereotypes of other cultures by allowing visitors to share a sense of the playfulness that all cultures demonstrate through their works of imagination and creation. Toys and crafts from diverse cultures, a phone booth/pen pal station, interactive video, and opportunities for hands-on and personal creativity, feature in the exhibition.

The CMC Children's Museum is not a carbon copy of other institutions, nor an adjunct to the school experience. It is a classroom of a sort, but not one in the conventional sense. Its emphasis is on exploration and enquiry as learning strategies. It has been designed as an informal and comfortable space where children's natural abilities to learn rapidly from their environment are given fuller scope than formal learning situations - which sometimes tend to inhibit individuality, active participation, and natural curiosity - can provide. Most children's museums are based on an *educational* paradigm : the belief that school-developed learning techniques are suitable for museums. This may have some validity, since most cover a wide range of subjects - humanities, science, nature - in which hands-on can be a good general learning technique. But for a museum of human history a somewhat different approach seems necessary, especially when, as in CMC's case, the mission is to foster in children positive attitudes towards people of different cultures and to stimulate an awareness, understanding, and appreciation of the contributions that each culture makes to human heritage.

An anthropological paradigm, based on methods of understanding and relating to others, seems appropri-ate. Touch, by itself, is not an adequate tool; all the senses need to be brought fully into play. The ways to convey multicultural concepts might include: exposure to images and sounds associated with other cultures, play with toys from other cultures, contact with living agents of those cultures, stimulation of taste and smell, and training to recognize differences and similarities in the various cultural styles. It is important to avoid becoming trapped in the western socialization process in which children's experiences are too highly structured by adults. The charac-teristics that CMC is infusing into its Children's Museum are : child-centered (rather than

Figure 97
'Hands-on' has long been recognised as a useful learning technique. But touch alone is not enough. CMC will enable children to learn through all of their senses and through free creative expression. Here, at the Indianapolis Children's Museum, two youngsters explore the sounds from a Trinidad steel drum, part of an exhibit on cultural forms of communication and creativity.

teacher-led), empowering, self-directed, creatively free, multisensory, open-ended, participative, often cooperative, interactive, and above all experiential. There may, of course, need to be some supervisory control exercised over the children, but subtly and unobtrusively, so as not to inhibit nor overly direct their creativity. It follows from this desire to encourage free expression of creative impulses that the traditional distancing of visitors from museum artifacts - both physically, by display cases, and psychologically, by putting people in awe of museum objects - must be avoided even more strenuously in the Children's Museum than in the main museum. CMC is building special collections whose objects are amenable to direct manipulation and exploration.

The mission of the Children's Museum, to teach the 'language' of culture and thereby enable intercultural understanding, and to project an image of Canadian multiculturalism as an expression of the Global Village, is the mission of CMC as a whole; but it may be in the Children's Museum where that mission can have its most profound effect. This is particularly true for its pre-school audience. In those early years a child's sense of self and of others develops and becomes fixed. Racism and bigotry are the end-product of a developmental process that seems to begin in infancy. Young children learn about themselves and their world through sensory, rather than intellectual, investigation; for them multi-sensory exhibits are a particularly effective form of communication, and a powerful learning tool since full engagement of the senses reinforces the memorability of an experience. Pre-schoolers are an audience which most children's museums have neglected, or treated superficially. Yet it is at this age, when they have neither fixed prejudices nor rigid learning styles, that they can incorporate into their world-view an unbiased appreciation of other cultures. To take one example, the phonemic structure of language is easily assimilated by pre-schoolers; exposing them to the sound of different languages may not *teach* them the languages, but *will* allow them to feel comfortable with that sound structure - whereas, if first contact comes at a later age, the language seems harsh and unnatural, and the hearer is unreceptive. Much the same is true of exposure to the different physical

Figure 98
Although designed primarily for a young audience, the Children's Museum will provide opportunities for parents to share experiences with their children, or to learn more about child development.

appearances of people from diverse cultures; again these can be accepted more easily by young children, without giving a sense of foreignness. Children's television has increasingly provided multicultural exposure for pre-schoolers (e.g. Sesame Street, Big Blue Marble) but tends to be unilingual. CMC may find a particular niche in helping young children develop the ability to acquire new languages.

This 'specialty of the house' (pre-schoolers) is a direction that the Children's Museum will develop more fully in a later phase. At first it is focusing upon its more general public and upon general messages, features, and programmes which are more typically found in children's museums. Whereas most children's museums focus on the 6-13 age-group, however, CMC sees a need to provide for the extremes : infants and parents. Many children who visit the museum will of course be accompanied by parents. Although some of the latter may leave their youngsters in the Children's Museum while they tour the other galleries, others will prefer to remain with them. Opportunities for shared experiences are provided, yet it is important to prevent parents from dominating their childrens' experiences - children must have freedom to develop their own agendas. Yet parents are themselves a valid target audience for the Children's Museum. The museum has access to children for only a short

visual, audio, and tactile stimuli. Even pre-natal infants can benefit from simulated multimedia environments : imagine having your first museum experience before you are even born!

Designing a museum for children demands different approaches than the design of exhibitions for adults. The environment must stimulate their imaginations, senses, and intellects to assure them of enjoyable, yet meaningful, experiences and at the same time to allow them to feel more comfortable than in the main museum. In the Children's Museum they are welcome and free to pursue their own objectives at their own pace, to study for school or personal interest projects, to interact with other children, to share experiences with their parents in a context in which *they* are in control, and to develop intimate relationships with the physical elements of past and present through hands-on and other sensory contacts. The physical surroundings and ambiance had to be designed much as if children had done the job themselves. Colours communicate a sense of warmth, welcome, and fun. Lighting adds to the brightness and attractiveness. Bright colours, large and numerous graphics, theatrical lighting, and varied textural surfaces all appeal to a young audience. Since colour stimulation influences behaviour, bright colours are used in areas where a high level of physical activity is called for; deeper

Figures 99 and 99a
Many of the artifacts used in the Children's Museum are replicas or items collected with the intention they be handled by visitors. However, there are some historical artifacts too, such as miniature carved wagons from the Bergeron circus model.

time; parents are continuing influences over the development of their children's attitudes. Therefore the Children's Museum will teach parents about the stages of child development so that they can under-stand their children better; this programme will also free children from their parents' supervision for a while. Some parents bring babies and toddlers. While the Children's Museum is not a day-care centre, programmes will exploit toddlers' natural inclinations to play (by providing toys from other cultures, and dedicated play-areas) and also the fact that babies' mental development can be aided by

and softer colours where calmer, mentally exacting tasks are performed. This contrast helps prevent overpowering children's senses by constant stimulation. The physical stature of the audience adds a further consideration : labels (kept to a minimum, and their typography designed to facilitate fast reading and easy comprehension), fixtures, furniture, all accommodate children's height and ease of use. The design also includes floors that are non-slip and free of obstacles that children might trip over, sound-absorbing material in the walls, and changing and nursing facilities in washrooms.

The layout and space allocation of the Children's Museum allows for maximum flexibility. All spaces work well for small and large groups as well as single visitors. None of the exhibitions here will be as permanent as the core exhibits in some of the galleries of the main museum. Children's Museum exhibitions will change with some frequency, to persuade children to return time and time again. Original objects will be used in exhibits and programmes where feasible; a characteristic that continues to distinguish children's museums from other children's centres is the availability of authentic objects from other cultures. Many of these originals have been specially collected by CMC for its educational collections, and it is hoped to obtain more through donations. High-quality reproductions will supplement originals in cases where objects are to be handled.

The Children's Museum occupies approximately 22,300 sq.' (2072 sq.m.) of space, of which about a third is an outdoor park. The museum is situated on the far side of the public wing from the Grand Hall, just off the main lobby. Its entrance lies halfway between CMC's main entrance and the sales shop, and just to the side of the Imax/Omnimax theatre. This is intentionally the *only* public access to the Children's Museum, to allow adults to position themselves with a view of the entrance/exit and ensure that their children do not wander out of the Children's Museum without them.

The Children's Museum will spill out into the main lobby, to make its location more apparent; a sense of excitement and anticipation begins to be built up at its entrance area. This is achieved partly through deployment of the Bergeron Circus, an artifact of hundreds of individual pieces acquired in 1988 specially for the Children's Museum. It is a miniature model of a circus parade, carved in wood by Quebec folk artist Gaston Bergeron, of circus wagons, horseback riders, wild animals, clowns and other circus entertainers. The long parade - 425' (127.5 m.) when fully laid out - will help entice visitors along the lobby and through the entrance and Reception Area of the Children's Museum. Sound effects, such as a steam calliope, the roar of lions and trumpeting of elephants, the laughter and applause of a circus audience, reinforce the alluring effect. The model is augmented by less fragile objects, such as larger-scale circus wagons, that children can touch or even climb upon - providing wonderful photographic opportunities.

Figure 100
The circus theme appears in several aspects of the Children's Museum. Cultural transformers, such as clowns, will animate the museum and capture the interest of visitors.

Figure 101
The Children's Museum has the facilities for intimate live performances

Another element, added at peak periods (notably weekends : the Children's Museum equivalent of the entertainment-focused nighttime mode of CMC), is live animators. They will play a pied piper-ish role, leading entranced visitors from one world to another, and will include clowns, as appropriate to the circus theme. Yet the circus motif symbolizes something more fundamental. It is a tool for engaging all the senses - for the circus is a multisensory world - but also a doorway to cultural transition, which reflects the underlying mission of the museum. Transformation techniques are often disguised in more culturally acceptable forms, with comedic elements. Clowns are a western representation of the transformer figure; magicians, jugglers, mummers, jesters, are other examples well-defined in European tradition, with a long and interesting folklore, and appealing to young and old alike. Other cultures have their counterparts, such as the trickster figures of native Canadian mythology; these will provide a link between the Children's Museum and other CMC exhibitions. Such figures, and the circus motif generally, will provide children with a gentle and gradual transition from the familiar world outside the museum to the unfamiliar cultures encountered inside the Children's Museum.

A meeting area, just beyond the Reception Area, is the central space into which all other parts of the Children's Museum empty out. The circus motif continues here in the form of banners and other decorations reminiscent of the Big Top. Here the transformers will give impromptu performances : clowning, magic shows, mime plays, street theatre, musical performances, juggling, and cultural rituals. Portable stage, simple stage furnishings, and moveable seating permit quick and easy reconfiguration of the area. The meeting area is also a rendezvous for adults and children who have, intentionally or otherwise, separated in the museum. Large objects placed here serve as rendezvous landmarks ("Meet you by the mini-bus!"). As the central space in the Children's Museum, the meeting area helps orient visitors to the other areas, and provides for general circulation.

The largest component of the Children's Museum is the General Exhibition Hall, although priority has been given to opening the other parts of the Children's Museum first. It will require a little time to translate CMC's unique vision of a human-history-focused children's museum into concrete terms for a major exhibition. In the interim, part of the General Exhibition Hall will be used to develop a temporary exhibition along the lines of those found in the Tropenmuseum Junior, with children engaged in roleplaying scenarios in large-scale reconstructions simulating other cultural environments. The exhibitions mounted here will be changed at least every two years, to address new themes and keep the interest of children who return periodically.

The hall has been designed as an open and very flexible area, to facilitate constant refurbishing; it is an area for experimentation and continuing modification as CMC's staff learn what children like and which elements of the exhibitions are most effective in promoting intercultural understanding. All exhibitions here will have participatory and interactive elements, and will provide opportunities for children to experience what it is like to be part of a particular culture and, by reflection, what it means to be Canadian. Thus the similarities and differences between cultures will become apparent, the concept of cultural change over time will be communicated, and children will be encouraged to learn to read the 'messages' of material culture and thereby how to exploit museum resources to the fullest.

One technique to be experimented with is the use of television. A TV studio in the Children's Museum will give them a tool for recording and studying their own behaviour, particularly in cultural roleplaying. It will also let them learn basic principles of video creativity, editing, and production, and thus may give them a better understanding of the nature of TV 'reality'. In this way, as well as by making accessible the authentic three-dimensional objects that provide reality anchors, CMC hopes to counteract some of TV's negative effects on children. CMC is also exploring the possibility of producing a regular children's television programme, using the Children's Museum as a base (much as the Vancouver Aquarium is the home-base in CBC's "Danger Bay"), through collaborative efforts with other organizations interested in quality children's television. Another possibility is linking up visitors in the Children's Museum with children of other cultures through the interactive telecommunications technologies described in chapter 6. These ideas may seem a little sophisticated for a children's museum, but children of today are more at home with new technologies than are most adults.

Kaleidoscope is the name of a more modest area of the Children's Museum, for mounting travelling and special exhibitions. "Kids Connect" will be hosted here in 1990. Other exhibitions to be brought in include : "Puppetronics", the Children's Museum's first guest exhibition, with hands-on opportunities, naturally; "Bubbles", a popular participatory exhibit from the Boston Children's Museum; "Science and Art in Flight", featuring kites ancient and modern; "Toys A to Zoo", whose artifacts illustrate toys Canadian children played with between 1824 and 1920, and which will run, appropriately, over Christmas 1989; "Soundtracks", conceived by the Staten Island Children's Museum, offering a chance to experiment with musical instruments - some typical, some unusual, and some do-it-yourself; and the Smithsonian's "Kaleidoscopes", an interactive exhibition which allows visitors to investigate optical principles and includes a large, walk-in kaleidoscope. As well as bringing images and treasures from across the world into the Children's Museum, the Kaleidoscope area provides a space in which children's work, created in other areas of the museum, can be displayed or where children can show their own collections if they wish.

Many museums created for general audiences have, since the mid-'70's, added areas aimed at children, under the title of Discovery Room. There museum objects can be handled and examined; often they are made available individually in special containers (e.g. discovery boxes) accompanied by printed materials which guide the examination. A Discovery

Room was part of the early plans for CMC's Children's Museum, but there were serious difficulties with the concept in a human history museum dedicated to intercultural understanding. Part of the problem was the title. 'Discovery' has acquired, in the context of the relationship between native and European cultures, a pejorative connotation suggesting a higher order of civilization discovering a lower order. The boxing of discovery items also suggests the 'capture' of heritage items of obsolete cultures and the neutralizing of any spiritual power attributed to them; whereas CMC seeks to reveal, and foster, the continuing vitality of ethnic cultures. Furthermore, it reflects western civilization's tendency to encapsulate, and fragment into categories, elements of reality, rather than to view the world in a holistic way as many non-western cultures do. Thus the 'discovery' approach tends to decontextualize objects from their cultural meaning - just the opposite of the goal sought by CMC. It is appropriate for science and natural history museums (which is where most Discovery Rooms exist) but not for human history museums.

CMC's vision of what was originally a Discovery Room has evolved into more of an 'exploration place'. The space introduces visitors to the material objects of other cultures and to the resources that help bring understanding of those objects and the cultures they reflect. It is a cross between an organized attic and a resource centre not unlike the Médiathèque in principle (although not in form). The aim is to stimulate children's feelings of wonder and desire to explore the contents through self-directed enquiry. Elements in the centre will appeal to all the senses, and to a variety of ages and interests, as well as providing for activities that children and parents can share. There are plenty of hands-on opportunities, although special exhibits from the main museum collections are available only for visual examination : bubble-gum cards, coins, stamps, marbles, easter eggs, for example. These exhibits introduce children to the idea of developing collections. Reproductions of card and board games - such as skiddles, dreidel, coddles, oware - also allow for interaction between visitors. A quieter area is available for children to pursue independent study and for parents to learn more about how to take full advantage of CMC's resources and facilities. The resources in this section will include reference books, pamphlets, charts and maps, photographic and audiovisual materials; computer terminals will offer interactive games and quizzes, as well as access to informational databases designed for children. A

Figures 102 and 102a
Several children's museums in the United States have included a 'television studio' among their exhibits. CMC plans to introduce a similar facility, to help children understand a medium that has so much influence over them, and to teach them rudiments of video production.

Figures 103 and 103a
In an area equipped as a studio,
children can watch demonstrations by
expert artists and craftspeople, learn
skills through workshops, or pursue
their own creative projects.

quiet corner for toddlers has wooden puzzles and pop-up picture books.

Adjacent to the Exploration Place is a studio roughly the same size as the Kaleidoscope. This is a multi-purpose room, but its main role is to establish in the minds of visitors that cultural material objects used elsewhere in the museum (e.g. masks used in performances in the Meeting Area) have a creative origin : they have to be made. Vibrant and attractively decorated, the area invites and inspires children to work, alone or with friends or family, on whatever creative projects interest them. The room

will become a showcase of their artwork, craft projects, and other creative endeavours.

In the informal and comfortable space of the Studio children can learn and practice new creative activities, usually bearing some relation to exhibits and programmes in the rest of the museum, notably the central theme of multiculturalism. Both self-directed and programmed instructional activities are bookable by groups, or visitors may just drop in. A moveable partition, dividing the Studio into two rooms, facilitates scheduling and space allocation. Classes, workshops, film presentations, puppet

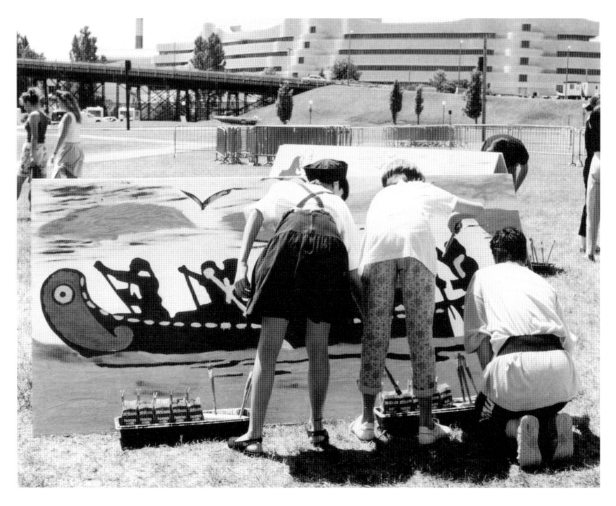

shows, weaving, modelling, carving, trying on costumes, demonstrations by experts, are some of the studio's activities. Activity units on various topics will guide children who visit the studio on a casual basis. These range from very simple to more complex activities, to cater to children of different ages; for example : stringing wooden beads into a pattern, origami, making a Christmas straw decoration, creating a paper cut-out. Activities requiring more space than a box can take place at tables and counters in the studio : soapstone carving, basket-weaving, carving a jack-o-lantern, and many others. A few activities, like loom-weaving, may be communal : a succession of individuals contributes to the ultimate creation of the finished product. Some activities - like making a cartoon, carving a mask, organizing and mounting a collection, printmaking, Chinese calligraphy, building a dollhouse, learning traditional folk songs - require participants to receive instruction. They will be scheduled during the week, as part of a workshop series, or presented on special occasions such as school breaks or ethnic festivals (e.g. a Kite Day during the week of Chinese festival). The dynamism and flexibility of the studio allows

children to explore topics of interest freely and to express their imaginations and their creativity in an unfettered way; it also enables CMC to provide diverse activities which reflect the seasonal and calendrical differences and thematic changes in its exhibitions and programmes.

The final component of the Children's Museum is an outdoor park of several acres, a fun but safe area where children can play. To control children's circulation, the park is accessible only from the Children's Museum : through a sheltered patio, and down a ramp; a fence surrounding the play area, concealed by shrubbery, ensures that children not wander off into the rest of Parc Laurier. Part of the purpose of the children's park is to provide a change from the indoor museum experience, in the form of either exercise or rest; most of the park is an active play area, but part is for passive play. Outdoor workshops, presentations or exhibits can take place there. The park will be developed from a simple grassy space. Options include a water play feature that symbolizes the importance of water-routes to Canada since the time of the voyageurs, and the erection of an Indian teepee which could host overnight camp-ins by children; CMC has commissioned three Plains teepees, authentically decorated with pictures that recount native legends. The park accommodates comfortably about 70 children at any given time, and is a supervised area.

The Children's Museum is envisaged only as the hub of CMC's programming for children. Only a limited amount can be accomplished within the museum itself, but the resources of the whole National Capital Region are open to exploitation. For many visitors a museum has only a few hours of contact in which to

Figure 104
One option for the enclosed park that is part of the Children's Museum is to erect a teepee for use in roleplaying or overnight camp-ins.

get across its message. To instill an understanding of other cultures, CMC hopes to encourage children to return frequently, so that its message take effect through cumulative exposure.

For these repeat visitors a type of club will be developed, as the nexus for in-depth explorations and outings. The Children's Museum will be simply the assembly point. Beyond its immediate threshold lies the main museum, where the environmental reconstruction exhibits will be the basis for roleplaying. Surrounding the museum is Parc Laurier, notably the children's park and the outdoor archaeological exhibit. The former offers potential for camp-ins on a year-round basis; in the winter, for example, a snow-house village can be constructed, with Inuit songs and shamanic performances in the evening. The latter will give children a chance to experience a real archaeological dig and try out techniques used by archaeologists to learn about the past. The next zone out is Parc Jacques Cartier - accessible from the museum without having to cross any roads - which is being developed by the National Capital Commission as a youth park. This presents possibilities for picnics, river rides, and living history events in the context of historic Charron House. On the opposite side of the museum lies the evolving Core Area West heritage theme park, with Victoria Island's parkland, boat-mooring area, totem pole, log chutes, historic industrial complex, and nearby Devil's Hole falls/whirlpool. Further afield are parks in the Gatineau Hills, at Lac Leamy, and Ottawa's Greenbelt, incorporating heritage sites such as the Wakefield Mill and the Old Log Farm, and offering opportunities for simulating large-scale voyageur or Indian encampments and allowing children to experience, perhaps over a stay of several days, the ways in which humans and nature interact. A minibus shuttle will connect the museum with these outlying sites.

The Children's Museum and the educational programmes, providing for the needs of the whole spectrum of CMC's users, are the core features of the museum's daytime mode of operations. In this mode the interpretive methods discussed in chapter 6 are integral parts of the educational programming of the museum; or the educational programmes are an integral part of CMC's approach to interpretation, stressing enquiry, interactivity, and experiential learning. Both perspectives are valid. At any rate, interpretation and education are then barely distinguishable. Each serves as a mediator or broker between the public and its material heritage, while the museum itself is facilitator or mentor in the process of learning : assisting and encouraging members of the public to explore their own interests through the museum's resources.

Figures 105 and 105a
The Children's Museum will be the home-base for field trips to regional heritage sites such as the Old Log Farm.

the museum as celebration

The public has a notion that museums provide only a rear-view mirror perspective on culture. Museums consequently seem to some people lifeless, with no relevance to the present. The Canadian Museum of Civilization aims at dispelling the negative image that museums are dull and dusty. As a record of the past a museum preserves inanimate objects; its image as a temple where the dead remains of the cultural past are honoured through the reverential behaviour of visitors suggests a form of ritualistic celebration. Yet culture cannot be relegated to the past; it is essential to the quality of life today and must not only be preserved but nourished. CMC is concerned not merely with material objects but with cultural traditions : traditions which continue to find expression in the present. It therefore devotes its energies to the display of such expressions no less than to the display of artifacts. In so doing, it seeks to celebrate life, to show how the past lives on in the present, and to strike the same note of confidence in the future that Douglas Cardinal has uttered through his architectural masterpiece. Programmes focusing on the performing and cinematic arts will allow CMC to redefine the role of the museum, as a place to celebrate the present as well as record the past. They will emphasize the museum as a vital and dynamic element of the community (be it local, national, or global), and will act as a cultural gener-ator by fostering creative impulses and providing facilities - laboratories for the living arts - to bring those creations before the public.

These ambitions are not wholly selfless. Museums must interest wider audiences if the important

Figure 106
Entertainment can be a valid vehicle for educating. This humorous vignette, "Canadians All", presented on Parliament Hill during the summer, was used to communicate messages about immigration and the multicultural character of Canada.

messages they wish to communicate are to reach all who should hear. The great investment of resources that the Canadian people have made in building a new national museum of human history can be justified, and repaid, only by that museum offering meaningful leisure opportunities that suit the tastes and needs of everyone. A museum that cultivates the image of a tower of learning will find its appeal limited to a small segment of the public. Today the competition for people's voluntary leisure-time is fiercer than ever : movies, television, theatre, theme parks, world's fairs all perform as well as or better than museums, in combining cultural and recreational dimensions. Many museums stubbornly refuse to see education and entertainment as compatible goals, ignoring the fact that the best teachers tend to be those who make their messages entertaining and fun, and thereby make their audiences receptive to the messages. Museums must similarly win the opportunity to educate by first entertaining, that is, capturing the imagination of the public. Introducing entertainment into the museum is not pandering to public taste and lowering the quality of exhibits, as some maintain; it is rather a matter of opening channels of communication with people who otherwise have no idea of what museums are about, by providing something that catches their interest.

CMC recognizes that enjoyment stimulates learning, and is in itself a worthy goal that does not necessarily require museums to relax high standards; excellence and popularity are mutually achievable. This enables CMC to come to terms with the realities of today's world and strive to attract new audiences by emphasizing the entertaining and often participatory qualities of some programmes. Using the theatres and other performance spaces built into the museum, these programmes should bring new visitors and encourage return visits, by offering frequent and various special events and presentations throughout the year, ensuring that there is always something new to see or do. In this way CMC will respond to people's needs for entertaining and for socializing opportunities. The many events will also fuel CMC's television production facilities, for outreach and the building of a national audience. CMC's Imax/Omnimax theatre, its interactive theatre, its performance-oriented plazas, its introduction of ritual and dramatic elements into the exhibitions themselves, the cultural festivals and other special events planned, should all help redefine the traditional image of a human history museum to reflect a lively and dynamic character and the full potential for meaningful use of leisure time.

It is essential that CMC develop large audiences, because of the federal government's insistence that cultural institutions become able to support some of their operations and programmes through self-generated revenues. One route to revenue generation is imposing admission charges. There is ample precedent for such charges, even among publicly-funded museums, but they discourage visitation, particularly in the local community which was not accustomed to paying. Yet everyone is accustomed to paying for entertainment - cable or Pay TV, movies, theatre, opera, theme park attractions - so long as the quality matches their expectations. Charges for entertainment elements introduced at CMC will help provide the funds needed to support its educational programmes and exhibitions, to ensure they remain free of charge and accessible to all. Thus the 'nighttime mode' of operations - so called because it is during the evening when people usually seek leisure activities for which they expect to pay - is CMC's key to revenue-generating strategy and to maximizing audiences. Hopefully, most visitors will frequent the facilities under both daytime and nighttime modes, to experience the full range of programmes offered.

The distinction between these modes is an oversimplification. It is more a question of the relative emphasis on educational and entertainment qualities within, or the purpose of or audience for, a programme. Essentially the same programme may be presented in both modes, but with slight differences to suit the time of day, day of the week, or season of the year; that is, to be suitable for school groups or tourists. Programmes whose goal is predominantly educational will be offered on weekdays during most of the school year; some may be extended into the evening in May and June when many school tour groups visit. Programme content will be geared towards the age level of the particular audience. On weekends programmes will be selected or modified to provide a more entertaining experience for family-based audiences. And in peak tourist season (July-August) the nighttime mode will really operate all day, with the emphasis on entertainment elements in keeping with the expectations of a vacationing tourist audience. Only during the summer and other major festivals (e.g. the National Capital Commission's Winterlude) will the most spectacular and most expensive events be put on by the museum. Nighttime mode programmes will not be devoid of educational content by any means, but will stress the type of culturally qualitative entertainment experiences for which audiences customarily pay. In this mode CMC will introduce

Figure 107
The Science Museum of Minnesota
production "Charles and Mrs.
Darwin" took actors into the midst of
the biology exhibits, for a theatrical
presentation about Darwin's theory of
evolution.

interactive and multiexperiential elements in their fullest formulation.

In seeking models for its nighttime mode programmes, CMC looked both inside and outside the museum world. Epcot Center offered examples of live animation done well; the reconstructed environments in its World Showcase are little more than stage sets, used as backdrops for performances by first-rate professionals : wonderful Moroccan musicians, Japanese food sculptors, Chinese dragon dancers, and so on. While the content of Epcot's programmes is not always worthy of emulation, the techniques they use often are. A closer model to the type of programme that CMC hopes to mount occasionally is the multiexperiential performance (at the Ontario Science Centre and later repeated in Holland) of "Ra", the creation of Canadian composer R. Murray Schafer. Taking the Egyptian *Book of the Dead* as the point of departure for his opera, he enhanced it with fabulous costumes, smells of incense and perfume, and a sumptuous banquet for performers and audience; the eight-hour event,

between sunset and sunrise, attracted over a thousand viewer/participants paying $150 apiece. CMC hopes to put on similar spectacles - not at such high prices - perhaps to re-stage "Ra" on the grounds of CMC and the National Gallery, or to commission a new work from Schafer, based on Canadian native rituals.

Another innovative, but more interactive, theatrical presentation has been created by Canadian Moses Znaimer, owner of the CITY TV and MuchMusic Pay TV networks. His play "Tamara" - which is highly experiential, calling for an unusual degree of audience participation - opened in Toronto and moved in 1983 to Los Angeles, where presented every night since to audiences averaging a hundred people, at about $110 a head; in 1987 a second production opened in New York. The play does not separate audience and performers, for the whole theatre is the stage set, in the form of a mansion. Audience members may follow any performers they choose to the several rooms where parts of the plot are acted out simultaneously. Viewers move from room to room as they wish - allowing them to

Figures 108 and 108a
Bringing the action off the stage and
into the audience can create a special,
memorable intimacy and provide
opportunities for actors and audience
to interact.

explore the set while experiencing different parts of the play - and can interact with the performers to an extent, which encourages roleplaying. At intermission, when a buffet is served, and at the end of the performance guests have opportunities to intermingle and discuss the different elements they have witnessed. The Tamara model demonstrated to CMC the potential for using the whole museum as one great theatre, and for using dramatic performances to fulfill visitors' needs to socialize and to stimulate

conversation; it also showed the effectiveness of creating an emotional involvement between performers and audience through interactivity.

Interestingly, theatre's origins lie in tribal rituals which typically took place on communal land and invited participation and involvement; there was no hint of specialized spaces for audience and performers. The rituals involved the whole community, and the 'set' was the natural scenic backdrop. McLuhan believed that the major influences on the development of theatre were the evolution of enclosed temples, and the creation of the phonetic alphabet allowing the translation of oral ritual into formalized text and converting expression to a linear, sequential process (separating memory from reality, and fragmenting experience into individual frames). Typical theatre architecture embodies a separation of audience from performers and the creation of a boundary separating art and life - a framed visual space which establishes that what happens on the stage is a separate reality from that of the audience. Viewing the world through frameworks - such as the theatre proscenium and the television or movie screen - is characteristic of Western culture, yet not of tribal cultures, which perceive the world in quite a different way. Thus it may be an obstacle to our understanding other cultures.[1] This is why CMC seeks to heighten the interaction of viewer and viewed by "dissolving the frame" in many of the exhibition, dramatic, and cinematic experiences it offers. Its reconstructed environments, interactive dramatic presentations, and giant-screen theatre are elements of this plan.

Traditionally, theatre has not been part of the museum experience, although some see an analogy between museums and theatres. It has been suggested that museum artifacts are the dramatic raw materials, or props, which visitors can use to create, mentally, their own plays; whereas in a theatrical performance the audience remains stationary while 'symbols' parade before them on stage, in museums the symbols remain static and the viewers move, controlling their own pacing, writing their own script, and selecting which set of symbols will be experienced and in which order.[2] There has been growing criticism of the highly objectified nature of the museum experience and a feeling that this should be countered by greater use of performance to communicate non-material elements of culture.[3]

Open air museums pioneered theatrical techniques many years ago; this style of interpretation has become standard in that type of museum, ranging

from unscripted first-person interpretation by individuals to larger-scale recreations of historical events. At King's Landing Historical Settlement, for example, troupes put on heritage productions in its theatrical hall. Plays of historical interest, as well as silent films, are presented in the Calgary Heritage Park opera house. Gay Nineties song-and-dance shows are regular features at the period theatres in Barkerville and Fort Steele. Old Fort William's annual Great Rendezvous pageant involves several hundred costumed performers in a series of inter-related presentations. Canada's National Historic Sites - especially the Fortress of Louisbourg - are also renowned for their use of live animation and mini-dramas.

Indoor museums have had less experience with theatrical programming. When they have ventured into the arena, the presentations have often been in spaces not really designed for the purpose. At least

two North American indoor museums, however, have reported successful theatrical productions.[4] Museums, of course, are not in the business of professional theatre, nor should they encourage their visitors to expect traditional theatre. Their educational mission, the presence of authentic icons rather than just props, and their preoccupation with heritage and cultural ritual, must inevitably influence the types of dramatic productions suitable for museums, giving them unique qualities that commercial theatrical productions have difficulty matching. CMC's goal is not to compete with existing theatres in the National Capital Region, but to offer theatre-going audiences alternative types of theatrical experience.

Widening its visitor population is therefore one benefit that CMC seeks by adding performing arts programmes to its existing attractions. Theatre is a high-profile medium, well-accepted in the

Figure 109
The huge semicircular plaza in front of the museum, its borders defined by vehicular access routes, meandering water-courses, and a serpentine terrace which can seat audiences for street entertainers, will be very much a 'people place', full of life.

177

community, and able to draw audiences from afar. It can help raise the profile of a museum in the community, and give an impression of liveliness and energy in the museum to combat unfavourable stereotypes. Furthermore, it creates 'events' that attract media attention and the promotional coverage that CMC needs. More importantly, theatre is an interpretive tool to add to CMC's repertoire for accomplishing its mission. Much more than static exhibits, and more than live interpretation, dramatic characters and plots can communicate emotions and ideas that might otherwise elude the visitor. By animating the cultural past - or, for that matter, the cultural present - museums can heighten public awareness of heritage and heritage issues, can breathe life into oral traditions, legends, and belief systems and represent the vitality of a culture in a

Figures 110, 110a, 110b, 110c and 110d
Parc Laurier's plazas can host a variety of performances. The bandura busker, juggling unicyclist, theatrical troupe (presenting "Stealing Home"), magician's act, and wandering commedia dell'arte players shown here are samples of what visitors may encounter in the outdoor plazas.

way no other technique can do quite so well. Furthermore, theatre can blend entertainment and education in a way with which the public is comfortable. Interactive theatre, by encouraging dialogue between audience and performers, can heighten the educational potential of theatre even further, and bring audiences back full circle to the time when there was no segregation of actors and audience; by so doing, a deeper understanding of the rituals and celebrations that underlie our cultural heritage may be engendered.

Theatrical space

CMC is well-endowed with facilities for hosting the performing arts. Some are outside the museum building. The Entrance Plaza sets the tone for visitors even before they enter the building; during the summer especially it will be a vibrant place - much like those in front of Paris' Musée de l'Homme or Centre Pompidou - where locals and tourists of many cultures congregate for any number of reasons. It may be to obtain information before embarking on their exploration of the museum; to take photographs of friends or relatives with the museum or

Figure 111
CMC's Theatre is designed to provide excellent acoustics for all types of performing arts events, and to allow those events to be recorded by television cameras for live or delayed transmission to other locations.

Parliament Hill as backdrop; to relax in the sun and perhaps enjoy an ice-cream sold by street-vendors; or to watch some informal entertainment : kids demonstrating their skateboarding skills, street musicians gathered for a jam session, clowns or mime artists animating the plaza with their acts. CMC will encourage and attract, as does the Centre Pompidou, performers of all types to display their talents. The Entrance Plaza will become a bustling marketplace of folk culture. On special occasions more formal entertainment may be presented; there is space for a temporary stage and conduits for power cables. Small concerts could be given to audiences of up to 1500 people.

Formal performances involving dialogue or music are mostly destined for the Central Plaza, at the foot of the Grand Stairway and on the threshold of the riverside park. Acoustics there are better. Intimate concerts or plays, craft fairs, demonstrations, and outdoor exhibits, can be accommodated there. The Stairway, outdoor benches, and the cafeteria and restaurant terraces provide viewing spots for perhaps 600-800 visitors. There is potential for something at every season : winter ice sculptures, spring rites, summer carnivals, fall festivals. Larger-scale, multimedia events can spill out beyond the plaza into the riverside park, and can be witnessed by several thousand people. Events in the Central Plaza, on the museum roofs in a kind of 'parapet theatre', in Theatre Canada (the area of Parc Laurier between the plaza and the river), and on the Ottawa River itself, will combine in a magnificent pageant of Canadian

history and cultural diversity. The park offers scope for numerous other independent events, such as puppet shows; the possibilities for events in the archaeological amphitheatre and the children's park have elsewhere been mentioned. It may prove feasible to use the roofs over the restaurant and public wing - the latter providing a large expanse, with strange sculpted structures towering overhead and suggesting tremendous ritual possibilities - for performances, receptions, or special events such as weddings. One by-product of all these outdoor performance areas is the lively advertisement they will provide for CMC to passers-by or persons observing them from the far bank of the river.

There are no fewer venues for theatrical presentations inside the museum. The space most specifically designed for them has been informally tagged the World Window Theatre, for reasons which shall become clear. The intent at the beginning of the New Accommodation project was to create a multi-purpose auditorium to host the types of programmes CMC had presented in the Victoria Memorial Museum Building's auditorium : small performances, films, demonstrations, lectures, and large group gatherings. As the potential for using theatrical techniques in museums became increasingly apparent, the architectural programme was modified to ensure that the space be designed as a theatre for dynamic events, rather than an auditorium for more passive lecture-style presentations. Now CMC's Theatre has the potential to be the most creative venue in the museum.

The Theatre takes up some 10,000 sq.' (929 sq.m.) of footprint space at the southwest corner of the museum. It has a proscenium stage with apron and full fly; the stage floor has been sprung to permit dance performances. Provision has been made for installation of elevation machinery to lower and raise the forestage; this will allow it to connect with storage areas under the auditorium, or to be brought to audience level to permit presentations or demonstrations in which the audience is in closer contact with the presenters. In lowered position the forestage also serves as an orchestra pit for up to 15 musicians. While not so grand as the stage in the National Arts Centre Opera, CMC's Theatre stage is perfectly suitable for a range of presentations, especially on the smaller scale of ethnic and native traditional performances that will be a focus of CMC's programmes. Theatre events will include not only dance but also : concerts ranging from solo performers up to small ensembles; local and international dramatic presentations of all kinds, including puppet theatre and interactive theatre; crafts demonstrations; special lectures by recognized authorities in support of other museum programmes, with slide or video presentations; national and international conferences; and films. Since the reverberation time required for different events varies - that needed for a motion picture soundtrack is not the same as for a live chamber orchestra, for instance - the Theatre's ceiling has been designed to allow acoustics to be adjusted to suit the event. A state-of-the-art sound system has been installed in the theatre. Two retractable screens, positioned up-stage of the proscenium, allow for front and rear projection; the theatre is equipped with 70 mm., 35 mm., and 16 mm. front projection equipment, as well as a high-resolution, rear video projector, and multiple slide projectors.

There is fixed audience seating for some 500 persons, tiered to provide clear views to stage or screen, and laid out in an intimate semicircle around the forestage; this arrangement should encourage interaction between performers and audience, and within the audience itself. Provision has been made for the needs of the mobility impaired; special boxes on either side and near the rear end of the auditorium each take at least three wheelchairs, and one row of seats in the middle of the house is removable to accommodate further wheelchairs. A ramp down one side of the theatre gives access to the stage itself. Simultaneous translation is available via a 6-channel system, which also offers sound enhancement for the hearing-impaired; infra-red transmission means that headsets do not require any wires or plug jacks. Infra-red transmission may also be the basis of an interactive polling feature planned for the theatre in the near future. Versions of this have been introduced to the public in Epcot's Horizons pavilion and in the Futures Theatre at Expo '86. In the former case peoplemover passengers select, by majority vote, which of several simulated experiences they will undergo. In the latter case, audience members were presented with optional scenarios for the future, and pushed buttons on their chairs to opt for which they thought most probable; a computer counted their responses and tabulated them on-screen. The CMC Theatre's electronic polling system will combine these features, allowing audience members to interact with presentations by registering, through keypads built into each seat, their responses (for tabulation and display) to questions; these answers then may determine the direction of the rest of the presentation.

Television facilities have been built into the Theatre : fixed camera pods on either side of the auditorium at stage level, and three open positions at the rear of the auditorium. A mobile studio can be accommodated in the theatre's loading dock. These facilities offer a number of benefits. During craft demonstrations overhead cameras can permit the projection of enlarged close-ups on a Theatre screen, to ensure the whole audience has an excellent view of what is going on. Events in the Theatre can be transmitted elsewhere in the museum, so that visitors resting in the lounges, lunching in the cafeteria, or watching other events, will have a chance to hook into what is happening in the Theatre. This is particularly useful for shows for which there is more demand than the auditorium can accommodate; temporary seating in the lobby outside the Theatre will allow overflow audiences to view performances on closed-circuit television.

Equally important is the ability to reach all Canadians, by recording performances for subsequent broadcasting or production of copies for sale, or by live broadcast : the interactive telecommunications potential described in chapter 6 will extend the size of the stage by some 25,000 miles! This is the first permanent theatre to employ the techniques pioneered by Mobile Image, by giving performers a world apart the ability to link up through satellite video. The technology may make it possible to see Inuit from Labrador settlements perform on CMC's stage drum dances with their counterparts in Siberia, or at New Year lion dancers in CMC dancing with partners in Hong Kong or Shanghai. This would truly be the Global Village of which McLuhan dreamed, and would give new meaning to the Bard's famous line "All the world's a stage." It could also help counteract the cultural drift - the tendency to fall out of touch with cultural developments in the homeland - that immigrants experience when they come to Canada.

The Theatre's various projection systems and potential for interactive programming offer the means to experiment with multimedia presentations, perhaps incorporating artifacts from CMC's collections when appropriate. The wide range of programmes possible, together with the intimate atmosphere, should make the Theatre an attractive venue for live performances and film festivals, catering to the interests of the local community, tourists, school groups, and special interest groups such as jazz clubs or film societies. Some events will be ticketed, others not; profits from events for which there is a charge will help finance the free ones.

Some programmes will be produced by CMC alone, some through cooperative (and co-sponsored) ventures with other agencies or organizations; for example a cooperative presentation with the Theatre Ballet of Canada is being negotiated and several organizations have joined CMC in sponsoring a performance of the Ningxia Yingchuan Beijing Opera Company. More will be presented by institutions or groups to whom CMC rents the Theatre, for a set fee and/or a percentage of the box-office takings. While priority for use of the Theatre will be given primarily to CMC-sponsored events, and secondarily to major national and international meetings related to CMC's mandate, as well as to the Friends of CMC for fundraising events or corporate evenings, other organizations will be able to rent the theatre during unprogrammed time-slots. The National Arts Centre and the Canadian Broadcasting Corporation, for example, have expressed interest in using CMC's Theatre for recitals and other small-scale presentations for which their own facilities are not as suitable. The City of Hull has commissioned from a local troupe an operetta, based on the legendary exploits of local lumberjack Jos Montferrand, to be performed at CMC.

There are other theatrical venues within the building. In fact within most galleries provision has been made

Figures 112 and 112a
The Theatre will present live performances of all kinds, from jazz concerts to Chinese opera.

for performance spaces. All the environmental reconstruction exhibits are potential stage sets, while the Grand Hall incorporates a multi-screen movie theatre, and the flexible Arts and Traditions Hall offers many opportunities for multimedia and multicultural presentations. Making the exhibition galleries suitable for theatrical programming naturally added complexity to the process of design, particularly since the present level of programming was not conceived of during the early stages of design. Theatrical possibilities need to be built into an exhibition at the conceptual stage for the most effective use to be made of them. Fortunately CMC's plans for theatre matured in time to allow them to be incorporated into the exhibit design process with relatively little disruption. It was necessary to design the galleries so that parts could be opened up at night, while other parts would remain securely protected. Also, to introduce computer-controlled lighting systems to produce different effects during the daytime/educational mode - when the focus is on the exhibits - and the nighttime/theatrical mode, as well as sound systems to serve dramatic performances.

Some modifications had to be made to the architecture to accommodate theatrical programmes. The presentations in most galleries will be relatively small-scale and intimate affairs, so that the necessary adjustments were not great. The Grand Hall, as the venue for larger presentations in front of the Pacific Coast Indian village, needed more significant changes. When a hall is defined as a multi-purpose area, there is inevitably compromise for all the purposes. The Grand Hall has to serve as reception and orientation area, exhibition gallery, banquet-hall, and theatre. This has meant providing lighting not only for the exhibits but for the areas in front of the exhibits where performances are given; at the same time the lighting hardware must be unobtrusive and avoid obstructing the view through the great window. Permanent lighting has been installed above the window-wall opposite the exhibition, while architectural provision has been made for temporary lighting to be installed, at need, in ceiling pits directly above the area in front of the village. The acoustic qualities of the hall were less than ideal for live performances. Reverberation has been brought more under control by upgrading the acoustic materials used in the fabric of the Hall and its exhibition. A further concern was adequate behind-the-scenes facilities to support theatrical programmes. These had been provided for the Theatre from an early stage : star and chorus changing and make-up rooms for 40 performers,

Figure 113
The Grand Hall is another space in the museum to be used for theatrical presentations. The Pacific Coast village provides a wonderful setting for dramatizing mythology and rituals of native cultures from that region.

showers, lounges, storage rooms, prop rooms, are under the Theatre. But these are too distant to serve the exhibition galleries. A second set of facilities has been supplied in a two-storey area running between the Grand Hall and the Native Peoples Hall, behind the village. Performers' facilities are on the lower level, and storage rooms on the upper. Performers can reach the galleries on other levels of the museum via a central (non-public) stairwell in the Native Peoples Hall.

Cinéplus

The twin of the World Window Theatre is a second theatre that is the most sophisticated cinematic space in the world. Cinema is a major attractor of leisure-time activities, and museums with cinematic facilities can tap into this audience, which includes many people who rarely or never visit museums. It would be pointless trying to compete with commercial movie theatres; however, the new giant-screen film technologies have offered an alternative area into which museums can venture. Almost no major museum has been constructed in the last decade without a super-cinema facility, and some existing museums have built extensions to house such theatres. They have also been among the most successful attractions at world's fairs since Expo '67. Now they are beyond being purely exotic amusements and are on the threshold of becoming part of the commercial cinematic establishment. Imax and Omnimax are the Canadian-developed versions of giant-screen cinema and are the dominant technology in the field; Canada's inability to capture world attention through traditional 35 mm. and regular 70 mm. film formats has been leapfrogged by its breakthrough with a new level film technology which is visionary yet reliable.

Figures 114 and 114a
The new museum incorporates the
world's first combined Imax/Omnimax
theatre. Such super-screen cinemas
are becoming increasingly common in
museums, due to the quasi-realistic
experiences they permit.

CMC considered Imax's potential for increasing its drawing-power and its educational effectiveness in 1977, when engaged in conceptual planning for a new museum at Brewery Creek, which never materialized. At the beginning of the '80's a private group's proposal to establish a Canadian Film Centre at a site in the Capital Core Area on the Ottawa River, with the world's first combined Imax and Omnimax facilities, interested the federal government. When the idea fell through, CMC took up the gauntlet and determined that the time was indeed ripe for the national capital to possess a facility that would be a flagship for Canadian film technology. Curiously there are relatively few of these theatres in Canada : Toronto's was the first, Vancouver had two built for Expo '86, others opened recently in Winnipeg and Montreal, and another in Edmonton was being built by Douglas Cardinal when he was selected to design the new CMC. After some consideration whether an Imax or an Omnimax theatre would be the better option, it was decided to build the first theatre ever that could convert back and forth between the two formats. The combined theatre allows access to more films and more potential for generating revenue through theatre rentals to other organizations, such as the National Capital Commission, the National Film Board, tourist agencies, or the national embassies in Ottawa. Although the Imax/Omnimax theatre is part of the CMC complex, in a sense it is a stand-alone attraction whose profile equals the many other tourist attractions along the ceremonial route. Its audiences may or may not include other components of the museum in their visit. Its independent drawing capabilities - demonstrated in recent years at Expo '86 and at Parc La Villette, where previews prior to opening of the main complexes brought a million people to each site - encouraged special efforts to ensure CMC's Imax/Omnimax would be ready for the museum's opening.

CMC's convertible Imax/Omnimax theatre represents a step forward in the technology. Its location in the museum, on the main entrance level between the Theatre and the sales shop, is conspicuous outside the museum owing to the huge, turtle-shaped, bronze dome which overtops it. With a 320-seat (ten-tier) capacity it is at the small end of the scale as Imax theatres go, but the large end of the Omnimax scale. In floor-area it is just a touch smaller than CMC's other theatre. Seating is arranged continental style, with aisles at the theatre's perimeter in the poorer viewing areas; as typical in these theatres, there is an enter-low, exit-high protocol which contributes to audience safety. Up to

14 wheelchairs can be accommodated, at the exit level, near the rear doors. In the lower part of the theatre, in front of the audience, is a small stage. The Imax screen is 62' (19 m.) high and 87' (26 m.) wide; it is made of flexible vinyl, perforated to improve sound transmission from speakers behind the screen. The Omnimax projection dome, which is not quite a hemisphere - it covers 165° - is constructed from 343 aluminum alloy panels which are overlapped and jointed, and riveted to a rib structure; the panels are painted a neutral, flat grey. The 76' (23 m.) diameter dome, weighing a staggering 33 metric tons, can be moved between a 36° downtilt (for projection) and a 4° angle above the horizon, by an ingenious hoist system. As the dome is partially transparent - some 20% of the total area is perforations, again an acoustical requirement - when it is lowered for projection the Imax screen (which would otherwise be visible through the perforations) is folded down into a storage pit. Water-sprinklers throughout the dome provide fire protection. House lights are at the back of the theatre, on either side of the upper projection room; others in the handrail risers light the stairs. Seats, carpets, and other features are all in dark colours, to prevent light bouncing off them onto the dome during screenings.

Figures 115 and 115a
This model of CMC's Imax/Omnimax theatre shows how the Omnimax projection dome can be stored overhead while the Imax screen is in use, or tilted down for an Omnimax presentation.

It is not CMC's role to showcase technology - a sister museum has that mandate - but for every rule there is a justifiable exception. The Imax/Omnimax system is that exception, as an important part of Canadian cinematic history and an exhibit-in-action

The Imax Story

Imax/Omnimax's roots lie in Expo '67, where two of the more successful attractions were the multi-screen films "Labyrinth" and "Polar Life".[5] Spurred on by these successes, the film-makers - Canadians Graeme Ferguson and Roman Kroitor - talked about making giant-screen entertainment commercially viable without relying on the cumbersome multiple-projector systems and disconcerting split-screen effect seen at Expo '67. When Kroitor was asked to make a film for the Fuji corporate pavilion at Expo '70 a race against time began, to develop a projector able to project sharp images on a screen larger than any in cinema history. The key to success was the discovery of, and purchase of patent rights to, an Australian invention : the 'rolling loop' mechanism, which allows film to be pushed through a projector gently and steadily without breaking. Funding from the Canadian government and Fuji ensured that the projector was completed in time to premiere at Expo '70 with the film "Tiger Child". Imax (which stands for maximum image) was born, and was an instant hit, drawing 30,000 visitors a day. Another stroke of luck followed the next year, when the newly-built Ontario Place theme park invited Imax Corporation to premiere its technology in North America in the park's Cinesphere, and commissioned a film. Imax set up shop in Toronto; its headquarters remain there, although it now has offices in Europe and Japan too.

Soon afterwards the San Diego Hall of Science approached Imax Corporation with a novel request for a theatre able to show both Imax films and planetarium presentations. A special fish-eye lens was created so the Imax projector could show movies on a planetarium-type dome. In 1973, with the opening of San Diego's Reuben H. Fleet Space Theater, Omnimax became a reality. The Smithsonian's acquisition in 1976 of an Imax theatre for its National Air and Space Museum - which has since become the most visited museum in the world (10 million visitors annually) - was a further market breakthrough. Subsequently, 15 more American museums or cultural centres, and 17 in other countries acquired Imax or Omnimax theatres. Since most of these institutions are science centres, they have favoured the Omnimax/planetarium format. Seventeen more theatres have been built in theme parks around the world, and 11 world's fairs or major expositions have boasted them; here, interestingly, Imax is more common than Omnimax. It is difficult to keep track of the numbers of theatres, as they are doubling about every five years. The

technology now having established itself, a surge of film-making is underway, and the 1987 opening of an Imax theatre in Winnipeg, in a downtown shopping mall where in direct competition with other movie theatres, signals the first foray into the commercial entertainment world.

Almost all Imax theatres have all been built in the same general proportions and share the same basic characteristics : the rectangular screen, slightly curved, fills the entire front wall of the theatre; seating is on steeply raked tiers, necessitating particular attention to safety in auditorium design; aisles are at the far sides of the auditorium. Theatres can be designed for either small or large audiences (up to 1000 seats), and screens may be up to 100' wide and 75' high; size is not the key factor, however. Omnimax film, on the other hand, is projected onto a tilted dome screen which is above the heads of the audience and is about 80% of a hemisphere; diameter can range from 40'-85'. Again, seating is steeply raked - reclining seats allow the audience to view upwards in comfort - and there is a strong feeling of space in Omnimax theatres. Projection onto such large screens while retaining exceptional sharpness and clarity of image is made possible by several factors. Imax and Omnimax use virtually the same film, but different lenses on the camera and projector. The film frame is ten times the size of a 35 mm. frame (three times that of a 70 mm. frame) which guarantees picture quality and allows the Imax screen to be wider and dramatically higher than the screen of a commercial movie theatre : up to ten times as large, depending on the size of the theatre; therefore, the effect is more compelling than wide-screen alone.

The Imax projector, seven times the size of a normal cinema projector, is the most advanced, highest precision, most powerful projector ever built. Its rolling loop mechanism advances the film horizontally through the projector, at 24 frames per second, in a smooth, wave-like motion, and as each frame is projected it is held steady against the rear element of the lens by a vacuum; this ensures a sharp image and protects the film from damage, substantially increasing its lifetime. High-wattage water-cooled lamps provide the light necessary to project large images with ample brightness; the shutter transmits one-third more light than a conventional projector. The Omnimax projector is similar, except for its fish-eye lens and its mounting on an elevator to lift it into a housing in the centre of the theatre when ready to project. The projectors have proven themselves 99% reliable; in 1986 the technology received an Academy Award in the Scientific and Engineering category. Film spool size allows for one-hour films; a recent advance lets projectors take larger spools, opening the door to feature-length films. Digital soundtracks, supplied from laser discs, is another recent development, as are three-dimensional films and slow-motion cameras.

The concept behind Imax/Omnimax is that each viewer has an unobstructed view of the screen and that the edges of the screen extend beyond the limits of viewers' peripheral vision; the image may cover up to 130° of the field of vision. The steep rake of seating ensures not only the clear views for everyone (including children) but also that even viewers in the back rows are very close to the screen, by normal standards. To see the entire picture - the limits of the screen - audiences have to move their eyes or even their heads. Every attempt is made to give the audiences horizontal and vertical viewing angles similar to those encountered in real-life. In Imax, front row eye-level is well above the bottom of the screen and rear row eye-level at roughly half the height of the screen; this places most viewers in a reasonably natural position in relation to the horizon

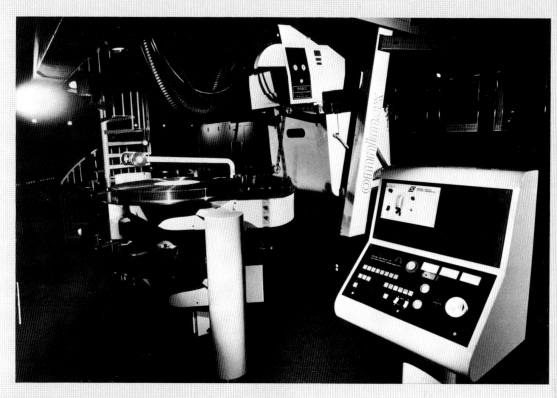

on the projected image. The varied tilting of seats for an Omnimax presentation helps achieve a similar result; front row seats slide to an almost horizontal position, in fact.

The objective is to give viewers the illusion of being part of the visual presentation, encompassed in the on-screen action, rather than merely allowed to look at a separate reality through the window, or frame, of a normal motion picture screen; there is consequently a participatory quality to the films, providing audiences with an unforgettable experience. "The nearest thing to being there" is the phrase commonly used to market the Imax/Omnimax experience; it was coined by astronaut Robert Crippen, after watching the film "The Dream is Alive", showing a shuttle mission.[6] The sense of realism is derived almost as much from sound as from sight. Sophisticated sound systems are integral elements of the theatres, dividing the audio signal from the dubber - which plays the soundtrack from a separate medium to the film, but is electronically interlocked for perfectly synchronized playback - into several distinct frequency bands, each individually amplified and reproduced through multi-speaker enclosures placed at several locations throughout the theatre. Theatres are designed to have very little of the natural reverberation which might interfere with the intelligibility of soundtracks.

Most Imax and Omnimax films now available are 30-40 minutes long. Depending on length, they cost between one to three million dollars to produce, hence there are not yet many more films than there are theatres. This ratio is beginning to change, as institutions become involved in collaborative, cost-sharing, film-making projects. Yet the inventory

of films is already rich and varied, being mostly of semi-documentary or experiential character. As one writer has pointed out :

Thrills and spectacles are the trademark of an IMAX film. In "Volcano", crimson flames and rocks erupt on the screen as the camera takes you over the lip of the inferno. Your knuckles whiten as you hurtle down an Olympic bobsled run in "An American Adventure". And the whole theater seems to shudder as the space shuttle blasts off the launch pad in "Hail Columbia!" But there are also moments of beauty and awe as you travel back billions of years, winding through perilous chasms of rock in the "Grand Canyon : The Hidden Secrets" .... [7]

And another describes these giant-screen films as :

The most viscerally exciting, mind-expanding movies being made today - the kind that provide windows on worlds previously undreamed of, or that discover the spectacular mysteries within something as commonplace as bird-flight.[8]

Most films made so far deal with science and technology (e.g. space exploration, flight, the mysteries of the atom) or geography and natural history (e.g. underwater exploration, the Arctic, the North African desert, wildlife); there are endless possibilities for films appropriate for a human history museum. No matter what the subject, audiences discover that descriptors such as panoramic, colossal, stupendous, magical, or breathtaking, have been applied to the films with just cause.

in its own right. Therefore the projection room walls arc floor-to-ceiling glass to allow visitors to see film preparation and projection operations and equipment: the room holds not only the massive projector weighing some 2000 lbs. (900 kg.) but also reel units, audio system equipment, and control console. The booth is on the theatre's entrance level, in the centre of the theatre under the seating. From here the projector must be raised by a hoist to a pod about two-thirds the way up the seating tiers; the projectionist operates it by remote control. The switch from Imax to Omnimax format, or vice versa, entails lowering the projector, changing lenses and reels, and raising it again. The noisy machinery required the projection booth to be acoustically insulated. Special attention was necessary to provide the desirable environmental conditions (18°-24° C and 40%-60% relative humidity) for the film, as well as a ventilation and vacuum system to combat dust, and a distilled water system to cool the projector's 15,000-watt xenon short arc lamp. A second (upper) projection room is equipped for presenting conventional video or slide shows; a water-cooled laser installation supplies special effects.

State-of-the-art components and sub-systems have been used in the Imax/Omnimax's audio set-up, which uses an 8-track tape recorder and 6-channel high quality, computer-controlled sound system. This provides for simplicity of operation during programme presentation, but flexibility of operation during film production. Its wide dynamic range and extra power-handling capability accommodate digital sound sources. Four loudspeaker clusters are positioned around the Imax screen : at its extreme left and right, centre and top centre; two more are at each side of the theatre's rear. To ensure high-fidelity sound it is important to control the theatre acoustics closely; although a dome presents problematic acoustical anomalies, a fibreglass treatment in the dome and under the wall carpeting, and padded floor carpets, help subdue reverberation.

Between the Imax/Omnimax and the World Window Theatre is a large area - the Salon Barbeau - facing onto Laurier Street. One role of this is as a lobby for the theatres, to prevent the museum's main entrance becoming congested with theatre-goers; line-ups for the Imax/Omnimax will be in the main lobby, however. Salon Barbeau is large enough to hold an audience waiting to enter the World Window Theatre plus those leaving a presentation and ticket lineups for later shows. It is also possible to use the lobby for overflow audiences, or as an extension of the main museum lobby when the need arises. Tickets

for both theatres are available from the box office in the main lobby (open day and evening), by phone, or through a city-wide computerized ticketing system.

The Imax/Omnimax theatre operates seven days a week with a new show starting on the hour each afternoon and evening. Morning programmes are targeted at school groups during the school year and at tourists in the summer. Other groups, such as corporations or community associations, can make group bookings or rent the whole theatre for special showings (e.g. company outings, Christmas parties). CMC particularly pursues group bookings during weekly and seasonal slow periods. There may be as many as 2500 shows a year - up to nine shows a day in peak tourist season - with new programmes being introduced on average every six months, and occasionally special film festivals. Each performance lasts roughly 45-50 minutes and comprises one film in each format; during the five minutes it takes to convert the theatres from one screen to another, a human interpreter on the front stage describes Imax/Omnimax technology to the audience. Tickets are priced higher than in commercial movie theatres, but lower than in opera houses; this is the usual market positioning of Imax and Omnimax theatres, and audiences always seem to feel they have had more than their money's worth from the unique film experience. Although most films shown will be rented, CMC is associating itself with other federal institutions, museums, and the corporate sector to co-produce new films, thus supporting the national film industry. Its first co-production is "The First Emperor".

Museums have adopted giant-screen technologies to attract new audiences, increase their revenues, and add a new dimension to their programmes. Museums possessing these theatres do usually experience significant increases in visitor attendance, their visibility in the local community is raised, tourism in the region as a whole is given a boost, and the overall experience of visitors to the museum is enhanced. The films are a powerful educational tool, combining learning with a thoroughly enjoyable experience. While the cost of installing the theatres is high, their revenue normally exceeds operational costs and can help fund other museum programmes. Furthermore their presence helps increase visitor expenditure in sales shops, eateries, and on memberships in Friends organizations. The drawing-power of the theatre is particularly important to CMC in its early years, by attracting visits from people not normally museum-goers and thus building a larger user-population for the future. At the same time, the Imax/Omnimax is

189

Figure 116
An artist's rendering of CMC's
Imax/Omnimax theatre interior suggest
how a presentation is "almost like
being there".

in its own right a major tourist attraction in the National Capital Region which will help promote an exciting and dynamic image of Canada's national institutions to visitors from abroad.

Performing arts and special events

As the extent of live performances planned for the new museum goes far beyond anything CMC has ever before attempted, a Performing Arts and Special Events (PASE) Section was established to develop, plan, coordinate, and realize live programmes in the museum's performance spaces. Through a series of symposia, CMC's staff consulted with experts in the theatre, television, interpretive, heritage, native, and anthropological communities to explore recent trends, issues, and techniques in implementing the performing arts in a museum context. Animated and performance events planned for CMC range from brief 'guerilla theatre' vignettes involving one or more actors in first-person interpretation in the exhibition halls, to multi-event, multimedia festivals lasting several days. Such programmes call for close coordination between PASE and other sections of the museum : educational programmers must identify which presentations are appropriate for each of their

Figures 117 and 117a
CMC will use a small in-house troupe,
volunteers, and guest performers to
give presentations.

target groups; volunteer assistance is sought from the Friends association, and sponsorship through the Development Directorate; public relations staff must provide promotion, while Design and Technical Services maintains and operates technical install-ations; ticket sales, ticket-taking, public queries, and hosting falls into the lap of CMC's Visitor Reception group; and Protection Services handles crowd and access control.

Professional performers and interpreters (both museum employees and guest artists) as well as semi-professional or amateur troupes and a corps of volunteers will be used in the live performance programmes. Leading Canadian playwrights, choreographers, or composers will be invited to create performance pieces for CMC - as seems only fitting, given the world-class character of the build-ing and the exhibits. Original works, in different languages, will be developed in consultation with ethnic and cultural groups they depict. Native participation will also come through the inclusion of native actors in CMC's acting troupe and the implementation of a Native Interpretation Pro-gramme bringing native students in the performing arts to CMC for field placements. In addition the artist-in-residence programme places studio and performance facilities at the disposal of artists in the fields of dance, music, theatre, and plastic arts; native participants will be encouraged to study CMC's Indian and Inuit collections for inspiration in interpreting their heritage. For example, a carver from British Columbia may work in the Grand Hall or one of the exterior site venues, or a playwright may create a script for a theatrical piece in the History Hall. CMC plans, in the long-term, to create a Centre for Native Performance Artists which would recruit and train performers, sponsor the creation of works, and stimulate the growth of a national network to present artists and their work.

Figures 118 and 118a
Some of CMC's theatrical presentations will have an ambulatory character, others will be fixed in a particular location.

Some of the goals for this type of programming have already been suggested :

- To attract increased visitation, particularly by persons who do not normally visit museums, through emphasizing entertaining and participatory qualities of live events over the traditionally passive educational museum experience.

- To generate revenues that will help support museum programmes for which the public is not charged; revenues may come directly through ticket sales or facility rentals, or indirectly through sales of events-related souvenirs and products created by artisans in demonstrations, or again through increased expenditure in the museum's eateries.

- To enhance the visitor's museum experiences and increase intercultural understanding by using both traditional and innovative theatrical techniques to make cultural heritage come alive.

- To attract media interest and coverage intended to stimulate increased public interest in, and visitation to, the museum.

- To create productions suitable for regional, national, or international distribution, especially by television or as audiovisual publications, and thereby to offer some of CMC's resources to all Canadians.

- To plan cooperative ventures with agencies, organiz-ations, groups, and individuals, locally, regionally, and nationally; this will increase CMC's programming potential and visibility, foster community support, and give CMC greater opportunity to stimulate the performing arts in Canada.

- To provide leadership for the Canadian museum community by developing and evaluating innovative techniques for live interpretation in a museum context.

The environmental reconstruction exhibits in the Grand Hall, History Hall, and the Native Peoples Hall, provide sets for both the guerilla theatre presentations and more major, scheduled theatrical pieces intended primarily as ticketed evening events. The New France town square or the Frontier sections of the History Hall, for example, offer very suitable spaces for presentations which audiences can view from floor and mezzanine levels while themselves remaining within the context of the stage set, so that there is no real barrier between them and the performers. The historical dramatizations here are modelled partly on presentations at Canadian National Historic Sites, which include interactive elements to bring audiences in close contact with the performance. Founded on careful historical research, some will focus on actual persons who lived in the past (not necessarily the famous) and who will describe their experiences in the period settings with which they are associated. From biographical files, performers recreate the personalities of historical figures for the audience, which can study the past through its human representatives.

Some dramatizations will take the form of free-flow ambulatory theatre, Tamara-style, involving 10-20 actors, beginning perhaps in the Grand Hall and followed by related performances in other museum locales. A presentation would involve touring parts of the galleries (where low lighting and special audiovisual effects enhance the dramatic mood), roleplaying by audience members provided with appropriate costumes and make-up, and an intermission in which food and drink is provided for participants. This type of event would host an audience of 100-200 persons, last for three to five hours, and be repeated a number of times over a season of several weeks. Its interactive character can make it a thought-provoking and emotionally-charged experience.

More fixed evening events focus on the Theatre and the Grand Hall. The latter's spaciousness and breathtaking Northwest Coast backdrop make it a marvellous setting for assembly and for theatrical presentations. A seated audience of several hundred can be accommodated in either venue. One- to two-hour performances, involving a cast of 5-10 performers, will be typical. Specially commissioned or existing productions, sponsored by CMC or hosted on a facility-rental basis, may run for several weeks and be repeated a few times a year, or a number of events may be organized as a series, with reduced prices when an entire series is purchased. The Grand Hall exhibition provides an excellent opportunity to animate a world-class heritage culture on a scale never before attempted by a museum; but not all the events there will be restricted to that theme. There, and in the Theatre, dramatic, film, dance, and musical performances may be tied to other exhibit themes - particularly those of the Arts and Traditions Hall - or simply be stand-alone events. The Theatre will be the main setting for dance, and for concerts of native, ethnic, classical, or contemporary music - soloists, small ensembles, or chamber orchestras. Yet the Grand Hall may also host such events on occasion : there is nothing incongruous in a classical concert in a Northwest Coast Indian village setting, for example, since the mix of two cultures reflects the universality of artistic communication.[9] The Theatre's presentations will highlight the wealth and diversity of Canada's cultural heritage, through

artists such as : the Théâtre de la Marmaille, a Montreal-based troupe with a special interest in Inuit culture; Vancouver's Green Thumb Theatre, which addresses issues such as unemployment and immigration; Katari Taiko, a Vancouver troupe of traditional Japanese drum performers; Native Earth Theatre, a Toronto group exploring the lives and aspirations of native women; Anjali, an Ottawa-based classical Indian dancer; and Edmonton's Shumka Dancers who perform traditional Ukrainian dances.

Live events and film presentations in the Grand Hall will be combined with receptions and banquets, the latter taking on the stature of State Dinners when visiting heads of state are received in an environment that ties them in to Canadian history; up to 350 guests for sit-down dinners, and twice that for buffets, can be accommodated. A Pacific Coast Potlatch is the model for official receptions, its centrepiece the magnificent feast bowl commissioned by CMC from Kwakiutl sculptor Calvin Hunt. Carved from a block of red cedar into the reclining mythical figure of a cannibal wild woman, the 26' (8 m.) long feast dish has a huge central bowl in its belly, while face and kneecaps cover secondary bowls; there are also removable bowls carved in the shapes of frogs, sculpins, and seals, as well as oversized serving spoons. The Salon Barbeau can be

Figure 119
The huge feast bowl (shown here with its sculptor, Calvin Hunt) displayed in the Grand Hall will be put to its intended use during banquets held in the hall.

used for smaller stand-up receptions or dinners; it is equipped with a pantry and roll-out food trolleys. A circular, sprung dance-floor has been installed in the centre of this space, and lighting and sound systems support dance or musical performances. Banquets may also be linked to other single events, such as ambulatory theatre, Imax/Omnimax shows, or multi-experiential events like those targeted at Ottawa's diplomatic community. Embassies promote their countries and encourage tourists to go there, but there has been no good public showplace in the national capital for them. CMC can provide that venue and offer them the visibility they would like; in return it would gain access to the Imax films that a number of countries have created to promote themselves. Not only embassies but other organizations - such as corporations, television/movie production companies, or special interest groups - can rent the Grand Hall, or other CMC facilities, for receptions, luncheons, banquets, weddings, VIP functions, board meetings, performance events, conventions, or trade shows; the rental revenue is, in effect, indirect sponsorship of the museum.

Not all of CMC's special events are for large groups. Major theatrical presentations are all very well, but to cover the spectrum of visitor needs museums must also provide small, meditative spaces allowing for intimate one-on-one relationships between individuals and artifacts, and for demonstrations or storytelling with only a few people as audience. Large-scale structured events need to be balanced by small-scale spontaneous ones. Large celebratory happenings, intimate theatre of the Tamara type, and small meditative experiences might all be choreographed together in a series of rituals to influence personal perspectives. Cardinal designed his building as a ritual structure, and different spaces within it can inspire different responses; there are live rituals, filmic rituals, artifact-rich rituals. Ritual rules are well enough known to allow the diverse experiences to be directed towards a central theme; individual contemplative spaces, with a single object as focus, could lead into a larger space/experience, with the two linked so that the latter expands upon the meaning in the former and opens the mind to wider horizons. Through this type of "designer ritual", CMC could produce new utterances, custom-designed myths.

Another approach to more personalized experiences is found in 'live-in' programmes : overnight stays in the museum galleries. Informal soundings by CMC indicate that members of the public frequently respond to the question "When would you most like to be in a museum?" with the answer "After midnight." Probing this response yields the impression people have that museums become magical places after the witching hour - like Giapetto's puppet workshop - where inanimate objects come to life and 'speak' to their human beholders. Many open air museums have programmes for visitors to live in over one or more nights, to enhance the effect of re-enacting lifestyles of the past. These programmes are generally directed at children. Children's museums in Boston, Indianapolis, and Cleveland have also recognized this extraordinary after-midnight attractiveness of museums and responded with camp-ins for organized groups of children. Closer to home, the National Museum of Natural Sciences' held a successful camp-in for staff and families in 1987; they slept in the dinosaur pit and mammal hall. And Murray Schafer's staging of "Ra" between sunset and sunrise was intended to inspire similarly mystical connections. CMC intends to offer to individuals overnight opportunities that will allow for an intensely personal communion with the cultural icons of Canadian history.

Not all CMC's special events are restricted to human performances. One potential of Cardinal's evocatively sculpted building is that parts can be used as screens for projection of symbolic images in son-et-lumière productions. This type of show has been around since the 1950's, derived from the illumination of châteaux in France; passive illumination gave way to 'games' of light, with accompanying soundtracks and/or narrations. Laser projection technology has now been added to incandescent light. CMC's new building lends itself well to son-et-lumière : the Grand Hall's curving parapet, the long vaults above the History Hall and Children's Museum, the Imax/Omnimax dome, the river facades at the ends of the two wings, the large expanses of window, the Entrance Plaza facades of the two wings. All these can serve as screens for sound and light shows that stand alone or are combined with live performances. Such shows permit interpretation of the building's symbolism and previews of themes to be encountered inside the building. They can promote the museum by attracting the attention of tourists on the south shore of the Ottawa River. CMC has at its disposal a palette of laser-projected and incandescent lights for use in converting the regular night lighting of the building to more creative productions, with light changing and undulating to set a certain mood, or on festive occasions to combine with sound in more formal presentations for specific audiences.

...ures 120, 120a, 120b, 120c and
...d
...tivals will highlight the many
...formance traditions that are part of
...nadian culture.

Canada Day, Christmas, and Winterlude are the occasions for major lighting programmes. Throughout each December the permanent architectural lighting will have certain lamps gelled with red and green to highlight sculptural features of the building in traditional Christmas colours, so that it will seem a jewel in contrast to the white landscape around it; this will be augmented by theatrical lighting, using computerized dimmer control, to heighten the festive quality. The February show is similar, except that blue and white (the official Winterlude colours) will be used; special effects will create a sense of drifting snow and glacial movement. For the evenings of July 1-3 a more ambitious show is programmed, with full soundtrack. It traces Canadian history from the dawn of time, through the Ice Age and glacial melt, to the era of native habitation, and on to the period of European settlement; sounds and images such as of animals and birds of the mesozoic era, native chants and artifacts, voyageur folk songs, church bells, and sounds of industrial machinery, provide accompaniment.

February and July son-et-lumière shows will be part of larger spectacles put on by CMC, with the cooperation of other federal agencies, ethnic groups, and cultural organizations. The February show will be an element of a Festival of the North which runs concurrently with Winterlude; the first is to be held in the early 1990's. It will address cultural and environmental issues of Canada's north and its people, to promote the north as a unique and viable component of Canada's cultural, economic, and social fabric. It may include a snow village, Inuit ice sculptures, games, crafts, and other activities characteristic of northern peoples. The July show is a component of a biennial Festival Canada. Each will focus on a specific region of Canada, a particular aspect of material culture (and its expression through the plastic and performing arts), and an individual ethnic group; within this format it will deal with issues and aspects of native, ethnic, and contemporary life, and provide for in-depth exploration of regional cultural variations. For example, the 1989 festival focuses on the West Coast, masks, and Chinese-Canadians; exhibitions in the Grand Hall and the Cultural Traditions Hall play key roles. In 1991 the emphasis will be on the Prairies, drums, and the Ukrainian community. Each festival will be opened on Canada Day by formal ceremonies

Figures 121 and 121a
The Ottawa River will be one of the 'stages' used in a Pageant of Canada, re-enacting historical events from Canadian history, such as those shown here (Champlain's arrival in the Ottawa area, and a landing of Loyalist troops defending Canada from American Revolutionary forces).

performed by elders of Indian tribes from the highlighted region; as elders of Canada's first peoples, they have the roles of hosts and of witnesses to the celebrations. Performances by native groups will also mark the opening ceremonies.

A longer-term goal for Canada Day is to develop a Pageant of Canada, a multimedia extravaganza with events in the museum's theatrical spaces, on the plazas around the site, and on the Ottawa River. The inspiration for such a pageant comes from a similar affair staged at the Chateau Frontenac in Quebec city in the late 'twenties by folklorist Marius Barbeau and others; this provided a broad panorama of Canadian history. The river particularly will be a focus of the pageant CMC envisages, with live presentations on riverbank or floating stages and on watercraft, a son-et-lumière show (some of it projected onto a sail shared by two 50' Haida war canoes which are tied together), and fireworks. However, events will go on all around a central audience in the Central Plaza and riverside park. The Pageant will be performed principally in the evenings, before crowds of some 2000, although a scaled-down version may be presented during the day.

CMC has plans for other, one-time festivals and events. It is hoped to involve local embassies in sponsoring festivals featuring the cultural attractions of their countries. A series of events related to CMC's dance exhibition will take on a festival-like appearance in 1989. In early 1990, CMC will co-host (with the Canadian Institute of the Arts for Young Audiences) the 12th International Showcase of Performing Arts for Young People. This will bring buyers from North American theatres to see 16 full-length children's productions. CMC will make available the Salon Barbeau, the Special Exhibitions Hall, the Grand Hall (for reception and dinner), and the Imax/Omnimax (for evening entertainment); performances will take place in the Theatre and Native Peoples Hall. It is hoped to follow with an International Children's Theatre Festival later in the year. A 10-day Drumming Festival is being considered for 1991. The forms, language, and cultural significance of drums and drumming will provide the conceptual theme for a festival and exhibition, the latter supported by : demonstrations; drum-making workshops for visitors, especially children; lectures by anthropologists, musicologists, and historians; films; and performances from around the world - such as African drummers, Caribbean steel drummers, Sami drummers from Sweden, Indian and Inuit drummers, military drum bands. A more distant idea is for a Celtic Festival in the mid-1990's.

In addition, CMC will commission the creation and production of several large-scale multimedia works over the next decade. The Theatre, Grand Hall, and Central Plaza present marvellous opportunities for leading designers, producers, performance artists, and others to combine new technology and live performers in innovative works sure to excite national and even international attention. The proposed Pageant of Canada would be one such major work. Another production - the creation of Evelyn Roth, Hunnelore Evans, and Gerry Thurston - is tentatively titled "The Old Woman of the Forest." The rain-forest and coastal vistas of the Northwest

Coast (reproduced in the Grand Hall) provided the inspiration for the work, and the catalyst for the performance is the Sea to Sea Drum, made by Haida artist Robert Davidson. The production will animate the Grand Hall's village by superimposing colour, motion, and sound to create a mythical landscape. Upon the touch of the storyteller, Forestwoman (a mythical character who has lived since the beginning of time), the drum releases elements of the story. Performers appear as dream-like echoes from another time, while a costumed dance-chorus interprets the meaning of the solo parts; 'dialogue' is in the form of costume, movement, masked puppetry, and sound. This concept exploits the unique characteristics of the Grand Hall, transforming it for visitors into a multiexperiential event.

The various and wide-ranging performance and special events programmes described above, combined with the less formal animation programmes, should make CMC a lively enough place to dispel the traditional image of museums as staid, solemn institutions which offer only passive experiences. By entombing the past, museums distance their visitors from it. Visitors to CMC, however, will find themselves challenged and inspired by the dramatic approach to interpretation and by the opportunities afforded them to participate physically and mentally in the communicative, conversational, and experiential elements of the interpretive animation in the reconstructed environment exhibits, the interactive theatrical productions, and the seemingly frameless Imax/Omnimax films. Museums have a responsibility not just to document past culture and interpret it to the present, but to demonstrate the reality of cultural continuity, and to encourage and support the development of culture into new forms and new products of expression. CMC accepts this responsibility and invites all who read these words to come and share in its ongoing celebration of the essence and life-force of Canada.

the museum as host

Know your audience. Walk in your visitors' shoes. These are two of Disney's ten commandments for its corporate operations. Disney knows that its success is based on audiences' opinions of its products. To no small degree the good reputation of Disney theme parks is founded upon person-to-person courtesy : the friendliness shown by park hosts to visitors, efforts to anticipate and provide for all the needs and concerns of visitors, and a well-evidenced and sincere desire that their guests enjoy everything about their visit. Why should museums, as public service institutions, not be similarly concerned about *their* visitors? Most have failed to be truly visitor-oriented.

A burning issue in the museum world is whether museums are to be 'artifact-friendly' or 'user-friendly'. Of course they should be both, but opposing camps hold the two stances to be incompatible; this is another manifestation of the "accessibility versus preservation" and "populism versus excellence" controversies already mentioned. The issue is whether museums ought to be responsive to the judgements made of them by their peers (the curatorial community) or by their public. The trend towards professionalization in museums has strengthened the attitude that they are best judged by their peers.[1] Yet those advocating democratization of museums stress greater involvement of, and accountability of institutions to, the public. CMC does not deny the importance of artifacts and their preservation to the museum's mission, nor that a commitment to excellence in all things is a worthy goal. But its existence cannot be justified unless it serves society, and its facilities and programmes must respond as fully as possible to their users' needs. To respond, it is necessary to identify more thoroughly than in the past the various user-groups and their diverse needs, and the relationship between a national museum and its community.

Museums and the public are, in respects, mutually dependent. The public relies on museums to provide access to, and understanding of, material heritage and the cultures associated with it. More than ever, museums rely on the public for the good opinion and support which, somewhere along the road, translate into the revenue vital for museums to operate at levels of excellence. In Canada there has been a tradition of government funding of cultural institutions, but over the last decade or so realization has grown that government resources are finite in the face of increasing and competitive demands for public money. The '80's were marked by cutbacks in public funding combined with widespread acceptance of the politico-philosophical perspective that the size of an institution's 'market' (its users) should determine the amount of resources allocated

Figure 122
Blockbuster exhibitions, such as The Vikings exhibition (shown here is the line-up to see it at the British Museum), were so called because their themes had particular popular appeal; their success was evaluated largely in terms of the number of visitors attracted and revenue generated.

to it. This policy has made it more difficult for museums to maintain services at levels and qualities the public has come to expect; often they have had to reduce support to clients just when they needed greater client support!

While it is the *quality* of the museum experience that is of real importance, government funding depends on the *quantity* of users, something more easily measured and considered by funding authorities as the criterion of success. Related to this is the policy requiring federal government agencies - including the national museums - to pursue increased cost-recovery for services from those who benefit most from the services. The amount of revenue generated from this "user-pays" source is a factor in deciding the financial support an institution can expect from government.

The necessity of supporting requests for government funding with statistical evidence of public interest, and of seeking alternative sources of revenue, including the user-community, help explain why CMC is more client-oriented than before and seeks a wider range of visitors through a greater diversity of attractions and programmes, both educational and entertaining. As Kenneth Hudson has observed, a

museum's financial base has much to do with the way it presents itself to the public, and with the priorities of its goals; the more it depends on direct revenues from its users, the more attention it must pay to showmanship and publicity.[2]

On the other hand, CMC is anxious to reach a greater public because it simply cannot fulfill its potential unless it is used. All efforts to provide access to its collections are wasted if no-one visits the museum; its message of intercultural understanding is meaningless without an audience to receive it. As a national museum, CMC must try to bring all Canadians within the definition of that audience, as well as represent Canada's cultural heritage to international audiences. This responsibility it can only now begin to undertake seriously, thanks to the expanded facilities at its disposal. Yet it will be able to continue that effort only through the enhanced revenues that can be generated by drawing larger audiences, of a million or more visitors annually. Maintaining these audiences depends largely on a positive public response to the museum. CMC, like the museum world generally, has come to a crossroads where it must opt to rise to greater heights or follow a downward spiral to who knows what end : there appears no viable middle option.

Figure 123
CMC is anxious to expand its audience, to communicate its messages to the greatest number of people. Many of the new visitors it hopes to attract will be tourists.

If part of the reason for appealing to wider audiences is revenue, it is also true that responding better to the needs of a larger market itself requires more money. To say that CMC's new facilities and programmes have been designed to satisfy public needs better implies a homogeneity of needs; in reality there is a whole spectrum of needs. To provide for them all is a very complex matter that requires CMC be much more than the conventional model of a museum. We have already discussed the sacred, social, intellectual, and recreational needs of visitors, and some of the types of museum visitors : Bob Kelly's New Visitor and Traditional Visitor, and the streaker, stroller, and student classification. In the next few years CMC will receive over its threshold francophones, anglophones, autochtones, foreign visitors, first-time visitors, regular visitors, visitors with special requirements because of age, social situation, physical or intellectual capabilities, and so on. Each category has definable needs to which CMC must respond effectively enough to make all visitors feel completely satisfied with their experience. This is the essence of hospitality, and the type of treatment the public has a *right* to expect from a public service institution of which they are the chief benefactors. Visiting a national museum is, in the sense of access to heritage, a privilege - particularly a privilege of citizenship, which defines national community - but also a right, the exercise of which it is CMC staff's task to facilitate.

Cultural tourism

Most museums primarily serve local, or at best regional, communities; a secondary market is visitors from other regions, to whom a museum represents the heritage of its locality. A national museum's community is, simply, the nation, and its secondary market the population of the rest of the world. This means that CMC will come in contact with most of its potential users only when they are tourists; as such they have particular needs, especially for recreation. Since the tourist market is of major importance to CMC, the museum has taken pains to cater for its needs and requirements. International tourism is the largest growth industry in the western world, accounting for some 5% of the gross world product.[3] In Canada tourism generates the same percentage of the gross national product, and is the seventh largest earner of foreign exchange (larger than crude petroleum or woodpulp). It is the second largest industry in most provinces, with some 61,000 tourist enterprises, employing 600,000 workers.[4]

Tourism and heritage were long seen as independent, or even antagonistic, interests; it was felt that tourism overexploited heritage resources and encouraged cultural stereotyping. However, over the last decade there has been growing awareness of the importance of cultural resources to tourism. Today people have more leisure-time and more disposable revenue than ever before, and higher educational levels have made them more demanding of leisure experiences. They continue to seek relaxational recreation but, when selecting travel destinations, are more inclined to consider the availability of meaningful, life-enriching experiences of the type that cultural institutions can best provide. Cultural tourism (defined in chapter 1, note 8) is the tourist industry's major new growth area. Tourism Canada estimates that of the $20 billion in Canadian revenues from international tourism in 1986, half had some cultural association; 50% of Canada's tourists visit arts or heritage attractions, and 29% plan their journeys specifically to visit them; a 1985 study identified such resources as a major motivator for Americans to visit Canada.[5] Federal, provincial, and local tourist agencies are now more actively promoting cultural tourism, as opposed to the 'wonders of nature'. Cities are competing for a share of the new market - for the artistic/cultural life of a city is a significant contributor to its image as a favoured tourist destination. New York established its economic recovery strategy on cultural tourism. Quebec City bolstered its position as a major Canadian destination with the recent opening of an important new museum. Toronto continues to add new attractions to its roster. Montreal has been advised to create new museums to establish a network of cultural institutions in its downtown.[6] Numerous studies show that museums can attract millions of tourist dollars to local economies.

The creation of three new national museums, and plans for further cultural institutions along the Ceremonial Route, enhances Canada's capital as a major cultural tourism destination. It is fitting that the capital should be a pilgrimage site for Canadians and the initial host for foreigners who come to discover Canada. Tourism is the National Capital Region's second largest employer, generating $375 million annually. A 1985/86 study of visitor characteristics, demand, behaviour, and attitudes, showed participation in cultural activities to feature heavily in visits to the capital : over 70% visited at least one national landmark, and half visited one or more national museums. Although most respondents saw the capital as a symbol of national identity, more than half felt that overall Canadian culture was underrepresented. The capital was perceived more as a political centre than a tourist destination.[7] The museum boom currently underway should shift the image towards a cultural centre. CMC will have a large role in creating a substantial increase in tourist visitation in 1989/90 and, in the longer-term, in spearheading a cultural renaissance in the city. This will benefit the whole National Capital Region in economic spin-off and visitation to other attractions. But CMC too is dependent on other cultural institutions in the capital to maintain the size of its initial audience in later years, for it is the total attraction of all combined that give a city a reputation as a premier tourist destination.

To exploit fully CMC's many experiential opportunities, a much larger and more diverse audience must be attracted to Parc Laurier than is typical of most museums in North America; CMC cannot be only a local or regional museum. It envisages a series of diffusion zones, each with a

particular audience. The immediate zone around Parc Laurier is the National Capital Region, where the museum's local community makes up a large proportion of its return visitors. Cultural institutions within this zone are perceived not as competitive, but as complementary, with a shared concern to make the capital a favoured tourist destination. It is in the interest of all institutions there to promote one another, to direct tourists from one facility to others.

The next zone is the one-day catchment area, holding day-trippers from Montreal and eastern Ontario, as far as Toronto. Again, this zone's cultural attractions can reinforce one another through mutual promotion and cooperative programming, such as the multi-location mega-festivals held by American cultural institutions.

A two-day zone covers Quebec-Windsor-New York State : weekend visitors, particularly bus tours; in this very large market the competition to attract

Figures 124, 124a and 124b
Experiencing the distinctive cultural elements - museums, arts events, historical structures, ethnic traditions - is now known to be a major attractor, both to Canada generally and to its capital, of tourists from other countries. It is the combination of features that determines the degree of popularity of any given destination.

Attracting larger audiences also means attracting more diverse audiences. About one-third of visitors to the National Capital Region come as tourists - or, at least, come seeking leisure opportunities. The typical visitor : comes usually from Ontario or Quebec (but is normally an Anglophone); is 26-45 years old; visits in a family group in summer, but at other seasons with spouse; comes to see national landmarks, or the natural environment, or to learn more about Canada.[8] While the 'Canadiana' visitors are already strongly museum-oriented, others (categorized by Kelly as 'City Spree' visitors) are more interested in shopping, theatre, and restaurants. Some visitors come as personal guests of residents; whatever the main reason for their visit, they often

tourists is fiercer. This triangle is the top of a much larger zone, the eastern seaboard corridor stretching down to Miami. Some 60 million Americans live in or near this corridor, within an hour's drive from a local airport; it is the main corridor bringing U.S. tourist dollars into Canada. The corresponding east-west axis, from St. John's to Victoria, holds about 20 million Canadians. Along these axes CMC can advertise by travelling exhibits, to tap into audiences such as those seeing the exhibits Epcot imports from the world's leading museums. Television is another way to reach these areas.

At the same time CMC will promote other Canadian cultural destinations by cross-referencing heritage sites in its History Hall and other exhibitions, and stimulating the creation of a pan-Canadian museum network that will promote Canada as a cultural tourism destination. Although the United States is a major target market, other countries' tourists are becoming increasingly important. Japanese tourists, for instance, have been increasing steadily through-out the '80's : in 1987 they rose by 24% over 1986, and half a million are expected to be visiting Canada by the mid-1990's.

Figures 125 and 125a
To develop larger audiences, museums must identify the various types of tourists and be able to respond to their diverse interests and inclinations. Some tourists, for instance, look for shopping, dining and theatre opportunities. Seniors also represent a special target-group that will increase in size as the baby-boom generation ages.

proportion of this segment in the visitor population, it represents 55% of those who stay in commercial accommodations. This type of visitor is especially important on weekdays outside peak tourist season, representing two-thirds of CMC's potential out-of-town visitors at those times. Business visitors possess the typical characteristics (e.g. high level of education, high status occupation, relatively cosmopolitan outlook) of museum visitors, and 43% claim to visit capital area museums, even though museums have made little effort to appeal directly to them. They also have more disposable income than the average tourist, and many are frequent return visitors to the city. They too have special needs : brief tours outside working hours, combined with opportunities to eat a meal, relax and enjoy a show, and buy tasteful gifts for family members.

Identifying the many audiences and assessing their characteristics and needs have been essential prerequisites for the design of comprehensive programming that gives people a rewarding visit, encourages them to return, and persuades them to

act as tourists, mostly during the day so that they can socialize at night. The key to attracting them is to persuade their hosts that CMC is a must-see place for their guests. Retired persons are another segment of the leisure/tourist group, well-defined, already motivated towards museum-visiting, often travelling in bus tours (mainly in the spring). Organized groups represent special market opportunities, since through one sale many tourists may be captured. The trick is to convince tour packagers, wholesalers, and agents that CMC and the National Capital Region are destinations preferable to others. Their selection of destinations is made on quite different grounds than individual visit decisions. School groups have dominated the bus tour segment of tourist visitation in the past; operators have indicated that the new museums increase the attractiveness of the National Capital Region to their clients. A key to the success of group visits is special accommodations - both for the groups and for their vehicles - and services to coordinate visits. Another type of group is the family, which seeks activities that strengthen parent-child relationships and/or enables parents to expose children to information of high educational value; this has long been an important type of visitor to CMC.

The *National Capital Region Visitor Survey* of 1985/86 identified an important, but underexploited, target market that visits Ottawa-Hull : the business visitor. Although it is hard to estimate the total

promote CMC as a worthwhile destination to their family and friends.

CMC's expanded facilities, its greater range of educational and recreational opportunities, and its ventures into new areas not traditionally associated with museums, are all necessary to maximize its total audience, and enhance the attractiveness of the

National Capital Region. The diversity of its features and experiences will almost give CMC the character of a heritage theme park. The building is an architectural monument that will attract visitors in its own right, as will the views of Parliament Hill from the site. For the Traditional Visitor and the Canadiana tourist the museum remains a showcase for authentic national treasures and a place to learn about their heritage - in the exhibitions, the Médiathèque, and behind-the-scenes. For the foreign tourist, who seeks different cultural experiences, CMC's environmental reconstructions, cultural animation, and ethnic celebrations will have appeal. For tourists generally, especially the New Visitor element, CMC's entertainment offers the qualitative cultural recreation now increasingly demanded by today's travellers; throughout peak tourist season Parc Laurier and CMC's plazas will be hives of colourful and enjoyable happenings, with festivals as seasonal highlights. Nighttime theatrical, cinematic and multi-experiential presentations, dining and socializing opportunities, and the cultural marketplace of CMC's sales shop, will attract City Spree visitors, couples who visit the capital in the winter, and business visitors. For the last and for school or special interest groups, custom-designed tours will respond to specific needs, and be supplemented by demonstrations, workshops, and so on. There are many routes for individual exploration of the museum's vast resources, notably through the interactive exhibits and databases, while families' need to experience together is met particularly in the Children's Museum. There is something for almost every taste and for every season.

Facilities and programmes are not enough to guarantee the reputation of CMC as a first-choice tourist destination. Word-of-mouth endorsements by visitors to family, friends, and business acquaintances, will help build a clientele; hence the importance of making every visitor's museum experience fully satisfying. In addition CMC must actively seek publicity and promotion, particularly by generating high-quality images, of its facilities and exhibits, that trigger interest among the media. By being more event-oriented, CMC expects to attract the attention of the mass media more often; its own foray into television will help it create the images that encourage viewers to visit in person. It must, furthermore, exploit cultural tourism fully through cooperative promotional ventures with other cultural agencies in the capital and across the country, since "the whole is greater than the sum of the parts". Also necessary are working partnerships - at least coordination, often formal cooperation -

Figures 126 and 126a
The experiences and attractions offered by CMC have been designed to cater to a range of tastes and interests. There is something for almost everyone.

between cultural agencies, tour package operators, transportation, accommodation, food services, and entertainment industries. Only a concerted effort can achieve the accelerated growth in visitation that benefits all parties. Again Disney points the way : to make its theme parks more attractive as vacation destinations, it has set up a travel company to create packages combining round trip transportation, accommodations, park admissions, meal coupons, car rentals, and excursions to other regional attractions.

If museums need tourism agencies, the reverse is no less true. Private enterprise tries to respond to the development of cultural tourism, but generally lacks the necessary expertise in cultural heritage and the access to many sources of cultural goods and experiences. Where they have tried to produce cultural tourism packages, the result has often been what anthropologists call 'staged authenticity' : a transparent attempt to fake a cultural experience. Cultural tourism also creates demands for supplementary goods and services, such as cultural appreciation training (lectures, readings, backstage access, film or videotape programmes, etc.), not readily available to the commercial tourism industry.

Museums, on the other hand, have a comparative advantage in designing cultural tourism packages. They know what is available, where, who can deliver it, who are the experts in given fields, and how best to explain meaningfully for tourists what they see and do. Museums also have better knowledge of the sources of authentic goods of the cultural market-place. Therefore they have the expertise to produce travel packages that tourism agencies can then market and operate. CMC envisages this type of cooperative venture not only to bring tourists to the National Capital Region, but to take them out on tours to distant and often exotic places, with museum experts as hosts/guides. Destinations might include archaeological sites, native villages, folk festivals across Canada, foreign places with links to Canadian heritage - such as the Ukraine or Iceland - or world heritage sites since CMC's mandate now encompasses the history of civilization. Such field trips can bring participants as close as most can hope to get to dreams of being an Egyptologist, say, or a paleontologist in the Gobi Desert. The experiential element of tourism is becoming increasingly important :

> In Bali ... tourists are no longer satisfied with watching the dancers, they want to learn the steps! In Morocco, where a replica of a mosque has just been opened for tourists, they are asking to take part in the ceremonies! ... the next 'adventures' sought after by tourists will be aimed at a better understanding of the people visited. Future tourists will be amateur ethnologists or anthropologists. They will no longer be satisfied merely to be shown things : they will want to participate, to try them out, to be initiated.[9]

Visitor services

Getting visitors to come to the museum in the first place is one thing; getting them to return is quite another. Part of the key is a wide range of programmes that cannot be experienced in one visit, and introducing new programmes often so that there is always something worth returning for. Another part is to ensure that the visitor's experience is in every way enjoyable, a goal to which museums have, traditionally, not devoted much effort, relying on exhibits and related programmes to create a favourable impression. A quite different philosophy drives international exposition and theme park operations where 'guest relations' are a dominating concern; the notion being that visitors are guests and the institution, as host, has the responsibility of ensuring that every aspect of the guest's stay is pleasant and

Figure 127
Providing a warm welcome to visitors as they enter a museum helps make a visit enjoyable. On its opening day, the National Gallery of Canada had clowns on hand to make the public feel welcome.

worry-free. This calls for detailed attention to such things as parking, how to load and unload tour buses, meeting and greeting visitors, providing guidance on what to see and do, making sure visitors can find their way around with ease, managing line-ups for tickets or presentations, and providing all sorts of amenities and services - not only the more obvious such as rest areas and eateries, but also conveniences such as diaper-changing facilities. These things are not peripheral to the museum experience but crucial to providing an environment that is welcoming and comfortable for visitors. It may be suggested that "No set of responsibilities are more critical to the

museum in its quest for large tourist/visitor populations than visitor services."[10]

CMC has established a Visitor Services section charged with those responsibilities. It coordinates the dealings that Protection Services, Public Relations, Educational Services, Performing Arts and Special Events, and the Volunteer Bureau have with visitors. Visitor Services staff usually represent the first interface between visitors and CMC's programmes. A warm and welcoming reception at the threshold of the museum from CMC's hosts can immediately make visitors feel at home and impart a

Figure 128
The museum's main entrance has been noted to resemble a face - its dramatic appearance is sure to make an impression on visitors. Visitors enter through the 'jaws'; the vestibule inside features a neon-lit glass sculpture by Brian Baxter that symbolizes the Aurora Borealis. Above the entrance is a large public rest area with views out, through the 'eyes', over the plaza.

humanizing touch to the building complex; a similar farewell, with invitation to return, will reinforce the feeling. Here and elsewhere hosts provide directions and other information to visitors, and a trouble-shooting service. They also welcome, and occasionally seek, visitors' comments on the museum.

After entering the museum, most visitors want to find out what there is to see and do, then decide on an itinerary. Visitor Services staffs an information desk in the main entrance lobby and, at times, posts at the group reception and river entrance areas. Visitors can obtain oral information or brochures answering questions such as the whereabouts of components of the museum, cafeteria hours, where to get strollers, times and places of theatre performances or special events, how to book tours, etc. Visitor Services is also responsible for the telephone enquiry service, electronic signs and kiosks providing directional and directory information, wall maps and other elements of the visitor orientation system. Information on other attractions and facilities in the National Capital Region, bus timetables, and lists of key telephone numbers (auto services, taxis, Para-Transpo, etc.) are also available. At the group reception area Visitor Services staff ensure tour groups have all the information pertinent to their needs (e.g. meeting and pick-up arrangements). All these services help guests organize their visit according to their particular needs and interests.

Another responsibility of Visitor Services is for access management. Staff direct the smooth arrival and departure of visitors who travel on foot, by bicycle (provision and supervision of bicycle racks), by car (supervision of garage, to handle problems such as lights left on), by city buses (timetable information), and by tour buses (provision of drop-off/pick-up points, summoning buses to pick-up points). An automobile drop-off area is near the museum's main entrance. To simplify traffic around the Entrance Plaza, the tour bus drop-off area is on the level below the plaza, accessed from a ramp; the group reception area here can handle up to ten bus-loads of visitors, and has coatcheck, washrooms, and group lunchroom. CMC's main lobby is a circulation hub, connecting with the group reception area, parking garage, Entrance Plaza, cafeteria wing, all exhibition levels, Children's Museum, sales shop, and theatres. In the lobby are visitor amenities as well as waiting and viewing areas. This marshalling yard sees arrivals and departures, information queries, reservation and purchasing of tickets, deposit and claiming of articles from the cloakroom, meetings with guides, rental of audiotours,

orientation, balcony viewing of activities down in the Grand Hall, families or other groups waiting for all their members to arrive. In peak periods as many as a thousand people may be standing in, or passing through, the lobby. CMC's hosts must ensure a smooth circulation flow and control line-ups.

Managing line-ups is a particularly prominent task, since events in the two theatres, guided tours, and some of the special exhibitions and presentations elsewhere on-site require pre-booking. Although reservations can be made by telephone or mail, many visitors buy or pick up tickets in person. It is also possible to reserve places for free but limited access events, programmes, or food services; in this way arriving visitors can coordinate several elements of their visit in one place. Visitor Services staff organize visitor queues and usher for theatre presentations and special exhibitions. They control circulation in outside areas where festivals or other events are underway, manage the overflow from facilities with limited capacity, and identify special routes through the building for large guided groups or the mobility-impaired.

Another responsibility is to coordinate the visits of VIPs and dignitaries. Such visits bring the museum recognition through media coverage, and boost public attendance during the visit. Each visit needs to be treated individually; they may vary in length and degree of formality. Yet even short visits may require large-scale preparations, and in all cases CMC's hosts must know the correct protocols and procedures. For every visit Visitor Services plans a suitable itinerary, perhaps coordinates the visit with External Affairs, reserves and prepares facilities - including a small but elegant VIP Lounge, just off the Grand Hall - ensures appropriate staff are available as hosts, and helps with security.

Visitor Services also helps manage, sometimes in coordination with other departments, amenities for the convenience and comfort of visitors. In the main lobby are the information/reception desk, the box-office, the audiotour rental desk, washrooms, and a cloakroom with a 1000-garment capacity. Other coat storage facilities are in the group reception area, the Children's Museum, the restaurant, and at the river entrance; lowered counter sections facilitate access from wheelchairs. CMC can supply visitors with wheelchairs, strollers, and folding seats. It also provides Lost & Found and First Aid services, postage stamps and letter-boxes, and assistance in calling for taxis and auto repair. All these are considered important elements of guest relations.

Rest areas are equally vital to the success of a museum visit, for the physical fatigue of touring, added to mental fatigue created by low-lit displays and spatial disorientation, is a notorious museum malady. Both the main lobby and Grand Hall are large open spaces where visitors may collect their thoughts, make decisions before touring the galleries, wait for other members of their parties, and so on. A large, circular salon near the History Hall, directly above the main entrance, is primarily a public rest area, although receptions may occasionally be held there; a few icons of Canadian history are on display. Windows to the outside provide all these areas with the visual orientation necessary to combat museum fatigue. Smaller rest areas are interspersed throughout the exhibitions; in the case of History Hall they are blended into the period reconstructions. Their strategic placement gives visitors the opportunity for a change of pace, and relief from what can be an intellectually and emotionally demanding experience.

Most museums, including Canada's national museums, have paid cursory attention to feeding their guests, often supplying only basic, unattractive cafeterias that add nothing to the museum experience, and sometimes even produce an unfavourable image. The tenets of 'guest relations' and 'multiexperientialism' demand a fresh approach to food services. A new breed of museum visitor expects something beyond standard cafeteria fare. Providing a special eating experience can (as Epcot has shown) augment and reinforce the core museum experience. Furthermore, it helps hold visitors in the building longer. As CMC has little expertise in food services, private firms were invited to make proposals for operating the cafeteria and restaurant. Only Crawley & McCracken Company Ltd. of Montreal bid on the complete food services package, and they now operate CMC's eateries, paying CMC a set annual fee plus a percentage of the sales. Crawley & McCracken bring to the museum over 80 years of experience in the food services industry, and an affiliation with the French firm Sodexho, the fifth largest food service company in the world; this enables them to promote CMC in Sodexho-affiliated restaurants in 48 countries. Wide-ranging menus will make CMC's food services independently attractive, help draw visitors to the museum, and contribute to the image of CMC as a source of enjoyable experiences. Revenues from the food services - both retail sales and facility rentals to private groups - will support CMC's core programmes.

Most services are based in the offshoot wing between public and curatorial blocks of the museum. On the lower level sits the cafeteria, accessible both from a corridor off the Grand Hall, and from Parc Laurier. It is a self-serve buffet with snacks, light and full meals (most prepared on-site), and licensed to serve beer and wine. Breakfast, lunch, and dinner are served. Some 300 guests can be accommodated - more in summer, when tables can be put out on the tree-lined terrace separating the cafeteria and the park. On the upper level, atop the cafeteria, the 60-guest restaurant enjoys an even better view of the

Figures 129 and 129a
CMC's principal food services are in the small wing projecting out into Parc Laurier. A large self-service cafeteria is topped by an intimate full-service restaurant which gives an excellent view of the river and Ottawa skyline. Ethnic dishes will be featured in the menus of each.

park, river, and Parliament Hill. It has full bar service and a more adventurous menu, featuring ethnic dishes from all regions of Canada. While the cafeteria, which may attract half to three-quarters of all the visitors to the museum, is a lively, bustling place, the restaurant offers a quieter and more leisurely eating atmosphere; it too has a terrace for *al fresco* dining. Adjacent to the restaurant - a moveable partition allows the two areas to become one for special occasions - is the Friends' Lounge, where a servery/bar is operated and free coffee supplied for members of the Friends association. Crawley & McCracken also manage Salon Barbeau's pantry, food vending machines in employee and group lunchrooms, and cater for the Grand Hall banquets and other special events which require refreshments. To relate food services to the total cultural experience offered by CMC, on 'theme days' customized menus of native or ethnic foods will complement the themes of exhibitions and programmes elsewhere in the museum; 'dinner theatre' packages combine restaurant and Imax/Omnimax shows. Light refreshment is also available in appropriate areas in the History Hall, such as the Louisbourg tavern, to enhance the exhibit experience.

An amenity more problematic than food services is visitor parking. The new building has underground

parking for 300 cars, but this is insufficient during peak visitations. Fortunately there is no shortage of nearby parking lots; efforts are underway to link these more closely with the museum complex. A shuttle bus service along the Ceremonial Route during peak tourist season helps bring tourists who have parked farther away. A more difficult access problem has been the large number of school and tour bus arrivals. In the past about 20% of CMC's visitors have come in organized groups; in May/June group attendance accounts for the greater part of weekday visitation. These groups travel to and within the capital by bus. During this peak period CMC requires parking space for some 40 buses, 3 or 4 drop-off locations, and 4-8 pick-up locations (since picking up passengers generally takes more time than dropping them off).[11] Space for three buses was built into the group reception area, accessible from a ramp leading down from the Entrance Plaza; supplementary lay-bys in front of the museum can accommodate several more buses, either as pick-up/drop-off points or for queuing to access the below-plaza reception area. For bus parking, CMC has been investigating short-term options such as an existing lot by Jacques Cartier park, nearby street parking, and creating a lot at the north end of the museum. This issue has yet to be fully resolved.

Marketing the museum

Marketing is another of those processes relatively new to the museum world.[12] Traditional elements heap scorn on it, as an operation which compromises the high values museums hold dear; the fear is that marketing inevitably commercializes. In the days when museums were content with only those elitist audiences who appreciated high culture, and when they could survive on government funding without concern about attendance figures, marketing may not have been necessary. Not so today. The cost of operating museums has grown beyond the ability of government funding alone to support it, and there is consequently greater reliance on attendance-generated revenues or private sector sponsorship (which is related to visitor attendance). Competition for the leisure-time of the public has intensified; some competitors are becoming quite sophisticated and integrating museum-like experiences into their repertoire.

If marketing means communication, museums have long engaged in it. However, only in recent years, in the face of increasing competition, have they realized that they are not very successful, for it requires

Figure 130
Promotional activities are increasingly vital to museums as the competition for public leisure-time intensifies.

management attitudes and staff skills upon which museums never placed high premiums - such as advertising, merchandizing, tour packaging, visitor services, fundraising. And it requires a mastery of the mass media which has been similarly lacking.

Marketing should be seen neither as anathema nor panacea. Properly implemented, it can deliver an organization's products and services more effectively and efficiently than if marketing practices are ignored. Marketing has a bad image, often equated with advertising or public relations. In reality it is a disciplined approach to acquiring resources (funds, volunteers, members, public support), by improving client service and satisfaction.[13] Its promotional messages need not be commercial, crass, or hype; they can be restrained and distinctive.

Museums need not be market-driven - they can hardly hope to be all things to all people. But they can and, as public service institutions, must be market-oriented; democratization of cultural programmes demands it. This means establishing an interactive relationship between client and producer : making a serious effort to acquire and maintain an awareness of the various audiences that comprise a museum's market; sensitivity to the needs of those audiences and to their reactions to a museum's offerings; and responsiveness to them as far as possible within institutional goals and values. It is in fact to disseminate those values that museums must develop the marketing skills needed to communicate with the public. It takes constant vigilance to meet the demands of marketing and yet not erode museums' standards of excellence : this is a challenge, not an impossibility. For example, in museum boutiques, the authenticity of crafts or art work and the accuracy of information products should be curator-approved before they are selected. The stamp of approval by experts declares items for sale to be information-rich and value-enhanced; discriminating selection of merchandize by staff assures customers that they are acquiring only outstanding or even unique objects.

CMC is forging closer links between the museum staff involved in marketing. Apart from the work of the sales shop, publishing programmes, and visitor services in communicating with the public, promoting awareness of CMC is the job principally of the Public Relations department; a new position, Director of Marketing, oversees this and other elements. Sponsorship is an aspect of marketing that falls under the responsibility of another relatively new department, the Development Directorate.

CMC is seeking to diversify its financial base through a healthy balance of public, private, and self-generated revenues. This diversification is a necessary response to the pressures of our time; as Sir Roy Strong points out, museums are in what is fundamentally "a sink or swim situation."[14]

Canadians have been less than generous in fulfilling their responsibility in supporting the cultural sector. The percentage of Canadian institutions and individuals claiming charitable deductions on their tax returns has diminished over the last three decades. Donations averaged 0.5% of pre-tax profits during the 1980's, compared with 1.5% in 1958; currently less than half of all firms with assets over $25 million claim any charitable donation at all. Many corporations have failed to seize the opportunity to serve and enrich the society of which they are a part. Canadian cultural institutions would be in dire straits if not for a few leading corporations and foundations; even these, receiving more funding requests each year, have become very discriminating in their donations. The arts community has actively sought private sponsorship for long enough that they are more skilled than museums. And in the museum world there is a tendency for corporate sponsors to give mostly to museums of their communities. In this sense CMC - perceived as a publicly funded institution - has found itself at a disadvantage in fundraising. On the other hand, the opening of a world-class building having innovative exhibits, marvellous facilities, and stimulating performing arts programmes provides an unprecedented opportunity to persuade private enterprise to engage in sponsorships and other joint endeavours, and to raise CMC's profile in the business community generally.

Appealing to altruism is no longer enough to attract significant charitable contributions. Corporations expect something in return for their support. The creation of a new museum allows CMC to reciprocate the generosity of sponsors, with benefits both tangible and intangible. It offers the immortality of association with a permanent institution destined for international acclaim, located in the national capital, and housing the national treasures; and the high visibility and public profile that such an association entails. Sponsors have their names on plaques prominently displayed in the sections of the museum they sponsor, and in the salon above the museum's main entrance. Major sponsors will have galleries or other facilities named in their honour. All sponsors may associate their name and logo with those of CMC in promotional products, and their names will be given visibility in CMC publications.

Figure 131
The generosity of sponsors is acknowledged publicly in a variety of ways, such as through commemorative plaques displayed in the salon (shown in this model) above the museum's main entrance.

Sponsorship also earns automatic corporate membership in CMC's Friends association and use of the Friends Lounge, as well as membership in the Director's Circle, a prestigious senior executives club whose members have special privileges. On the more tangible side, sponsors' benefits include : special access to sponsored areas, CMC executive boardrooms, and other areas, for corporate functions or promotional events; reserved underground parking; invitations to previews of special exhibitions and shows; reserved tickets for the Imax/Omnimax theatre; and special programmes or events created for the sponsor's employees.

A by-product of a sponsorship programme is that the museum cultivates contacts in the business community. To achieve the same results in a wider sphere, CMC established in 1987 the Friends of the Canadian Museum of Civilization. Many museums, especially in the United States, have come to depend on their Friends associations. They build and formalize supportive relationships, and bring into the museum a sampling of public opinion and expect-ations from all parts of the country, in return creating an informed constituency whose members' act as ambassadors to local and national communities.

They give interested individuals or organizations an opportunity to share in the development of the mus-eum and gain a fuller understanding of its purposes, activities, and products. They bring to the assistance of the museum the talents and abilities of volunteers from all walks of life, and undertake activities of a charitable nature. They can act as lobby groups, advocating the interests of the museum to politicians and to the public. And they generate revenue, via membership fees, donations, fundraising events, and by expanding the market for museum products and programmes. The members of Friends associations range from major corporations to private citizens of ordinary means; all have in common a strong interest in their nation's cultural heritage.

Those are the roles which CMC's Friends will play. The association is devoted to the well-being of the museum, its programmes, its role in the community, and to spreading awareness of CMC and its mission. The money it raises helps CMC develop new exhibitions, arrange lectures by leading scholars, create innovative programmes, and acquire new technology to experiment in cultural communication. CMC provides a lounge and office-space to the Friends, and a staff member to liaise between the association and CMC's divisions and to coordinate training of members. Membership has benefits such as : discounts on boutique merchandize; pre-purchase of museum publications at reduced prices; discounts on theatre tickets; invitations to previews and exhibition openings; special events (tours, seminars, etc.) exclusively for Friends; social activities; special tours of CMC exhibitions that travel to the localities of members; a newsletter; and limited membership privileges in other museums' Friends associations. Membership fees are set at different levels for individuals, families, youths, out-of-towners, corporations, and for those able to make larger contributions. CMC welcomes everyone who wishes to join, but has particularly targeted for recruitment all mayors in the region, federal and provincial politicians, members of the diplomatic corps, members of Quebec and Ontario's museum associations, regional educational and cultural institutions, community organizations and service clubs, ethnic associations and native groups, and major businesses and corporations in the area.

One of the Friends' most valuable services is to provide volunteers to help museum staff. Without such voluntary aid CMC could not undertake many of its present services and public programmes. With Protection Services staff and CMC's professional animators, volunteers represent the principal public face of the museum, as hosts, ushers, tour guides, educational programme coordinators, demonstrators, and so on. The public encounters them staffing information and reception desks in the lobbies and the Médiathèque, selling tickets, coordinating activities in the Children's Museum, conducting visitor surveys, and in numerous other roles. Behind the scenes they assist in research projects and other curatorial duties, prepare mailings of invitations to special events, operate the boutique's mail-order service, prepare promotional packages, produce newsletters, and run the Friends association, among other tasks. CMC plans to build a corps of some 500 volunteers, all drawn from the Friends association, but managed through a Volunteer Bureau like an employment agency. Museum divisions specify their needs in job descriptions, and the Bureau matches them with its inventory. The new building has lunch-room, locker room, and work/lounge areas where volunteers can relax, train, or plan programmes and activities.

What do volunteers get in compensation for their time and talents? Of course they get a sense of achievement and the satisfaction of contributing to a good cause. But many today seek more benefit than this from voluntary activities. Some value the high-quality training CMC provides; it enriches their lives, develops skills, and gives valuable work experience. Others, especially retired persons, welcome the opportunity to put existing skills to good use, sometimes easing their boredom or re-establishing self-esteem; this pool of talent in the National Capital area is particularly valuable to CMC. Then again there are the opportunities for public recognition, through museum newsletters and annual reports, or simply for social interaction.

Voluntarism brings the museum in closer contact with the local user community. Its importance to CMC, as a source of frequent visitors, as well as providers of oral endorsements to potential visitors from afar, is not in the least diminished by the museum's interest in markets far beyond the capital. CMC remains committed to maintaining an environment in which local residents may make a significant contribution to, and derive meaning from, the museum; and it hopes that its existence will be a source of pride for all Canadians but especially for the populace of the National Capital Region. Its increased concern with marketing itself nationally and internationally, to attract tourists in greater numbers, is to ensure that its message of intercultural understanding reaches as many people as possible, and that the museum can earn the enhanced revenues needed to fund the dissemination of that message. That increased visitation also benefits the residents of the capital, through economic spin-offs for local businesses. To maximize its user-community in this competitive world necessitates the museum acquiring new skills and new attitudes, directed at tourism planning, guest relations, marketing. These are facts of life. Museums can no longer afford to be aloof institutions, but must come to terms with their sym-biotic relationship with their users. They must be aware of, genuinely concerned with, and responsive to the needs of their diverse audiences. Museums must, in sum, get people *involved* with them, in a welcoming and a sharing environment, and involved with cultural heritage, if they are to have a valid and viable role in tomorrow's world, and if society of the future is to remain conscious of its roots in, and debt to, the past.

the museum as resource

The 'Information Society' that we are beginning to see emerge will give rise to a world in many respects significantly different from that of today. Increasingly, information is a commodity that will be the foundation of wealth and social status; many developed countries, including Canada, are becoming major producers of information-based services, rather than material goods. Information expands our understanding of our environment, ourselves, our past achievements, and our future potential. It takes many forms, ranging from the crisp, clean, computer-manipulable data on which science is founded, to the essence of experience grasped as much by our senses and intuition as by our intellect, and less easily captured by language - at best an imperfect tool.

Yet an equally important characteristic of tomorrow's world is *communication.* Information is of little value unless shared, and no sustainer of *democratic* society unless freely accessible. The new technologies driving society's transformation are as much instruments of communication as of information storage and retrieval. These technologies are gradually creating a Global Village much along the lines of McLuhan's vision. Instant communication and the ability to transmit, with high efficiency, huge quantities of information - in a diversity of forms - over great distances is linking communities within a framework of shared knowledge. The larger community thus created, the Global Village, will be defined by the knowledge base (and the values inherent in it) which is made common to all members by the communication process.

Museums have a valid role in this future, for their basic resource is information : whether implicit within material objects, made explicit through research and interpretation, or communicated to visitors through the medium of experience. All their core functions exist to support the increase of human knowledge by managing that information in ways that maximize its accessibility and its intelligibility.

But, if they are to become more than just relics of the twentieth century, they must keep pace with the changing needs of society. Although museums' *generic* mission, of increasing human knowledge, remains constant through time, their *temporal* mission must evolve reactively to social change and be able to respond appropriately. By definition, museums have no real resources to offer society *unless* those resources meet genuine needs.

It is perhaps in times of change that museums are most vital to society, supplying that lifeline to the past, that sense of continuity, which humans seem to need to proceed - confidently and peaceably - in forging a worthwhile future. This may be particularly true of societies where modernization, urbanization, and growth of tourism must be compensated for by institutions dedicated to the preservation and strengthening of material and non-material elements of traditional cultural heritage.[1] The creation of a global community need not be a threat to local, regional, or national cultures. The technologies that are creating it also offer the means to preserve the information resources of cultural heritage : by enabling their replication on new, durable media; and by disseminating them to a wider audience - which in turn may foster greater appreciation of human heritage and the need to preserve it. Museums are still the best-equipped institutions to interpret the significance of heritage in a changing world, by building a bridge between past and future and by providing a forum for conversation between representatives of different cultures. The form in which society emerges from its present metamorphosis may depend much upon how successful heritage institutions are in instilling understanding between the various cultures of the Global Village.

At its most fundamental level the Canadian Museum of Civilization is no more, and no less, than a resource open to exploitation. How valuable a resource depends partly upon the extent of use made of it. Therefore part of CMC's task is to encourage that use - by, for example, introducing entertainment elements that draw new audiences formerly distanced by the solemn image of the traditional museum - and to make it practicable for as many people as possible to have access to its collections, programmes, facilities, and services. Two elements lie at the core of the 'museum-without-walls' concept. One is the Médiathèque, which serves as the repository of the databases that are not only accessible to on-site users of the facility, but will become so to every corner of the globe, twenty-four hours a day. The other is the networking capability built into the new museum; this is the key to disseminating CMC's informational resources. These represent memory and communication which, together, create cultural consciousness : the essence of a museum.

The intimate connection between the Médiathèque and the Network Control Centre is reflected in their physical adjacency in the building. This is the spatial focus of CMC's 'information technology', a term used to describe the meshing of computing and tele-communications technologies; it is also the core for much of the 'media technology' used throughout the building - that is the systems that blend computers and audiovisual media. Over the last decade it has become increasingly evident that a new literacy is developing, based on visual and auditory media, in response to the output of the entertainment industry. Witness : the pervasiveness of popular music - not merely in leisure contexts but as a background to everyday activities (symbolized by the portable cassette players that allow one to listen while travelling, working, etc.); the swift adoption of VCRs in North America as a standard household appliance, and the growth in home computers - marketed largely on their abilities to produce ever more realistic graphics; and above all the dominant role of television in our leisure-time. The average Canadian watches 24 hours of TV a week, and listens to 18 hours of radio.[2] Museums have begun to respond, tentatively, to these factors - hence the greater use of video screens as a language of display - but few have seriously addressed the real issue.

Part of that issue is that more and more people are forming relationships with machines, of various sorts, for the purpose of gaining knowledge of their world and their fellow-humans. It has been pointed out that "People have long 'understood' other cultures not through actual contact but through mediated experience and imagination."[3] Museums are no different from television in their mission of mediating between everyday life and experiences which are, to most, arcane or inaccessible.[4] The

other part of the issue is that the next generation of computerized technologies will be more affordable, more powerful, easier to use, and more easily linkable to telecommunications channels, with the likely result that they will become much more common in the home environment; perhaps 30%-40% of North American households in the 1990's will have access to information services via computers.[5] At the same time, technological advances continually raise public expectations regarding fidelity of image and sound, and challenge of content.

Museums are deluding themselves if they believe they can pursue audience development while standing aloof from our mass-mediated culture, or ignoring the fact that the home will increasingly become the focus of education, work, and leisure - a phenomenon too lightly dismissed as the 'couch potato' syndrome. The museum-without-walls is a museum able to reach out to multiple locations great distances apart to supply comparable information, programmes, and services to those available to on-site visitors, and thus provide larger numbers of people with that shared experience which is central to the definition of cultural identity.[6]

The highly visual nature of museums makes them eminently appropriate media for a society dominated by televisual forms. After its artifactual collections, CMC's most important resource is perhaps its collection of audio and visual materials. Many of these have been, or are being, transferred to laser disc, to facilitate preservation, access, and dissemination. Audio recordings from field research (some 15,000 hours), an image inventory of the entire collection of artifacts, and the photographic archive held in CMC's Photothèque, have been replicated on laser disc. Other, more specialized discs have also been created; for example, an archive of the photographs and other documentation of Canadian native art gathered in the course of developing "The Spirit Sings" exhibition, and an interactive learning disc with images of some 600 paleoeskimo carvings.

CMC intends to develop its collection of films and videos into a major national resource, with particular emphasis on ethnographic materials, as there is a growing number of institutions and individual anthropologists active in this area. Part of the rationale for this is to furnish content for the exhibitions. The filmic needs of the new museum have developed well beyond initial expectations. Early exhibition concepts called for extensive but static dioramic scenes to be painted on walls and ceilings. To achieve greater realism and programmability, and introduce a sense of change or movement, however, it was decided to employ instead multi-image slide or film presentations projected onto the 'architectural screens'. For instance, visitors who look out of certain windows in some of the History Hall's period structures will appear to see dynamic representations of the environment or daily life appropriate to the historical context. These will actually be rear-screen video projections, using footage shot on location at historic sites across Canada. Life-size projections, as backdrops for 3-D settings with live animation, will also be used to simulate historical environments; this is the first time this combination of media has been used in a museum.

A second rationale for building such a collection is to assist CMC in addressing its expanded mandate to deal with the story of civilization. It would be far too expensive, at this time, to build a collection of artifacts fully representative of world cultures. But a collection of films and videos showing different cultures can be developed cost-effectively. Many of these would be copies. CMC is not looking to compete with the National Archives or National Film Board. Instead its special task will be to make visual materials more easily accessible to the general public. The Médiathèque will be the chief point of access to the collection. But there will be other layers of access. Excerpts will be seen in the galleries : supporting the exhibitions, or available from the electronic information kiosks - visual indexes to capture visitors' interest, indicate what is available for further study in the Médiathèque, and help them select materials they would like to see in full. The Médiathèque has viewing facilities for individuals or small groups, while screenings for large groups can be provided through the World Window Theatre; when no other special programming is scheduled, it is hoped to provide almost continuous showings of films from CMC's collection. In addition, videocassette copies of materials for which copyright clearance can be obtained will be made available for public purchase.

A further possibility is allowing visitors to produce their own videos, on personal cameras or camcorders rented from CMC, in the context of the environmental reconstruction exhibits. Replica period costumes would be provided for visitors to dress up and create their own mini-dramas, stimulated by one of CMC's professional animators. Period photographer's studios, where visitors dress up and have daguerrotypes taken, have proven popular features of several open air museums. To add animation would supply a means for encouraging visitors to get into roleplaying scenarios (otherwise a hard thing to do with adults), and leave them with an interesting souvenir.

Another way in which the public might use CMC's audiovisual collection is to 'preview' the cultural features of possible travel destinations, to help them make a selection or to provide a cultural orientation to a selected destination. At a recent conference on tourism the distinction was made between 'outward bound' travel (the tourist physically transported to a destination) and 'inward bound' travel, in which a destination is brought to the tourist through physical simulation - that is, environmental reconstructions - or a communication medium which induces a mental simulation.[7] An outstanding example of the latter is New York's Bank Street College's Palenque Project, an interactive video programme allowing users to 'tour' an ancient Maya site, thanks to a full-motion film shot with a 360^0 lens; the images, once unwrapped and undistorted by computer, enable the user to look or move in whatever direction desired. Special features allow users to capture any scene in a digitized 'photograph' and download their photos to take home, or to enter a 'museum' - actually a multimedia database - at any time to view artifacts associated with Mayan civilization or delve into a library of information. By developing programmes such as this, and through its environmental reconstructions and audiovisual collections, CMC hopes to provide inward bound travellers with a substitute experience of many cultures, and encourage those who can afford it to visit the real thing.

CMC will also address its international mandate by bringing in travelling exhibitions. During the next few years the Special Exhibitions Hall will host shows on Eastern and Oriental Orthodox folk and canonical rituals, Himalayan ritual costumes, Benin women of the royal court, the art of indigenous peoples of New Guinea, Angolan and West African cultures, and cultural values communicated by Latin American costumes. The Native Art Gallery will present an exhibition of African art. And a reconstruction of a rural Hispanic-Indian village from Mexico will be set up in the Children's Museum. CMC will mount special film programmes to complement the themes of these exhibitions. It will of course also continue to mount its own travelling exhibitions, to reach remote audiences, as well as to augment this through longer-term decentralization of elements from its material collections, in the form of controlled 'repatriation' to museums across Canada.

All the features described above will help make CMC an invaluable learning resource, aimed at cultivating a global perspective in its users. Museums should not seek to teach 'facts' - for facts are too often actually culturally-biased interpretations - so much as to encourage people to open up their minds, free themselves as much as possible from the constraints of their culture-specific world-views, and make independent judgements. As Tomislav Sola notes : "by acquiring a wider intellectual approach and understanding of historical experience one becomes *tolerant*, and that is what is needed so desperately in this world."[8] What CMC seeks to impart is communicative competence : the ability to converse with people of different cultures in a common language. A language founded upon cultural literacy, which requires understanding each other's value system, social, historical, and political background.[9] The proper learning environment is not a classroom, but rather a workshop : experiential learning is the key. Several educational institutions in the United States are already offering "global education" curricula to children, employing multimedia presentations, simulations, telecommunications links to other countries, and field trips, to raise intercultural awareness.[10] This approach is needed in Canada, not just because of its multicultural character, but because Canada will need, to compete and prosper in the new global economy that is developing, leaders in business, government, and the professions who have a good ability to communicate with their counterparts in other nations.

However, it is important that museums avoid being purely didactic machines. They require their own version of 'artificial intelligence', that combines the

Figure 132
To achieve its temporal mission of improving intercultural understanding, CMC will find ways of bringing representatives of different cultures together to converse with each other. An exchange of understanding, in the cause of global harmony, was the purpose of this peace-pipe ceremony, in 1988, in which a representative from each of red, yellow, white, and black races (seated on blankets) participated.

analytical with the intuitive. The latter comes from their role as ritual spaces; ritual too is a traditional vehicle for communication, especially for sub-conscious, sensory information. CMC is trying to acquire this balance, that recognizes the value of both right and left brain faculties - whereas, historically, societies have tended to let one side dominate. There are many examples of rituals in museums. Visiting itself is quite ritualized, as the reverential and meditative behaviours of visitors evidence. Group visits, such as school classes or bus tours, are even more highly developed rituals : membership, group behaviour, and leadership are carefully prescribed, and the motivation of cultural participation is more clearly defined. More obvious examples of museum rituals are the formal cere-monies such as exhibition or museum openings.

It is an even greater challenge to develop the sensory function of museums than the analytical one. It means recognising the rituals that exist, and deter-mining which contribute to the museum and which do not. The old and useless ritual of paramilitary guards parading through the galleries is one to be eliminated, superseded partly by the newer rituals performed by live animators - these are less intimidating and more participatory for visitors. Museum spaces should be ritual-friendly : places suitable for the 'display' of rituals. The Arts and Traditions Hall will be a particularly important site for this display, since its flexibility makes it highly programmable. Most galleries are primarily artifact-rich, however. The ritual-rich spaces in CMC may prove rather to be its theatres, its plazas, the large open spaces of the entrance lobby, Salon Barbeau, and Grand Hall, and even the rooftop areas of the museum; these are most amenable to performance or celebrative rituals, strengthened by sensory-based technologies such as the powerful visual experience of Imax/Omnimax cinema.

But there is no reason why rituals have to be only on-site. Electronic rituals are emerging, especially through television. Television has imported rituals such as evangelistic gatherings, coronations, weddings, sports, and has created its own in game shows and soap operas. Children's television is especially ritualized; Sesame Street, for instance, borrows the frenetic - one might say ecstatic - pacing of commercials. Rock videos are electronic myths that are quite participatory, calling for physical and emotional responses. The ritual aspects of popular culture are one of several reasons why museums need to devote more attention to that face of our culture. CMC's plans to use television as an inter-pretive medium, and plans for future exhibitions on popular culture themes, such as hockey, are a response to this need.

To exploit to the fullest their potential as places where people can interact and learn to communicate with each other, museums need to transcend their functions as repositories of material heritage and educational centres. They must play a more extroverted and more central role in everyday social life - active in the cultural present, not just the past. Technology and simulations are useful tools but, ultimately, no substitute for people learning to relate directly to their fellow travellers in this global ark. An awareness of this is evident particularly in the United States and Europe, where new museums are coming equipped with large theatres with their own lobbies, lounges, conference rooms, spaces to host gala events, full-service restaurants, learning centres, studios, and large book and gift shops.[11] The trans-ition from museum to cultural centre is characterized by making museum facilities available to community or private groups and associations for social gatherings and events, such as weddings, concerts, films, fashion shows. It is in a museum's interest - and in the interest of its educational mission - to encourage the public to feel welcome and comfort-able inside its walls. Furthermore, it is appropriate to make the museum a source of inspiration for the generation of cultural events, for the past is a firm foundation for producing new cultural expressions.

CMC intends to pursue the model of "cultural centre as dynamo". The ways in which the public makes use of the museum, in addition to the travelling shows brought in, the programmes put together by CMC itself, and the ritual possibilities of the archi-tecture and topographical setting of the museum, all contribute to the building of an 'event structure'. This event orientation is the key to reaching out across the nation with content that will attract the attention of a populace raised on television.

Cultural networking

Networking is not a new concept, as the history of postal services shows, but is only now beginning to come into its own as telecommunications technology matures. Whereas in the past it has been necessary to transmit different forms of information (voice, text, image) by independent communication routes, the evolving Integrated Services Digital Network (ISDN) promises to alter all that.[12] This technology and the relatively cheap transmission of data via satellite will change both the types of services institutions can provide and the way in which they present those services to users. There is a shift of emphasis from static forms of information (e.g. printed text) to dynamic (digital) forms, and greater concern with accessibility to information in terms of user interface technologies that do not demand a functional literacy, such as touch screen and menu-driven programmes.

However, the costs of hardware, of database development, and of nationwide dissemination are, and will remain, too high for any single cultural institution - even a national institution - to finance alone the setting up of an information network. Only through collaborative ventures to share costs, expertise, and applications can museums hope to take advantage of the immense benefits of cooperation : sharing information resources, offering a wider range of services thanks to those expanded resources, yet avoiding unnecessary duplication of services and programmes.

Nonetheless, the cost factor has not deterred France from forging ahead, in its determination to defend cultural sovereignty against the threat of trans-border data flow, and an equal determination to be at the forefront of the Information Society. Faced with a commercial direct broadcast satellite transmitting English-language programmes across Europe, France launched its own satellite to service a government-subsidized channel using programming from five French-speaking countries. At the beginning of the 80's the French government, as an experiment, put a great deal of money into replacing the old telephone system in Biarritz with a new fibre optic based system supporting videophones and an interactive telecommunications network. Soon after, France Telecom handed out four million Minitel terminals to telephone subscribers. This videotex terminal with attached telephone gives access to thousands of services, retail outlets, and information databases, including national inventories of art museum collections and archival records. The programme was viewed as an integral element in creating a population accustomed to computer access to information. At the same time, massive government support was given to the building, at Poitiers, of a complex focusing on the latest communications and information processing technologies, and how they are affecting society. Parc du Futuroscope incorporates pavilions with public exhibitions, giant-screen theatres, a conference centre, teleport to link the complex with other parts of the country, an international research institute, and a school for

teaching France's next generation about new technology and media. Surrounding it is an industrial park.

Based on the dispersal of its population and its past preoccupation with telecommunications, Canada ought to have a natural leadership position in networking. Yet, despite its tradition of innovation in communications technology, it has not taken a concrete initiative since setting up the Canadian Heritage Information Network to serve as a national inventory of museum collections. CMC, part of the department standing at the intersection of culture and communications, hopes to remedy that situation by acting as a catalyst in the creation of a Canadian cultural network. Most cultural institutions are mandated to serve only local communities, therefore it is natural that the lead in forming a national network be taken by a national institution. The model envisaged, however, is not one with centralized control. CMC's role as national museum does not give it any authority over other museums - nor does it seek such authority - but it does give a certain responsibility to cut a path that others may follow. Nor would centralization be very practical, given the multiplicity of local applications, software, and hardware. Fortunately the growing acceptance of Open Systems Interconnection standards makes it feasible to have a tight communications coupling between institutions, permitting free exchange of information resources, while leaving each network participant the autonomy to make its own decisions on equipment and applications. The role of CMC in a cultural network, apart from that of major repository of information, would be to direct queries to the destinations having the appropriate resources to provide answers, and to provide certain common services such as access to communications media not locally available at all institutions.

A cultural network is something that must be built up in stages. CMC has already achieved the first plateau, in that it is wired up as an 'intelligent building'. This alone qualifies it as the best prepared cultural institution in Canada to take the lead in forming a cultural network. The Museum of Civilization Applications Supported Intelligent Network (MOCASIN) was in the planning stages for three years before A.T.&T. Canada was selected, through a process of narrowing down from over 250 major suppliers, to provide CMC with the advanced network incorporating the new generation of IBM microcomputers. In mid-1988 the installation of the network began, in the cable conduits permeating the new museum building. MOCASIN supports telephones, computers, audio and video equipment, laser disc hardware, and television monitors at over 1000 locations throughout the museum. Each of these wall- or floor-mounted Universal Cable Outlets (UCOs) has dedicated cables - multiple twisted-pair, coaxial, and multiple element fibre optic - running to the Network Control Centre. There the signals through each cable can be switched to go from any UCO to any other, and can be kept independent or be integrated with each other. The network has been designed to accommodate traditional voice and data requirements, needs for transition from narrowband to wideband applications, and future planning for fibre optic communications as new technologies come forward. Although optical fibre cabre is still relatively expensive, it is a good investment in the future and avoids costly and complex retro-fitting. It can carry more information than copper cable - MOCASIN could support all of the telephone conversations in the country, and has the equivalent throughput of 100 Ethernets. It accommodates a wider variety of information types, retains signal strength better over distances, is not subject to electromagnetic interference, and has a longer life. It is particularly important for transmitting full motion, full colour, high resolution video. CMC will adopt HDTV technology, once one of the many standards proposed becomes widely accepted; until then, however, it will rely on the existing (NTSC) tele-vision transmission standard in North America.

As part of CMC's intelligent building structure, trunk lines can link the Network Control Centre, and thereby all CMC's information resources, to on-site satellite dishes. From there CMC could reach out, via Telesat Canada's Anik satellites, to other museums across Canada. Simple point-to-point services could be provided on a pre-scheduled basis between CMC and sites equipped as downlinks. Point-to-multipoint programming is equally feasible, with CMC acting as the central host. Through video-conferences, -workshops, -seminars, or -lectures CMC could share, for example, the results of its visitor research and so help build museum visiting across the country; or it could provide training to small museums in a cost-effective fashion. By using the K frequency band, terrestrial microwave inter-ference would be avoided, and network nodes could minimize downlink costs by using VSAT (very small aperture) receiving antennae. The structure of such a network is much the same as the direct broadcast satellite systems delivering TV entertainment to homes equipped with small dishes. An outreach network of this nature will allow CMC to make its information resources - including its educational and entertainment programmes - more widely available without incurring the cost of physically duplicating those resources at multiple sites. Hopefully some of the network participants will be able to equip themselves for uplinking too, so that *their* resources can be similarly shared. Such a network would greatly magnify participating museums' ability to serve existing audiences and attract new ones.

CMC is currently seeking to identify partners in this project, and eagerly awaits expressions of interest from other museums. Only a concerted effort, in these times of funding stringency, will enable Canadian museums to achieve their ambitious goals. If they fail to work together in the service of the public, the private sector will surely fill the gap, and subordinate public interest and quality of content to profit-seeking from information products. An ability to act in unison at this crucial juncture may be the greatest, and most important, challenge Canada's museums have yet faced.

To maximize the effectiveness of a cultural network, however, other institutions must also be drawn in from the cultural and educational sectors. There are already educational television services in several provinces, and a number of universities have cable-TV channels for outreach to their communities. Although CBC is presently seen as the central instrument of the government's cultural policy, new broadcasting policy being formulated recognizes the need for alternative programming that is innovative and better reflects Canada's regions, its multicultural character, and its aboriginal peoples.[13] This alter-native service could be a component of a Canadian cultural network. Another element might be a 'knowledge network'. Many universities have their own LANs for linking resources internally; a national network would interconnect them. And Canada, the United States, and Europe are all giving serious consideration to creating supercomputer-based networks to link scientific research institutions.[14] The library community would be another natural participant. The National Library of Canada is proceeding with its own plans for a decentralized library network, but it would be advantageous for all to tie this into the cultural network, so that museum databases were accessible to the broad clientele libraries serve. In the area of high culture a lead is being taken by the National Arts Centre, whose director-general is pursuing the possibilty of establishing, in the immediate future, a Canadian network of HDTV equipped auditoriums to which the NAC can transmit, via satellite, its live performances. Although CMC is not convinced that

Mocasin

What makes MOCASIN an 'intelligent network' is its flexibility in being able to adapt to differing requirements and demands of users. If the user requires traditional telephone service, the network can take on that role in a guise to which the user is already accustomed. Similarly MOCASIN can respond as a modem-equipped analogue terminal, a fully integrated digital (ISDN) device, or a highly interactive, full motion, colour display device. Coaxial cabling provides broadband capability to each UCO, and is intended primarily for full-spectrum multi-channel TV - similar to a cable television system. Twisted-pair wiring supports all of the ISDN services, such as telephones and Local Area Networks, wherever broadband capabilities are not required; specialized LAN installations in particular parts of the museum

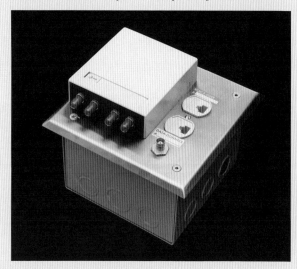

are unnecessary, since various LAN topologies can easily be constructed, to serve any given cluster of outlets, at the Network Control Centre. These two cable technologies are transitional.

The versatility and capacity of fibre optic cable makes it the ultimate solution for information movement. Although this pathway is not being greatly used as yet - mostly for field-trials of applications - it would have been difficult and expensive to rewire CMC later, once optical fibre becomes the standard communication medium. And it is expected that user requirements for information will be increasingly picture-oriented, especially for real-time motion video; this will demand the enormous communication speed and elegance of bandwidth that fibre optic cables can supply. At present, integrated services are provided over the three different types of cable; to interface seamlessly the signals from the different cabling domains requires a complex intelligence in the Network Control Centre. Museum visitors can watch the Centre's operations for themselves from the corridor linking the Grand Hall and the cafeteria.

A very important aspect of MOCASIN is its selectivity. Each of the numerous UCOs can be identified and addressed individually, to receive or transmit application-specific information. A request for video information, for example, can originate at any outlet from devices such as telephone or computer terminal, and be sent via twisted-pair or fibre optic interface to the Network Control Centre. From there the request is routed to video sources and the appropriate information directed, via coaxial cable, to a TV monitor at the requesting UCO. Each UCO supports all three cable types, so that the user does not have to move from one location to another to receive different types of information; it is simply a question of plugging workstation devices into the right UCO connections, combined with a reconfiguration at the Centre to reflect exactly what a particular UCO is supporting at any given time. Thanks to the dedicated, end-to-end connection of each UCO to the Centre, a user at any location can access any of the museum's databases, centralized modem pooling, centralized file-servers, office automation services, publishing, video and audio information, laser disc servers, etc. At the same time, a workspace need not be physically stationary, or geographically defined; that is, special applications are not necessarily bound to a specific UCO for support. By providing such flexible and universal access, each workstation becomes a sort of 'virtual space', adaptable to the personal requirements of the user.

HDTV is financially feasible as a start-up technology, since it requires nodes to have expensive display and signal decompression hardware, it recognizes the commonality of interest between itself and the NAC and has been in discussion with the NAC in hopes that a cooperative effort can be undertaken.

The vision of a cultural network that goes beyond the museum community has a rationale that is, in part, pragmatic. To be flexible in serving network members' needs as they arise means owning transmitter equipment, rather than renting a portable transponder for occasional, pre-scheduled transmissions. The high cost of ownership can only be justified if the uplink is in continuous use, which would require a higher content of programming than the museum community may be expected to produce. One promising prospect for finding other contributors of input and money, with CMC charging for services on a cost-recovery basis, lies in the proposal for a network of government departments and agencies in the Capital Core Area. MetroNet would be a very high capacity, broadband, fibre optic ring linking institutions situated around the ceremonial route - such as Parliament, CMC, the National Library, the National Gallery, NAC, the Supreme Court, CRTC, and Hull's Maison du Citoyen. Some of the agencies

Figure 133
CMC is taking the initiative in the development of a network of museums across Canada and around the world. Only by interlinking and resource-sharing can museums realize their full potential for shaping cultural consciousness. Part of the network may be the bridging, by fibre optic cable, of national institutions located around the capital's ceremonial route, with CMC as teleport serving those nodes.

that would be connected are already developing internal networks. Much of the physical route of MetroNet is ready now, in the form of conduit-equipped tunnels linking various buildings; some already has fibre optic cable installed.

As an intelligent building, CMC would be the natural choice to act as teleport - that is, a permanent tele-communications gateway - for this network, sending government communications and services across the country. CMC's site has a clear and unobstructing signal path to satellite transceivers. CMC would thus become an 'information utility' channelling requests for information and responses to and fro between nodes. The concept of information utility is founded on a comparison with services supplying natural resources :

> "In the case of the electric company, the user merely plugs into an electrical outlet; he does not have to consider the source of the current or how it gets from here to there. Just so, the users of the information utility will be able to plug in to the information source, locally or remotely, in a manner almost as standardized as an electrical outlet, a telephone set, or for that matter, as the standard interface to the proposed Integrated Services Digital Network."[15]

Ultimately, as prices of VSAT antennae drop, many Canadian homes could hook into the network, taking information directly instead of having to go to the institution housing the resources. Consideration is being given to an initial linkage of CMC, the National Gallery, and NAC to demonstrate the potential of such a network.

One important consequence of having teleport facilities is that CMC would then have the flexibility to extend the envisaged cultural network across the globe. Through Telesat, CMC could reach Gander and thereby link to Europe via Intelsat; or go westwards across the Pacific, or southwards into the United States, in a similar leapfrogging fashion. A truly multicultural network could be created, a wonderful tool for connecting peoples of different countries in live and even interactive shared experiences and conversations that contribute towards the development of a Global Village. And the size of the information resources that could be put at the fingertips of network users would be greatly multiplied. It might be possible, for instance, to link into the educational television network for which the Smithsonian is currently looking for partners. Or, again, into the Woods Hole Oceanographic

Institute's Jason Project, an undersea search for ancient shipwrecks televised live to network participants. A good deal of 'armchair travel' to remote parts of the world might be made available via a global information utility such as CMC could become.

In its search for institutions to collaborate in the formation of a global network CMC has already signed a three-year agreement with France's Futuroscope to work together in creating exhibitions, audiovisual programmes, multimedia spectacles, and in exchanging such programmes - as well as technical and museological information that can help the two institutions realize common goals - via electronic highways. This 'twinning' for the purpose of cultural exchanges CMC hopes to be the first of many partnerships that will enable it to bring the cultural resources of the world to Canada's doorstep.

Canada's museums must be responsive to changing realities, and must recognize their responsibility not merely to present passively the collective memory, but to shape social consciousness actively, to achieve a common vision of the future. Up to now museums have largely been passive recipients of information; the emerging Information Society requires that they focus henceforth upon getting that information out to people, in ways that are effective and are convenient to the users. Providing better access to information is itself an aid in the generation of new knowledge and improved understanding. If museums can encourage and enable people to use that information creatively, then they are making a worthy contribution to the continued vitality of the cultures they commemorate. As Canada enters an era of freer commercial exchange with its southern neighbour, there is an added need to reinforce Canadian cultural identity through the sharing of images, ideas, and experiences.

As a national resource, and an institution contributing to the definition of national identity, CMC has the responsibility to make itself and its products accessible to all Canadians. But it cannot, practically, achieve this without the collaboration of other cultural institutions across the country - institutions with the foresight to perceive the benefit to the public derived from pooling resources. Through an outreach network the assets of one become the assets of all. Cultural performances, for example, could be broadcast from one institution to others; festivals could be created from events originating in diverse locations, but brought together for all audiences on the video screen. Such combined efforts would have promotional benefits for contributing institutions, and for Canada generally as a cultural tourism destination, by making tourists more aware of museum resources across the country, and leading them from one heritage centre to another.

Furthermore, through an ongoing programme of cultural exchanges the traditional image of museums, as resting-places of dead cultures, may be dispelled, and replaced with an image as cultural dynamos :

vehicles supportive of culture as a living entity constantly inspired to new utterances. By offering itself as a forum for the creative forces in Canadian culture - artists, craftspeople, performers, playwrights, film-makers, etc. - CMC proposes to demonstrate that our cultural heritage not only has a past but also a future. And that that future holds the brightest promise if it is founded upon mutual understanding, appreciation, respect, and acceptance.

Figure 134

ENDNOTES

CHAPTER 1

1 *Giving our past a future : a discussion paper prepared for the Ontario Heritage Policy Review,* Toronto : Ministry of Citizenship and Culture, April 1987, p.7.

2 In a lecture given on 22 September 1987 by the Minister of Communications, Flora MacDonald, in the series *Towards the 21st century : new directions for Canada's National Museums,* (sponsored by Carleton University and the National Museums of Canada).

3 Robert Sullivan, "The museum as moral artifact," *Moral Education Forum,* vol.10, nos.3-4 (fall/winter 1985), p.2.

4 Ekos Research Associates, *National Capital Region visitor survey : final report,* Ottawa : National Capital Commission, November 1986, p.39.

5 John McAvity, "Museums bloom in Ottawa," *Christian Science Monitor,* 10-16 November 1986, p.B10.

6 Douglas J. Cardinal Architect Limited, *The National Museum of Man,* Unpublished and unpaginated report submitted to the Canada Museums Construction Corporation, January 1983.

7 Described in more detail in Duncan Cameron, "Museums and public access : the Glenbow approach," *International Journal of Museum Management and Curatorship,* vol.1 (1982), pp.177-196.

8 This has been defined by the Ontario Heritage Policy Review (*Giving our past a future ....,* p.21) as "tourism in which the activities, during a stay at destinations outside one's place of residence, include attendance at art events or such involvement with heritage resources as visiting museums, experiencing a historical re-enactment, or admiring the buildings of a small town."

9 Flora MacDonald, *op. cit*; McAvity, *op. cit.,* p.B12.

10 Ekos Research Associates, *op. cit.,* passim.

11 Summarized in the NCC booklet *A capital in the making : reflections of the past, visions of the future,* Ottawa, June 1984.

12 The results are in the report by Roger du Toit Architects, *Five museum sites : comparative site evaluation, the National Gallery of Canada and the National Museum of Man,* Toronto, November 1982.

13 Summaries of the proposals are in *Twelve proposals for the National Gallery and for the National Museum of Man,* a special supplement of the periodical *Section A,* published in August 1984.

14 For example, William Bernstein and Ruth Cawker, *Contemporary Canadian Architecture,* Toronto : Fitzhenry & Whiteside, 1982, pp.130-32,139; Trevor Boddy, *Modern architecture in Alberta,* Alberta Culture and Multiculturalism and the Canadian Plains Research Center, 1987, passim.

15 The first quotation is from George MacDonald and Douglas J. Cardinal, "Building Canada's National Museum of Man : an interpersonal dialogue," *Museum,* no.149 (1986), p.14, the second from *Frozen Music,* a CTV documentary (producer Dan Kauffman) televised in May 1985. Much text and all quotations in the following section are derived from these sources, Cardinal's design proposal, and unpublished biographical and project notes relating to Cardinal and his work. The authors thank Carole Philippe, Mr. Cardinal's executive assistant, for supplying some of these materials.

16 See Abraham Rogatnick and Alvin Balkind, "The work of Douglas Cardinal : an evolving Indian architecture," *Arts Canada,* (October/November 1976), pp.35-40.

17 The results of the survey are embodied in an unpublished report by Erica Claus, *Findings report : "Sharing the Challenge",* September 1982.

18 National Museums of Canada, Architecture and Planning Group, *Architectural programme : National Museum of Man, Parc Laurier, Hull, Quebec : volume one,* Ottawa, January 1983, p.3.5.

19 Douglas J. Cardinal Architect Limited et/and Tétreault, Parent, Languedoc et Associés Inc., *Design development report,* Ottawa : National Museum of Man, May 1984 (unpublished), p.2.

20 Such is the explanation in the CMCC's *Fifth annual report 1986-87,* (Ottawa, 1987), pp.9-10.

21 Its results are in an unpublished report by Les Recherches ARKHIS, *Archéologie des sites du Musée de l'Homme et de la Galerie Nationale,* Quebec, 1984. The archival investigation has been published, however : Francine Brousseau, *Historique du nouvel emplacement du Musée national de l'Homme à Hull,* National Museum of Man Mercury Series, History no.38 (1984).

22 In a speech given 28 November 1983 by Jean Sutherland Boggs, then chairman of the Canada Museums Construction Corporation.

23 The conceptual design is in the unpublished report by Howard Brandston Lighting Design Inc. & Gabriel/design, *Lighting design for the new National Museum of Man,* Canada Museums Construction Corporation, April 1984.

CHAPTER 2

1 *Old images / new metaphors : the museum in the modern world,* (transcript of a radio broadcast on the 'Ideas' programme, hosted by Jeanne Cannizzo), Toronto : Canadian Broadcasting Corporation, 1982, passim.

2 Neil Cossons, "The new museum movement in the United Kingdom," *Museum,* no.138 (1983), p.83; Peter Swann, "The trouble with Canada's museums," *Muse,* vol.4, no.1 (April 1986), p.10; John R. Kinard, "The neighbourhood museum as a catalyst for social change," *Museum,* no.148 (1985), p.217; Tom Sherman, "Museums of tomorrow," *Parachute,* March-May 1987, p.78.

3 For recent representations of this viewpoint see Philip Ward, "Museums : commitments to the future," *Echo*, vol.2, no.2 (February 1982), p.5; Yorke Edwards, "Museums must decide : hands-on or hands-off?" *Muse*, vol.5, no.1 (Spring 1987), pp.18-23; Margaret Graham-Bell, "Preservation paramount to museum mission," *Muse*, vol.5, no.1 (Spring 1987), p.5.

4 See for example letters to the editor in response to Ward's article, cited above; also Lorin I. Nevlin, "On public understanding of museum research," *Curator*, vol.27, no.3 (September 1984), pp.189-93.

5 Elliot Eisner and Stephen Dobbs, *Silent pedagogy : how museums help visitors experience exhibitions*, paper presented at the American Association of Museums Annual Meeting, San Francisco, June 1987.

6 Edwards, *op. cit.*, p.21.

7 See, for example : Joseph Veach Noble, "Museums in the real world," *Gazette*, vol.15, no.4 (Fall 1982), pp.4-5; Sheila Stevenson, "Balancing the scales : old views and a new muse," *Muse*, vol.5, no.1 (Spring 1987), p.30; Thomas Leavitt and Dennis O'Toole, "Two views on museum education," *Museum News*, vol.64, no.2 (December 1985), pp.26-31; Gordon M. Ambach, "Museums as places of learning," *Museum News*, vol.65, no.2 (December 1986), pp.35-41.

8 This criticism is by Michael M. Ames, "De-schooling the museum : a proposal to increase public access to museums and their resources," *Museum*, no.145 (1985), p.29.

9 Kenneth Hudson, *Museums of influence*, Cambridge : University Press, 1987, pp.176-79. See also Roy Strong, "The museum as communicator," *Museum*, no.138 (1983), pp.74-81.

10 Supporters of this view include Tomislav Sola, "The concept and nature of museology," *Museum*, no.153 (1987), pp.45-49; Robert Sullivan, "The museum as moral artifact," *Moral Education Forum*, vol.10, nos.3-4 (Fall/Winter 1985), pp.2-18; Deidre Sklar, "Making belief : the Museum of the American Indian as a cultural performance," *Muse*, vol.5, no.2 (Summer 1987), pp.26-30; Sheldon Annis, "The museum as a staging ground for symbolic action," *Museum*, no.151 (1986), pp.168-71; Marjorie M. Halpin, *Quality and the post-modern museum*, paper presented at the Canadian Museums Association Trainers Workshop, Ottawa, August 1987.

11 Sullivan, *op. cit.*, p.2.

12 The views of a number of these critics were expressed in the radio broadcast *Old images / new metaphors ...*, (see fn.1).

13 Kinard, *op. cit.*, p.218; *The future of the museum system in Canada : a series of three national conferences sponsored by the National Museums of Canada*, Val Morin (Quebec), June 1985 (unpublished report).

14 *Old images / new metaphors ...*, pp.23-24. This may be the modern version of the museum as 'sacred grove' role.

15 Sklar, *op. cit.*, p.29; Halpin, *op. cit.*, p.15.

16 Sullivan, *op. cit.*, passim.

17 See for example Stephen Weil, "Questioning some premises," *Museum News*, vol.64, no.5 (June 1986), p.23.

18 *Ibid.*, pp.26-27.

19 Hudson, *op. cit.*, p.194.

20 *Giving our past a future ...*, p.10.

21 *Giving our past a future ...*, p.8.

22 *University of the Air : a new interactive curriculum on intellectual and cultural history of the 20th century*, Washington : Smithsonian Institution, 1987 (unpublished), p.1.

23 Robert F. Kelly, *Museums as status symbols II : attaining a state of "having been"*. Read in its 1984 draft form, but subsequently published in *Advances in non-profit marketing*, vol.2, ed. R. Belk, Greenwich (Conn.) : JAI Press, 1987.

24 *Giving our past a future ...*, p.9. For a critical look at the effect the mass media has on our way of thinking, see Neil Postman, *Amusing ourselves to death : public discourse in the age of show business*, New York : Viking, 1985.

25 On these matters see Kinard, *op. cit.*; Chris Miller-Marti, "Local history museums and the creation of 'the past'," *Muse*, vol.5, no.2 (Summer 1987), pp.36-39; Kenneth Hopkins, "Let's chatter in the trees," pp.27-35 in *Twentieth-century popular culture in museums and libraries*, ed. F. Schroeder, Bowling Green (Ohio) : University Press, 1981; Mary Tivy, "The trend towards specialized museums in Ontario," *Museum Quarterly*, vol.12, no.3 (September 1983), pp.19-24; Shona McKay, "Corporate museums : taking pride in the past," *Report on Business Magazine*, December 1986, pp.71-81.

26 According to Flora MacDonald (see ch.1, fn.2).

27 *Giving our past a future ...*, p.7.

28 *Old images / new metaphors ...*, p.9; Miller-Marti, *op. cit.*, passim.

29 Strong, *op. cit.*, p.79; *Old images / new metaphors ...*, p.8; D.R. Richeson, *At the crossroads : the museum's dilemma*, paper presented at the Canadian Museums Association Annual Conference, May 1987, p.1; Noble, *op. cit.*, p.6; Duncan F. Cameron, "Museums and public access : the Glenbow approach," *International Journal of Museum Management and Curatorship*, vol.2 (1982), p.178; Weil, *op. cit.*, p.26; Kelly, *Museums as status symbols II ...*, pp.20-22; Ames, *op. cit.*, pp.25, 30.

30 These projects are described in Cameron, *op. cit.*, pp.177-96, and Ames, *op. cit.*, pp.25-31.

31 Robert F. Kelly, *Tourism master plan : Canadian Museum of Civilization*, Vancouver : Kelly Consultants, November 1987 (unpublished), p.9.

32 Most notably in *Museums as status symbols II*, (see fn.24), and in an as yet unpublished paper *International tourism : pilgrimage in the technological age*, (1986). Most of the section that follows borrows heavily from those sources.

33 On this see also John Theilmann, "Medieval pilgrims and the origins of tourism," *Journal of Popular Culture*, vol.20, no.4 (Spring 1987), pp.93-102.

34 H.H. Nelson Graburn, "The museum and the visitor experience," in *The visitor and the museum*, ed. L. Draper, American Association of Museums Annual Conference, 1977. See also the Graburn-inspired distinction of museums roles as cognitive space, dream space, and pragmatic space, made by Annis, *op. cit.*, pp.169-70.

35 See Cossons, *op. cit.*, pp.83-89.

36 On these see Stuart Silver, "Almost everyone loves a winner : a designer looks at the blockbuster era," *Museum News*, vol.61, no.2 (November/December 1982), pp.24-35; Joseph Veach Noble, "The megashows are coming," *Curator*, vol.30, no.1 (March 1987), pp.5-10.

37 For example, see Edwards, *op. cit.*, p.23.

38 One example is reported in Mary Ellen Munley, *Evaluation study report : Buyin' Freedom, an experimental live interpretation program, March 20 - May 1, 1982*, Washington : National Museum of American History, 1982 (unpublished).

39 A readable, if dated, history of this type of museum is Richard W.E. Perrin, *Outdoor museums*, Milwaukee Public Museum Publications in Museology, no.4 (1975). Jay Anderson's *Time machines : the world*

of living history, Nashville : American Association for State and Local History, 1984, is more up-to-date.

40 Stephen Alsford, *The looking-glass world : a study of reconstructed-community museums in Canada*, Ottawa : National Museum of Man, 1984 (unpublished).

41 Descriptions of the philosophy may be found in Georges Henri Rivière, "The ecomuseum - an evolutive definition," *Museum*, no.148 (1985), pp.182-83; Pierre Mayrand, "The new museology proclaimed," *Museum*, no.148 (1985), pp.200-201; "Declaration of Quebec : basic principles for a new museology," *Museum*, no.148 (1985), p.201; Stevenson, *op. cit.*, pp.30-31.

42 Kinard, *op. cit.*, p.221.

43 Noble, "Museums in the real world," p.6.

44 L. Thomas Frye, *Museum collecting for the 21st century*, paper presented at the Conference for a Common Agenda for History Museums, 1987.

45 Halpin, *op. cit.*, pp.11-12.

46 *Harbourfront : Toronto's waterfront vision*, Toronto : Harbourfront Corporation, 1987.

47 George F. MacDonald, "Epcot Centre in museological perspective," *Muse*, vol.6, no.1 (Spring 1988), pp.27-37.

48 Noble, "Museums in the real world," pp.3-4.

49 In Canada 48% of the population visits a museum or historical site at least once a year, but only 4% make museum-going a frequent leisure activity; Jean-Louis Coté and Carlos Ferrand, *The museum visits you*, Ottawa : Canadian Museums Association, 1985 (unpublished), p.4.

50 The argument is that tourism overexploits heritage resources and may encourage cultural stereotyping; *Giving our past a future ...*, p.21.

51 Ambach, *op. cit.*, p.41.

52 Sola, *op. cit.*, p.49.

53 Halpin, *op. cit.*, p.16.

54 Richeson, *op. cit.*, p.5; this leaves plenty of scope for interpretation, of course.

55 Cuyler Young, "Value driven, market oriented," *Rotunda*, vol.19, no.1 (Summer 1986), pp.6-7.

56 Halpin, *op. cit.*, pp.8-9.

CHAPTER 3

1 See for example Edwards, *op. cit.*, passim; Duncan Cameron, *Museumscapes or streetscapes*, (unpublished paper), October 1985, p.9.

2 Corcoran, Frank et al., *Provisional exhibition master plan*, Ottawa : National Museum of Man, March 1983 (unpublished).

3 For further information on the development of CMC's craft collections, see Angela Marcus, "A glimpse at craft's future at the Canadian Museum of Civilization," *Ontario Craft*, vol.12, no.2 (June 1987), pp.13-15.

4 'Streetscape' is a commonly-used term for such exhibitions, but strictly speaking the Grand Hall exhibition is rather a villagescape. 'Environmental reconstruction' is a more general term, used to cover replicated total environmental settings of historical, ethnological, and natural characters.

5 This phase of the development of the History Hall exhibition is discussed in : George MacDonald, "Streets are in at this museum," *Canadian Heritage*, vol.10, no.5 (December 1984 - January 1985), pp.30-33, 49; D. T. Ruddel, "Streetscape : dead end or signpost to the future?" *Muse*, vol.2, no.4 (winter 1985), pp.18-27.

CHAPTER 4

1 Stefan Michalski, *A survey of conditions in buildings housing the collection of the National Museum of Man*, Ottawa, 1981 (unpublished); Stefan Michalski, *A survey of the housekeeping for the collections, National Museum of Man, August 1981 : museum responsibilities*, Ottawa, 1982 (unpublished).

2 This design is described in detail (as too is the general planning of CMC's collections holding system) in Denis Alsford and Stephen Alsford, *Housing the reserve collections of the Canadian Museum of Civilization*, Hull : Canadian Museum of Civilization, 1989.

3 Cameron, "Museums and public access," p.178.

4 See Ames, *op. cit.*, pp.25-31.

5 See Cameron, "Museums and public access," pp.177-96.

6 The University of British Columbia Museum of Anthropology has also experimented with the technology; see Margaret Stott, "Videodisc : museums and the future," *Muse*, vol.3, no.4 (winter 1986), pp.44-46.

7 An account of the pilot project and of subsequent early operations of the system, as well as the general applications of the technology in CMC and the museum world as a whole, is available in Frederick Granger and Stephen Alsford, *The Canadian Museum of Civilization Optical Disc Project*, Hull : Canadian Museum of Civilization, 1988. A briefer account may be found in Stephen Alsford and Frederick Granger, "Image automation in museums : the Canadian Museum of Civilization's Optical Disc Project," *International Journal of Museum Management and Curatorship*, vol.6 (1987), pp.187-200.

8 See, for example, Manfred Lehmbruck, "Museum architecture : functions : space and circulation," *Museum*, vol.26, nos.3/4 (1974), p.232.

9 Stephen Alsford, *An exploratory study of the feasibility of the use of people-mover systems to provide tours to visitors of the future National Museum of Man*, Ottawa, 1985; this unpublished report is summarized in Stephen Alsford, "The use of people-mover systems in museums and associated cultural institutions," *International Journal of Museum Management and Curatorship*, vol.4 (1985), pp.329-44.

CHAPTER 5

1 Stevenson, *op. cit.*, p.30.

2 Lorna Kee, *Case study : new directions in interpretation and education*, a lecture given in November 1987 in the series *Towards the 21st century : new directions for Canada's National Museums*, (sponsored by Carleton University and the National Museums of Canada).

3 See, for example, Sherman, *op. cit.*, pp.79-80.

4 This is embodied in an unpublished report by the Davies Flaman Partnership, *Canadian Museum of Civilization comprehensive informatics master plan 1987/88 - 1999/2000*, Ottawa, May 1987.

5 This philosophy, referred to simply as IRM, requires that an institution define systematically the information needed to accomplish its missions, goals, and objectives, and manage its information resources efficiently and economically to meet the defined needs.

6 For further information on the La Villette system, see Francoise Bony, "14 mars : le public entre à la Cité des sciences de La Villette," *Livres Hebdo*, no.11 (10 mars 1986), pp.77-80; Francoise Bony, "La Villette a ouvert sa médiathèque enfants," *Livres Hebdo*, no.42 (13 octobre 1986), pp.104-106; Marie-Pascale Chatras and Francois Favre, "Médiathèque :

l'audiovisuel robotisé," *Sonovision*, no.309 (November 1987), pp.95-97.

7 For further information see George Smith, "A new information retrieval system : Got a question? Just touch the screen!" *Bell Laboratories Record*, October 1982, pp.206-13.

8 Strong, *op. cit.*, p.76.

9 Jerzy Wojciechowski, "Computing systems in an Ecology of Knowledge perspective," *Future of Computing Systems*, v.1, n.4 (1986), p.343.

CHAPTER 6

1 Strong, *op. cit.*, p.76. A similar sentiment was expressed in 1984 in the Declaration of Quebec (published in *Museum*, no.148, 1985, p.201), setting out basic principles of the 'new museology' movement.

2 Marilyn Sara Cohen, *The state of the art of museum visitor orientation : a survey of selected institutions*, Washington : Smithsonian Institution Office of Museum Programs, 1974 (unpublished), p.1.

3 Manfred Lehmbruck, "Museum architecture : psychology : perception and behaviour," *Museum*, vol.26, nos.3/4 (1974), p.194; S.A. Griggs, "Orientating visitors within a thematic display," *International Journal of Museum Management and Curatorship*, vol.2 (1983), p.121.

4 Some of the following paragraph is based on the ideas of Lorna Kee, as expressed in her lecture *Case study : new directions in interpretation and education*, (cited in ch.5, fn.2).

5 Ron Pears and Phil Aldrich, "Interactive exhibit design," *New frontiers : Interpretation Canada's ninth annual conference, September 25-29, 1982, Banff, Alberta : proceedings*, p.21.

6 On these see Robin Dunitz, "Interactive museums," *Media & Methods*, vol.21, no.8 (1985), pp.8-11.

7 Cameron, "Museums and public access," p.181.

8 Gene Youngblood, "Virtual space : the electronic environments of Mobile Image," *IS Journal*, vol.1, no.1 (1986), pp.15-16.

9 Halpin, *op. cit.*, p.16.

10 As expressed in Linda Champoux-Ares, *History Hall communications plan : working document*, Canadian Museum of Civilization, 1987 (unpublished), p.16.

11 Munley, *op. cit.*, p.26.

12 Ron McRae, "Interpretation and performance at the museum," *Canadian Museum of Civilization*, vol.1, no.2 (1987), p.3.

13 Chandler G. Screven, "Learning and exhibits : instructional design," *Museum News*, vol.52, no.5 (Jan./Feb. 1974), p.75; Randal Washburne and Allan Wagan, "Evaluating visitor response to exhibit content," *Curator*, vol.15 (1972), p.250; National Museums of Canada, Evaluation Directorate, *Evaluation study report : dissemination activities, Canadian Museum of Civilization, Canadian War Museum, National Museum of Natural Sciences*, February 1987 (unpublished), p.22.

14 David Dunn, Andra Akers, Allyn B. Brodsky, and Lizbeth Rymland, *Electronic dreamtime and vernacular TV : rationale for a planetary television network*, Los Angeles : International Synergy Institute, 1987, pp.1-2.

15 Kit Galloway and Sherrie Rabinowitz, "Long distance relationships : comments on the history and potential of video teleconferencing," *Videography*, March 1986, pp.49-50, 54.

16 These and other projects are described in more detail in *Ibid.*, pp.50-54.

17 For a description of these projects, see Youngblood, *op. cit.*, pp.9-20.

18 Coté and Ferrand, *op. cit.*, p.4; David Collison, "Making money for your museum," *Museums Journal*, vol.77, no.4 (March 1978), p.169.

CHAPTER 7

1 Museological journals are full of literature on this subject. See, for example, the articles by Ambach and by Leavitt and O'Toole cited in chapter 2, fn.7.

2 Michel Pichette, "New directions in continuing education : what are the stakes in today's 'New technological revolution'?" *Learning in society : towards a new paradigm*, Canadian Commission for Unesco Occasional Paper 51 (May 1985), pp.11-12. The publication contains several interesting papers contrasting education and learning; see particularly Guy Bourgeault, "Learning : toward a new paradigm," pp.37-46.

3 *Museums for a new century : a report of the Commission on Museums for a New Century*, Washington, D.C. : American Association of Museums, 1984, p.59.

4 *Ibid.*, p.66.

CHAPTER 8

1 Much of this paragraph's information is from an unpublished paper of Robert Scott, *Theatrical space from the Stone Age to the Space Age*, Ryerson Polytechnical Institute, 1986, which he kindly provided to the authors.

2 *Old images / new metaphors ...*, p.23; Annis, *op. cit.*, p.168.

3 See, for example, Sklar, *op. cit.*, p.29.

4 Lynette Harper and Tom Graff, *Museum on stage : readers and musicians theatre*, Vancouver : Vancouver Museum, 1984; Tessa Bridal, *Using theatre as an interpretive technique in museums*, Minnesota : Science Museum of Minnesota, 1987.

5 The history and technology of Imax/Omnimax is well-documented. A few examples of articles are : Victor Danilov, "Imax/Omnimax : fad or trend?" *Museum News*, vol.65, no.6 (Aug. 1987), pp.32-39; Charles Smith, "It's colossal! It's stupendous! It's IMAX!" *Reader's Digest*, Aug. 1985, pp.83-87; William Shaw and J. Creighton Douglas, "Imax and Omnimax theatre design," *SMPTE Journal*, vol.92, no.3 (Mar. 1983), pp.284-290. Good case studies (the latter unpublished) are : Juan Stoleson and Audley Lemmenes, "Countdown to lift-off : launching Chicago's Henry Crown Space Center and Omnimax Theater," *The Big Frame*, vol.4, no.1 (spring 1987), pp.5-8; Steven Fitch, *Samuel P. Langley Theater : the theater of the National Air & Space Museum : experience and recommendations*, Washington, D.C. : NASM, ca.1986.

6 Smith, *op. cit.*, p.83.

7 *Ibid.*, pp.86-87.

8 Vincent Canby, "'Big screen' takes on new meaning," *New York Times*, 19 April 1987, p.H18.

9 Classical concerts have been held in the Haida house at the University of British Columbia Museum of Anthropology; Max Wyman, "The twain meet in Haida house," *Vancouver Province*, 15 April 1987, p.46.

CHAPTER 9

1 Weil, *op. cit.*, p.26.

2 Hudson, *op. cit.*, pp.166-67.

3 Kelly, *Tourism master-plan ...*, p.12.

4 *Giving our past a future ...*, p.21.

5 *Ibid.*, p.22; Kelly, *loc. cit.*

6 Task Force on Cultural Industries, *The cultural industry and an international vision for Montreal,* Montreal : Chambre du commerce de Montréal and Montreal Board of Trade, 1987, passim.

7 Ekos Research Associates, *op. cit.,* passim.

8 *Ibid.,* p.i.

9 Stated by Marc Laplante, in an address to the Heritage Canada Foundation 14th Annual Conference (Quebec City, 1987), and quoted in a paper, entitled *A new tourism for Canada : can we meet the challenge,* presented by Heritage Canada at the National Conference on Tourism, Culture and Multiculturalism, Montreal, April 17-19, 1988.

10 Kelly, *Tourism master plan ...,* p.50.

11 DS-Lea Associates Ltd., *Tour bus parking study,* Ottawa : National Capital Commission and National Museums of Canada, 1987, p.12.

12 A series of interesting discussions on the topic was published in *Muse,* vol.4, no.2 (July 1986); see particularly Elizabeth Addison, "Is marketing a threat ... or is it the greatest challenge that museums have ever face?", pp.28-31.

13 Philip Kotler, *Marketing for nonprofit organizations,* 2nd ed., Englewood Cliffs, N.J. : Prentice-Hall, 1982, p.18.

14 Strong, *op. cit.,* p.77.

CHAPTER 10

1 Sivagamie Verina Obeyeschere, "The role of a craft museum in marketing/ promoting crafts, and the Lakpahana experience," *Museum,* no.157 (1988), p.10.

2 Communications Canada, *Canadian voices, Canadian choices : a new broadcasting policy for Canada,* Ottawa, 1988, p.5.

3 Margaret King, "Disneyland and Walt Disney World : traditional values in futuristic form," *Journal of Popular Culture,* vol.15, no.1 (1981), p.128.

4 Roger Silverstone, "Museums and the media : a theoretical and methodological exploration," *International Journal of Museum Management and Curatorship,* vol.7, no.3 (September 1988), p.232.

5 Nicholas Vitalari and Alladi Venkatesh, "In-home computing and information services : a twenty-year analysis of the technology and its impacts," *Telecommunications Policy,* vol.11, no.1 (March 1987), pp.66, 76.

6 The electronic outreach concept is more advanced in the educational sphere; see, for example, Henry Swope and Charles Worsley, "The media center of the future : transforming media centers : the Montgomery County experience," *Media & Methods,* vol.24, no.5 (May/June 1988), pp.12-14.

7 Donald MacLean and D. Craig Taylor, *Communications and tourism : new dimensions in space and time,* presentation to Tourism - A Vital Force for Peace : First Annual Conference, Vancouver, October 1988.

8 Tomislav Sola, "From education to communication," *ICOM News,* vol.40, nos.3/4 (1987), p.8.

9 Bracha Klein, "Communication in cross cultural settings," *Tourism - A Vital Force for Peace,* ed. L. J. D'Amore and J. Jafari, Montreal : First Global Conference, 1988, p.144.

10 Jonathan Swift, "Making time and space dissolve ... using media in global education," *Media & Methods,* vol.24, no.4 (March/April 1988), pp.9-14.

11 See Ellen Posner, "The museum as bazaar," *Atlantic Monthly,* August 1988, pp.67-70; "Museums : a global view," *Museum News,* vol.67, no.1 (September/ October 1988), passim. 12 See Larry Learn, "Networks : the telecommunications infrastructure and impacts of change," *Library Hi Tech,* vol.6, no.1 (1988), pp.13-31.

13 *Canadian voices, Canadian choices ...,* pp.33, 45.

14 Gordon Bell, "Steps towards a national research telecommunications network," *Library Hi Tech,* vol.6, no.1 (1988), pp.34, 36.

15 Jacob Slonim et al., "The information utility : a conceptual scheme for the library of the future," *Canadian Journal of Information Science,* vol.12, no.2 (1987), p.37.

INDEX